THE LIVING LANDSCAPE
AN ECOLOGICAL APPROACH TO LANDSCAPE PLANNING

Frederick Steiner

Arizona State University

McGraw-Hill, Inc.

New York   St. Louis   San Francisco   Auckland   Bogotá   Caracas
Hamburg   Lisbon   London   Madrid   Mexico   Milan   Montreal   New Delhi
Paris   San Juan   São Paulo   Singapore   Sydney   Tokyo   Toronto

For Anna

THE LIVING LANDSCAPE
An Ecological Approach
to Landscape Planning

1 2 3 4 5 6 7 8 9 0 DOH   DOH 9 5 4 3 2 1 0

ISBN   0-07-061133-5

Cover and chapter opener photos courtesy of Philip Maechling.

This book was set in Optima by Monotype
Composition Company.
The editors were B. J. Clark and Jean Akers;
the designer was Karen K. Quigley;
the production supervisor was Richard Ausburn.
R. R. Donnelley & Sons Company was printer and binder.

Library of Congress Cataloging-in-Publication Data

Steiner, Frederick R.
   The living landscape: an ecological approach to landscape
   planning/Frederick Steiner.
      p.   cm.
   Includes bibliographical references.
   ISBN 0-07-061133-5
   1. Land use—Planning.   2. Land use—Environmental
aspects.   3. Landscape architecture.   4. Landscape
protection.   I. Title.
HD108.6.S74   1991
333.73'17—dc20   90-30908

ABOUT THE AUTHOR

FREDERICK STEINER is professor and chair, Department of Planning, Arizona State University. Previously, he taught in programs of planning, landscape architecture, and environmental science at Washington State University (1977–1987) and the University of Colorado at Denver (1987–1989). Professor Steiner has worked for city, county, state, federal, and Indian agencies as well as private companies and nonprofit organizations. He served as a city planning commissioner and as a board member of a downtown renewal district. As an involved citizen, he helped to initiate a local civic improvement organization. His projects and research include the areas of new community development, farmland protection, international planning, soil conservation policy, greenline planning, watershed planning, suitability analysis, environmental assessment, and landscape design. In 1980, he was a Fulbright-Hays scholar at the Agricultural University Wageningen in The Netherlands. Professor Steiner received his planning and design education at the University of Pennsylvania and the University of Cincinnati.

CONTENTS

PREFACE ix

ACKNOWLEDGMENTS xi

CHAPTER 1   INTRODUCTION   3

BASIC CONCEPTS   4
THE TRADITIONAL FRAMEWORK OF PLANNING
   IN THE UNITED STATES   5
A NEW APPROACH   8
ECOLOGICAL PLANNING METHOD   9
   Step 1:   Identification of Planning Problems and
            Opportunities   10
   Step 2:   Establishment of Planning Goals   11
   Step 3:   Landscape Analysis, Regional Level   12
   Step 4:   Landscape Analysis, Local Level   12
   Step 5:   Detailed Studies   14
   Step 6:   Planning Area Concepts, Options, and
            Choices   17
   Step 7:   Landscape Plan   17
   Step 8:   Continued Citizen Involvement and
            Community Education   18
   Step 9:   Detailed Designs   18
   Step 10: Plan and Design Implementation   18
   Step 11: Administration   19
WORKING PLANS   19

**CHAPTER 2   IDENTIFYING ISSUES AND
              ESTABLISHING PLANNING GOALS   23**

TECHNIQUES FOR INVOLVING PEOPLE IN THE
   IDENTIFICATION OF ISSUES AND THE
   ESTABLISHMENT OF GOALS   24
   Task Forces   24
   Citizens Advisory Committees and
     Technical Advisory Committees   24
   Neighborhood Planning Councils   24
   Group Dynamics   25

Nominal-Group Workshops   25
Delphi   26
PUBLIC OPINION POLLS   27
TOWN MEETINGS AND PUBLIC HEARINGS   30
GOAL SETTING   31
TWO EXAMPLES OF GOAL-ORIENTED PLANNING   32
The Oregon Comprehensive Planning Law   32
New Jersey Pinelands Comprehensive
Management Plan   35

**CHAPTER 3   INVENTORY AND ANALYSIS OF
THE BIOPHYSICAL ENVIRONMENT   41**

MAKING A BASE MAP AND A REGIONAL
CONTEXT MAP   43
INVENTORY ELEMENTS   43
Regional Climate   43
Geology   48
Physiography   51
Hydrology   53
Soils   60
Microclimate   63
Vegetation   67
Wildlife   71
Existing Land Use and Land Users   72
ANALYSIS AND SYNTHESIS OF
INVENTORY ELEMENTS   76
Bivariate Relationships   76
Layer-Cake Relationships   80
The Holdridge Life-Zone System   80
TWO EXAMPLES OF BIOPHYSICAL INVENTORY
AND ANALYSIS   81
The New Jersey Pinelands Comprehensive
Management Plan   81
The Makah Coastal Zone Management Plan   87

**CHAPTER 4   HUMAN COMMUNITY INVENTORY
AND ANALYSIS   95**

SOURCES OF EXISTING INFORMATION   97
Land-Use Maps and Settlement Pattern Diagrams   97
Histories   97
Census Data   97
Newspapers and Periodicals   99
Phone Books   99
Community Organizations and Clubs   99
Colleges and Universities   99

Government and Public Agencies   100
Synopsis of Information Sources   100
USE OF EXISTING DATA TO GENERATE NEW
INFORMATION   100
Population Trends, Characteristics, and
Projections   100
Development Projections   106
Economic Analyses   110
User Groups   111
GENERATION OF NEW INFORMATION   115
Mail and Telephone Surveys   116
Face-to-Face Interviews   118
Participant Observation   119
ANALYSIS AND SYNTHESIS OF
SOCIAL INFORMATION   120
Establish Visual and Landscape Patterns   120
Identification of Interactions and Relationships   121
Community Needs Assessment   122
TWO EXAMPLES OF HUMAN COMMUNITY
INVENTORY AND ANALYSIS   124
New Jersey Pinelands Comprehensive
Management Plan   124
Makah Coastal Zone Management Plan   125

CHAPTER 5   SUITABILITY ANALYSIS   131

APPROACHES TO SUITABILITY
ANALYSIS—METHODS   132
Soil Conservation Service Systems   132
The McHarg, or University of Pennsylvania,
Suitability Analysis Method   141
Dutch Suitability Analysis   145
COMPUTER APPLICATIONS   145
THE CARRYING-CAPACITY CONCEPT   150
TWO APPLICATIONS OF SUITABILITY ANALYSIS   152
The Development of Performance Requirements in
Medford Township, New Jersey   152
Locating Areas for Rural Housing in
Whitman County, Washington   155

**CHAPTER 6   PLANNING OPTIONS AND
CHOICES   161**

OPTIONAL PLANS   162
TECHNIQUES FOR SELECTING PREFERENCES   162
The Charrette   162
Task Forces, Citizens Advisory Committees, and
Technical Advisory Committees   165

Citizen Referendum and Synchronized Surveys   165
Goals-Achievement Matrix   166
Scenario Writing   167
Public Hearings   167
TWO EXAMPLES OF SELECTING PREFERENCES   168
The Walworth County, Wisconsin, Farmland
   Protection Program   168
Portland, Oregon, Alternative Land-Use Plans   169

CHAPTER 7   LANDSCAPE PLANS   173

RECOGNITION AND ADOPTION OF PLAN   175
STATEMENT OF POLICIES   176
STRATEGIES TO ACHIEVE POLICIES   178
LANDSCAPE PLAN MAP   180
TWO EXAMPLES OF PLANS   182
Comprehensive Management Plan for
   the New Jersey Pinelands   182
Teller County/City of Woodland Park, Colorado,
   Growth Management Plan   184

**CHAPTER 8   CONTINUING CITIZEN INVOLVEMENT
                      AND COMMUNITY EDUCATION   191**

CITIZEN INVOLVEMENT   192
CLASSIFICATION OF CITIZEN PARTICIPATION
   TECHNIQUES   193
CONTINUING COMMUNITY EDUCATION   194
Information and Education   194
Publications   196
Television and Radio   197
TWO EXAMPLES OF EDUCATION PROGRAMS   197
University of Wisconsin-Extension Community
   Development Program   197
The Davis, California, Energy Planning Program   200

CHAPTER 9   DETAILED DESIGNS   207

SITE DESIGN   208
INDIVIDUAL LAND-USER DESIGNS: FARM
   CONSERVATION PLANS   209
SIMULATION   210
CONCEPTUAL DESIGN OF NEW FACILITIES   210
The Concept Design   212
Phase 1   214
Phase 2   216

Summary of the Concept Design   219
DEMONSTRATION PROJECTS   219
TWO EXAMPLES OF DETAILED DESIGNS   221
Connecticut River Valley, Massachusetts   221
Teller County, Colorado   226

**CHAPTER 10   PLAN AND DESIGN
                         IMPLEMENTATION   241**

POWER TO REGULATE   242
Zoning   242
Planned Unit Developments (PUDs)   244
Performance Standards   244
Critical or Environmentally Sensitive Areas   248
Subdivision Regulations   252
Building Codes   255
Covenants   256
POWER TO SPEND   258
Easements   258
Development Rights Purchases and Transfers   259
Property Acquisition   261
Capital Improvement Programming   262
Public Property Management   263
POWER TO TAX   263
INTERAGENCY COORDINATION FOR GROWTH
   MANAGEMENT   266
PROGRAM LINKAGE AND CROSS COMPLIANCE   267
NONGOVERNMENT STRATEGIES   267
IMPLEMENTATION MATRIX   268
THREE EXAMPLES OF PLANNING
   IMPLEMENTATION   269
Innovative Zoning for Agricultural Land Protection in
   York County, Pennsylvania, and Black Hawk
   County, Iowa   269
The Snohomish County, Washington, Growth
   Management Strategy   273

**CHAPTER 11   ADMINISTRATION OF PLANNING
                         PROGRAMS   279**

CURRENT PLANNING   280
The Role of Planning Commissions and
   Review Boards   280
The Role of Planning Staffs   281
The Impact of Procedural Requirements   281
THE BUDGET   286

Planning, Programming, and Budget System
(PPBS) 286
Zero-Base Budgeting 289
Capital Improvement Programming 289
ENVIRONMENTAL IMPACT ASSESSMENTS 290
Environmental Impact Analysis 292
Economic Impact Analysis 294
Fiscal Impact Analysis 296
Social Impact Analysis 299
TWO EXAMPLES OF PLANNING
ADMINISTRATION 299
Boulder, Colorado, Residential Allocation System 299
Court-Mandated Plan Review and Administrative
Procedures in Oregon 305

CHAPTER 12   CONCLUSION   311

GLOSSARY OF ECOLOGICAL PLANNING TERMS 319

ACRONYMS 329

REFERENCES 331

INDEX 347

PREFACE

Two fundamental reasons to plan are to influence equitable sharing among people and to ensure the viability of the future. Because we cannot function by ourselves, each of us is required to share time and space. Sharing is necessary for the well-being of our neighbors and of future generations. This book is about a specific kind of planning; it is about how to share physical space in communities.

The rather abstract notion of human spatial organization manifests itself in the use of land. But the term *land use* oversimplifies the organization of human communities. *Landscape* I find to be a better word. Working with landscapes, planners can begin to understand the connectivity of settlement patterns and functions over time and space. The lines between urban and rural as well as between natural and cultural have become blurred, if indeed such lines were ever clear. With the intermixing of the distinctions between urban/rural and natural/cultural, understanding landscapes from a spatial, functional, and dynamic perspective becomes a key to balancing conflicting uses of land, water, and air.

The landscapes of this planet need help. Conflicts over the use of land and about environmental and social degradation abound. Complex and often seemingly contradictory questions must be addressed: Where should new communities be located? How do new community developers accommodate housing that is affordable? Can new communities be designed that are safe, healthy, and beautiful? How can existing communities be revitalized and restored? Where can new development and open space be located in the existing built-up areas of metropolitan regions? Can we dispose of our hazardous and solid waste in a responsible manner? What about the alternatives of recycling our waste or simply using fewer hazardous products? How do we protect prime agricultural areas in urbanizing regions?

Agriculture and urban uses often conflict, as do many old and new uses—retirement communities and mining, tourism and timber harvesting. Must such old and new uses always conflict? People often move to suburban and rural areas for open space and recreational amenities. In addition to causing problems for existing inhabitants, the new land uses created by the new residents often disrupt wildlife habitat and other environmentally sensitive areas. How do we plan open space that will allow both recreational uses and wildlife habitat? Sometimes new land uses are sited in areas that are susceptible to natural hazards. Can we use our growing knowledge about earthquakes, forest fires, hurricanes, and flooding to direct human uses to the safest locations?

In seeking to address these questions, it is tempting to adopt a global perspective. Certainly many issues that prompt these questions exist internationally. But, because the legal, political, economic, and cultural forces vary widely from nation to nation, I have chosen to focus on planning in the United States. United States' citizens share a common boundary and cultural heritage with Canadians. Canada made many advances in environmental planning during the 1980s, when the national leadership in the United States retreated from environmental concerns. Because I have been influenced by Canadian policy and because several Canadian colleagues have read and reviewed portions of this book in its manuscript form, I hope that some Canadians may find it useful for their work. I also hope that my international work filters through the pages that follow. The focus, however, is on the United States.

Americans seem to have an especially difficult time sharing when it comes to the land. We have set aside spectacular natural landscapes, but despoil other beautiful places with garish signage, trash, and just plain ugly buildings. We Americans produce garbage at an unequaled pace, yet resist the location of waste dumps in our neighborhoods. We seek to live in the countryside but, once we settle in a rural area, try to prevent farmers from continuing their normal, sometimes dirty and smelly, activities. We do not want the government to tell us what to do with our land, but we seek help from the government in times of natural disaster. We want our neighborhoods to be squeaky clean but turn our backs to poor people who live in substandard housing, or in trailers, or on the street.

To more fairly share the bounty of natural resources in the United States, we must ask: Who suffers and who benefits from our decisions? In making and adopting public policy, we must analyze who benefits and who pays for the decisions that elected leaders make. This book presents a framework for presenting information to decision makers. The preparation of the book grew out of my need to explain the planning process to my students. Most of these students have pursued degrees in planning, landscape architecture, and environmental science, but they and I have been enriched by others from geography, architecture, soil science, forestry, civil engineering, business, and sociology. Although written by a teacher, the book is based on my experience as a practitioner and researcher. Through my practical experience and research, I have sought to plan for places that are fit, adaptable, and delightful.

Planning is more than a tool or a technique; it is a philosophy for organizing actions that enable people to predict and visualize the future of any land area. Moreover, planning gives people the ability to link actions on specific parcels of land to larger regional systems. It is up to us to plan with vision. Our responsibility is to retain what we treasure, because we are merely guests on those spaces of the earth that we inhabit. We should leave good impressions about our visit.

Frederick Steiner

ACKNOWLEDGMENTS

There are several colleagues at Washington State University and the University of Colorado at Denver who have supported my work and have offered helpful advice and criticism. In this regard, I thank Paul Rasmussen, Hamid Shirvani, Bill Budd, Mack Roberts, Jack Kartez, Tom Bartuska, Don Satterlund, Yuk Lee, Lois Brink, Lauri Johnson, and Peter Schaeffer. I owe much to my former students in landscape architecture, regional planning, and environmental science. Donna Hall, George Newman, Doug Osterman, and John Theilacker stand out as four to whom I owe the greatest debts.

I studied planning at the University of Pennsylvania and was influenced by several of Penn's fine planning and design faculty, especially Ian McHarg, Ann Strong, John Keene, Jon Berger, Dan Rose, Art Johnson, and Robert Coughlin. Lenore Sagan is a constant, steady influence at Penn, and I value her friendship.

Several Dutch friends have influenced my thinking about landscape planning, especially Ingrid Duchhart, Hubert van Lier, Nico de Jonge, and Meto Vroom of the Dutch Agricultural University, Wageningen.

I benefited greatly from the helpful criticisms by Elizabeth Watson and Sam Stokes on a draft of this manuscript. Others who have contributed to my ideas in one way or another include: Mark Lapping, Ron Eber, Chuck Little, Max Schnepf, Bill Toner, Lee Nellis, Warren Zitzmann, Lloyd Wright, Cecily Corcoran Kihn, J. Glenn Eugster, Jean Tarlet, Christine Carlson, Dennis Canty, Larry Larsen, Kip Petersen, and Terri Morrell. In addition, I am indebted through their published works to the pioneers in ecological planning—Patrick Geddes, Aldo Leopold, Lewis Mumford, Benton MacKaye, Artur Glickson, and G. Angus Hills.

The typing of the manuscript for this book was done by various people including Brenda Stevens, Angela Briggs, Gail Rise, Telisa Swan, Nita Thomas, Jane Bower, Doris Birch, and Penn Clerical Services of Philadelphia. The final version was typed by Pam Erickson and Kathy Saykally of the School of Architecture and Planning, University of Colorado at Denver. I thank them for preparing the manuscript in its final form.

The illustrations were completed by a number of people including Lonnie Kennedy, Mark Woods, Gary McMath, Brandon Burch, Clint Keller, Christine Carlson, Doug Osterman, Louis Burwell, Chuck Watson, Brad Nelson, Richard Van De Mark, Brad Pugh, Gary Christensen, Elizabeth Slocum, Joseph Bell, and Gretchen Schalge. I appreciate their diligence and hard work. I also thank the many others who allowed me to use their illustrations and photographs and to quote from their work. Robert Yaro and Chris Reid of the Center for Rural Massachusetts; Martin Bierbaum and Michael Neuman of the New Jersey Office of State Planning; George Bowechop of the Makah Tribal Council, Chuck Warsinske of David Evans and Associates of Bellevue, Washington; Annemarie and Hans Bleiker of the Institute for Participatory Management and Planning in Monterey, California; the New Jersey Pinelands Commission; and the late Narendra Juneja were especially generous.

Philip Maechling's photographs help portray the essence of the living landscape and make an invaluable contribution to this book for which I am grateful. B. J. Clark and Jean Akers of McGraw-Hill have been the kind of editors that every author dreams will bring a manuscript to fruition.

I would also like to thank the following reviewers for their many helpful comments and suggestions: Nicholas Dines, University of Massachusetts; Patrick Mooney, The University of British Columbia; and William Shepherd, Virginia Polytechnic Institute and State University.

Four friends have had a substantial influence on this book, each in their distinct way. They are Joanne Barnes Jackson, Jerry Young, Ken Brooks, and Bill Wagner. I am indebted to each of them in many ways.

Finally, I owe special thanks to Anna, Halina, and Andrew for their love and tolerance.

THE LIVING LANDSCAPE

AN ECOLOGICAL APPROACH
TO LANDSCAPE PLANNING

1

INTRODUCTION

Conventionally the planning process is presented as a linear progression of activities. Decision making, like other human behavior, seldom occurs in such a linear, rational manner. Still, it is a logical sequence of activities and presents a convenient organizational framework. The common steps include the identification of problems and opportunities; the establishment of goals; inventory and analysis of the biophysical environment, ideally at several scales; human community inventory and analysis; detailed studies like suitability analysis; the development of concepts and the selection of options; the adoption of a plan; community involvement and education; detailed design; plan implementation; and plan administration. This book is organized around these conventional steps but with an ecological perspective. The chapters that follow cover most of the steps in the process.

Each chapter includes a section of "how to" accomplish the step and a few examples where such activities have been successfully undertaken. For many of the chapters, various planning efforts undertaken in the Palouse region of eastern Washington and northern Idaho will be used to illustrate each step. The author was involved in the Palouse planning work for a decade. Because this work is largely rural and because ecological planning is useful for urban and suburban areas as well, several additional prototypical efforts were selected to illustrate the principles described in each chapter and to compare them with the more conventional approach to planning.

Before discussing each step, it will be helpful to first define a few key terms. It will then be necessary to provide a brief overview of traditional planning in the United States. The ecological planning method, the subject of this book, can then be described and the difference of its approach better understood.

BASIC CONCEPTS

Planning has been defined as the use of scientific and technical knowledge to provide options for decision making as well as a process for considering and reaching consensus on a range of choices. As John Friedmann (1973) has succinctly put it, planning links knowledge to action. There is a difference between project planning and comprehensive planning. *Project planning* involves designing a specific object such as a dam, highway, harbor, or an individual building or group of buildings. *Comprehensive planning* involves a broad range of choices relating to all the functions of an area. Resolution of conflicts, often through compromises, is the inherent purpose of comprehensive planning.

Management has been defined as the judicious use of means to accomplish a desired end. It involves working with people to accomplish organizational goals. For practical purposes, many see the distinction between planning and management as largely semantic. The management of resources, such as land, may be a goal of a planning process. Conversely, planning may be a means of management.

Land use is a self-defining term. One can debate if a harbor is a land use or a water use, but land generally refers to all parts of the surface of the earth, wet and dry. The same area of that surface may be used for a variety of human activities. A harbor, for instance, may have commercial, industrial, and recreational purposes. A farm field may be used for speculation and recreation as well as for agriculture. All human activity is in one way or another connected with land.

Landscape is related to land use. The composite features of one part of the surface of the earth that distinguish it from another area is a *landscape*. It is then a combination of elements—fields, hills, forests, water bodies, and settlements. The landscape encompasses the uses of land—housing, transportation, agriculture, recreation, and natural areas—and is a composite of those uses. A landscape is more than a picturesque view; it is the sum of the parts that can be seen with one's eye.

The English word *ecology* is derived from the Greek word for house, *oikos*. The expanded definition is the study of the reciprocal relationships of all living things to each other and to their biotic and physical environments (Ricklefs, 1973). Obviously, humans are living things and thus are engaged in ecological relationships.

The use of ecological information for planning has been a national policy since late 1969 when the U.S. Congress, through the National Environmental Policy Act (NEPA), required all agencies of the federal government to "initiate and utilize ecological information in the planning and development of resource-oriented projects." The act, signed into law by President Richard Nixon on January 1, 1970, is a relatively recent development in American planning. In spite of NEPA and other laws, ecological information has not been integrated adequately into the planning process. Although much work is necessary to realize an ecological approach to planning, NEPA represents an important step. To begin to understand its importance, it is useful to quickly review the status of American planning.

Landscape is the sum of the parts that can be seen with the eye. *(David C. Flaherty, Washington State University College of Engineering and Architecture)*

THE TRADITIONAL FRAMEWORK OF PLANNING IN THE UNITED STATES

The function of planning in the United States has been much debated. There are diverse opinions about the purpose of planning, whether it is to achieve a specific physical project or comprehensive social, economic, or environmental goals. The traditional role of planning in the United States is responsible for many of its divisions. In England, for instance, planning is done by statute. Statutory planning gives English planners more authority in the decision-making process. In contrast, American planners generally have more limited statutory power than in England and other European nations.

There are several reasons for the differences between European and American planning. First, land is recognized as a scarce commodity in Europe and in many other parts of the world. In land-hungry Europe over the last century, public officials have been granted increasing planning powers over use of land (and other resources) through the governing process. In the democracies of Western Europe, there is much concern about the quality of the environment. This concern has resulted in complex systems of planning that address a broad range of issues, including housing, recreation, aesthetics, open space, and transportation.

Another reason emerges from the origins of the United States. Thomas Jefferson and the other founding fathers were influenced strongly by John Locke, who viewed the chief end of establishing a government as the preservation of property. Locke, in his *Two Treatises of Government,* defined property as "lives, liberties, and estates" (Laslett, 1988). Elsewhere, Locke wrote of the "pursuit of happiness." It was Jefferson who combined Locke's terms, "life, liberty, and the pursuit of happiness." But it has been the view of property as possession, rather than Locke's predominant version—life, liberty, and estate—that has prevailed. The constitution of the Commonwealth of Pennsylvania states in Article 1, Section 1, "all . . . men have certain inherent and indefeasible rights, among which are those of enjoying and defending life and liberty, of acquiring, possessing and protecting property." And, in the Fifth Amendment of the U.S. Constitution, there is this clause: "No person shall . . . be deprived of life, liberty, or property, without due process of law; nor shall private property be taken for public use without just compensation." Property rights were seen as a fundamental freedom to those in the new republic who had fought against the landed elite of the mother country.

When Jefferson who wrote the Declaration of Independence and the others who authored the Constitution rode on horseback or in a carriage from their Virginia estates, their hinterland Pennsylvania farms, or their New England towns to Philadelphia, they traveled through a seemingly endless expanse of woodlands, rich farmlands, and rolling pastures with fresh, clear creeks and rivers, abundant game, and pristine coastlines. In Philadelphia, they were concerned foremost with human rights and freedoms. Even the most foresighted of the framers of the Constitution could not have envisioned the environmental and social crises that came with the industrialization and urbanization of America.

However, the U.S. Constitution does give the states and their political subdivisions the power of regulation. Police powers, which provide the basis for state and local regulation, were derived by the states from the Tenth Amendment, which reads: "The powers not delegated to the United States by the Constitution, nor prohibited by it to the States, are reserved to the States respectively, or to the people."

The states, in the use of police powers, must consider the Fifth Amendment because the U.S. Supreme Court has held that the "taking clause" is embodied in the due process clause of the Fourteenth Amendment and hence applies to the states. In addition, state constitutions contain taking clauses, some with rather interesting twists. For instance, Article I, Section 16 (the Ninth Amendment) of the Washington Constitution states: "No private property shall be taken *or damaged* for public *or private use* without just compensation having first been made" [emphasis added]. A person's private use of property cannot damage the property of another person in Washington State.

Given this constitutional backdrop, the federal and several state legislatures have slowly but steadily increased statutory authority for planning. In addition, the courts have consistently upheld land-use regulations that do not go "too far" and thus constitute a taking. In addition, courts have increasingly supported restrictions on the use of environmentally sensitive areas, such as wetlands and stream corridors. However, planning remains a fragmented effort in the United States, undertaken primarily by powerful vested business interests and sometimes by consent. Planning by consent, which depends largely on an individual's persuasive power, has caused several adaptations on the part of American planners. These adaptations can be broken down into two broad categories: administrative and adversary.

Administrative planners are realists who respond directly to governmental programs either as bureaucrats in a city or regional planning agency or as a consultant. Successful administrative planners build political power in the city or metropolitan region where they work. They administer programs for voluntary community organizations and health, education, and welfare associations designed to support the political-economic structure of the nation-state. They may also administer transportation or utility programs deemed necessary by the same structure. By building political power, administrative planners serve the power structure of the city or region. The result is that often the unpowered groups of an area suffer. Poor people suffer the most, bearing the brunt of the social costs, when planners and others administer the programs of the status quo.

Advocacy planners are idealists and respond to issues, such as those resulting from social or environmental concerns. They usually work outside the power structure, forming new coalitions among the previously unorganized in order to mobilize support for their cause. Often advocacy planners work for veto groups—ad hoc organizations opposed to a controversial project or proposal such as a highway, a high-density housing project, a dam, or a nuclear power plant.

The rights of people have a deep-seated heritage in American history, from the Declaration of Independence, the Constitution, and the Bill of Rights through the Thirteenth and Nineteenth Amendments to the labor and civil rights movements. Human rights has been the important issue for one group of advocacy planners called by various terms including community organizers, adversary planners, and change agents. In *Reveille for Radicals,* Saul Alinsky (1946) best articulated the philosophy for the latest crest of this movement, which began to ebb when Richard Nixon cut off funding for a variety of programs created during the 1960s. Many of the social programs created during the 1960s were concerned with making basic changes in the urban power structure. The programs were a result of the civil rights movement and the attention brought to the poor living conditions in urban ghettos by the riots that occurred there. The withdrawal of the federal commitment to domestic human rights programs begun by President Nixon continued through most of the 1970s, except during the presidency of Jimmy Carter. During the Ronald Reagan administration, the social programs created in the 1960s were almost completely dismantled.

With the passage of the NEPA, the Congress of the United States put into motion the machinery for the protection of the environment by setting forth certain general aims of federal activity in the environmental field, establishing the Council on Environmental Quality, and instructing all federal agencies to include an impact statement as part of future reports or recommendations on actions significantly affecting the quality of the human environment. Subsequent regional, state, and federal actions—such as state environmental policy acts, land-use legislation, and the Coastal Zone Management Act—have furthered this commitment.

As with the heritage for human rights, these environmental measures are deeply rooted in the American tradition. Laced throughout the social criticism of Henry David Thoreau, the novels of Mark Twain, the poetry of Walt Whitman, the photography of Ansel Adams, the films of John Ford, and the music of Woody Guthrie is the love for nature.

Even before the recent governmental action, both administrative and adversary planners have been concerned with degradation of the environment. In the nineteenth century, the young Frederick Law Olmsted traveled to England where he witnessed the efforts of reformers to use techniques of the English landscape garden tradition to relieve the pressures of urban blight brought on by the industrial revolution. The resulting public parks were viewed as natural refuges from the evils of the surrounding industrial city. Public parks in English cities were pastoral retreats and escapes from urban congestion and pollution. Olmsted and American reformers adopted the idea. The first result was Central Park in New York. Eventually, these efforts became known as the City Beautiful Movement, after the World's Columbian Exposition of 1893 in Chicago. The City Beautiful Movement resulted in numerous parks and public facilities being built in the early twentieth century.

From the late nineteenth into the early twentieth centuries a great national parks system was formed and blossomed under the leadership of President Theodore Roosevelt. Also in the late nineteenth century, the use of river drainage basins or watersheds as the basic geographical unit for planning was initiated. An advocate of the watershed conservancy idea, the humanist engineer Arthur Morgan, helped organize the Miami

Conservancy District near Dayton, Ohio, and later directed the Tennessee Valley Authority. During the New Deal, greenbelt new towns—new satellite communities surrounded by parks and accessible to cities by automobile—were created by economist Rexford Tugwell and other leaders of the New Deal. Urban parks, national parks, watershed conservancies, greenbelt new towns—each was a response designed to maintain some portion of the natural environment during periods of increased human settlement.

Ian McHarg (1969) is Saul Alinksy's environmentalist counterpart, the author of a manifesto for ecological planning similar to the one Alinsky wrote for community advocacy. Although separate (and sometimes conflicting) American traditions, social activism and environmentalism share common problems. Environmental programs were as vulnerable in the 1980s as social programs were a decade earlier. Ronald Reagan chose not to enforce many environmental laws enacted during the 1970s. He appointed people to key positions in environmental and natural resource management agencies who were opposed to the functions of those agencies. Legally established environmental goals will not be achieved unless governmental enforcement is supported by the public. In spite of actions of the Reagan administration, the American public has generally continued to favor the protection of water, air, and land resources. In addition, President Reagan's successor, George Bush, has declared himself an environmentalist, and has endorsed the creation of a cabinet-level environmental protection agency.

Neither administrative nor advocacy planners have been totally effective. While administrative planners may be able to get things done, unpowered groups often suffer. While advocacy planners may win important civil rights struggles or stop flagrant abuse of the natural environment, overall problems persist and people remain poor— frequently poorer—and environmental degradation continues, too often at a more rapid rate.

A NEW APPROACH

There is a need for a common language, a common method among all those concerned about social equity and ecological parity. This method must be able to transcend disciplinary territorialism and must be applicable to all levels of government. It is imperative that this approach incorporate both social and environmental concerns. For, as the poet Wendell Berry has observed, "The mentality that destroys a watershed and then panics at the threat of flood is the same mentality that gives institutionalized insult to black people then panics at the prospect of race riots" (1972, p. 73).

What is needed is an approach that can assist planners to analyze the problems of a region as they relate to each other, to the landscape, and to the national and local political economic structure. This might be called an applied human ecology. Each problem is linked to the community in one or more specific ways. Banking is related to real estate is related to development pressure is related to schools is related to rising tax base is related to retirees organizing against increasing property taxes. This approach identifies how people are affected by these chain reactions and presents options for the future based on those impacts.

Aldo Leopold, the University of Wisconsin wildlife biologist, was perhaps the first to advocate an "ecological ethic" for planning, doing so in the 1930s (1933; 1949). He was joined by such individuals as Lewis Mumford and Benton MacKaye (1940). Mumford and MacKaye were strongly influenced by the Scottish biologist and town planner Patrick Geddes and the English garden city advocate Ebenezer Howard. Others who have proposed or developed ecological approaches for planning include the Canadian forester G. Angus Hills (1961); the Israeli architect and town planner Artur Glickson (1971); the American landscape architects Philip Lewis (1969), Ian McHarg (1969), and Anne Spirn (1984); the American regional planner Jon Berger (with Sinton, 1985); and the French geographer and planner Jean Tarlet (1985).

ECOLOGICAL PLANNING METHOD

What is meant by ecological planning? Planning is a process that uses scientific and technical information for considering and reaching consensus on a range of choices. Ecology is the study of the relationship of all living things, including people, to their biological and physical environments. *Ecological planning* then may be defined as the use of biophysical and sociocultural information to suggest opportunities and constraints for decision making about the use of the landscape.

Ian McHarg has summarized a framework for ecological planning in the following way:

> All systems aspire to survival and success. This state can be described as synthropic-fitness-health. Its antithesis is entropic-misfitness-morbidity. To achieve the first state requires systems to find the fittest environment, adapt it and themselves. Fitness of an environment for a system is defined as that requiring the minimum of work and adaptation. Fitness and fitting are indications of health and process of fitness is health giving. The quest for fitness is entitled adaptation. Of all the instrumentalities available for man for successful adaptation, cultural adaptation in general and planning in particular, appear to be the most direct and efficacious for maintaining and enhancing human health and well-being. (1981, pp. 112–113)

Arthur Johnson explained the central principle of this theory in the following way:

> The fittest environment for any organism, artifact, natural and social ecosystem, is that environment which provides the [energy] needed to sustain the health or well-being of the organism/artifact/ecosystem. Such an approach is not limited by scale. It may be applied to locating plants within a garden as well as to the development of a nation. (1981, p. 107)

The ecological planning method is primarily a procedure for studying the biophysical and sociocultural systems of a place to reveal where specific land uses may be best practiced. As Ian

McHarg has summarized repeatedly in his writings and in many public presentations:

> The method defines the best areas for a potential land use at the convergence of all or most of the factors deemed propitious for the use in the absence of all or most detrimental conditions. Areas meeting this standard are deemed intrinsically suitable for the land use under consideration.

As presented in Figure 1.1, there are eleven interacting steps. An issue or group of related issues is identified by a community—that is, some collection of people—in step 1. These issues are problematic or present an opportunity to the people or the environment of an area. A goal(s) is then established in step 2 to address the problem(s). Next, in steps 3 and 4, inventories and analyses of biophysical and sociocultural processes are conducted, first at a larger level, such as a drainage basin or an appropriate regional unit of government, and second at a more specific level, such as a watershed or a local government.

In step 5, detailed studies are made that link the inventory and analysis information to the problem(s) and goal(s). Suitability analyses are one such type of detailed study. Step 6 involves the development of concepts and options. A landscape plan is then derived from these concepts in step 7. Throughout the process, a systematic educational and citizen involvement effort occurs. Such involvement is important in each step but especially so in step 8 when the plan is explained to the affected public. In step 9, detailed designs are made that are specific at the individual land-user or site level.

These designs and the plan are implemented in step 10. In step 11, the plan is administered. The heavier arrows in Figure 1.1 indicate the flow from step 1 to step 11. Smaller arrows between each step suggest a feedback system whereby each step can modify the previous step and, in turn, change from the subsequent step. Additional arrows indicate other possible modifications through the process. For instance, detailed studies of a

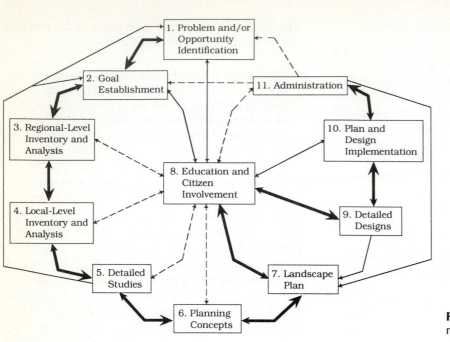

FIGURE 1.1 Ecological planning model.

planning area (step 5) may lead to the identification of new problems or opportunities or the amendment of goals (steps 1 and 2). Detailed designs (step 9) may change the master plan, and so on. Once the process is complete and the plan is being administered and monitored (step 11), the view of the problems and opportunities facing the region and the goals to address these problems and opportunities may be altered, as is indicated by the dashed lines in Figure 1.1.

This process is adapted from the conventional planning process and its many variations (see, for instance Hall, 1975; Roberts, 1979; McDowell, 1986; Moore, 1988; & Stokes et al., 1989), as well as those suggested specifically for landscape planning (Lovejoy, 1973; Fabos, 1979; Zube, 1980; Marsh, 1983; & Duchhart, 1989). Unlike some of these other planning processes, design plays an important role in this method. Each step in the process contributes to and is affected by a plan and implementing measures, which may be the official controls of the planning area. The plan and

implementing measures may be viewed as the results of the process, although products may be generated from each step. The approach to ecological planning developed by McHarg at the University of Pennsylvania differs slightly from the one presented here. The Pennsylvania, or McHarg, model places a greater emphasis on inventory, analysis, and synthesis. This one places more emphasis on the establishment of goals, implementation, administration, and public participation, yet does attempt to do so in an ecological manner.

Step 1: Identification of Planning Problems and Opportunities

Human societies face many social, economic, political, and environmental problems and opportunities. Since a landscape is the interface between social and environmental processes, landscape planning addresses those issues that concern the interrelationship between people and nature. The planet presents many opportunities for people, and there is no shortage of environmental problems.

Problems and opportunities lead to specific planning issues. For instance, suburban development is occurring on prime agricultural land, which local officials consider a problem. A number of issues arise, such as land-use conflicts between new suburban residents and farmers as well as who will pay the costs of public services for the newly developed areas. Another example is an area with the opportunity for new development because of its scenic beauty and recreational amenities, like an ocean beach or mountain town. One issue will be how to accommodate the new growth while protecting the natural resources that are attracting people to the place.

Residents can help to identify local environmental issues that require future planning. *(Washington State University College of Agriculture and Home Economics)*

Step 2: Establishment of Planning Goals

In a democracy, the people of a region establish goals through the political process. Elected representatives will identify a particular issue affecting their region—a steel plant is closing, suburban sprawl is threatening agricultural land, or a new power plant is creating a housing boom. After issues have been identified, then goals are established to address the problem. Such goals should provide the basis for the planning process.

Goals articulate an idealized future situation. In the context of this method, it is assumed that once goals have been established there is a commitment by some group to address the problem or opportunity identified in step 1. Problems and opportunities can be identified at various levels. Local people can recognize a problem or opportunity and then set a goal to address it. As well, issues can be national, international, or global in scope. Problem solving, of which goal setting is a part, may occur at many levels or combinations of levels. Although goal setting is obviously

dependent on the cultural-political system, the people affected by a goal should be involved in its establishment.

Goal-oriented planning has long been advocated by many community planners. Such an approach has been summarized by Herbert Gans:

> The basic idea behind goal-oriented planning is simple; that planners must begin with the goals of the community—and of its people—and then develop those programs which constitute the best means for achieving the community's goals, taking care that the consequences of these programs do not result in undesirable behavioral or cost consequences. (1968, p. 53)

There are some good examples of goal-oriented planning, such as Oregon's mandatory land-use law (see, for instance, Pease, 1984; & Eber, 1984). However, although locally generated goals are the ideal, too often goals are established by a higher level of government. Many federal and state laws have mandated planning goals for local government, often resulting in the creation of new regions to respond to a particular federal program. These regional agencies must respond to wide-ranging issues that generate specific goals for water and air quality, resource management, energy conservation, transportation, and housing. No matter at what level of government goals are established, information must be collected to help elected representatives resolve underlying issues. Many goals, those which are the focus of this book, require an understanding of biophysical processes.

Step 3: Landscape Analysis, Regional Level

This step and the next one involve interrelated scale levels. The method addresses three scale levels: region, locality, and specific site, with an emphasis on the local. The use of different scales is consistent with the concept of levels-of-organization used by ecologists. According to this concept, each level of organization has special properties. According to Novikoff, "What were wholes on one level become parts on a higher one" (1945; as quoted by Quinby, 1988). Watersheds have been identified as one level of organization to provide boundaries for landscape and ecosystem analysis. Drainage basins and watersheds have often been advocated as useful levels of analysis for landscape planning and natural resource management (Doornkamp, 1982; Young et al., 1983; Steiner, 1983; Dickert & Olshansky, 1986; Easter et al., 1986; & Fox, 1987).

Essentially, drainage basins and watersheds are the same thing (catchment areas), but in practical use, especially in the United States, drainage basins generally are used to refer to larger regions and watersheds to more specific areas. Lowrance et al. (1986), who have developed a hierarchial approach for agricultural planning, refer to watersheds as the landscape system, or ecologic level, and the larger unit as the regional system, or macroeconomic level. In the Lowrance et al.

hierarchy, the two smallest units are the farm system, or microeconomic level, and field system, or agronomic level. The analysis at the regional drainage-basin level provides insight into how the landscape functions at the more specific local scale.

Drainage basins and watersheds, however, are seldom practical boundaries for American planners. Political boundaries frequently do not neatly conform with river catchments, and planners commonly work for political entities. There are certainly many examples of plans that are based on drainage basins, such as water quality and erosion control plans. Several federal agencies, such as the U.S. Forest Service (USFS) and the U.S. Soil Conservation Service (SCS), regularly use watersheds as a planning unit. Planners who work for cities or counties are less likely to be hydrologically bound.

Step 4: Landscape Analysis, Local Level

During step 4, processes taking place in the more specific planning area are studied. The major aim of local-level analysis is to obtain insight about the natural processes and the human plans and activities. Such processes can be viewed as the elements of a system, with the landscape a visual expression of the system.

This step in the ecological planning process, like the previous one, involves the collection of information concerning the appropriate physical, biological, and social elements that constitute the planning area. Since cost and time are important factors in many planning processes, existing published and mapped information is the easiest and fastest to gather. If budget and time allow, then the inventory and analysis step may be best accomplished by an interdisciplinary team collecting new information. In either case, this step is an interdisciplinary collection effort that involves search, accumulation, field checking, and mapping of data.

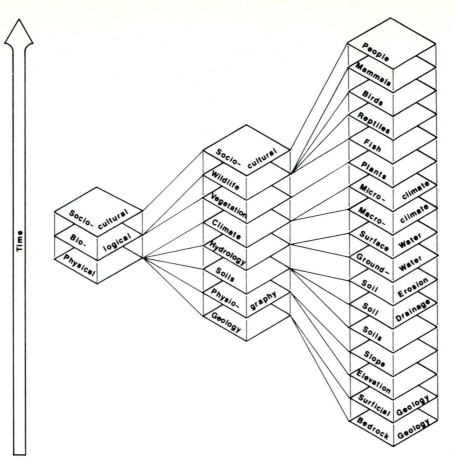

FIGURE 1.2 Layer-cake model.
(Source: Adapted from Wallace, McHarg, Roberts, & Todd, 1971–1974)

Ian McHarg and his colleagues have developed a layer-cake model (Figure 1.2) that provides a central group of biophysical elements for the inventory. Categories include geology, physiography, groundwater, surface water, soils, climate, vegetation, wildlife, and people. UNESCO, in its Man and the Biosphere Programme, has developed a more exhaustive list of possible inventory elements (Table 1.1).

Land classification systems are valuable at this stage for analysis because they may allow the planner to aggregate specific information into general groupings. Such systems are based on inventoried data and on needs for analysis. Many government agencies in the United States and elsewhere have developed land classification systems that are helpful. The SCS, USFS, the U.S. Fish and Wildlife Service, and the U.S. Geological Survey (USGS) are agencies that have been notably active in land classification systems. However, there is not a consistency of data sources even in the United States. In urban areas, a planner may be overwhelmed with data for inventory and analysis. In remote rural areas, on the other hand, even a Soil Conservation Service survey may not exist or it may be old and unusable. An even

TABLE 1.1
UNESCO TOTAL ENVIRONMENTAL CHECKLIST:
COMPONENTS AND PROCESSES

Natural Environment—Components

Soil	Energy resources
Water	Fauna
Atmosphere	Flora
Mineral resources	Microorganisms

Natural Environment—Processes

Biogeochemical cycles	Fluctuations in animal and plant growth
Irradiation	
Climatic processes	Changes in soil fertility, salinity, alkalinity
Photosynthesis	
Animal and plant growth	Host/parasite interactions, and epidemic processes

Human Population—Demographic Aspects

Population structure:
- Age
- Ethnicity
- Economic
- Educational
- Occupational

Population size
Population density
Fertility and mortality rates
Health statistics

Human Activities and the Use of Machines

Migratory movements	Mining
Daily mobility	Industrial activities
Decision making	Commercial activities
Exercise and distribution of authority	Military activities
	Transportation
Administration	Recreational activities
Farming, fishing	Crime rates

Societal Groupings

Governmental groupings	
Industrial groupings	Information media
Commercial groupings	Law-keeping media
Political groupings	Health services
Religious groupings	Community groupings
Educational groupings	Family groupings

Products of Labor

The built-environment:
- Buildings
- Roads
- Railways
- Parks

Food
Pharmaceutical products
Machines
Other commodities

Culture

Values	Technology
Beliefs	Literature
Attitudes	Laws
Knowledge	Economic System
Information	

SOURCE: Boyden, 1979.

larger problem is that there is little or no consistency in scale or in the terminology used among agencies. A recommendation of the National Agricultural Lands Study (1981) was that a statistical protocol for federal agencies concerning land resource information be developed and led by the Office of Federal Statistical Policy and Standards. One helpful system that has been developed for land classification is the USGS Land Use and Land Cover Classification System (Table 1.2).

The ability of the landscape planner and resource manager to inventory biophysical processes may be uneven, but it is far better than their capability to assess human ecosystems. An understanding of human ecology may provide a key to sociocultural inventory and analysis. Since humans are living things, *human ecology* may be thought of as an expansion of ecology, of how humans interact with each other and their environments. Interaction then is used as both a basic concept and an explanatory device. As Gerald Young (1974; 1978; 1983; 1989), who has illustrated the pandisciplinary scope of human ecology, noted:

In human ecology, the way people interact with each other and with the environment is definitive of a number of basic relationships. Interaction provides a measure of belonging, it affects identity versus alienation, including alienation from the environment. The system of obligation, responsibility and liability is defined through interaction. The process has become definitive of the public interest as opposed to private interests which prosper in the spirit of independence. (1976, p. 294)

Step 5: Detailed Studies

Detailed studies link the inventory and analysis information to the problem(s) and goal(s). One example of such studies is suitability analysis. As explained by McHarg (1969), *suitability analyses* can be used to determine the fitness of a specific place for a variety of land uses based on thorough ecological inventories and on the values of land

TABLE 1.2
U.S. GEOLOGICAL SURVEY LAND-USE AND LAND-COVER CLASSIFICATION SYSTEM FOR USE WITH REMOTE SENSOR DATA

Level I	Level II
1 Urban or built-up land	11 Residential
	12 Commercial and services
	13 Industrial
	14 Transportation, communications, and services
	15 Industrial and commercial complexes
	16 Mixed urban or built-up land
	17 Other urban or built-up land
2 Agricultural land	21 Cropland and pasture
	22 Orchards, groves, vineyards, nurseries, and ornamental horticultural
	23 Confined feeding operations
	24 Other agricultural land
3 Rangeland	31 Herbaceous rangeland
	32 Shrub and brush rangeland
	33 Mixed rangeland
4 Forest land	41 Deciduous forest land
	42 Evergreen forest land
	43 Mixed forest land
5 Water	51 Streams and canals
	52 Lakes
	53 Reservoirs
	54 Bays and estuaries
6 Wetland	61 Forested wetland
	62 Nonforested wetland
7 Barren land	71 Dry salt flats
	72 Beaches
	73 Sandy areas other than beaches
	74 Bare exposed rocks
	75 Strip mines, quarries, and gravel pits
	76 Transitional areas
	77 Mixed barren land
8 Tundra	81 Shrub and brush tundra
	82 Herbaceous tundra
	83 Bare ground
	84 Mixed tundra
9 Perennial snow ice	91 Perennial snowfields
	92 Glaciers

SOURCE: Anderson et al., 1976.

users. The basic purpose of the detailed studies is to gain an understanding about the complex relationships between human values, environmental opportunities and constraints, and the issues being addressed. To accomplish this, it is crucial to link the studies to the local situation. As a result, a variety of scales may be used to explore linkages.

A simplified suitability analysis process is provided in Figure 1.3. There are several techniques that may be used to accomplish suitability analysis. Again, it was McHarg who popularized the "overlay technique" (1969). This technique involves maps of inventory information superimposed on one another to identify areas that provide, first, opportunities for particular land uses and, second, constraints (Johnson, Berger, & McHarg, 1979). MacDougall (1975) has criticized the accuracy of map overlays and made suggestions on how map overlays may be made more accurate. Steinitz et al. (1976) have provided a history of the use of hand overlays of mapped information, and Neckar (1989) has written a profile of Warren Manning, who was responsible for the idea of overlaying maps to represent natural systems.

Although there has been a general tendency away from hand-drawn overlays, there are still occasions when they may be useful. For instance, they may be helpful for small study sites within a larger region or for certain scales of project planning. It is important to realize the limitations of hand-drawn overlays. For instance, after more than three or four overlays, they may become opaque; there are the accuracy questions raised by MacDougall (1975) and others that are especially acute with hand-drawn maps; and there are limitations for weighting various values represented by map units. Computer technology may help to overcome these limitations.

Numerous computer program systems have been developed that replace the technique of hand-drawn overlays. Some of these programs are intended to model only positions of environmental processes or phenomena, while others are designed

STEP 1
MAP DATA FACTORS BY TYPE

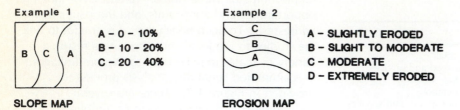

Example 1

B C A

A – 0 – 10%
B – 10 – 20%
C – 20 – 40%

SLOPE MAP

Example 2

C
B
A
D

A – SLIGHTLY ERODED
B – SLIGHT TO MODERATE
C – MODERATE
D – EXTREMELY ERODED

EROSION MAP

STEP 2
RATE EACH TYPE OF EACH FACTOR FOR EACH LAND USE

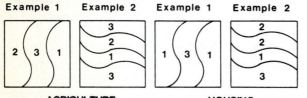

Factor Types	Agriculture	Housing
Example 1		
A	1	1
B	2	1
C	3	3
Example 2		
A	1	1
B	2	2
C	3	2
D	3	3

1 – PRIME SUITABILITY
2 – SECONDARY
3 – TERTIARY

STEP 3
MAP RATINGS FOR EACH AND USE ONE SET OF MAPS FOR EACH LAND USE

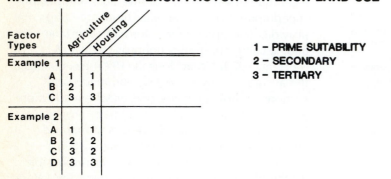

Example 1   Example 2   Example 1   Example 2

2 3 1

3
2
1
3

1 3 1

2
2
1
3

AGRICULTURE   HOUSING

STEP 4
OVERLAY SINGLE FACTOR SUITABILITY MAPS TO OBTAIN COMPOSITES. ONE MAP FOR EACH LAND USE

5	6	4
4	5	3
3	4	2
5	6	4

3	5	3
3	5	3
2	4	2
4	6	4

AGRICULTURE   HOUSING

LOWEST NUMBERS ARE BEST SUITED
FOR LAND USE

HIGHEST NUMBERS ARE LEAST SUITED
FOR LAND USE

FIGURE 1.3 Suitability analysis procedure.

as comprehensive information storage, retrieval, and evaluation systems. These systems are intended to improve efficiency and economy in information handling, especially for large or complex planning projects.

Step 6: Planning Area Concepts, Options, and Choices

This step involves the development of concepts for the planning area. These concepts can be viewed as options for the future based on the suitabilities for the use(s) that give a general conceptual model or scenario of how problems may be solved. This model should be presented in such a way that the goals will be achieved. Often more than one scenario has to be made. These concepts are based on a logical and imaginative combination of the information gathered through the inventory and analysis steps. The conceptual model shows allocations of uses and actions. The scenarios set possible directions for future management of the area and therefore should be viewed as a basis for discussion where choices are made by the community about its future.

Choices should be based on the goals of the planning effort. For instance, if it is the goal to protect agricultural land yet allow some low-density housing to develop, different organizations of the environment for those two land uses should be developed. Different schemes for realizing the desired preferences also need to be explored.

The Dutch have devised an interesting approach to developing planning options for their agricultural land reallocation projects. Four land-use options are developed, each with the preferred scheme for a certain point of view. Optional land-use schemes of the area are made for nature and landscape, agriculture, recreation, and urbanization. These schemes are constructed by groups of citizens working with government scientists and planners. For instance, for the nature and landscape scheme, landscape architects and ecologists from the *Staatsbosbeheer* (Dutch

Forest Service) work with citizen environmental action groups. For agriculture, local extension agents and soil scientists work with farm commodity organizations and farmer cooperatives. Similar coalitions are formed for recreation and urbanization. What John Friedmann (1973) calls a dialogue process begins at the point where each of the individual schemes is constructed. The groups come together for mutual learning so that a consensus of opinion is reached through debate and discussion.

Various options for implementation also need to be explored, which must relate to the goal of the planning effort. If, for instance, the planning is being conducted for a jurisdiction trying to protect its agricultural land resources, then it is necessary not only to identify lands that should be protected but also the implementation options that might be employed to achieve the farmland protection goal.

Step 7: Landscape Plan

The preferred concepts and options are brought together in a landscape plan. The plan gives a strategy for development at the local scale. The plan provides flexible guidelines for policymakers, land managers, and land users about how to conserve, rehabilitate, or develop an area. In such a plan, enough freedom should be left so that local officials and land users can adjust their practices to new economic demands or social changes.

This step represents a key decision-making point in the planning process. Responsible officials, such as county commissioners or city council members, are often required by law to adopt a plan. The rules for adoption and forms that the plans may take vary widely. Commonly in the United States, planning commissions recommend a plan for adoption to the legislative body after a series of public hearings. Such plans are called *comprehensive plans* in much of the United States, *general plans* in California and Arizona. In some states like Oregon, there are specific, detailed elements that local governments are required to include in such plans. Other states permit much flexibility to local officials for the contents of these plans. On public lands, various federal agencies, including the USFS, the U.S. National Park Service (NPS), and the U.S. Bureau of Land Management (BLM), have specific statutory requirements for land management plans.

The term *landscape plan* is used here to emphasize that such plans should incorporate natural and social considerations. A landscape plan is more than a land-use plan because it addresses the overlap and integration of land uses. A landscape plan may involve the formal recognition of previous elements in the planning process, such as the adoption of policy goals. The plan should include both written statements about policies and implementation strategies as well as a map showing the spatial organization of the landscape.

Step 8: Continued Citizen Involvement and Community Education

In step 8, the plan is explained to the affected public through education and information dissemination. Actually, such interaction occurs throughout the planning process, beginning with the identification of issues. Public involvement is especially crucial as the landscape plan is developed, because it is important to ensure that the goals established by the community will be achieved in the plan.

The success of a plan depends largely on how much people affected by the plan have been involved in its determination. There are numerous examples of both government agencies and private businesses suddenly announcing a plan for a project that will dramatically impact people without consulting those individuals first. The result is predictable—the people will rise in opposition against the project. The alternative is to involve people in the planning process, soliciting their ideas and incorporating those ideas into the plan. Doing so may require a longer time to

develop a plan, but local citizens will be more likely to support it than to oppose it and will often monitor its execution.

Step 9: Detailed Designs

To design is to give form and to arrange elements spatially. By making specific designs based on the landscape plan, planners can help decision makers visualize the consequences of their policies. Carrying policies through to arranging the physical environment gives meaning to the process by actually affecting change in the spatial organization of a place. Designs represent a synthesis of all the previous planning studies. During the design step, the short-term benefits for the land users or individual citizen have to be combined with the long-term economic and ecological goals for the whole area.

Step 10: Plan and Design Implementation

Implementation is the employment of various strategies, tactics, and procedures to realize the goals and policies adopted in the landscape plan. On the local level, several different mechanisms have been developed to control the use of land and other resources. These techniques include voluntary covenants, easements, land purchase, transfer of development rights, zoning, utility extension policies, and performance standards. The preference selected should be appropriate for the region. For instance, in urban areas like King County, Washington, and Suffolk County, New York, traditional zoning has not been effective to protect farmland. The citizens of these counties have elected to tax themselves to purchase development easements from farmers. In more rural counties like Whitman County, Washington, and Black Hawk County, Iowa, local leaders have found traditional zoning effective.

One implementation technique especially well suited for ecological planning is performance standards. Like many other planning implementation measures, *performance standards* is a general term that has been defined and applied in several different ways. Basically, performance standards, or criteria, are established and must be met before a certain use will be permitted. These criteria are usually a combination of economic, environmental, and social factors. This technique lends itself to ecological planning because criteria for specific land uses can be based on suitability analysis.

Step 11: Administration

In this final step, the plan is administered. *Administration* involves monitoring and evaluating how the plan is implemented on an ongoing basis. Amendments or adjustments to the plan will no doubt be necessary because of changing conditions or new information. To achieve the goals established for the process, planners should pay especial attention to the design of regulation review procedures and of the management of the decision-making process.

Administration may be accomplished by a commission comprising citizens with or without the support of a professional staff. Citizens should play an important role in administering local planning through commissions and review boards that oversee local ordinances. To a large degree, the success of citizens boards and commissions depends on the extent of their involvement in the development of the plans that they manage. Again, Oregon provides an excellent example of the use of citizens to administer a plan. The Land Conservation and Development Commission (LCDC), comprising seven members who are appointed by the governor and supported by its professional staff, is responsible for overseeing the implementation of the state land-use planning law. Another group of citizens, 1000 Friends of Oregon, monitors the administration of the law. The support that the law has from the public is evidenced in the defeat of several attempts to

abolish mandatory statewide land-use planning in Oregon.

WORKING PLANS

A method is necessary as an organizational framework for landscape planners. Also, a relatively standard method presents the opportunity to compare and analyze case studies. To adequately fulfill their responsibilities to protect the public health, safety, and welfare, actions of planners should be based on a knowledge of what has and has not worked in other settings and situations. A large body of case study results can provide an empirical foundation for planners. A common method is helpful for both practicing planners and scholars who should probe and criticize the nuances of such a method in order to expand and improve its utility.

The following chapters are organized roughly parallel to the method. The identification of planning problems and opportunities is not discussed independently because it is assumed that once an issue has been defined, then a process such as the one described here is triggered. In addition, many of the techniques described in the next chapter can be used to both define issues and establish goals. Also, there are no separate discussions of regional- and local-level ecological inventories (steps 3 and 4) because the techniques used are similar. Instead, there are separate detailed descriptions of inventories and analyses of the biophysical environment and the human community.

The approach suggested here should be viewed as a working method. The pioneering forester Gifford Pinchot advocated a conservation approach to the planning of the national forests. His approach was both utilitarian and protectionist, and he believed "wise use and preservation of all forest resources were compatible" (Wilkinson & Anderson, 1985, p. 22). To implement this philosophy, Pinchot in his position as chief of the U.S. Forest Service required "working plans."

Such plans recognized the dynamic, living nature of forests. In the same vein, the methods used to develop plans should be viewed as a living process. However, this is not meant to imply that there should be no structure to planning methodologies. Rather, working planning methods should be viewed as something analogous to a jazz composition: not a fixed score but a palette that invites improvisation.

The method offered here has a landscape ecological, specifically human ecological, bias. As noted by the geographer Donald W. Meinig, "Environment sustains us as creatures; landscape display us as cultures" (1979, p. 3). As an artifact of culture, landscapes are an appropriate focus of planners faced with land-use and environmental management issues. Ecology provides insight into landscape patterns, processes, and interactions. An understanding of ecology reveals how we interact with each other and our natural and built environments. What we know of such relationships is still relatively little but expanding all the time. As Ilya Prigogine and Isabelle Stengers have observed, "Nature speaks in a thousand voices, and we have only begun to listen" (1984, p. 77).

2

IDENTIFYING ISSUES AND ESTABLISHING PLANNING GOALS

The most straightforward means of deciding planning goals in a democratic society is by voting. However, before goals reach a vote, they must be defined. In addition, many issues do not reach a popular vote and are decided through actions by the legislative and/or the administrative branches of government. As a result, a variety of means have been developed to identify issues, to establish goals, and to assess public opinion about potential issues and goals. Some techniques include task forces, citizens and technical advisory committees, neighborhood planning councils, group dynamics, nominal-group workshops, and Delphi (Gil & Lucchesi, 1979). Once potential goals are set, politicians and public officials often depend on opinion polls for public reaction. Public opinion polls are also used to survey the problems and opportunities of an area and thereby to identify issues. An alternative to impersonal polling is the noisy, often emotional American tradition of the town meeting, or its stepchild, the public hearing. Two examples of planning that are goal-oriented and that emphasize ecological concerns are the Oregon statewide land-use planning law and the comprehensive management plan for the New Jersey Pinelands.

TECHNIQUES FOR INVOLVING PEOPLE IN THE IDENTIFICATION OF ISSUES AND THE ESTABLISHMENT OF GOALS

Task Forces

A *task force* is an ad hoc agency-sponsored citizen committee with a well-defined problem-solving or specific task and charge relating usually to a single problem or subject (Gil & Lucchesi, 1979). Such a specific task may be establishing goals for a plan. The existence of task forces is temporary. The directed purpose of a task force means membership is limited in number to allow all members to participate actively and effectively. The size of task forces varies from eight to twenty participants. Task forces usually rely on planning agencies for technical assistance and support but sometimes engage outside experts (U.S. Department of Transportation, 1976).

Citizens Advisory Committees and Technical Advisory Committees

Citizens advisory committees are groups presumed to represent the ideas and attitudes of local groups. Their purpose is to advise some decision-making body such as a planning commission, an agency staff, or a developer (Gil & Lucchesi, 1979). *Technical advisory committees* are groups that represent bodies of technical or scientific information important to a planning commission, agency, or developer. Often these groups are interdisciplinary or multidisciplinary. Citizens and technical advisory committees may be organized similar to task forces. However, their role encompasses a broader scope than an individual task. These groups may be involved in identifying issues, setting goals, and later establishing preferences as well as implementing the plan.

Citizens advisory committees have become increasingly popular for goal setting and policy-making by legislative bodies (Institute for Participatory Planning, 1978). Citizens advisory committee is a generic term that covers a variety of committees and councils differing in type, membership, and operations. Most have the following similar characteristics: limited power and authority, large membership (50 to 100 members), agency staff providing technical assistance, a life tied to the program or project, and infrequent meetings of full membership (U.S. Department of Transportation, 1976).

Technical advisory committee is also a generic term. It may be an intraagency committee made up of representatives from various staffs involved with or interested in a specific program or project, or it may be a group outside an agency from universities or consulting companies.

Neighborhood Planning Councils

Neighborhood planning councils are organizations formed by citizens or an outside community organizer that engage in a number of neighborhood programs as well as in advocacy and advice (Gil & Lucchesi, 1979). Neighborhood planning councils came into wide use during the 1960s as a result of federally funded programs such as urban renewal and model cities. These locally based councils serve as advisory bodies to elected officials and public agencies in identifying neighborhood problems and issues, formulating goals and priorities, and implementing and evaluating plans (U.S. Department of Transportation, 1976). Neighborhood councils are purely advisory in nature and seldom have any decision-making authority.

Organizing neighborhood groups is a complex skill. Two approaches familiar to many planners are the Alinsky approach and organization development. The former was developed by the famous Chicago organizer Saul Alinsky. The steps in the Alinsky (1946) approach include entering the community, sizing it up, making contacts, bringing people together, developing leadership, working with organizations, setting priorities, developing power tactics, building political power, working on self-help strategies, and exiting from the community.

Organization development is a discipline that evolved from group dynamics and field theory, which were established by psychologist Kurt Lewin. Students and followers of Lewin, including Chris Argyris, Warren Bennis, Carl Rogers, Edgar Schein, and other behavioral scientists, differ from traditional social scientists in that their role as practitioners, or change agents, occurs in organizations outside the academic environment. Organization development has been used extensively in large corporate structures. Some community planners have adapted these techniques for neighborhood-level organizing. Bolan explains organization development in the following way:

> The change agent, together with the client group, analyzes the forces available in support of, and resistant to, change. Such techniques stress awareness of the need for change and levels of change, methods for developing the goals of change, and the overcoming of resistance to change. (1979, p. 538)

Once organized, neighborhood-level planning councils may assist in the setting of goals for larger communities and provide public participation in other stages of the planning process. Their effectiveness is dependent on the skill with which they are organized and the level of interest in the neighborhood. Pitfalls include the inability of neighborhood groups to connect local issues to the needs of the larger society and the ephemeral nature of some of these groups.

Group Dynamics

Group dynamics is a generic term for a variety of problem-solving techniques used to clarify goals, encourage group interaction, and resolve conflicts within citizen groups (Gil & Lucchesi, 1979). The many techniques vary in their level of sophistication and degree of activity but share some common characteristics, including:

- *Small-group involvement.* Techniques are designed for small groups ranging from five to twenty-five members. If used with a larger membership, then participants are divided into small groups.
- *Skilled leadership.* Techniques require the direction of a group leader knowledgeable in and comfortable with the use of the particular technique. The role of the leader involves setting the stage for the technique by providing a general introduction and rationale, directing the process and specific activities that may be required, and generally keeping the process going to its conclusion.
- *Structured process.* Each technique involves a controlled, specified activity or series of ordered activities and/or tasks for all members of the group.
- *Timing.* Each technique covers a specific time span ranging from 30 to 90 minutes for completion. (U.S. Department of Transportation, pp. 104–105, 1976)

Group dynamics can be employed at almost any stage of the planning process, including issue identification and goal setting, in which the public is participating in an advisory committee, a task force, or a neighborhood council. Some strategies employed through group dynamics include empathy, feedback, video-taped group interview, brainstorming, nominal-group workshops, and role playing (U.S. Department of Transportation, 1976).

Nominal-Group Workshops

Nominal-group workshops are one form of group dynamics. The Institute for Participatory Management and Planning explains the concept in the following way:

> This technique is built on the premise that any reasonably representative group of people who are concerned with a project [or issue], identify virtually all of the problems associated with a project [or issue],

During the planning process, members of a group present issues identified as important by listing them on large sheets of paper. *(Washington State University College of Agriculture and Home Economics)*

3 × 5 cards without consulting others in the group. On each card, the individual writes one major issue and several reasons why this issue is important.

Afterward, each person presents one issue and why it was considered important to the group. These issues are listed on a blackboard or on a large sheet of paper. Members of the group take turns presenting issues until all issues are exhausted. The nominal group's issues are then presented to the whole body. Often only the top five or ten issues from the nominal groups are presented to the larger group. Next a vote is taken. Each person ranks what he or she considers the most important issues. Often the top five or ten issues are listed on the ballot. This may be done with paper ballots; it is also becoming popular to vote using computers that give an instant tally (Delbecq et al., 1975; Institute for Participatory Planning, 1978).

Next, the ballots are counted and ranked. This ranking is followed by general discussion. People lobby for and against issues. Another vote is taken, and the results are listed in priority. If the ranking has drastically changed, then another round of discussion, lobbying, and voting ensues. This continues until a consensus is reached (Delbecq et al., 1975; Institute for Participatory Planning, 1978). Nominal-group workshops have been used effectively to first identify problems and opportunities for an area and then to set goals.

Delphi

Delphi, developed by the RAND Corporation, is a technique that relies strongly on experts. Originally used as a means of technological forecasting, the name *Delphi* is taken from the ancient Greek city where travelers went to consult the oracle about the future (U.S. Department of Transportation, 1976). The idea is to conduct several rounds of argument offering different points of view about a project or issue until a consensus is reached. It is an indirect technique compared to

and can make the individual compromises that are necessary for coming up with a single list of priorities or preferences. (1978, p. V-6)

The nominal-group technique works in the following manner. A large group is brought together and given a balanced presentation of the project or subject being addressed by the workshop. This large group is then divided into nominally small groups of five to twelve people. Each person then individually fills out several blank

the direct citizen participation approaches involved in group dynamics.

Delphi works in the following manner. Experts are chosen. The Institute for Participatory Management and Planning suggests this may be done by conducting a survey among people knowledgeable about a particular issue. This can be accomplished through a bibliographical search of the literature about the issue. From the survey, a name is suggested. That person is contacted and asked to nominate a list of people who are knowledgeable about the subject. Each person on the list is contacted and asked to nominate her or his own list of experts. After a while, the same names keep reappearing. Experts representing different points of view are sought. For instance, if one is trying to establish land-use goals for a reclaimed strip mine, one expert from the mining industry may be sought, while another may be from a nature conservancy, another from agriculture, and so on. These people become a Delphi panel of experts that is never to meet or know who the other members of the panel are (Institute for Participatory Planning, 1978).

This panel of eight to twelve experts is asked to predict the future of the project or issue. These predictions are compiled and distributed to the panel without identifying the authors. The panel reviews the prophesies and is given the opportunity to change its own. If the predictions are changed, then a second round is conducted. The process is continued until the panel members remain firm in their forecasts or a consensus is reached. The predictions then may be used by a citizens advisory committee, technical advisory committee, neighborhood council, planning commission, and/ or agency staff to establish goals and policy for the project or issue.

These are the major techniques used for identifying issues and establishing goals. The techniques reviewed here and the others may be used in the subsequent stages of the planning process. The Institute for Participatory Management and Planning of Monterey, California,

has developed a matrix of citizen participation techniques and their relative effectiveness (Figure 2.1). Each planning issue or project should help to determine the appropriate participation technique. An effort should be made to keep people involved in the subsequent steps of the planning process. Sign-up sheets should be collected at all meetings and those lists used to keep people informed over time. Continual communication between the public and the planning agency or consultant can create knowledgeable citizens who will support decisions that result from the process. Some planners have found it helpful to maintain a newspaper article clipping file about public meetings to document public involvement and the planning process.

PUBLIC OPINION POLLS

Preference surveys, or *public opinion polls* as they are more commonly known, have become a ubiquitous part of American life. Surveys can be conducted through the mail, over the telephone, or by face-to-face interviews. Public opinion polls can be used to identify issues and to set goals. One of the leading practitioners of preference surveying, Don Dillman, a professor of sociology at Washington State University, has suggested that there are three schools of thought concerning public opinion polls. The first is do not conduct polls. The second is that surveys are fundamental for community participation. Finally, they can be useful, if done well.

Preference surveys are popular for a number of reasons. First, they are convenient for planners and other researchers. A researcher does not have to leave the comforts of her or his office to write a survey or compile the results. Second, results are relatively simple to tabulate. In this age of computers it is important that research results can be tabulated for statistical analysis. Finally, polls can be used to illustrate that the government pays attention to whatever the people say; thus because

Citizen Participation Objectives

Citizen Participation Techniques 1-7

Column headings (Citizen Participation Objectives):
1. Establish the legitimacy of your agency
2. Maintain the legitimacy of your agency
3. Establish the legitimacy of your process
4. Maintain the legitimacy of your process
5. Maint. Legit. of assumptions & earlier decisions
6. Get to know all affected interests
7. See the project through their eyes
8. Identify problems
9. Generate solutions
10. Articulate & clarify the key issues
11. Nurture & protect your credibility
12. Have your communications received & understood
13. Receive & understand communicated info.
14. Search for consensus
15. Mediate between polarized interests

Technique	1	2	3	4	5	6	7	8	9	10	11	12	13	14	15
1. Holding or attending meetings & public hearings															
1A. Working meetings	○	○	○		●	●	●	●	●	●	○	●		●	●
1B. "Open" meetings	●	●	●	●	●	●		○		●	●	●	○		
1C. Forums	●	○	○	○	●	●	●	●	●	●	●	●		○	
1D. Public mass meetings					○			○			○	●			
1E. Public hearings	●	●	●	●	●	○		○		●	●	○	○		
2. Using citizen advisory committees	○	○	○	○	●	●		○	○	○	○	○		●	●
2A. Committee of "Gofers"	●	●	●	●	●	●	●	●	●	●	●	●		●	○
3. Conducting a nominal-group workshop					●		●	●	●	○				●	●
4. Producing & releasing materials for communication to the public	●	●	●	●	●						●	●	●		○
5. Publishing a project newsletter	○	○	●	●	○						●	●	●		
6. "Napoleon's Idiot"											●		●		
7. Educating the public about your decision-making process	●	●	●	●	●						●	●	○	○	○
8. Mapping socio-political and environmental data							○	●	●	○		○	○		
9. Presenting the public the full range of feasible alternatives		○		○	○	○	○	●	●	●	○	●	●	○	○
10. Illustrating the final form of a proposed alternative in laymen's terms							●	●	○	○		●	○		
11. Dealing with the public in the agency offices	○	○	○	○		●	○	○					●		
12. Installing an ombudsman						○	○	○					●	○	○
13. Encouraging internal communication					○			●	●			○			
14. Gaming and role-playing	○	○	○	○		○	●	○							●
15. Operating a field office	○	○	○	○		●	●	○			●	○			
16. Making the most of existing organizations	●	●	●	●	●	○	○	●	○	●	●	●	○	●	●
17. Opening a channel of communication with each potentially affected interest	○	○	○	○		●	○	●	○		○	●	●		
18. Monitoring the mass media & other non-reactive learning						○	●	●	●	●			●		
19. Collecting data; carrying out surveys						○	○	●	○				●		
20. Examining past actions of an interest						○	○	●	●	○			○		
21. Experiencing empathy							●	●	●			○	○		
22. Being a "participant-observer"						○	●	●	●	●	○		●	○	○
23. Employing local citizens on the project			○			○	○	○	○		○	○	○	○	
24. Monitoring new developments in systems that may affect your project						○		●	●				○		
25. Conducting a background study					●		○	○	○	●		●	○		
26. Hiring an advocate for one or several affected interests		○	○	○		●	●	●	●		●	●	○		
27. Looking for analogies								○	○		●	●		○	○
28. Cataloging of solution concepts								●			●				
29. Conducting a "Charrette"					○		●	●	●	●	●	●	●	●	○
30. Mediating a conflict between different interests	○	○			○	●	○	○		○	○	○	○	●	●
31. Being a "good samaritan" by helping solve problems outside your scope of responsibility	●	●	●	●	○	○	●	○		●	○		○	○	○
32. Monitoring the actual impacts of a project		○		○	●	●	○	●	○	○	●		○		○
33. "Delphi" technique					●		○	●	●	●	○		○	○	

● Productive technique vis à vis objective
○ Moderately Productive   "   "
  Ineffective   "   "

Responsibility	Responsiveness	Effectiveness

Citizen Participation Objectives

FIGURE 2.1 Citizen participation techniques and their relative effectiveness.
(Source: Institute for Participatory Management and Planning, 1978)

the government is responsive, democracy is working.

The first of the arguments used by people pessimistic about the usefulness of polls is that "people are not well enough informed or otherwise capable of stating their real preferences" (Dillman, 1977, p. 31). Dillman questions if people who never went to high school can assess the needs of higher education or if people whose medical experience consists of an annual checkup can determine community health care needs. Land-use and natural resource management issues are equally complicated and may require technical information difficult for the average citizen to understand, as, for example, the siting of a nuclear power plant or a hazardous waste disposal site. Social and environmental issues are becoming more complex, requiring more specialized knowledge, and may not lend itself to simple yes, no, maybe, or no opinion responses.

The second basis of criticism raised by Dillman concerning the use of surveys is the belief that "people's stated preferences are superficial and likely to change; thus, they can provide an inadequate basis for making decisions with long lasting consequences" (1977, p. 32). A community's perception of a need for a service—a school, hospital, or highway—may be higher than its willingness to pay for the same service. A citizen may want the convenience of cheap electrical power or plastic garbage bags but resist the siting of a power generating plant or chemical factory in her or his community.

The final criticism is a technical one: "The procedures used for assessing people's preferences are inevitably inadequate, leaving a very large gap between survey questions and policy questions they were supposed to address" (Dillman, 1977, p. 32). Dillman (1978) gives several examples of this final point. For instance, a survey may attempt to ask very general questions, such as, "Do you consider juvenile delinquency to be a serious, moderate, slight, or no problem in this community?" and use them to address a specific issue: "Should we

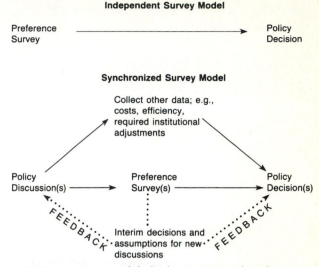

FIGURE 2.2 Two models for bringing stated preferences to bear on policy decisions. *(Source: Dillman, 1977)*

increase the parks and recreation budget by 25 percent?"

Dillman observes there is often a gap between survey questions and uses that are attempted to be made of the answers. He presents two models for policy surveys (Figure 2.2). The first, the independent survey, is illustrative of the typical, simplistic one-shot survey. His alternative, the synchronized survey, is one that can be used as an integral part of the entire planning process. In Chapter 4, surveys are discussed as a community inventory technique, while in Chapter 6, the synchronized survey will be presented as a means for the selection of preferences among various choices.

Another form of opinion polling is the community self-survey. In a less scientific approach the people of an area write and collect survey themselves instead of an outsider. The benefit of a self-survey is that it allows and even encourages people to think about the area in which they reside (Littrell, 1976). The disadvantages include possible biases in drafting the survey and inaccuracies that may result in tabulating and analyzing the results.

TOWN MEETINGS AND PUBLIC HEARINGS

The origin of the American tradition of town meetings is in New England. According to planning historian John Reps, in New England "the complete rural-urban settlement was called a town, a word that encompassed not only the nucleated urban-type settlement but the entire community of village lots and farm fields as well" (1970, p. 147). This form of town continues in New England and has had enduring influence in American politics.

The New England town meeting was an outgrowth of the need to provide defense and settle agricultural matters. It was strengthened by the religious bond that brought the Puritan settlers from England to the New World and their special political adeptness. The topography and hostile Indians reinforced the group consciousness already forged by religious persecution and military fraternity.

While the village became the focus of the New England community, agriculture became its chief occupation. Lots were drawn for house sites in the village, and the surrounding farmland was divided into long strips also assigned by drawing lots. Reps explains the unique farming structure:

> While the strips themselves were not fenced, it was the usual practice to enclose an entire field by a wooden fencing. Each farmer then became responsible for his proportionate share of the fencing. . . . [The group had to determine] what would be grown, when they would be harvested and what land should be left in fallow. Common cultivation was thus carried on. . . (1970, p. 148)

The Puritans who developed this system of common fields, or proprietor's commons, were not a politically naive group. They had risen in the sixteenth century in the Church of England, demanding greater strictness in religious discipline.

During part of the seventeenth century, they constituted a powerful political party, ruling England briefly after its bloody civil war. As a result, the New England town meeting was a sophisticated forum where defensive, agricultural, and other political matters were decided after open debate and discussion. Town meetings continue to be an integral part of local government in New England.

The contemporary heir of the New England town meeting for most of the United States is the *public hearing*. City planners have advocated public hearings as an essential part of good government and comprehensive planning since the beginning of the twentieth century. Hearings are now a part of most municipal and county governments in the United States and are often mandated by federal and state law. Planning commissions as well as the local legislative body—the city council or board of county commissioners—are often required to hold hearings in order to make plans and to amend them. Nowadays, many local issues are debated at public hearings and goals are discussed. A group of citizens may raise an issue at a public hearing, and as a result the planning commission, city council, or county commission may resolve to address the issue.

Often public hearings can be the best entertainment in town. Certainly they have more dimensions than the average television fare but require leaving the comfortable confines of one's own home. Many local governments have experimented with televising public hearings, but such programs seldom dent the Nielsen ratings. The result is that public hearings become dominated by single-issue adversary groups or special interests.

Efraim Gil and Enid Lucchesi explain this situation in the following way:

> Citizen participation is most often stimulated by existing social problems coupled with a lack of confidence in official solutions—and it varies with economic and social conditions. When citizens feel

that officials are making decisions similar to those that they themselves would make, or that these decisions necessitate special knowledge that the official has and the citizens do not have, or when they feel the decision is economically sound, they are not likely to actively participate in government. It is when these criteria of government performance are not being met that citizens lose confidence in government officials and the demand for the active participation arises. (1979, pp. 553–554)

Public hearings are a difficult forum in which to involve citizens in goal setting. Because such hearings are often a legal requirement, they may often assume a legal aura, which may intimidate citizens. Because officials have limited time, goals are often written before such hearings. This means the goals may be composed by a planning staff, perhaps only with the advice of vested interests. Therefore, people must be involved through task forces, advisory committees, or workshops before goals are set.

The role of citizen involvement is much debated. One school of thought holds that citizens are a nuisance that should be avoided. Another viewpoint is that public participation programs are little more than tokenism, ineffective because citizens are excluded from actual decision making. Many feel there is a gap between government agencies and grass roots community organizations. Ray MacNair (1981) has proposed a model to link agency planning and citizen organizing (Figure 2.3).

GOAL SETTING

Often more than one citizen involvement technique will be used by planners to identify issues and to set goals. For example, the local planning commission may believe rapid growth is causing problems such as linking new public services to new development and raising the funds to pay for those additional public services. Furthermore, members of the planning commission may have observed that the quality of the new development is

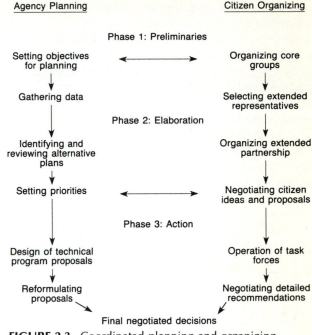

FIGURE 2.3 Coordinated planning and organizing. *(Source: MacNair, 1981)*

below existing community standards, thus creating safety hazards for new residents and negatively impacting the property values of existing homeowners. They may also observe that some new development is sited in locations where environmental damage is caused and potential health and safety problems are created. The planning commissioners may then request the staff planner or a consultant to study the situation. The staff or consulting planner may conduct a mail survey of the planning area to determine if indeed these perceptions are accurate. If the findings of the survey are affirmative, then a task force may be organized to recommend goals for addressing the problems created by the growth. These suggested goals are presented at hearings before the planning commission, who in turn can recommend that goals be established by the county commission or city council. At this step in the planning process, goals should be considered preliminary. Still there should be some agreed-upon goal statement to guide the rest of the process. To address the growth issue, for instance, the goal could be "to provide for planned and orderly development within the planning area, while balancing basic human needs of a changing population and maintaining a healthy environment for future generations."

In an ecological planning process, goals should be approached in an evolutionary manner. At this early step in the planning process, some consensus should be reached about the direction to be taken to address the problems and opportunities facing the area. These aims should be debated and refined throughout the planning process, as suggested by the central position of step 8 in Figure 1.1. At some point, goals need to be adopted formally. In Chapter 7, it is recommended that goals become part of a landscape plan.

TWO EXAMPLES OF GOAL-ORIENTED PLANNING

The Oregon Comprehensive Planning Law

Beginning in the 1960s and continuing to the present, several states adopted ambitious, new land-use planning laws. These new laws often prescribe that local governments adopt specific goals. Among the most far-reaching statewide planning efforts are those of Hawaii, Vermont, Oregon, and Florida (Bosselman & Callies 1971; Bosselman et al., 1973; Callies, 1980; & DeGrove, 1984). The Oregon comprehensive law provides one of the best examples of statewide goal-oriented planning. With the late Governor Tom McCall providing the leadership, this law was created by the Oregon legislature in 1973. The law established the Land Conservation and Development Commission (LCDC), authorizing the governor to appoint citizen members to the LCDC and the LCDC to coordinate planning in Oregon. Nineteen

goals were set as regulations to be followed by city and county governments throughout the state. Since some goals are specific to coastal counties or those along the Willamette River, the number of goals that local governments must follow varies somewhat. The goals were established in 1975 after a program of 127 citizen workshops that involved 10,000 participants (Pease, 1984). Each of these goals reveals much about the problems and opportunities facing Oregon and the policies established to address the planning issues raised by those problems and opportunities.

The nineteen statewide goals are printed in a twenty-four-page newsprint tabloid that has been continuously distributed throughout the state and reprinted since 1975. The tabloid offers an accessible easy-to-read format. Definitions of the technical terms are provided. As a result, the Oregon comprehensive plan is a familiar document in the state, rather than a thick technical report that has languished and been forgotten on someone's office bookshelf. A review of several of Oregon's goals helps illustrate the thrust of the plan. The first goal addresses citizen involvement; it is a statewide goal:

> To develop a citizen involvement program that insures the opportunity for citizens to be involved in all phases of the planning process. (Land Conservation and Development Commission, 1980, p. 3)

This goal statement and the ones that followed are accompanied by specific planning and implementation guidelines. The guidelines for the first goal include standards for citizen involvement, communication, citizen influence, technical information, feedback mechanisms, and financial support (see Chapter 8). Citizens are to be involved throughout the planning process in inventorying, recording, mapping, describing, analyzing, and evaluating the elements necessary for the development of local plans. The public is to participate in the preparation of local plans and the adoption process, plus the implementation, evaluation, and revision of plans.

The second statewide goal addresses land-use planning. It is the second goal of Oregon:

> To establish a land-use planning process and policy framework as a basis for all decisions and actions related to the use of land and to assure an adequate factual base for such decisions and actions. City, county, state, and federal agency and special district plans and actions related to land use shall be consistent with the comprehensive plans of cities and counties and regional plans. . . . (Land Conservation and Development Commission, 1980, p. 4)

The land-use planning goal is accompanied by a statement explaining where exceptions could be made under certain circumstances. An integrated framework is required for the preparation of plans and implementation measures; the conformance of regional, state, and federal plans; the content of the plan; the filing of plans; revisions during the planning process; implementation measures; and the use of the statewide planning goals (Land Conservation and Development Commission, 1980) (see Chapter 7).

The LCDC specifies the plan contents including its factual basis and the planning elements. The factual base is to address data concerning natural resources, human-made structures and utilities, population and economic characteristics, and the roles and responsibilities of governmental units. The planning elements are the applicable statewide planning goals, any critical geographic areas designated by the Oregon legislature, elements that address any special needs or concerns of the people of the planning area, and time periods. Furthermore, the LCDC requires that all these elements should fit together and relate to one another to form a consistent whole at all times.

The guidelines for land-use implementation include management measures like ordinances controlling the use and construction on the land such as building codes, sign ordinances, subdivision regulations, and zoning ordinances. Oregon statutes require subdivision and zoning ordinances to be consistent with a comprehensive

plan. Additional management measures are specific plans for public facilities, capital improvement budgeting, state and federal land-use regulations, and annexations and other governmental boundary reorganizations. Site and specific area implementation measures include building permits, septic tank permits, driveway permits, subdivision review, zone changes, conditional use permits, the construction of public facilities, the provision of land-related public services such as fire and police, the awarding of state and federal grants to local governments to provide these facilities and services, and the leasing of public lands (Land Conservation and Development Commission, 1980). Plan implementation measures will be discussed in greater detail in Chapter 10.

The statewide third goal is to preserve and maintain agricultural lands. This goal states:

> Agricultural lands shall be preserved and maintained for farm use, consistent with existing and future needs for agricultural products, forest, and open space. These lands shall be inventoried and preserved by adopting exclusive farm use zones. . . . Such minimum lot sizes as are utilized for any farm use zones shall be appropriate for the continuation of the existing commercial agricultural enterprise with the area. Conversion of rural agricultural land to urbanizable land shall be based upon consideration of the following factors: (1) environmental, energy, social, and economic consequences; (2) demonstrated need consistent with LCDC goals; (3) unavailability of an alternative suitable location for the requested use; (4) compatibility of the proposed use with related agricultural land; and (5) the retention of Class I, II, III, and IV soils in farm use. (Land Conservation and Development Commission, 1980, p. 6)

The SCS land capability classification system is used to define agricultural land in Oregon. Guidelines are established for both the planning and implementation of the agricultural goal. The first planning guideline states that urban growth should be separated from agricultural lands by buffer, or transitional, areas of open space. The second planning guideline states that plans providing for the preservation and maintenance of farmland for agricultural use should consider as a major determinant the carrying capacity of the air, land, and waste resources of the planning area. There are four guidelines for the implementation of the agricultural lands goal. First, nonfarm uses permitted within farm-use zones should be minimized to allow for maximum agricultural productivity. Second, extension of services, such as sewer and waste supplies, into rural areas should be appropriate for the needs of agriculture, farm use, and permitted nonfarm use. Third, special provisions are made for services that need to pass through agricultural lands to protect the farm-use integrity of the area. Finally, forest and open space uses are to be permitted on farmlands that are set aside for future agricultural development (Land Conservation and Development Commission, 1980).

The fourth statewide goal of Oregon is to conserve forestlands for forest uses. The goal states:

> Forest land shall be retained for production of wood fiber and other forest uses. Lands suitable for forest uses shall be inventoried and designated as forest lands. Existing forest land uses shall be protected unless proposed changes are in conformance with the comprehensive plan. (Land Conservation and Development Commission, 1980, p. 4)

The designation of forestlands is based on a classification system used by the USFS. Forest-lands are existing and potential areas suitable for commercial forest uses. Other forested lands needed for watershed protection, wildlife and fisheries habitat, recreation, and special ecological consideration are also to be included. In addition, forested areas in agricultural and urban areas necessary to provide buffers are to be considered (Land Conservation and Development Commission, 1980). Again, there are specific guidelines for the

During October the Pinelands bogs are flooded to loosen cranberries from their vines, a step in the harvesting of this crop, which yields more than $9 million a year.
(Photo by Norma Martin Milner of the New Jersey Pinelands Commission)

planning and implementation of the forestlands goal.

Goals 5 through 9 address open spaces, scenic and historic areas, and natural resources; air, water, and land resources quality; areas subject to natural disasters and hazards; recreational needs; and the economy of the state. The tenth goal is "to provide for the housing needs of citizens of the state" (Land Conservation and Development Commission, 1980, p. 10). To achieve this goal, buildable land for home sites is to be identified. Plans are to encourage the development on those lands of "adequate numbers of housing units at price ranges and rent levels which are com-mensurate with the financial capabilities of Oregon households," and the plans are to "allow for flexibility of housing location, type and density" (Land Conservation and Development Commission, 1980, p. 10).

The remaining nine goals include:

11. Public facilities and services
12. Transportation
13. Energy conservation
14. Urbanization
15. Willamette River greenway
16. Estuarine resources
17. Coastal shoreline
18. Beaches and dunes
19. Ocean resources

Each of these nineteen goals is explained in a succinct statement. Each goal is accompanied by specific guidelines for planning and implementation. Key terms are defined with several of the goal statements and in a glossary on the two final pages of the tabloid. This is the most comprehensive statement of goals ever developed for an American state, and it is printed on 24 pages of newsprint. The achievement of these goals has required the careful balancing of often conflicting demands. Because of the difficulty of this task and the success of the Oregon planning effort, it will be used as an example throughout this book, as will the plan for the New Jersey Pinelands.

New Jersey Pinelands Comprehensive Management Plan

The New Jersey Pinelands, or Pine Barrens as it is known by its inhabitants, is a substate, multicounty region (Figure 2.4). The Pinelands is a 1-million-acre (407,000-hectare) forest located in the midst of the most densely populated region in the United States. The New Jersey Pinelands Comprehensive Management Plan was a result of both federal and state legislative action. The federal action was the designation by Congress in 1978 of the Pinelands as a national reserve. This legislative mandate was set forth in the National Parks and Recreation Act of 1978, signed by President Jimmy Carter. The state action was the 1979 New Jersey Pinelands Protection Act (Pinelands Commission, 1980).

As a result of these actions, Governor Brendan T.

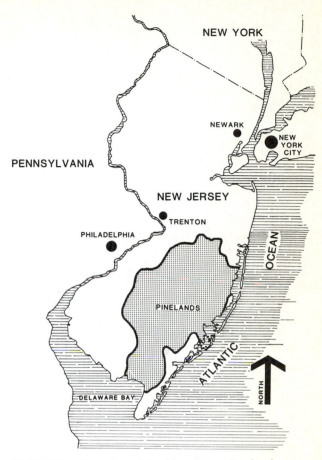

FIGURE 2.4 Location of the New Jersey Pinelands.

Byrne issued an executive order that established the Pinelands Planning Commission. The commission's composition was prescribed in both the federal and state laws as follows: fifteen members, including one appointed by each of the governing bodies of the seven Pinelands counties, seven appointed by the governor of New Jersey, and one designated by the U.S. Secretary of the Interior. The overriding goals of the acts are to preserve, protect, and enhance the significant values of the land and water resources in the Pinelands. The state act speaks of the need to maintain a contiguous tract of land in its natural state, safeguard the essential character of the Pinelands

TABLE 2.1
PINELANDS GOALS AND POLICIES

Natural Resources Goal	**Preserve, protect, and enhance the overall ecological values of the Pinelands, including its large forested areas, its essential character, and its potential to recover from disturbance.**

Policy 1: Preserve, protect, and enhance the quality and quantity of surface and groundwater.
Policy 2: Preserve, protect, and enhance the diversity of plant and animal communities and their habitats.
Policy 3: Preserve, protect, and enhance existing soil conditions.
Policy 4: Preserve, protect, and enhance existing topographic features.
Policy 5: Preserve, protect, and enhance existing air quality.
Policy 6: Protect natural scenic qualities.

Historic and Cultural Goal	**Maintain and enhance the historic and cultural resources of the Pinelands.**

Policy 1: Maintain opportunities for traditional lifestyles that are related to and compatible with the overall ecological values of the Pinelands.
Policy 2: Maintain the social and cultural integrity of traditional Pinelands communities.
Policy 3: Maintain and enhance historic and archeological areas and sites of national, state, and local importance.

Agricultural and Horticultural Goal	**Preserve and enhance agricultural and horticultural uses that are compatible with the preservation and protection of the overall ecological values of the Pinelands.**

Policy 1: Reserve for agricultural purposes prime agricultural soils and soils of statewide significance in or adjacent to established agricultural areas
Policy 2: Reserve unique agricultural soils and protect water quality and quantity necessary for cranberry and blueberry cultivation.
Policy 3: Protect the long-term economic viability of agricultural activities.
Policy 4: Require the use of recommended management practices in areas of substandard water quality.

environment, protect the quality of the surface and ground water, promote compatible agricultural and recreational uses, and encourage appropriate residential, commercial, and industrial patterns of development (Pinelands Commission, 1980).

Based on the state and federal legislation, the Pinelands Commission adopted five resource and use goals and twenty-five policies. The goals and policies were not as comprehensive as those goals and guidelines developed by the LCDC. The resource goals and policies adopted for the Pinelands are in Table 2.1. As can be seen from Table 2.1, the Pinelands goals emphasized the protection of natural, historical and cultural, and agricultural resources. Development is to be encouraged in a manner compatible with these resources. The overall goal of the Pinelands plan is to balance resource conservation and development. (The plan is discussed further in Chapter 7.)

The Pinelands and Oregon cases are two examples of planning goals with a strong emphasis

Policy 5: Protect agricultural operations and other private landowners from trespass and vandalism.

Policy 6: Encourage horticulture of native Pinelands plants.

Development Goal	**Accommodate residential, commercial, and industrial development in a way that is compatible with the preservation and protection of the overall ecological and cultural values of the Pinelands.**

Policy 1: Permit infill development in existing communities.

Policy 2: Direct new residential, commercial, and industrial development into environmentally suitable areas in orderly patterns which are with or adjacent to existing developed areas.

Policy 3: Assure opportunities for housing for all economic groups.

Policy 4: Allow economic development which supports existing community needs but does not generate new development outside those areas designated for future development by the Comprehensive Management Plan.

Policy 5: Permit growth-generating capital improvements only within those areas designated for future development.

Recreation Goal	**Protect and enhance outdoor recreational uses and the natural resources on which they depend.**

Policy 1: Preserve, protect, and enhance those natural resources, including forests, waters, and wildlife habitats, necessary for compatible recreational uses.

Policy 2: Promote diverse recreational opportunities in a manner that minimizes land-use conflicts.

Policy 3: Assure that recreational uses in undeveloped areas be of low intensity and compatible with the protection of the natural resources.

Policy 4: Assure that, insofar as possible, intensive recreational uses be located in or near developed areas.

Policy 5: Protect and enhance opportunities for proprietary recreational facilities in areas that are suitable for such uses.

SOURCE: Pinelands Commission, 1980.

on environmental protection and natural resource management. These examples have been criticized for not adequately considering local values (for a critique of the Pinelands in this regard, see Berger & Sinton, 1985). The effectiveness of the resultant planning programs has also been questioned (see, for example, Daniels & Nelson, 1986, regarding Oregon). Nevertheless, both are examples of goals for ecological planning that have been established by state and federal governments.

These goals were set because issues were identified and governments responded. The Pinelands region and the state of Oregon face a range of problems and opportunities because of their ecological and scenic resources. In the Pinelands, the threat to these resources was recognized at the state level, which prompted actions by New Jersey and the federal government. The actions set goals for the region and local governments. In Oregon, the environment is highly valued by citizens throughout the state. Grass roots concerns resulted in statewide legislation that initiated a citizen involvement process to set goals for local governments in Oregon.

This emphasis on ecological values differentiate the Pinelands and Oregon goals from those of conventional planning processes. As compared with conventional programs, the Pinelands and Oregon goals are linked more directly to specific policies and implementation guidelines, which also emphasize environmental protection and natural resource management.

3

INVENTORY AND ANALYSIS OF THE BIOPHYSICAL ENVIRONMENT

After a community has identified the problems and opportunities that it faces and has reached some consensus concerning its goals to address those issues, then it is necessary to collect the information needed to achieve community goals. Information about nature has often been used in an ad hoc manner in American planning. Only that information needed to achieve a specific goal is collected—so too often it is disconnected information. For instance, since flooding is recognized by a community as a hazard to human safety, the responsible elected officials adopt a goal to prevent buildings in flood-prone areas. These areas are mapped and building restricted. The goal is one-dimensional.

The basic premise of ecology is that everything is connected to everything else. As a result, the ecological approach differs from more traditional methods. Whereas in conventional planning only the flood-prone areas are identified, in contrast, the complex matrix of factors related to flooding would be considered in ecological planning. Flooding is the result of the interaction of several natural phenomena—rainfall, bedrock, terrain, temperature, and vegetation, for instance. Since ecological planning rests on an understanding of relationships, broader-range information about the biophysical processes of an area must be collected and analyzed. Moreover, the sequence of collecting it is important.

Older, larger-scale components of the landscape exert a strong influence on more ephemeral elements. Regional climate and geology help determine soils and water drainage systems of an area that, in turn, affect what vegetation and animals will inhabit a place. As a result, in ecological planning one begins to inventory the older elements and proceed to the youngest.

When conducting such an inventory, it is useful to identify boundaries so that the various biophysical elements can be compared with each other over the same spatial area and at the same scale. Often such a planning area is defined by legislative goals, as, for instance, with the New Jersey Pinelands.

Ideally, several levels of inventories from regional to local are undertaken. A hierarchy of levels is identified so that the planning area may be understood as part of a larger system and specific places may be seen as parts of a whole. The drainage basin at the regional level and the watershed more locally are ideal units of analysis for ecological planning. A *watershed* is an area drained by a river or river system, also called a *catchment area* or, in the United States at a larger scale, a *drainage basin*. Eugene Odum suggests the watershed as "a practical ecosystem unit for management that combines natural and cultural attributes" (1971, p. 512), while Peter Quinby (1988) notes that watershed boundaries can be used as ecosystem boundaries. The watershed is a handy unit that contains biological, physical, social, and economic processes. Watersheds have discrete boundaries yet can vary in scale. This

provides flexibility to adapt to social, economic, and political issues. Watersheds also offer linkages between the elements of regions. One reason they can be considered an ideal is that the flow of water, the linkage, throughout the watershed may be easily visualized.

The use of watersheds for planning is not new. John Wesley Powell, who introduced the term *region* to North America, essentially suggested the use of watersheds in his 1879 plan for the American west. The use of watersheds is also consistent with past efforts of watershed conservancies and river basin commissions, such as the Delaware River Basin Commission, the Columbia River Basin Commission, and the Tennessee Valley Authority, and with programs of the SCS, Army Corps of Engineers, NPS, and USFS. But, more often than not, units other than watersheds—political boundaries most frequently—are used. Still the principle of hierarchy can apply to political boundaries, with counties forming the regional scale and cities or towns being used as the unit for local landscape analysis.

In this chapter, a method for the inventory, analysis, and synthesis of the biophysical components of the landscape in the planning process is presented. This approach to data collection can be used at the regional, local, and even site-specific scales. To illustrate this chapter, an example of a small area around the town of Albion in Whitman County, eastern Washington State, is used. This biophysical inventory and analysis was conducted as a part of a larger planning process to help implement goals adopted by a county government. This chapter presents methods for making base maps, inventorying elements of the landscape, and analyzing and synthesizing this information. Two examples, the New Jersey Pinelands and the Makah Indian Reservation in Washington State, are used as illustrations.

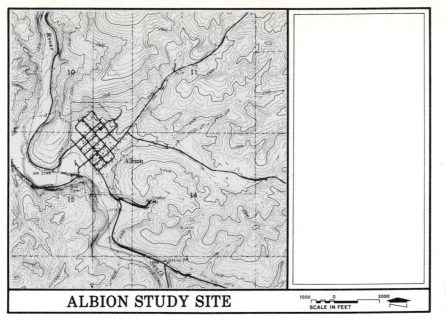

ALBION STUDY SITE

SCALE IN FEET

FIGURE 3.1 Base map of Albion, Washington. *(Source: U.S. Geological Survey)*

MAKING A BASE MAP AND A REGIONAL CONTEXT MAP

The starting point for collecting information in a graphic format is the *base map,* a map from which copies are made. The most convenient source for a base map is the USGS 7.5-minute quadrangle maps with a scale of 1:24,000. USGS maps are available for most areas in the United States. They give the location of all buildings (except in urban areas), bodies of water, elevations, contour lines, roads, rail lines, political boundaries, and some woodlands. A portion of a quadrangle map or several quadrangle maps mosaicked (pieced) together can be photographically reproduced on polyester film. Additional information can be added to the polyester film to form the base map. The most important information includes a north arrow, a proportional scale, a map title, a legend, the source of the information displayed, the name of the planning area, and the names of the company, university group, and/or agency performing the study (Figure 3.1). In addition to the familiar 7.5-minute quadrangle maps, ortho aerial photographs at the same scale are now available from the USGS in many areas (Figure 3.2). These photographs are helpful for both performing inventories and displaying information.

Next, the study area needs to be placed in a regional context. This is important because people who read a planning report often come from outside the area described. Often it is necessary to place the area in a subregional context, perhaps a county or other governmental jurisdiction, then in a larger regional context, such as the state or multistate region (Figure 3.3).

INVENTORY ELEMENTS

Regional Climate

Climate is the set of meteorological conditions characteristic of an area over a given length of time. The regional, or macro, climate is the big picture, the meteorological conditions and patterns over a large area. Macroclimate is measured at about 2 meters above the ground and is affected by physical conditions such as mountains, ocean currents, prevailing winds, and latitude. Macroclimate, in turn, affects the formation of the physiographic region. As observed by Pielke and Avissar (1990), the atmosphere is responsive to the landscape, and landscape ecology will change in response to atmospheric alterations. Changes in land use cause major alterations in both regional and local climate (Pielke & Avissar, 1990).

The Albion study area illustrates the types of macroclimate information that should be inventoried as well as the other elements that follow. The town of Albion is located in the region known as the Palouse of eastern Washington and northern Idaho (Figure 3.3). The macroclimate of the Palouse is influenced by both continental and marine weather patterns (Figure 3.4). Located in

the inland basin between the Cascade Range and the Rocky Mountains, the region is defined by the Köppen climatic classification system as a middle-latitude steppe. The Palouse is sheltered by the Cascades from the moderating influence of the Pacific. Most of the cold waves sweeping down from Canada are blocked by the northern highlands and Rockies—most stay to the east of the Rockies but do occasionally "slop over" the Bitterroot Range. As a result of these factors, the Palouse experiences a wide temperature range (Figure 3.5). Hot, dry, and sunny summer days with cool evenings are common, with a maximum temperature of 110°F (43.4°C) having been recorded. Meanwhile, winters are cold with frequent periods of cloudy or foggy weather. During an average winter, the maximum temperatures range from 30 to 40°F (−1.1 to 4.4°C), and minimums range from 15 to 30°F (−9.4 to −1.1°C). Colder temperatures occur

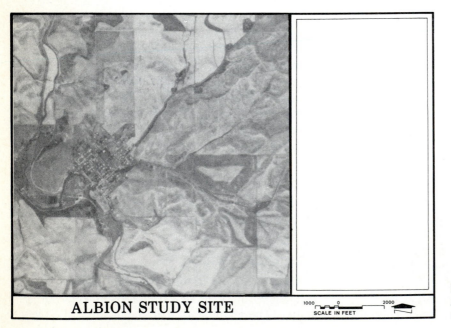

ALBION STUDY SITE

1000   0   2000
SCALE IN FEET

FIGURE 3.2 Aerial photograph of Albion, Washington. *(Source: U.S. Geological Survey)*

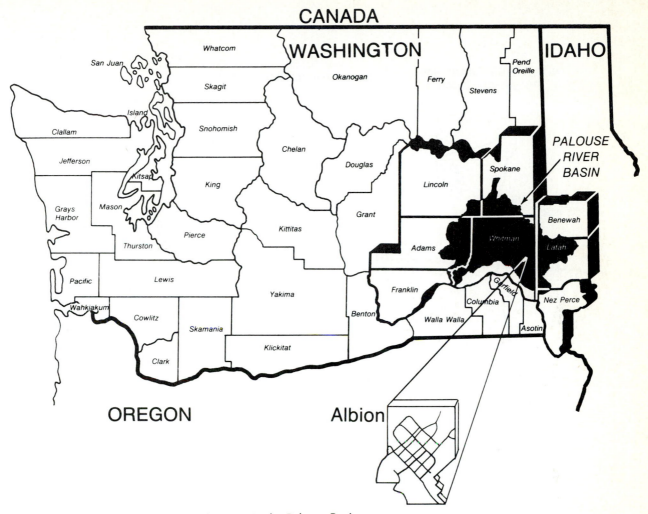

FIGURE 3.3 Context of Albion, Washington, in the Palouse Region.

when arctic air moves into the area, usually for brief periods. The lowest temperature recorded was 37°F below zero (−38.8°C) (Ledwitz, 1977; U.S. Department of Agriculture, 1978).

Precipitation in Whitman County ranges from 11 inches (27.9 centimeters) annually on its western border to above 22 inches (55.88 centimeters) annually on its eastern border. Most of this

precipitation occurs in the winter months (Figure 3.6). In Whitman County, the prevailing direction of the wind is generally from the southwest but is from the northwest in winter. The higher velocities in both winter and summer vary from southerly to westerly directions. Rapidly moving weather systems cause blowing dust during the spring and fall. In summer, there is a wide range in the

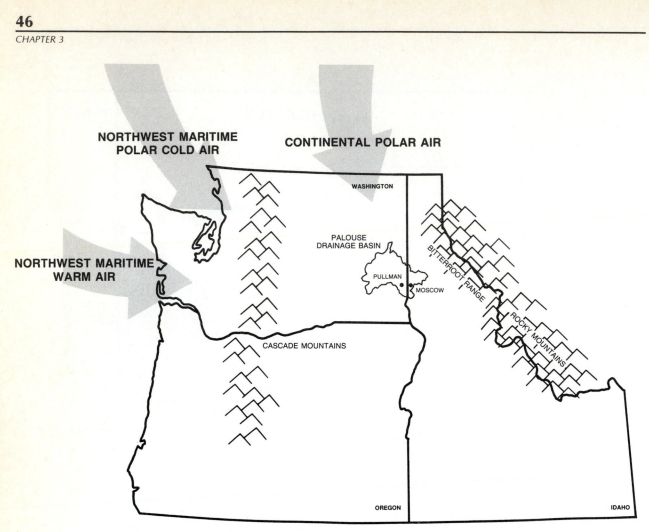

FIGURE 3.4 Macroclimatic influences of the Palouse Region.

relative humidity from the low morning temperatures to the warmer afternoons (Ledwitz, 1977; U.S. Department of Agriculture, 1978).

SUMMARY OF REGIONAL CLIMATE INVENTORY ELEMENTS

1. Köppen classification
2. Average temperatures
3. Average precipitation
4. Prevailing winds
5. Relative humidity

MAJOR SOURCES OF INFORMATION

1. National Weather Service
2. National Oceanic and Atmospheric Administration (NOAA)

The best source for climate information is:

National Climatic Data Center
National Oceanic and Atmospheric
  Administration
Federal Building
Asheville, NC 28801

Regional information is available concerning monthly precipitation, temperature, and wind data

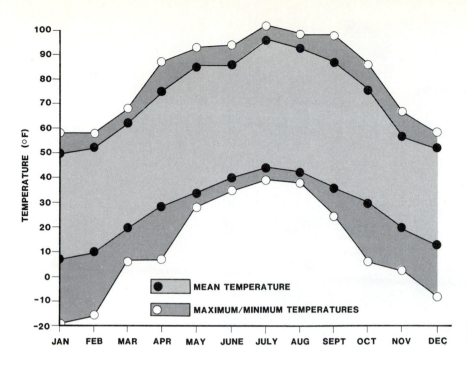

FIGURE 3.5 Average temperature ranges of Pullman, Washington.

FIGURE 3.6 Average precipitation by month for Pullman, Washington, and precipitation ranges for Whitman County.

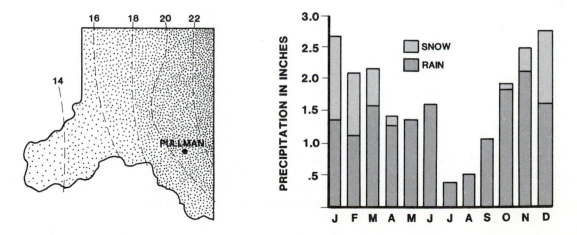

FIGURE 3.7 Typical Palouse landscape. *(Courtesy of USDA)*

3. Federal Aviation Administration (FAA)
4. Local weather stations and/or airports
5. College or university libraries
6. Farmers

Geology

Geology is the study of the earth. This study involves both what has happened in the past, or geological history, and what is happening on and in the earth today, or process. The inventory of a place requires an understanding of the geological history and processes of the region.

Located in the inland basin between the Cascade Range and the Rocky Mountains, Albion is in the physiographic region commonly known as the Palouse. The unique dunelike topography of the Palouse is a result of windblown loess deposits that cover the area (Figure 3.7). Through the eolian (windblown) deposition and erosion by rain and runoff, the landscape has developed into a complex formation of small hills and valleys.

A geology map of Albion reveals that the area is characterized by two types of subsurface and two types of surface formations. Crystalline granite rocks, which underlie the area, were formed about 70 million years ago. These protrude through the younger formations at a few high points throughout the region (Figure 3.8). Over the crystalline rocks are *basalts*. Better known as Yakima basalts, they originated as subsurface lava flows during the Miocene and Pliocene Periods. Largely as a result of erosion they are exposed as outcrops at the surface in many locations, especially along stream banks and steep slopes. These subsurface basalts and granite are covered by eolian silts called *loess*. They were carried into the area from the Columbia River basin by prevailing southwest winds. The

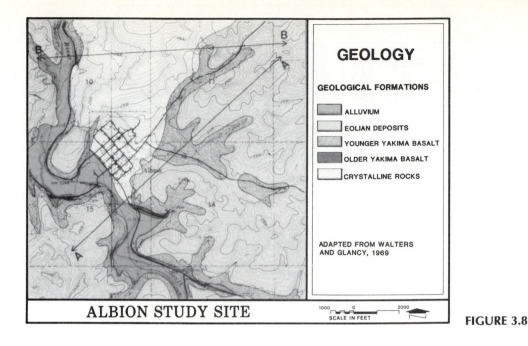

ALBION STUDY SITE

FIGURE 3.8

resulting loess soils, known collectively as the *Palouse formation,* are fertile and support some of the nation's most productive dryland agriculture. Alluvial (waterborne) deposits are predominant along streams and valley bottoms. In some cases, they are merely relocated loess, and, in other cases, they range from coarse sands to gravels and are principally basalt rubble (Walters & Glancy, 1969; Nassar & Walters, 1975).

The geology map is illuminated by a columnar section and a lithologic description that explain the depositional or intrusive sequence and the composition of the rock units (Figure 3.9). Rock is a natural mixture or aggregate of materials and can be classified into three general types on the basis of origin: (1) igneous rocks, which cool from molten liquid; (2) sedimentary rocks, which are derived from preexisting rock or rock materials by surficial geological processes of weathering, transportation, and deposition or as a result of chemical and biological processes; and (3) metamorphic rocks,

which form from existing rocks as a result of heat or pressure changes in the crust of the earth. A columnar section can be accompanied by a geologic history that explains the origin of rock units. Two columnar sections of Albion are used to illustrate both a hilltop and a streambed area.

In some regions, it is helpful to produce separate maps for bedrock and surficial deposits or regolith. A bedrock geology map shows the continuous solid rock of the continental crust, while the surficial geology map illustrates the distribution of deposits on the surface of the landscape. In the Albion demonstration area, most of the geologic units are surficial (i.e., the windblown loess and the alluvium). In many places, it is important to map geologic hazards, such as radon-prone deposits and active fault zones. Such information may be included on the geology map or a separate hazards map.

The most important aspect of a geological analysis is the ability to visualize the units in three

STREAMBED SECTION

HILLTOP SECTION

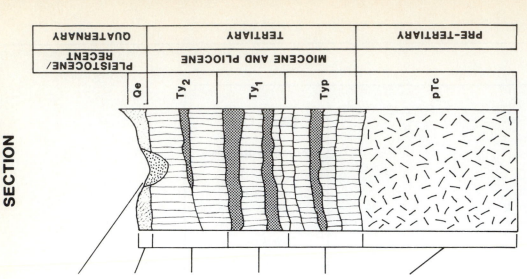
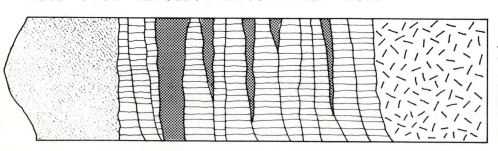

	QUATERNARY	TERTIARY	PRE-TERTIARY
	PLEISTOCENE/RECENT	MIOCENE AND PLIOCENE	
	Qe	Ty₂	Ty₁	Typ	pTc

COLUMNAR SECTION

ALLUVIUM

Fluvial deposits consisting of some rock fragments, sand, silt, and clay. Unit also includes windborne volcanic ash deposits visible in some freshly cut arroyos. Includes alluvial terrace deposits of possible Pleistocene age along Snake River upstream from Riparia. Deposits restricted mainly to major flood plains, and range in thickness from a few feet to 170 feet.

EOLIAN DEPOSITS

Tan to brown deposits of silt and clay-size particles that contain some prominent caliche zones in the western part of the country. Individual deposits not differentiated. Eolian deposits (principally loess) are extensive throughout the county, although erosion has removed considerable quantities in channeled scabland region. Thickness ranges from a few feet to about 300 feet.

YAKIMA BASALT & SEDIMENTARY INTERBEDS OVER ROZA MEMBERS

Includes flows of Priest Rapids Member and flows of possibly younger age. Exposures are dark-gray to black and range from massive- to medium-bedded, depending on the thickness of individual flows. Some vesicular zones are present, but much basalt is very dense. Basalts of this unit are distinguished by lack of megascopically developed plagioclase phenocrysts. Some flows impinge on steptoes of pretertiary crystalline basement rocks that were only slightly covered or never completely buried by basalt flows. Interbeds consist essentially of sand and finer size particles derived mainly from crystalline rocks and pyroclastic detritus. Thickness exceeds 100 feet in many places.

YAKIMA BASALT & INTERBEDS WITH ROZA MEMBER AS UPPERMOST UNIT

Basalt of Roza Member chiefly characterized by distinctive plagioclase phenocrysts ranging from reddish-brown to gray to black. Roza basalt is variable in content, ranging from sparsely to highly vesicular. Interbeds consist of sand and finer sized particles derived mainly from crystalline rocks and pyroclastic detritus. Unit is thousands of feet thick over most of the county; not differentiated in extreme southeast corner, where Roza Member apparently pinches out.

YAKIMA AND (OR) PICTURE GORGE BASALT & SEDIMENTARY INTERBEDS

Includes basalt flows that range from thin- to thick-bedded. Composition of individual flows appears to vary only slightly within project area. Individual lithographic units fine- to coarse-grained basalt, porphyritic basalt, flow breccias, cinder beds, and sedimentary interbeds. Interbeds consist essentially of sand and finer size particles derived mainly from crystalline rocks and pyroclastic detritus. Thickness ranges from hundreds to thousands of feet.

CRYSTALLINE ROCKS

Principally quartzite, phyllite, schist, granite gneiss, granite pegmatite, and granite igneous rocks. Includes a distinctive granitic body exposed along Snake River at Granite Point. Metamorphic rocks, probably metasediments, generally chemically altered, in many places extensively. Unit locally protrudes above all basalt flows in eastern part of county. In other exposures it has been exhumed by recent erosion.

FIGURE 3.9 Columnar section and a lithographic description of the Palouse geology.

dimensions. Topographic profiles, geologic cross sections, and block diagrams are three-dimensional illustrative devices that are shown in Figure 3.10. Figure 3.11 indicates symbols commonly used to show structure on geologic maps and representative patterns commonly used to show kinds of rocks in geologic cross sections. The geologic cross sections and block diagrams of the Albion area show the same information as the columnar section. Geologic cross sections, however, are more specific and show where a formation occurs beneath the landscape. Block diagrams are also especially helpful in visualizing the physiography of an area.

SUMMARY OF GEOLOGIC INVENTORY ELEMENTS

1. Depth to bedrock
2. Outcrops
3. Bedrock types and characteristics
4. Cross sections
5. Surficial deposits (regolith)
6. Mineral resources
7. Major fault line and earthquake zones

MAJOR SOURCES OF INFORMATION

1. USGS. The best source for obtaining information is the circular titled *A Guide to Obtaining Information from the USGS* (Geological Survey Circular 900). It is available from:

   Branch of Distribution
   U.S. Geological Survey
   Box 25286, Federal Center
   Denver, CO 80225

2. *Bibliography of Geology.* Published annually and compiled every 10 years by the USGS.
3. State departments of natural resources, mining, and ecology.
4. College or university libraries.

Physiography

The world is a myriad of peaks and depressions, ridges and valleys, rolling hills and flat areas, small bumps and slight slumps; it is uneven, varied. *Physiography* deals with the physical conditions of the surface of the land. The broad physiography of an area can be determined by the knowledge of the physiographic region in which it lies. For instance, Albion lies in the Palouse physiographic region. A helpful resource for determining physiographic regions is Charles B. Hunt's *Physiography of the United States* (1967).

The important aspects of physiography are elevation and slope. Slope, soils, geology, hydrology, microclimate, plants, and animals may be strongly related to elevation. This means that elevation is an important feature in analyzing landscapes. Elevation maps are easily constructed by selecting intervals from the base maps. Altitudes can be represented by coloring spaces between topographic intervals. Elevation changes are depicted in shades of browns, yellows, or grays with felt markers, colored pencils, crayons, or through the use of computer technology, becoming lighter or darker as elevation increases (Figure 3.12). In the Albion area, the highest point is slightly over 2,700 feet (822.7 meters) above sea level, while the lowest benchmark is 2,232 feet (680.3 meters). In the Albion study, 100-foot (30.48-meter) intervals were used to illustrate the location of the town in the low-lying valley among the higher Palouse hills. In other inventories, depending on the scale and location of the study, different intervals may be necessary. For instance, the New Jersey Pinelands cover a much larger and flatter area than the Albion example. As a result, a large-scale map with 1,000-foot (304.8-meter) intervals may be more revealing in the Pinelands.

Because of the dunelike topography of the Albion area, there are many steep slopes (Figure 3.13). The slopes of Albion fall largely into two categories: 7 to 12 percent and 12 to 25 percent. The notable exceptions are drainage areas that are

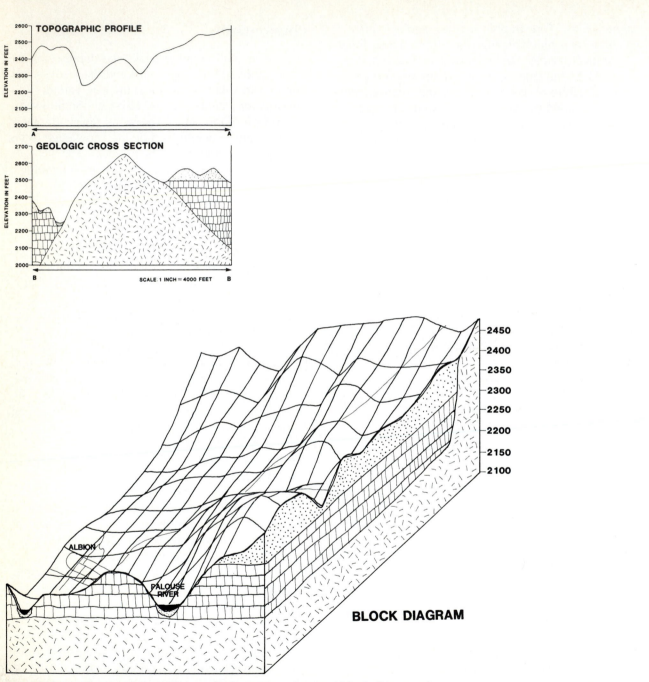

FIGURE 3.10 Topographic profiles, geologic cross section, and block diagram of Albion area.

SYMBOL   DESCRIPTION

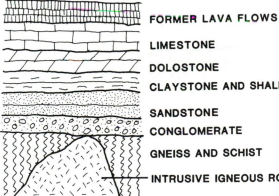

Strike and dip of strata

Strike of vertical strata; tops of strata are on side marked with angle of din

Structure of horizontal strata; no strike, dip=O

Strike and dip of foliation in metamorphic rocks

Strike of vertical foliation

Anticline; arrows show directions of dip away from axis

Syncline; arrows show directions of dip toward axis

Anticline, showing direction and angle of plunge

Syncline, showing direction and angle of dip

Normal fault; hachures on downthrown side

Reverse fault; arrow shows direction of dip, hachures on downthrown side

Dip of fault surface; D, downthrown side; U, upthrown side

Directions of relative horizontal movement along a fault

Low-angle thrust fault; barbs on upper block

FORMER LAVA FLOWS

LIMESTONE

DOLOSTONE

CLAYSTONE AND SHALE

SANDSTONE

CONGLOMERATE

GNEISS AND SCHIST

INTRUSIVE IGNEOUS ROCK

FIGURE 3.11 Common geologic symbols.

relatively gentle and flat—less than 3 percent in the floodplains. Slopes may be subdivided into steepness and direction. Slope direction is referred to as *aspect,* or orientation. Steepness may be important for such activities as agriculture or the construction of buildings, while the direction of slopes is an important factor for such activities as siting housing for solar energy collection. As with the elevation map, the division of slope categories will depend on the study. In the rolling hills around Albion, there are many small changes in the steepness of slope. In another area, the changes in topography may require different slope categories.

SUMMARY OF PHYSIOGRAPHY INVENTORY ELEMENTS

1. Physiographic region
2. Elevation
3. Slope: steepness and direction

MAJOR SOURCES OF INFORMATION

1. USGS
2. College or university libraries
3. *Physiography of the United States* (Hunt, 1967)

Hydrology

Bernard Palissy first explained in the sixteenth century that springs originate from and are fed by rain alone. He showed how this happens: seawater evaporates and is condensed to form rain, which falls, percolates into the ground, and emerges later as springs and rivers that return the water to the sea. This is the hydrologic cycle (Figure 3.14). The *hydrologic cycle* expresses the balance of water in its various forms in the air, on land, and in the sea (Morisawa, 1968, p. 12).

A water budget can be constructed for an average year, which represents the inflow and outflow through the hydrologic cycle. Figure 3.15 illustrates the water budget for Albion. As can be seen, there is a water surplus early in the year followed by a period when moisture in the soil is

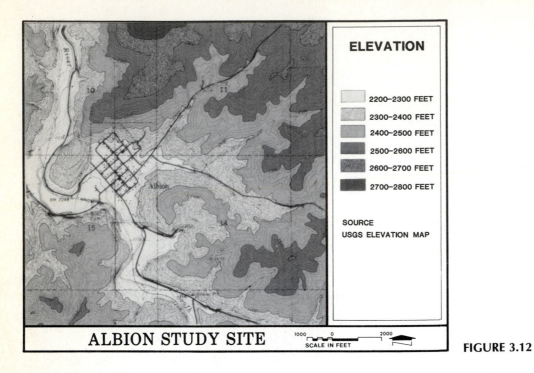

ELEVATION

2200–2300 FEET
2300–2400 FEET
2400–2500 FEET
2500–2600 FEET
2600–2700 FEET
2700–2800 FEET

SOURCE
USGS ELEVATION MAP

ALBION STUDY SITE

1000 0 2000
SCALE IN FEET

FIGURE 3.12

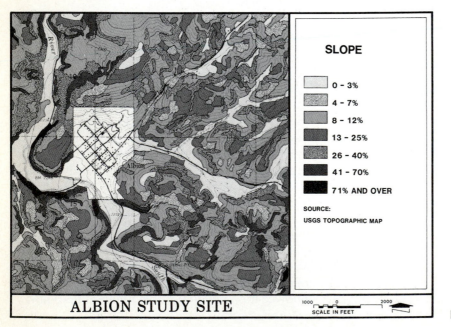

SLOPE

0 - 3%
4 - 7%
8 - 12%
13 - 25%
26 - 40%
41 - 70%
71% AND OVER

SOURCE:
USGS TOPOGRAPHIC MAP

ALBION STUDY SITE

1000 0 2000
SCALE IN FEET

FIGURE 3.13

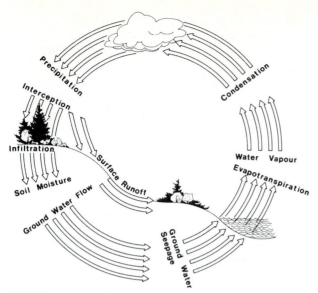

FIGURE 3.14 Hydrologic cycle.

illustrates, *hydrology* deals with the movement of water through the landscape both on the surface and in the ground. *Groundwater* is water that fills all the unblocked pores of materials lying beneath the surface. *Surface water* is water that flows above the ground. Depth to water table, water quality, aquifer yields, direction of movement, and the location of wells are important groundwater factors. Data concerning these factors can be obtained from various sources including the U.S. Environmental Protection Agency (EPA), the USGS, the SCS, various state agencies, and individual well owners. From the geology map, the location of aquifers can be determined. An *aquifer* is a water-bearing layer of permeable rock, sand, or gravel.

The Albion surface-water map reveals several things about the area including its drainage, stream orders, and floodplains. Drainage basins, or watersheds, are the morphological units of surface water. Albion is located within the South Fork of the Palouse River watershed, which is in turn part of the greater Palouse River drainage basin.

Although several methods have been suggested for stream ordering, that proposed by Strahler

being utilized. Then through the summer and early autumn there is a period of water deficiency, and finally moisture is recharged in the soil.

As the hydrologic cycle and water budget

FIGURE 3.15 Water budget for Albion, Washington.

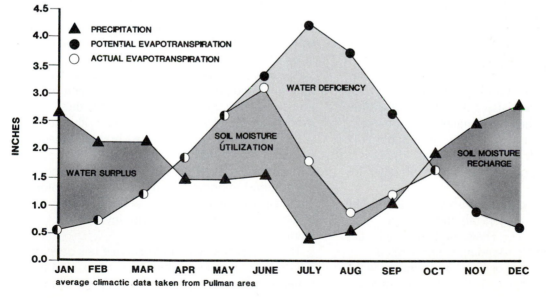

average climactic data taken from Pullman area

(1957) is the most straightforward. According to his system, stream orders are designated as first, second, third, and so on. *First-order streams* are primary drainageways; they are fingertip tributaries at the head of the stream system. *Second-order streams* are formed by the confluence of two first-order streams, and *third-order streams* are formed by the confluence of two second-order streams, and so on (Figure 3.16).

First-order streams are usually at higher elevations and travel a shorter distance over a steeper grade than second-order streams. Second-order streams are at higher elevations and travel a shorter distance over a steeper grade than third-order streams, and so on. Gravity causes this manner of stream movement toward a steady state. This can be expressed graphically by plotting elevation versus stream length for the streams in the study area (Figure 3.16). Average stream length can also be plotted against stream order. Streams develop along a location determined by a balance between available energy and resistance. Thus, the patterns of stream drainage in the landscape are determined by the regional geologic structure. Common types of drainage patterns are also shown in Figure 3.16.

Flooding is the general and temporary condition of a partial or complete inundation of normally dry land areas either from the overflow of streams, rivers, and other inland water (Figure 3.17) or from abnormally high tidal water or rising coastal water resulting from severe storms, hurricanes, or tsunamis. Flooding is also any relatively high flow as measured by either gauge height or discharge quantity (Waananen et al., 1977). The South Fork of the Palouse River that flows through Albion is prone to periodic flooding, so part of the town lies in the floodplain.

Limnology is the study of fresh waters in all their physical, chemical, geological, and biological aspects (Odum, 1971). There are two broad types of freshwater habitats: standing-water habitats (lakes, ponds, swamps, or bogs) and running-water habitats (springs, streams, or rivers). For purposes

of hydrological inventory and analysis, the chemical and biological aspects of aquatic ecosystems and the types of freshwater habitats are important.

The Palouse region has a severe erosion problem that has an impact on runoff. Runoff from the farm fields can contribute sediments, plant nutrients, pesticides, and microorganisms to the surface streams near Albion (Johnson et al., 1973). As a result, the water quality is poor and few fish species are found in the streams. The sediment carried from the area has many regional consequences. For instance, the Palouse River flows into the Snake River, which in turn enters the Columbia River. A complex network of dams on the Columbia and Snake Rivers provides hydroelectric power, water transportation, and recreational opportunities to the northwest. The high amount of sediment affects the operation and maintenance of these dams.

In coastal areas, a hydrologic inventory may be replaced or supplemented by an analysis of oceanography and/or estuarine ecology. *Oceanography* is the study of the sea in all its physical, chemical, geological, and biological aspects (Odum, 1971). For purposes of inventory and analysis of hydrology, the chemical and biological aspects of oceanography are important, while the physical and geological aspects may be covered in other inventory steps.

According to Eugene Odum, an estuary "is a semi-enclosed coastal body of water which has a free connection with the open sea; it is thus strongly affected by tidal action, and within it sea water is mixed (and usually measurably diluted) with fresh water from land drainage" (1971, p. 352). Again the chemical and biological aspects are the most important for hydrological inventory and analysis, while the physical and geologic aspects may be covered in other inventory elements.

The U.S. Fish and Wildlife Service has developed a useful classification system of wetlands and deep-water habitats of the United States (Cowardin et al.,

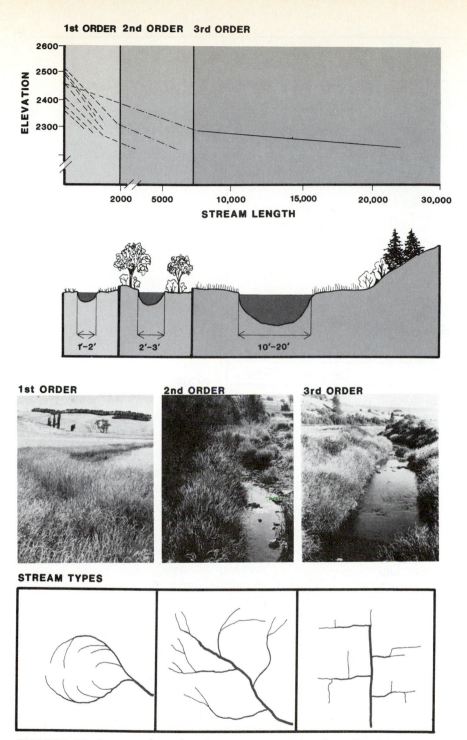

FIGURE 3.16 Stream orders, elevation versus stream length, and common drainage patterns.

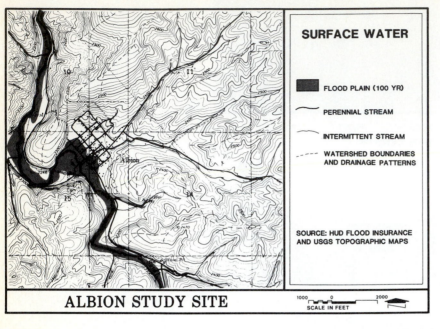

SURFACE WATER

FLOOD PLAIN (100 YR)

PERENNIAL STREAM

INTERMITTENT STREAM

WATERSHED BOUNDARIES
AND DRAINAGE PATTERNS

SOURCE: HUD FLOOD INSURANCE
AND USGS TOPOGRAPHIC MAPS

ALBION STUDY SITE

1000   0   2000
SCALE IN FEET

FIGURE 3.17

1979). This classification system was especially designed to be used for biophysical inventories. It describes ecological taxa, arranges them in a system useful for resource managers and planners, furnishes units for mapping, and provides uniformity of concepts and terms. Five systems form the highest level of classification hierarchy, including marine, estuarine, riverine, lacustrine, and palustrine. These systems are further sub-divided into subsystems and classes. Figure 3.18 summarizes these systems, subsystems, and classes.

SUMMARY OF HYDROLOGIC INVENTORY ELEMENTS

A. Groundwater systems
   1. Aquifer recharge areas
   2. Consolidated and unconsolidated aquifer location and yield
   3. Well locations and yields

   4. Water quality
   5. Water table, artesian supplies
   6. Seasonally high water table
   7. Water-bearing characteristics of geologic units

B. Surface water systems
   1. Watershed and drainage basins
   2. Stream, lake, estuary, coastline, and wetland locations
   3. Stream volumes
   4. Lake levels, tides
   5. Floodplains, flood-hazard areas
   6. Physical water-quality characteristics (sediment loads and temperature)
   7. Chemical water-quality characteristics (such as pH, nitrogen, phosphorus, chlorine, boron, and electrical conductivity)
   8. Bacteriological water-quality characteristics
   9. Freshwater or marine flora and fauna (may also be included in the vegetation

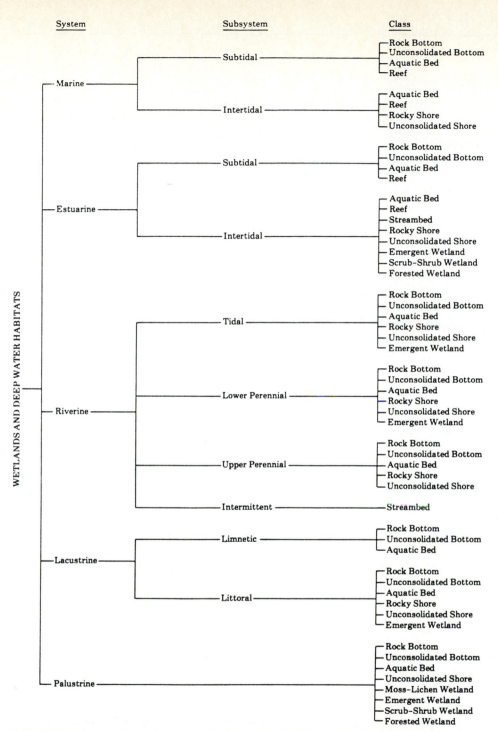

FIGURE 3.18 Classification hierarchy of wetlands and deep-water habitats, showing systems, subsystems, and classes. The Palustrine system does not include deep-water habitats. *(Source: Cowardin et al., 1979. Courtesy of U.S. Fish and Wildlife Service.)*

and wildlife parts of the inventory and analysis process)

10. Eutrophication
11. Water supply systems
12. Sewage treatment systems
13. Existing industrial disposal and discharge points
14. Existing solid-waste disposal sites affecting water quality
15. Existing storm sewer systems and discharge points
16. Algal bloom problems
17. Aquatic weed problem areas
18. Fish hatcheries and stocking areas (may also be included in the land-use portion of the inventory and analysis process)

MAJOR SOURCES OF INFORMATION

1. USGS
2. U.S. Fish and Wildlife Service
3. SCS
4. Agricultural Stabilization and Conservation Service (ASCS)
5. U.S. Army Corps of Engineers
6. U.S. Department of Housing and Urban Development (National Flood Insurance Program)
7. USFS
8. EPA
9. National Marine Fisheries Service (U.S. Department of Commerce)
10. Office of Coastal Zone Management (NOAA, U.S. Department of Commerce)
11. FAA
12. U.S. Coast Guard
13. State departments of fisheries and coastal management
14. State sea-grant universities
15. College and university libraries
16. River basin commissions
17. State departments of natural resources, mining, and ecology
18. Individual well owners

Soils

Soils occupy a unique position in the lithosphere and atmosphere. They are a transition zone that is linked to both the biotic and abiotic environments. *Soil* is a natural three-dimensional body on the surface of the earth that is capable of supporting plants. Its properties result from the integrated effect of climate and living matter acting upon parent material, as conditioned by relief over periods of time. Many processes are linked within the soil zone, so soils often can reveal more about an area than any other natural factor. Fortunately, many dedicated conservationists have mapped soil information for most of the United States.

These conservationists, working for the SCS, an agency of the U.S. Department of Agriculture (USDA), have compiled map information in soil surveys for much of the nation. The soil survey includes the research and information necessary:

- To determine the important characteristics of soils
- To classify soils into defined types and other classificational units
- To establish and to plot on maps the boundaries among kinds of soils
- To correlate and to predict the adaptability of soils to various crops, grasses, and trees, their behavior and productivity under different management systems, and the yields of adapted crops under defined sets of management practices

The principal purposes of the soil survey are:

- To make all the specific information about each kind of soil that is significant to its use and behavior available to those who must decide how to manage it
- To provide such descriptions of the mapping units that the survey can be interpreted for those purposes requiring the fundamental facts about the soil

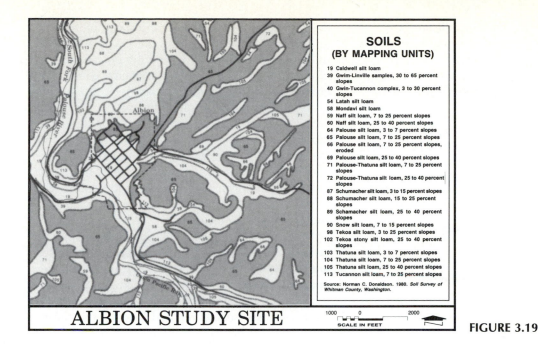

SOILS (BY MAPPING UNITS)

19 Caldwell silt loam
39 Gwim-Linville samples, 30 to 65 percent slopes
40 Gwin-Tucannon complex, 3 to 30 percent slopes
54 Latah silt loam
58 Mondavi silt loam
59 Naff silt loam, 7 to 25 percent slopes
60 Naff silt loam, 25 to 40 percent slopes
64 Palouse silt loam, 3 to 7 percent slopes
65 Palouse silt loam, 7 to 25 percent slopes
66 Palouse silt loam, 7 to 25 percent slopes, eroded
69 Palouse silt loam, 25 to 40 percent slopes
71 Palouse-Thatuna silt loam, 7 to 25 percent slopes
72 Palouse-Thatuna silt loam, 25 to 40 percent slopes
87 Schumacher silt loam, 3 to 15 percent slopes
88 Schumacher silt loam, 15 to 25 percent slopes
89 Schamacher silt loam, 25 to 40 percent slopes
90 Snow silt loam, 7 to 15 percent slopes
98 Tekoa silt loam, 3 to 25 percent slopes
102 Tekoa stony silt loam, 25 to 40 percent slopes
103 Thatuna silt loam, 3 to 7 percent slopes
104 Thatuna silt loam, 7 to 25 percent slopes
105 Thatuna silt loam, 25 to 40 percent slopes
113 Tucannon silt loam, 7 to 25 percent slopes

Source: Norman C. Donaldson. 1980. *Soil Survey of Whitman County, Washington.*

ALBION STUDY SITE

SCALE IN FEET

FIGURE 3.19

These surveys include information about soil associations, catenas, series, phases, capability classes, profiles, erosion, and drainage. A landscape has a distinctive proportional pattern of soils. Such a pattern is called an *association*. It normally consists of one or more major soils and at least one minor soil and is named for the major soil or soils. A related, but different, grouping is that of a *catena*, a sequence of soils of about the same age, derived from similar parent material, and occurring under similar climate conditions but having different characteristics due to variation in relief and drainage.

A *soil series* is a group of soils having soil horizons similar in characteristics and arrangement in the soil profile, except for the texture of the soil, and developed from a particular type of parent material. Each soil series generally is named for a town or other geographic feature near the place where a soil of that series was first observed and mapped. All the soils having the same series name are essentially alike in those characteristics that affect their behavior in the undisturbed landscape.

Soils of one series can differ in texture of the surface layer and in slope, stoniness, or some other characteristic that affects human use of the soil. On the basis of such differences, a soil series is divided into phases. The name of a soil phase indicates a feature that affects management. For example, in Whitman County, Tekoa silt loam, 3 to 25 percent slopes, is one of several phases of the Tekoa series. A mapping unit is usually equivalent to a phase. In a soil survey, these units are numbered (Figure 3.19).

Soil capability classification is a general way of showing the suitability of soils for agricultural purposes. Soils are grouped according to their limitations, the risk of erosion under use, and the way they respond to treatment. Capability classification will be described further in Chapter 5.

The *soil profile* is an important part of the description of each soil series and is defined as the sequence of layers (horizons) from the surface downward to rock or other underlying material. These layers, or horizons, include:

O—Organic horizons (litter derived from dead plants and animals)

A—Eluvial horizons (mineral horizons that lie at or near surface and are characterized as zones of maximum leaching)

B—Illuvial horizons (the layers of accumulation into which the above minerals are washed)

C—Unconsolidated material under A and B layers

Bedrock

Soil *erosion* is the searing away of the land surface by running water, wind, ice, or other geologic agents and by processes such as gravity. Erosion hazard may be considered the susceptibility of soils to these factors. The rate of erosion caused by water is measured by the universal soil-loss equation

$$A = RKLSCP$$

A = computed soil loss per unit area, which is a product of the other factors
R = rainfall
K = soil erodibility
L = slope length
S = slope gradient
C = crop management (vegetative cover)
P = erosion-control practice

There is also a universal wind-erosion equation that considers similar factors for wind erosion. Some soil erosion occurs naturally, so the question can be raised: What rate is tolerable? *Tolerable soil loss* can be defined as the maximum rate of annual soil erosion that will permit a high level of crop productivity to be sustained economically and indefinitely. These T values vary from soil to soil,

depending on how fast new topsoil can be formed to replace the soil lost to erosion. Typically the universal soil-loss equation and the universal wind-erosion equation are used to determine what cropping and tillage practices are necessary to keep soil loss within a tolerable level.

Soil drainage may be defined as the relative rapidity and the extent of the removal of water from the surface and from within the soil under natural conditions. Soil series in a soil survey will include a description of drainage. Some of this soil survey information will be explored further using the Albion area as an example.

The soils map (Figure 3.19) shows the mapping units in the Albion area. The soils of the Palouse are silt loam in texture and were formed in the very deep loess deposit. Figure 3.20 shows the soil textural classes. There are four basic texture groups—sands, silts, clays, and loams—that can be subdivided further to reflect various mixtures, for instance, loamy sands and sandy loams. *Sand* is coarse-textured and comprises loose, single-particle grains that can be easily seen or felt. *Silts* have a

FIGURE 3.20 Soil textural classes.

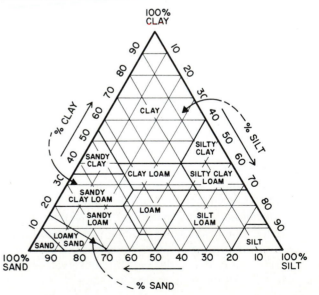

medium texture, while fine-textured clay comprises very small particles. *Loams* have a relatively balanced mixture of different sand, silt, and clay particles (Rogers, Golden, & Halpern, 1986).

Soil number 65 on Figure 3.19 is named Palouse silt loam, 7 to 25 percent slope, and is one of the most common near Albion and in the region. The soil survey describes this soil as a strongly sloping and moderately steep soil on uplands. The landscape is mainly smooth and rolling but in places is hilly (Donaldson, 1980).

Soil profiles can illustrate these characteristics in two dimensions (Figure 3.21). Palouse and Thatuna soils are shown in these examples. Soil surveys include information about drainage that can be compared with information about physiography and hydrology. Poor drainage, for instance, occurs in the lower elevations at 3 to 15 percent slope where runoff from the higher areas has produced rivers, streams, and gullies. Caldwell silt loams and Latah silt loams are the poorest drained soils near Albion. Moderate drainage areas in Albion are usually found on northeast facing slopes from middle to high elevations. These soils are formed just below the crest of hills and ridges on 15 to 25 percent slopes. The dominant soil type in the area, Palouse silt loam, is well-drained. These soils occur on various slopes at various elevations (Donaldson, 1980).

Soil erosion is a serious problem in the Palouse region, which has been rated one of the ten most critically eroding areas in the United States. The erosion hazard for the Albion area is mapped in Figure 3.22, based on information from the soil survey. The hazards range from little or no potential for erosion to high or very high. Much of the area has been rated as moderate, including the Palouse silt loams (number 65 on the soils map, Figure 3.19). But this rating is somewhat deceptive. The capability classification for these soils is IIIe for 7 to 15 percent and IVe for 15 to 25 percent slopes. The "e" indicates a risk of erosion unless close-growing plant cover is maintained. Roman numeral III indicates that the soils have

severe limitations, and IV indicates very severe limitations that require special conservation practices. Without these conservation practices, soil erosion increases, which has been the case in the Palouse. This discussion about erosion in the Palouse helps illustrate the wealth of information in soil surveys. The example also shows that this information should be analyzed thoroughly.

Soil surveys provide data that can be used to produce additional graphic representations of the environment. For instance, a typical Palouse hill is shown in Figure 3.23. All the soil types were derived from the same parent material, loess. South-facing and west-facing slopes are generally longer and less steep than north and east exposures. The hilltops or ridgetops have lost nearly all the original topsoil by the combined action of water and tillage erosion (Kaiser, 1967).

As the drawing of the Palouse hill helps to show, soil, the transitional zone between the abiotic and biotic environments, is strongly related to geology and physiography. The orientation of slopes begins to show how soil and climate are related.

SUMMARY OF SOILS INVENTORY ELEMENTS

1. Soil series
2. Permeability
3. Texture
4. Profiles
5. Erosion potential
6. Drainage potential
7. Catenas and/or associations

MAJOR SOURCES OF INFORMATION

1. SCS
2. ASCS
3. Soil and Water Conservation Society
4. College or university libraries
5. County extension agents

Microclimate

Meteorological elements are subject to vertical changes and vary horizontally within short distances

PALOUSE SILT LOAM

A11 0-3" Black (10YR 2/1m) silt loam; moderate medium and fine granular; slightly sticky, nonplastic, friable, slight hard, abundant roots; clear wavy boundary.

A12 3-5.5" Black (10YR 2/1m) silt loam; weak coarse platy, reducing to moderate fine subangular blocky and coarse granular; slightly sticky, nonplastic, friable, slightly hard; numerous roots; clear wavy boundary.

A13 5.5-13" Very dark grayish brown (10YR 3/2d), or very dark brown (10YR 2/2m) silt loam; moderate coarse platy, reducing to medium subangular blocky; slightly sticky, nonplastic, friable, slightly hard; numerous roots; clear wavy boundary.

A3 12-21" Dark brown (10YR 3/3m) silt loam; moderate medium and fine angular and subangular blocky; slightly sticky, nonplastic, slightly firm, slightly hard.

B11 21-28" Dark brown (7.5YR 3/2m) silt loam; moderate medium and fine angular blocky; sticky, slightly plastic, slightly firm, slightly hard, numerous worm casts and channels; frequent roots; streaks and splotches of dark organic matter straining; clear wavy boundary.

B12 28-37" Brown (7.5YR 4/2m) silty clay loam; moderate medium and fine angular and subangular blocky; sticky, slightly plastic, firm, hard; with frequent siliceous coatings on ped faces; occasional roots; clear wavy boundary.

B21 37"+ Brown (7.5YR 4/2m) silty clay loam; moderate medium prismatic, reducing to strong medium and fine subangular blocky, with intense siliceous coatings on pores and ped faces; occasional roots.

THATUNA SILT LOAM

A11 0-9" Black (10YR 2/1m) silt loam; weak fine granular; slightly sticky, slightly plastic, friable, soft; abundant roots; clear wavy boundary.

A12 9-19" Very dark brown (10YR 2/2m) silt loam; weak medium granular; slightly sticky, slightly plastic, friable, soft; numerous roots; clear wavy boundary.

A13 19-33" Dark brown (10YR 3/3m) silt loam; moderate medium and fine subangular blocky, reducing to medium granular; slightly sticky, slightly plastic, slightly firm, slightly hard; numerous roots; clear wavy boundary.

A3 33-44" Dark brown (grayish), (10YR 4/2m) silt loam moderate medium and fine subangular blocky, slightly sticky, slightly plastic, slightly firm, slightly hard; numerous roots; clear wavy boundary.

A2 44-50" Grayish brown (10YR 5/2m) silt loam; moderate fine angular blocky, with conspicuous gray siliceous coatings on ped faces and in pores; slightly sticky, slightly plastic, firm, slightly hard; frequent roots; clear wavy boundary.

B21 50-55" Brown (10YR 4/3m) silty clay loam; moderate medium and fine subangular blocky, with conspicuous gray siliceous coatings on ped faces; sticky, plastic firm, hard; occasional roots; clear wavy boundary.

B22 55"+ Dark yellowish brown (10YR 4/4m) silty clay loam; moderate medium and fine prismatic, reducing to fine prismatic and medium angular blocky; sticky, plastic, firm, hard; occasional roots.

FIGURE 3.21   Soil profiles. *(Source: Adapted from U.S. Soil Conservation Service information)*

64

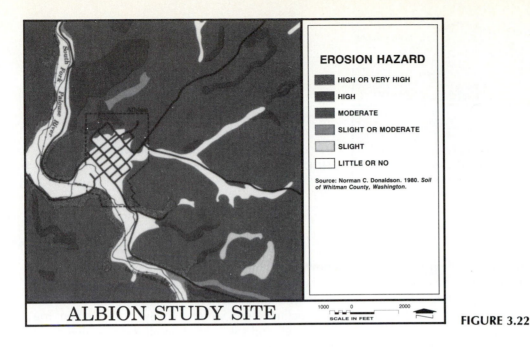

ALBION STUDY SITE

EROSION HAZARD

HIGH OR VERY HIGH

HIGH

MODERATE

SLIGHT OR MODERATE

SLIGHT

LITTLE OR NO

Source: Norman C. Donaldson. 1980. *Soil of Whitman County, Washington.*

1000   0   2000
SCALE IN FEET

FIGURE 3.22

as well. Small-scale variations are brought about by changes in slope and orientation of the ground surface, soil type and moisture, and vegetation type and height. These different climates found within a small space are grouped together under the general description of *microclimate*. The term *topoclimate* is used when the topographic variations of the land on the microclimate are considered. Generally, topoclimate is an extension of microclimate into higher layers of the atmosphere, depending on the relief of the land. Therefore, topoclimate can be considered an intermediate scale between macroclimate and microclimate. Some important microclimate elements to consider are ventilation, fog and frost, solar radiation, and vegetative changes.

Ventilation is the circulation of fresh air across the landscape and is largely dependent on landforms and wind direction. The calculation of ventilation is "important in determining local climate; furthermore, wind pressure and eddy formation largely depend on the degree of landform relief" (University of Pennsylvania, 1985, p. B1.4). Ventilation is greatest in those areas where the terrain is aligned with the prevailing wind. Rudolf Geiger, a German scientist who studied the effects of topography on climate, developed the formula in Figure 3.24 to determine the relative values of ventilation. The formula relates wind direction to landform. The *d* in the formula is determined by the direction of seasonal regional winds; thus different ventilation calculations may be necessary for the various seasons. It has been noted that, in general:

The greater or more pronounced the relief [then] the greater the wind pressure on the slopes perpendicular and facing the wind (windward) and the greater the formation of eddies on the lee side. These factors influence temperature and humidity and, therefore, have important influence on local microclimate. (University of Pennsylvania, 1985, p. B1.4)

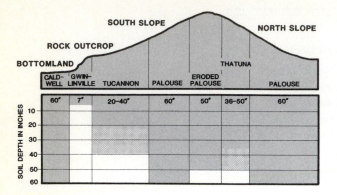

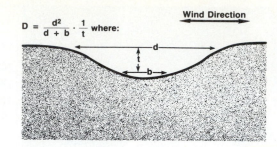

$$D = \frac{d^2}{d + b} \cdot \frac{1}{t} \text{ where:}$$

FIGURE 3.24 Geiger ventilation formula. *(Source: Adapted from Geiger, 1965, via the University of Pennsylvania, 1985)*

Subtle topographic changes and their relative elevation greatly affect temperature near the ground surface. These changes in temperature, in turn, influence the susceptibility of an area to fog and frost. The complex topography of the Albion area results in varying degrees of fog and frost susceptibility (Figure 3.25).

Solar radiation is a result of slope steepness and direction. Satterlund and Means (1979) have observed that solar radiation is the primary variable in energy exchange processes that determine ecosystem distribution, composition, and productivity. In addition, radiation melts snow and powers the hydrologic cycle and significantly influences agricultural productivity.

Vegetation influences and results from microclimate in a variety of ways. Ventilation, fog and frost, and solar radiation all are modified by changes in vegetation. Figure 3.26 illustrates some of the ways vegetation influences microclimate near Albion.

SUMMARY OF MICROCLIMATE INVENTORY ELEMENTS

1. Ventilation
2. Fog and frost

FIGURE 3.25 Fog and frost susceptibility.

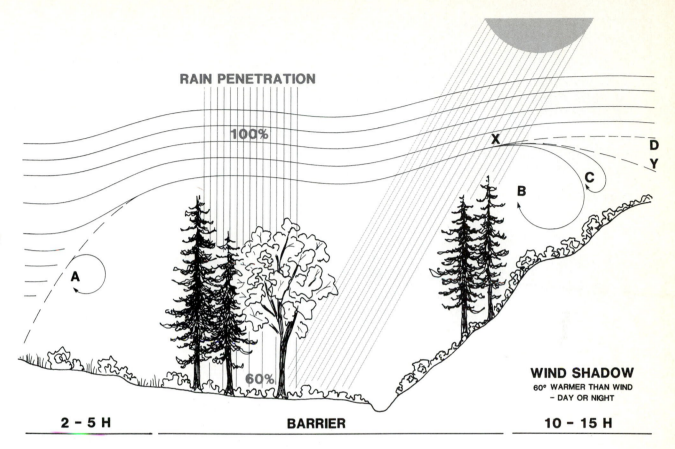

FIGURE 3.26 Vegetation influences on microclimate. *(Source: Adapted from Higashi et al., 1978)*

3. Solar radiation
4. Vegetation changes

MAJOR SOURCES OF INFORMATION

1. National Weather Service
2. NOAA
3. FAA
4. Local weather stations and/or airports
5. College or university libraries

6. County extension agents
7. Farmers

Vegetation

The ecologist Robert E. Ricklefs observed that "life is an extension of the physical world" (1973, p. 81). This observation is reinforced by J. E. Lovelock's Gaia hypothesis that suggests "the

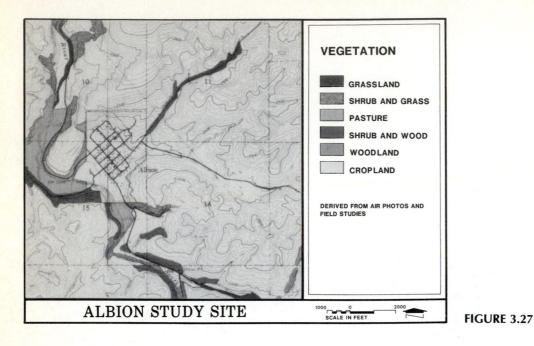

ALBION STUDY SITE

SCALE IN FEET
1000   0   2000

FIGURE 3.27

biosphere is a self-regulating entity with the capacity to keep our planet healthy by controlling the chemical and physical environment'' (1979, p. xii). Living things are a result of the physical processes that have been discussed thus far plus their interaction with other life-forms. Vegetation refers to plant life—trees, shrubs, herbs, and grasses. Because of the omnipresence of vegetation, it would seem that plants would be simple to inventory. This, however, is not the case. For various reasons, naturally occurring vegetation has not been inventoried to the extent that geology, hydrology, soils, or climate have. As a result, plants are too often ignored in the planning process in the United States.*

* An obvious exception is that work done by the U.S. Forest Service or state agencies responsible for forestry and range programs. In this case, vegetation is viewed as an economic resource.

The Albion vegetative unit map shows the major communities of the area (Figure 3.27). There are several ways to classify land cover. One helpful system is the USGS Land-Use and Land-Cover Classification System that was developed for use with remote sensor data (Anderson et al., 1976) (see Table 2.1). Once a system is selected, it is necessary to identify the specific units. The most straightforward method is to use aerial photographs to identify the areas, then field-check the units.

In Albion, the units that were identified include shrubland, woodland, grassland, mixed shrub and woodland, mixed shrub and grassland, pastures, croplands, riparian, and farmsteads. After the units are identified and mapped, it is often helpful to list the individual species in the area. Table 3.1 is a list of some of the plant species in the Palouse. The ecologist Rexford Daubenmire (1970) spent a large portion of his career identifying communities in the Palouse. Because of his efforts, compiling a

TABLE 3.1
SOME PLANT SPECIES IN THE PALOUSE

Scientific Name	Common Name	Scientific Name	Common Name
		Pastures	
Agropyron spicatum	Bluebunch wheatgrass	*Festuca idahoensis*	Idaho fescue
Collinsia parviflora	Small-flowered blue-eyed Mary	*Poa pratensis*	Kentucky bluegrass
Eriogonum heracleoides	Wyeth buckwheat	*Thlaspi arvense*	Field pennycress
		Grasslands	
Achillea millefolium	Yarrow	*Gaillardia aristata*	Blanket-flower
Agropyron spicatum	Bluebunch wheatgrass	*Geranium viscosissimum*	Sticky purple geranium
Antennaria luzuloides	Woodrush pussytoes	*Geum triflorum*	Prairie smoke avens
Artemisia frigida	Pasture sagebrush	*Haplopappus liatriformis*	Palouse goldenweed
A. tridentata	Big sagebrush	*Helianthella uniflora*	Rocky Mountain helianthella
Aster sp.	Aster	*Hieracium albertinum*	Western hawkweed
Astragalus spaldingii	Spalding's milkvetch	*Iris missouriensis*	Western blueflag
Balsamorhiza sagittata	Arrowleaf balsamroot	*Koeleria cristata*	Koeler's grass
Brodiaea douglasii	Douglas' Brodiaea	*Lithophragma bulbifera*	Rocketstar
Bromus japonicus	Japanese brome-grass	*L. parviflora*	Small-flowered fringecup
B. mollis	Soft brome-grass	*Lithospermum ruderale*	Western gromwell
Calochortus elegans	Northwest mariposa lily	*Lomatium triternatum*	Nine-leaf lomatium
Castilleja cusickii	Cusick's paintbrush	*Lupinus sericeus*	Silky lupine
Centaurea cyanus	Cornflower	*Microsteris gracilis*	Pink microsteris
Carex geyeri	Elk sedge	*Montia linearis*	Narrowleaved montia
Collinsia parviflora	Small-flowered blue-eyed Mary	*Potentilla gracilis*	Cinquefoil
Draba verna	Spring Whitlow-grass	*Senecio integerrimus*	Western groundsel
Epilobium paniculatum	Autumn willow-weed	*Sisyrinchium inflatum*	Purple-eyed grass
Erigeron corymbosus	Long-leaf fleabane	*Stellaria nitens*	Shining chickweed
Eriogonum heracleoides	Wyeth buckwheat	*Thlaspi arvense*	Field pennycress
Festuca idahoensis	Idaho fescue	*Zigadenus venenosus*	Deadly zigadenus
Fritillaria pudica	Yellow bell		

SOURCE: Adapted from Daubenmire, 1970, and other regional descriptions.

vegetative unit list for Albion was relatively easy. In other areas, this task may be more difficult.

The Albion physiognomic profiles show these units in three dimensions (Figure 3.28). Peter Skaller has noted that "besides revealing a great deal about ecosystem processes, physiognomy affords a quick look at the structural components of wildlife habitat" (in Berger et al., 1977, p. 101). Between the units are boundaries (Figure 3.28) whose edges form ecotones. *Ecotones* are transitional areas between two ecological communities, generally of greater richness and equitability than either of the communities it separates. Albion has many such areas. One of the most common is the transition between the *Festuca idahoensis* and *Symphoricarpos albus* (Idaho fescue and snowberry) and the *Pinus ponderosa* and *Symphoricarpos albus* (ponderosa pine and snowberry) communities (Daubenmire, 1970).

The Idaho fescue and snowberry association is most common on well-drained soils, while

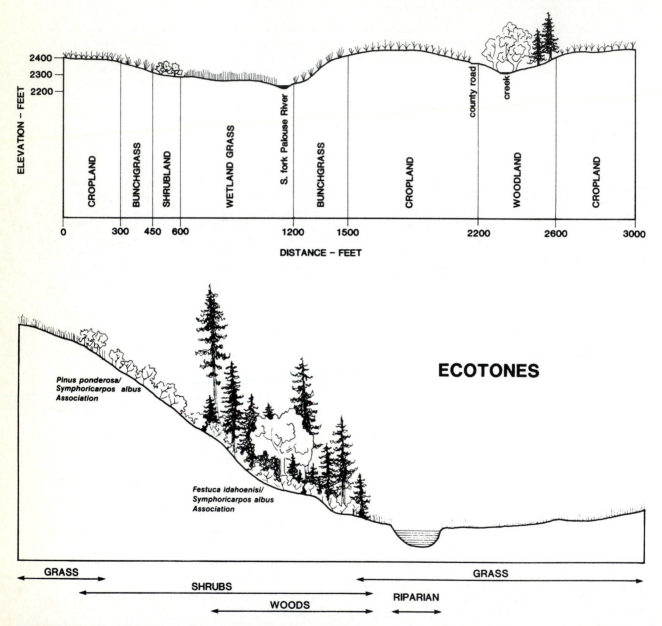

PROFILE OF VEGETATIVE UNITS

SOURCE: VEGETATIVE UNITS MAP

FIGURE 3.28 Physiognomic profiles, ecotones, and edge profiles. *(Source: Adapted from Brunton et al., 1977)*

ponderosa pine and snowberry communities occur in more moist sites (Churchill et al., 1986). Ponderosa pines are found on many of the steeper north-facing slopes in the Palouse. These areas are relatively colder and thus retain moisture. The cover provided by the pines and the moisture help produce a favorable habitat for several wildlife species.

SUMMARY OF VEGETATION INVENTORY ELEMENTS

1. Vegetative units
2. Species list
3. Physiognomic profiles
4. Ecotone and edge profiles

MAJOR SOURCES OF INFORMATION

1. USGS
2. SCS
3. USFS
4. National, state, and local conservation and environmental groups
5. College or university libraries

Wildlife

Broadly, *wildlife* is considered to be animals that are neither human nor domesticated. Insects, fish, amphibians, birds, and mammals are more mobile than plants. While closely linked to vegetative units for food and shelter, wildlife often uses

G—GRASS   S—SHRUB   W—WOODS   C—CROP   R—RIVER

SPECIES	ANIMAL HABITAT			OCCURRENCE					COMMENTS
	BREED-ING	LIVING	EATING	COMMON	UN-COMMON	RARE	MIGRANT	RESI-DENT	
American Robin *Turdus migratorius*	W	W	G S	●			●		
Barn Owl *Tyto alba*	W	W	W S	●				●	
Mourning Dove *Zenaida macroura*	G S	G S	G S C	●				●	
Red tailed hawk *Buteo jamaicensis*	W	W	G W S C R		●			●	
Porcupine *Erethizon dorsatum*	W	W	W			●		●	
Norway rat *Rattus norvegicus*	G S	G S	G S C	●				●	
Beaver *Castor canadensis*	W R	R	W R		●			●	
White tailed deer *Odocoileus virginianus*	W	W S	W S G C	●				●	

FIGURE 3.29 Species-habitat matrix.

different areas to reproduce, eat, and sleep. Like vegetation, wildlife has not been extensively inventoried except where the animals have some commercial value. Because animals are mobile, they are even more difficult to inventory and are even more often ignored by planners than is vegetation.

A starting point again is to compile a list of species in the area. State departments of game are useful sources of information for hunted or fished species. A few state game departments have begun to conduct research on some nongame species as well, but this is still the exception rather than the rule. Conservation groups and academic facilities are usually the best resources for nongame species.

Once such a list is compiled, which can be a substantial task in itself, it is important to analyze where the species live. One helpful tool is a matrix (Figure 3.29). For the Albion area, species were listed with both their common and scientific names. The individual species were then matched with the vegetative units they use for breeding, living, and eating. It was noted if the species was common, uncommon, or rare and what its seasonal occurrence was. Additional remarks for each species were also included. For example, the northwestern whitetail deer (*Odocoileus virginianus*) is a common resident of the area. This species uses a variety of habitats year-round and is a vegetarian.

Next, it is important to rate the habitats for their relative value (Figure 3.30). This can be done through a series of interviews with game officials, conservation club representatives, landowners, and wildlife biologists. Again, this task can be as complex as the planning issue requires. In the Palouse, there is some debate between farmers and state game officials about the value of various habitats. Though farmers enjoy hunting, many consider some game birds and deer pests. Game officials argue that habitats need to be preserved for these species. The value of inventorying wildlife lies in gaining an understanding of the ecosystem of

	GRASSLAND AND PASTURE	SHRUBLAND	CROPLAND	WOODLAND
GAME OFFICIALS	◐	◐	●	◐
CONSERVATIONISTS	◐	●	●	◐
BIOLOGISTS	◐	●	●	◐
HUNTERS	◐	◐	●	◐
LAND OWNERS	◐	◐	○	●

● VALUABLE
◐ MODERATELY VALUABLE
○ NOT VALUABLE

FIGURE 3.30 Habitat value matrix. *(Source: Adapted from Brunton et al., 1977)*

an area. Food webs (Figure 3.31) are useful illustrations that help show people of an area how the living things use the region.

SUMMARY OF WILDLIFE INVENTORY ELEMENTS

1. Species list
2. Species-habitat matrix
3. Habitat value map
4. Food web

MAJOR SOURCES OF INFORMATION

1. State departments of game and/or fisheries
2. USFS
3. SCS
4. National, state, and local conservation and environmental groups
5. College or university libraries

Existing Land Use and Land Users

Existing land use refers to the physical arrangement of space utilized by humans. Almost all the land on the planet is used by people in some way—from the wilderness areas of Alaska to the alleyways in Philadelphia. The human ecology, the living network of an area, is much more complex than how land is used. However, land and other resource utilization is a significant component of human ecology. Human impact on the environment is great. So it is important when inventorying and analyzing an area to recognize how people are using land as well as to distinguish land use from land users.

Land use is fairly simple to discern. A particular area of land is either used for agriculture or it is not. However, different users may view that area of land for different purposes. For instance, farmland may be used for a variety of crops or pasture; it may be used for hunting or other forms of recreation. Its owners also may see it as an investment.

Land use is only the beginning in the establishment of user groups. A particular person

FIGURE 3.31 Food web.

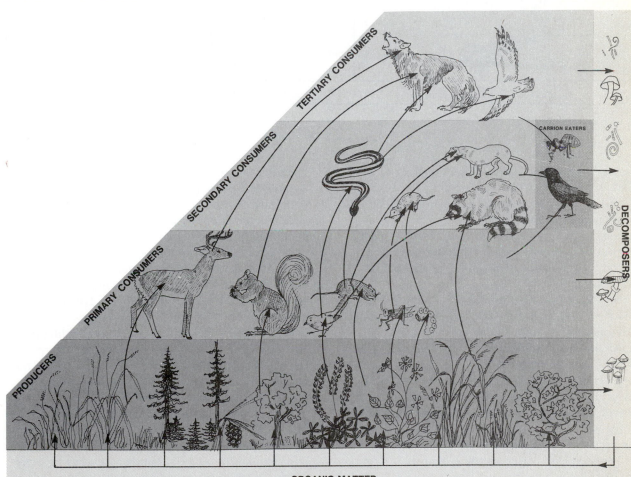

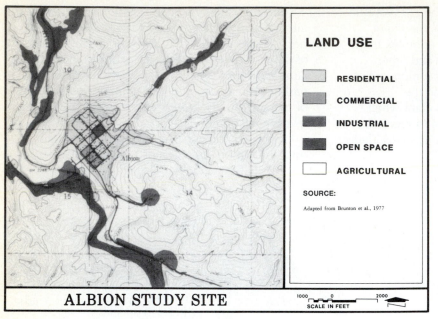

LAND USE

RESIDENTIAL

COMMERCIAL

INDUSTRIAL

OPEN SPACE

AGRICULTURAL

SOURCE:

Adapted from Brunton et al., 1977

ALBION STUDY SITE

1000 0 2000
SCALE IN FEET

FIGURE 3.32

in a given location will use many parcels of land. Part of the land used by an individual will be called *home* (residential); another part will be called *work* (commercial or industrial); many parts may be labeled *play* and be tennis courts, restaurants, the homes of friends, or roads for either driving or jogging (recreation, commercial, residential, transportation).

A helpful starting point for identifying existing land use and land users is the history of an area. Albion was first used by Indians as a campsite. Later, it was developed as a farming community. Today, Albion retains its rural character while serving as a bedroom community for nearby Washington State University. Information about the history of a place can be gathered from various sources including interviews with older residents and research in community libraries.

The next step is to determine land-use categories. As with the vegetation inventory, the USGS Land-Use and Land-Cover Classification System provides

helpful standard categories (Anderson et al., 1976). Again aerial photographs and field checking are necessary to compile a land-use map (Figure 3.32). For many planning processes, this is just the beginning of analyzing land use—property ownership, housing condition, and farm management maps also may be required. Some of this information can be gathered from the local tax assessor and the county SCS office. For other information, fieldwork will be necessary.

While census information is a good starting point for understanding who uses the land, it is even better to go out into the community and talk to the people. By talking with people in their homes or places of work and by taking photographs or making sketches, an idea of settlement patterns (Figure 3.33) and concerns or issues can be gained. As Allan Jacobs of the University of California, Berkeley, has observed, "Planners tend to be more careful in deciding on policies and actions when they associate real people's faces and images of

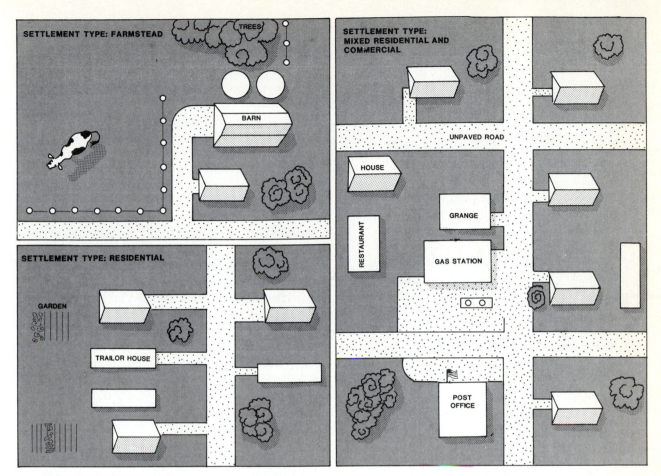

FIGURE 3.33 Settlement patterns. *(Source: Adapted from Brunton et al., 1977)*

places with the decisions'' (1985, p. 8).

The Albion settlement patterns include farmsteads, a mixed mobile-home and single-family-house arrangement, and a mixed residential and commercial pattern. The groups of people who live in the area can be listed, then a matrix can be made with those groups and the various settlement types (Figure 3.34). While, on the one hand, the idea that we belong to an identifiable group seems to run contrary to the American ideals

of the melting pot and individualism, on the other hand, our work ethic seems to dictate a certain amount of identity with our work peers. In the Albion area, groups in which people identified themselves included farmers, students, retirees, university professionals, and laborers.

By identifying land use and land users and analyzing who uses what, an elementary understanding of the social organization of an area can be gained. How these groups are linked to resources and issues is more complex, but this understanding is crucial to planning. These relationships will be explored in Chapter 4.

SUMMARY OF EXISTING LAND-USE AND LAND-USER ELEMENTS

1. Historical development
2. Existing land use
3. Settlement patterns
4. Land-user groups
5. Settlement pattern–groups matrix
6. Groups-issues matrix

MAJOR SOURCES OF INFORMATION*

1. Individual interviews
2. Interviews with groups and associations
3. Local newspapers and libraries
4. Tax assessors
5. U.S. Bureau of the Census
6. SCS
7. USGS
8. College and university libraries

ANALYSIS AND SYNTHESIS OF INVENTORY INFORMATION

Bivariate Relationships

If it is true that everything is connected to everything else, then to be helpful for planning, those connections need to be made explicit. The first step in making those connections is to analyze how the inventory elements relate to each other. A useful guide is to identify bivariate relationships of all possible pairs of landscape elements (Figure 3.35).

In the Palouse, as in most regions, geology influences elevation and slope (bivariate rela-

* Refer to Table 4.1 for a more complete list.

tionship 1 in Figure 3.35) in several ways. The old crystalline rocks are at the highest elevations in the Albion area. The sloping Palouse hills are a result of deposition, while the basalt has been exposed through erosion. Those exposed basalt outcrops result in steep slopes. In lower elevations, there are alluvial deposits along the streams. These kinds of relationships between geology and physiography are almost always an important factor in analyzing the broad physical pattern of a region. The effect of geology on elevation and slope can be quite striking, as with the Front Range of the Colorado Rocky Mountains, or obvious, as with the New Jersey Coastal Plain, or more subtle, as in the Great Plains.

Locally in the Albion area, geology influences microclimate, and there is also a regional influence (2). The microclimate is affected by both the Palouse hills and the basalt valleys. The north sides of the hills are cooler than the south sides. Fog pockets hug the valley areas. In the Palouse, these relationships are quite important to agriculture. In other regions, forestry, tourism, or shipping may be affected by how geology and climate are related.

Geologic parent material is an important ingredient to the soil-forming process (3). The most important parent material in the Palouse is the wind-deposited loess. Through time, as erosion from the hills occurred, these soils became the parent material for alluvial soils. Basalt and crystalline rock also add parent material to soils. Because of the relationship with geologic materials, all soils are not of equal value for human use. Some soils, including those from loess and alluvium, are more fertile than others.

Certain rock formations make better aquifers and aquicludes than others (4). Clay areas between basalt layers hold water. Fissures in the crystalline rock provide some good local water supply. In addition to groundwater, surface water is also affected by geology (5). Near Albion, ephemeral streams occur mostly in the eolian deposit,

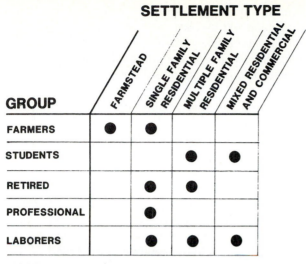

FIGURE 3.34 Settlement patterns-groups matrix.

FIGURE 3.35 Bivariate relationships.

	GEOLOGY	PHYSIOGRAPHY	CLIMATE	SOILS	GROUNDWATER	SURFACE WATER	VEGETATION	WILDLIFE	LAND USE
GEOLOGY		1	2	3	4	5	6	7	8
PHYSIOGRAPHY			9	10	11	12	13	14	15
CLIMATE				16	17	18	19	20	21
SOILS					22	23	24	25	26
GROUNDWATER						27	28	29	30
SURFACE WATER							31	32	33
VEGETATION								34	35
WILDLIFE									36
LAND USE									

intermittent streams occur where the soil is thinner and the basalt closer to the surface, and the rivers and streams that flow year-round occur where the basalt has been cut away. Alluvium has been deposited along most of the streams. The interrelationships between geology and hydrology are important for determining available water supplies and understanding stream flows.

Geology influences vegetation and wildlife (6, 7) through its effect on physiography, climate, and soils. In the Palouse region, the eolian deposits support primary grass and shrubland. Where basalt is closer to the surface, there are more woodland and shrubs such as hawthorn and roses. The alluvial areas support marsh grasses, shrubs, and some willows. The geology also provides burrowing habitats (in the eolian deposits) and cliff habitats (in the basalt outcrops).

Land use is influenced in several ways by geology (8). The eolian deposits provide the parent material for the fertile Palouse soils. These areas are used extensively for farming. The town of Albion is located over the crystalline formation. There are several dirt roads in Albion supported by this crystalline base. In some regions, geologic conditions can cause hazards to human settlement, as in the case of earthquakes and volcanoes, and thus can be important when determining the location of various land uses.

The physiography is the surface expression of geology. As a result, the influence of physiography on climate (9) is similar to that of geology. Physiography influences soils (10) in several ways. In the Palouse, deeper soils occur on gentler slopes, while the shallower soils occur on steeper slopes that are usually north-facing. In even steeper regions, like the Rocky Mountains, such relationships will be more dramatic. In flat regions, such as the New Jersey Coastal Plain, physiography will exert a more subtle influence.

Physiography is related to groundwater through recharge (11) especially in relationship to steepness. Near Albion, it is common after a rainfall to see water being discharged between the basalt layers along steep valley walls. Surface water flows at different levels in relationship to elevation and slopes (12). Ephemeral streams occur in the highest elevations, on the steepest slopes. Intermittent streams occur at lower elevations; they have eroded more distinct channels into the more gentle slopes. In the lowest and flattest area near Albion flows the South Fork of the Palouse River.

Physiography exerts a strong influence on vegetation (13). Steeper north-facing slopes and valleys support the majority of the Albion area's woody vegetation. The lowlands along the Palouse River support wetland grasses, some shrubs, and a few willow trees. The remaining areas of native grasses and herbaceous plants are in the higher elevations. The placement of roads and utility lines is influenced by the physiography of an area. In other regions, the influence of physiography on land use is also evident, as, for example, in the San Francisco Bay area. Too often in the United States land use has been poorly adapted to physiography. In the Palouse region, this contributes to the erosion problem; in other regions poorly sited houses may be vulnerable to landslides.

Climate plays a strong role in soil development through a number of processes (16). Frost action, precipitation, and wind play major roles in soil development, affecting soil texture and drainage characteristics. Erosion in the Palouse area is influenced by a number of soil-climate relationships. Palouse soils are impermeable, thus increasing surface runoff. Serious erosion problems result in the winter when snow collects on the hillsides. Intermittent warm Chinook winds can quickly melt the snow, causing water to wash the soil down the hillside.

There are obvious relationships between climate and hydrology (17, 18). Precipitation is the source of groundwater and surface water. Water that does not infiltrate into the ground is contained in the Albion area ponds, streams, and rivers until it flows

out of the area or evaporates. Vegetation is also greatly affected by climate (19). Water and solar radiation are the key influences on plant development. Likewise, climate influences wildlife (20) through precipitation and solar radiation. Reproduction, migration, hibernation, and feeding are all influenced by the variation in climate through the seasons.

The major land use in the Albion area is dependent on climate (21). Farmers probably talk as much about the weather as they do the price of wheat. Climate also influences housing through such things as heating bills and road access during snowstorms. An understanding of climate in planning and design can help conserve energy and water resources. In the southwestern United States, such relationships are especially dramatic, but land use is affected by climate everywhere.

Soils influence the amount of water that flows through the ground to feed aquifers (22). Water flowing across the land surface is a major factor in erosion and drainage in the Palouse (23). Water also deposits material that develops into alluvial soils. Soil characteristics such as texture, pH level, and cation exchange capacity are interrelated to vegetation (24). Coniferous trees, such as the ponderosa pine, help to create acidic soils. Soil in turn helps determine what will or will not grow in an area. Wildlife species use soil as a habitat (25). Again, it is hard to separate the influence of soil on vegetation from wildlife. Agriculture is dependent on good soils (26). Crops are plants and as such have the same relationship with soil as other vegetation. Soils also influence lawns and shrubs around housing, the septic tanks used by many rural residents, and Albion's sewage treatment plant.

Groundwater recharge influences stream flow (27). It also provides the supply of water available for vegetation, wildlife, and humans (28 to 30). Except in low-lying areas, vegetation in the Palouse is largely independent of groundwater (phreatic water). Instead, it is dependent on soil moisture

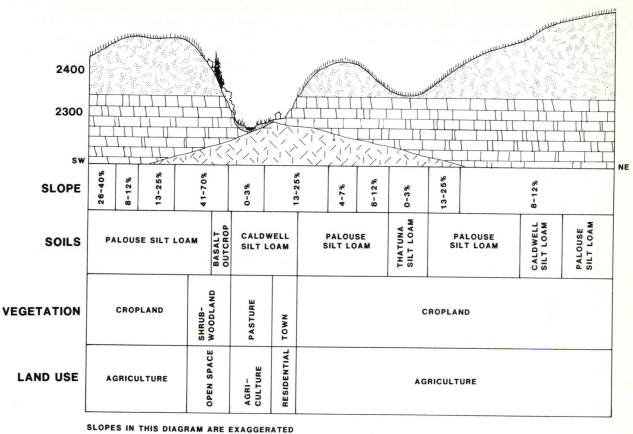

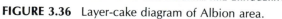

FIGURE 3.36 Layer-cake diagram of Albion area.

(radose water). Surface water is related again to water supply for animals and people (31 to 33) as well as providing a habitat for certain types of plant and animal life. Surface water is of concern to agriculture in the Palouse because of erosion and to other land uses because of flooding. In other regions, irrigation or land drainage will be important.

The interrelationship between vegetation and wildlife is strong (34). Vegetation provides food and shelter for animals. Animals, in turn, may affect the reproduction and growth of plants.

Energy-flow and food-web diagrams are good ways to visualize these relationships. Plants and animals influence how land is used by people (35, 36). Certain species conflict with agricultural crops, which requires special management by farmers. Other types of vegetation, such as trees, provide energy-efficient home sites that make pleasant places to live. Animals relate to land use and users both as pests and as sources of recreation.

By reviewing bivariate relationships in such a manner, linkages between different elements of the landscape can be made more explicit. One can also start to view each element as it relates to other elements. This perspective should be helpful when contemplating options in the use of resources.

Layer-Cake Relationships

One useful tool to help show how these elements interrelate across the landscape is layer-cake relationships (Figure 1.2). Each element is considered one "layer" in the landscape as a whole. The layer-cake diagram of the Albion area (Figure 3.36) was built on the topographic profile. The diagram was constructed by using the same set of points overlaid on each of the inventory maps. The collected information was then stacked to form a "layer cake."

This layer cake helps illuminate bivarite relationships and aids in analyzing multiple interrelationships between elements across the landscape. For instance, the relationship between the Palouse silt loam soils and agricultural land use is readily apparent. It is evident also that where the basalt outcrop occurs on a northeast-facing slope there is more vegetation. This steep area is used as open space. In the valley, the town of Albion is located on a less steep area over the crystalline rock.

Depending on the study area, several such layer-cake diagrams should be constructed to analyze how the different elements interrelate at different places in the landscape. In addition to being a useful analytical device, layer-cake diagrams can help a planner explain complex relationships to elected officials and to the public.

The Holdridge Life-Zone System

L. R. Holdridge (1967) of the Tropical Science Center in Costa Rica devised an objective system for classifying life, or bioclimatic, zones. His goal was to develop a means of determining the basic natural units for ecology. Holdridge observed that:

Among plant ecologists, the usual definition of association has restricted the unit to a given set of plant species. Such a definition not only places complete emphasis on vegetation alone, but renders difficult the mapping of associations. (1967, p. 7)

Holdridge took a broader view. He contended that:

The association must be thought of as a natural unit in which the vegetation, the animal activities, the climate, the land physiography, geological formation and the soil are all interrelated in a unique recognizable combination which has a distinct aspect or physiognomy. (1967, p. 7)

The system he developed is helpful for analysis and synthesis in planning because of this wider perspective.

Holdridge based his life zones on equivalently weighted divisions of three major climatic factors: heat, precipitation, and moisture. Based on his work in the Caribbean region, he developed the chart shown in Figure 3.37. According to Holdridge:

The life zone permits the groupings into natural units of several hundred or perhaps well over one thousand associations of the earth. The life zone chart, considered as a three dimension representation, separates 120 distinct life zones, provided that the subunits of the Subtropical region and Premontane belt are counted life zones. (1967, p. 14)

Life zones are then defined by Holdridge as a group of associations related through the effects of the three major climatic factors—heat, precipitation, and moisture. His system is applied in the following manner. By construction of a triangle (Figure 3.37), using the three parameters of temperature, precipitation, and evapotranspiration as the three axes of the triangle, any spot on earth with climatic records can be placed in one of the Holdridge life zones. The life-zone designations are those of the "climatic association" charac-

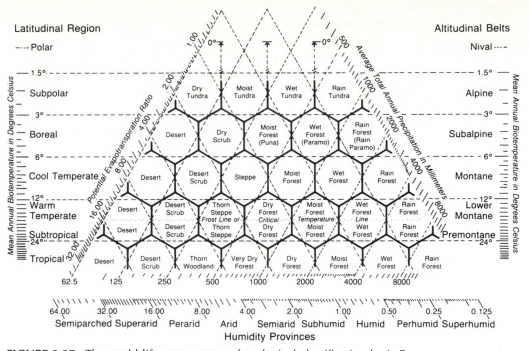

FIGURE 3.37 The world life zone system of ecological classification by L. R. Holdridge. *(Source: Adapted from Holdridge, 1967)*

teristics of the zone, that is, the normal climatic vegetation. This can be much modified by edaphic soil factors so that many plant associations are possible within each life zone, but there should be only one type of climax vegetation.

The life zone of Albion can be determined by locating its average temperature 47.7°F (8.72°C) and average precipitation 22.1 inches (561.34 millimeters). According to Holdridge's chart, Albion is on the interface between the Steppe and Moist Forest zones. The life-zone system may be especially helpful in larger, more complex planning areas. For instance, the system was used for an inventory and analysis of a large county in southeastern Washington (Beach et al., 1978). The layer-cake models in Figure 3.38 illustrate how the life zones related to other inventory elements.

TWO EXAMPLES OF BIOPHYSICAL INVENTORY AND ANALYSIS

The New Jersey Pinelands Comprehensive Management Plan

New Jersey is one of the most densely populated states in America. Yet, after 300 years of settlement by Europeans, Afro-Americans, and their descendants as well as by more recent immigrants, there remain natural areas in the state. The Pinelands is the largest of such areas. The basis for the New Jersey Pinelands Comprehensive Management Plan was a natural resource inventory.

This inventory summarizes reports by several consulting firms, state agencies, and environmental organizations. The Pinelands Commission's work,

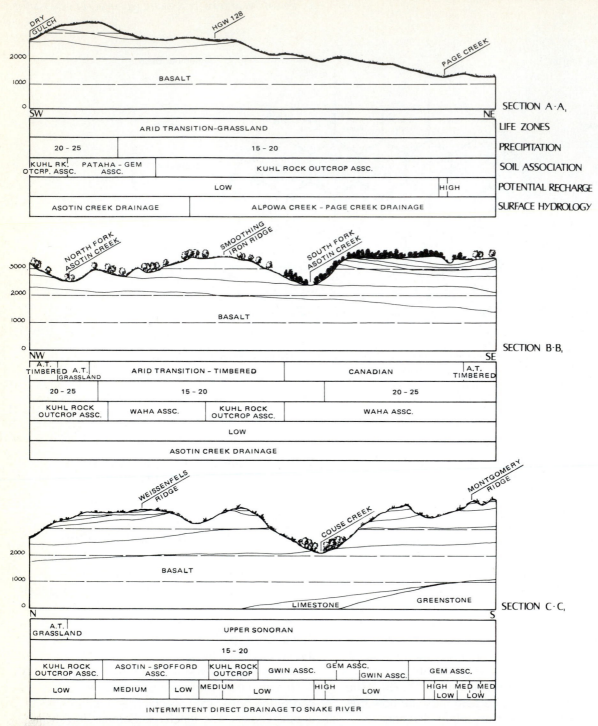

FIGURE 3.38 Layer-cake diagrams related to life zones. *(Beach et al., 1978)*

The largest known population of the rare Pine Barrens Treefrog, bright green with a lavender and white side stripe, thrives in its boggy, southern white cedar habitat of the New Jersey Pinelands. *(Photo by Norma Martin Milner of the New Jersey Pinelands Commission)*

including the reports that constituted the biophysical inventory, was supported with state and federal funds in addition to grants from private organizations. For instance, the Geraldine R. Dodge Foundation contributed $200,000 to the effort (Pinelands Commission, 1980).

The biophysical inventory and analysis sections in the management plan included a discussion of the evolution of the Pinelands ecosystem and a review of geology, hydrogeology, surface hydrology, soils, vegetation, aquatic communities, wildlife, climate, and air quality. The evolution of the Pinelands ecosystem was a broad review from the early geologic processes and the Pleistocene ice age through 10,000 years ago and the time of European colonization to the present. A summary of human influences was also included. Land users were included in the human inventory and analyses sections and will be discussed in Chapter 4.

The Pinelands is located in the Atlantic Coastal Plain formation. Much of the description of the Coastal Plain in the management plan was based on the work of the geologist E. C. Rhodehamel. The Coastal Plain has developed over the past 170

to 200 million years as a result of deposition and erosion. The region is characterized by a gently rolling terrain with sandy, droughty soils with no rock outcrops, steep slopes, or mountain peaks. The geology of the Coastal Plain comprises a wedged-shaped series of unconsolidated layers of sands, clays, and marls on a gently southeastward-dipping bedrock (80 to 100 feet per mile) that is 1,300 to 6,000 feet (397 to 1,830 meters) below the surface. These layers extend seaward into the submerged continental shelf (Pinelands Commission, 1980). A thorough description of the geological components of the Coastal Plain was included in the plan with a foldout map of the surficial geology and a foldout geologic cross section.

The hydrogeology of the Coastal Plain is characterized by extensive sand aquifers. According to the comprehensive management plan (1980), this groundwater supports 89 percent of the flow in the Pinelands streams, discharging primarily through the many swamps and marshes in the region. The aquifers are replenished solely by precipitation, of which about 44 percent of the annual total percolates through the sandy surface.

TABLE 3.2
MAMMALS OF THE PINELANDS AND THEIR HABITATS

Species	Status*	Pine-oak	Oak-pine	Pitch pine lowland	Cedar swamp	Hardwood swamp	Water	Bog	Marsh	Non-Pine Barrens	Agricultural	Urban	Non-forested	Borrow pit	Old fields
Opossum, *Didelphis virginiana*	C	•	•	•	•	•		•	•	•	•	•			•
Raccoon, *Procyon lotor*	C	•	•	•	•	•		•	•	•	•	•			•
Long-tailed weasel, *Mustela frenata*	C	•	•	•	•	•		•	•	•	•				•
Mink, *Mustela vison*	C	•	•	•	•	•		•	•	•	•				•
River otter, *Lutra canadensis*	C						•							•	
Striped skunk, *Mephitis mephitis*	C	•	•	•		•			•	•	•	•			•
Red fox, *Vulpes fulva*	C	•	•	•		•			•	•	•				•
Gray fox, *Urocyon cinereoargenteus*	A	•	•	•											•
Black bear†, *Ursus americanus*	Ex					•					•				•
Bobcat†, *Lynx rufus*	Ex					•				•					
Eastern coyote, *Canis latrans*	P/UC	•	•			•				•					
Gray squirrel, *Sciurus carolinensis*	C		•	•		•				•	•	•			•
Red squirrel, *Tamiasciurus hudsonicus*	A	•	•								•	•			
Woodchuck, *Marmota monax*	UC					•				•					•
Beaver, *Castor canadensis*	C				•	•	•	•			•				
Muskrat, *Ondatra zibethica*	C			•	•		•	•	•		•				
Eastern cottontail, *Sylvilagus floridanus*	C	•	•	•						•	•				•
White-tailed deer, *Odocoileus virginianus*	C	•	•	•	•					•	•	•			•

84

Species	Status*
Masked shrew, *Sorex cinerus*	UC
Short-tailed shrew, *Blarina brevicauda*	UC
Least shrew, *Cryptotis parva*	UD
Eastern mole, *Scalopus aquaticus*	C
Starnosed mole, *Condylura cristata*	UC
Little brown bat, *Myotis lucifugus*	UD
Eastern pipistrelle, *Pipistrellus subflavus*	UD
Big brown bat, *Eptesicus fuscus*	UD
Eastern chipmunk, *Tamias striatus*	C
Flying squirrel, *Glaucomys volans*	C
Rice rat, *Oryzomys palustris*	UD
White-footed mouse, *Peromyscus leucopus*	C
Red-backed vole, *Clethrinonomys gapperi*	C
Meadow vole, *Microtus pennsylvanicus*	C
Pine vole, *Pitymys pinetorum*	C
Southern bog lemming, *Synaptomys cooperi*	UD
Norway rat, *Rattus norvegicus*	C
House mouse, *Mus musculus*	C
Meadow jumping mouse, *Zapus hudsonius*	UD

* Explanation of status codes:

Abundant (A)—The species reaches its highest population densities in the Pinelands when compared to other areas of New Jersey.

Common (C)—The species population is at a level consistent with the habitat available in the Pinelands, but the density here is exceeded in other areas of New Jersey.

Uncommon (UC)—The species population level is below the level which the Pinelands is capable of supporting, or the species is rarely encountered because of a scarcity of habitat.

Undetermined (UD)—A species about which there is not enough information available to determine status.

Extirpated (Ex)—A species that occurred in the Pinelands within the last 300 years but no longer exists within the region.

Peripheral (P)—The species reaches the limits of its distribution in the Pinelands. It may be uncommon to abundant. This designation will be used along with another status.

† Potential habitats exist for these extirpated species.

SOURCE: Pinelands Commission, 1980.

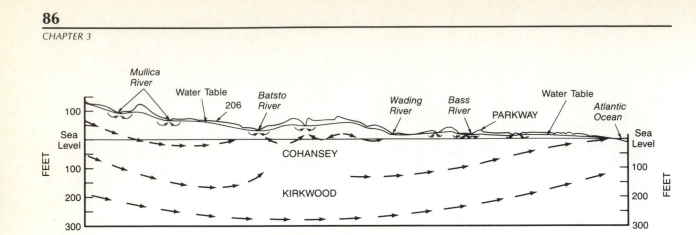

FIGURE 3.39 Hydraulic flows of the Cohansey-Kirkwood aquifer system. *(Source: Pinelands Commission, 1980)*

The major Coastal Plain groundwater systems are the Potomac-Raritan-Magothy, the Englishtown formation, the Wenonah formation, and Cohansey-Kirkwood. These systems and their relative importance to the Pinelands are described as are hydraulic flows (Figure 3.39), groundwater quality, and groundwater contamination.

Surface water is a distinctive character of the Pinelands. The Pinelands streams are typically slow-moving and shallow because of the flat topography. The components of surface hydrology considered by Pinelands planners include drainage basins, a hydrologic budget, surface-water quality, and drainage basin water quality. This information is discussed and summarized in tables and maps in the management plan.

The soils have developed from a parent material of the sandy geologic deposits. These soils are unusually porous and acidic. Pinelands planners analyzed information about soil classification, development and mineralogy, characteristics and interpretations, depth to water table, hydrologic soil groups, factors that limit use for septic tank absorption fields, and waste treatment information. Chemical aspects such as nitrogen, phosphorus, pH, and organic matter were considered as well to gain an understanding about the potential soil

productivity. SCS soil survey information was used for mapping and description. The Pinelands Commission utilized the SCS important farmland system to describe prime, unique, and statewide important farmlands (Pinelands Commission, 1980).

The Pinelands contains one of the largest natural areas in the northeastern United States. The authors of the Pinelands management plan characterize it as "low, dense forests of pine and oak, ribbons of cedar and hardwood swamp bordering drainage courses, pitch pine lowlands, bogs and marshes" (1980, p. 58). There are two distinct floristic complexes in the Pinelands, the uplands and the lowlands. Pine-oak and oak-pine forests are characteristic of the uplands complex, while cedar and hardwood swamps and pitch-pine lowland forest dominate the lowland complex (Pinelands Commission, 1980). The management plan included analysis of vegetation trends and patterns, the value of wetlands, endangered and threatened plants, forest fire management, and forestry.

The general aquatic habitat types in the Pinelands include streams, lakes and ponds, and bogs. The components of these aquatic habitats discussed in the management plan include algae, macrophytes, macroinvertebrates, and fish. Factors influencing

Pinelands aquatic communities, human influences, and a watershed inventory were also included (Pinelands Commission, 1980).

Several wildlife studies were summarized in the management plan. Table 3.2 lists the mammals of the Pinelands and their habitats, while Table 3.3 lists the total number of Pinelands mammals associated with each habitat. Similar species lists and habitat relationships were developed for birds, reptiles, and amphibians. There were also discussions about arthropods, wildlife, and fisheries resources and management practices (Pinelands Commission, 1980). Regional climate characteristics were analyzed by planners, including information about temperature, precipitation, and winds. The brief description of climate was followed by a review of air quality. Chemical air pollutants were reviewed—particulates, lead, sulfur dioxide, carbon monoxide, ozone, and nitrogen dioxide—as were point, area, and line sources of air pollution (Pinelands Commission, 1980).

The Pinelands Commission relied on a series of consultants to develop studies incorporated into their management plan (see, for instance, Berger & Sinton, 1985). These consultants utilized both existing data and fieldwork. This information was presented in such a way as to illustrate the interrelationships between the biophysical components of the Pinelands.

The Makah Coastal Zone Management Plan

The coastal zone management plan prepared for the Makah people also relied on collecting and analyzing existing data. The Makahs used a single consultant, Pacific Rim Planners, Inc., of Seattle, Washington, to prepare this plan, which included a natural resource inventory. The Makah Indian Reservation covers approximately 44 square miles

FIGURE 3.40 Location of the Makah Reservation.

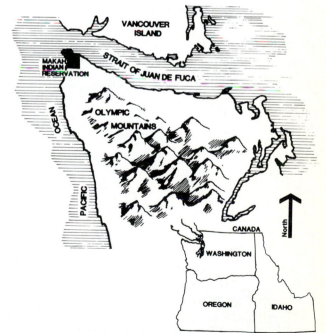

TABLE 3.3

TOTAL NUMBER OF PINELANDS MAMMALS
ASSOCIATED WITH EACH HABITAT

Habitat	Number of Species
Pine-oak forest	23
Oak-pine forest	24
Pitch pine lowland	25
Cedar swamp	18
Hardwood swamp	27
Water	6
Bog	20
Marsh (inland and coastal)	13
Non-Pine Barrens forest	15
Agricultural	26
Urban	13
Nonforested	3
Borrow pits	4
Old fields	24

SOURCE: Pinelands Commission, 1980.

(113.9 square kilometers) on the northwestern corner of the Olympic Peninsula in Washington State (Figure 3.40). The Makah people have historically looked to the sea for their livelihood. The federal Coastal Zone Management Act (CZMA) requires states to develop and coordinate programs for their coasts. This act excludes federal trust lands from the coastal zone but makes special funding available for Indian people to develop their own CZMA programs. The Makah program was funded through the U.S. Department of Commerce Office of Coastal Zone Management, the Washington State Department of Ecology, and the U.S. Department of Interior Bureau of Indian Affairs (Pacific Rim Planners, 1980).

This natural resource inventory was organized as follows:

Physical features

Climate

Geology

Soils

Upland ecological communities

The freshwater environment

    Stream flow and water quality

    Freshwater wetlands

    Salmonid use

Marine resources

    Rocky shores

    Sandy beaches

    Tidal marsh and mudflats

The physical features of the Makah Reservation are dominated by the rugged, mountainous terrain. While there are two large low-lying valleys, there

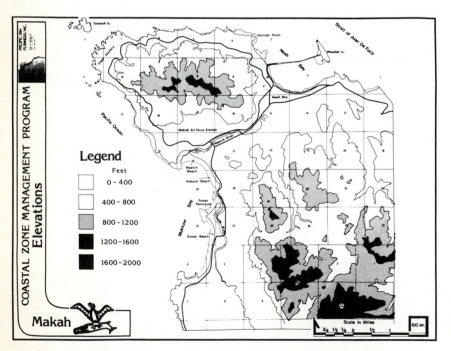

FIGURE 3.41 Elevation of the Makah Reservation. *(Source: Pacific Rim Planners, 1980, courtesy of Olympic Associates Co., Seattle, Washington)*

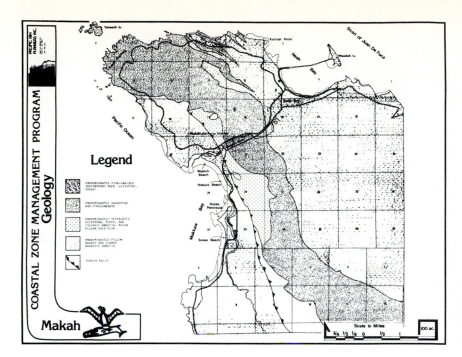

FIGURE 3.42 Geology of the Makah Reservation. *(Source: Pacific Rim Planners, 1980, courtesy of Olympic Associates Co., Seattle, Washington)*

are many mountains, hills, and ridges that range from 500 to 2,000 feet (152.5 to 610 meters) in elevation (Figure 3.41). The abundant rainfall in the Olympic Peninsula has created numerous small streams that have eroded the mountains, causing many steep slopes (Pacific Rim Planners, 1980).

The Makah Reservation has a marine climate characteristic of the Olympic Peninsula—very wet with a moderate temperature. The geology of the Olympic Peninsula is a result of marine volcanism that was gradually uplifted. More recent geologic action includes erosion and deposition of sediments by glaciers and streams (Figure 3.42). The soils information was derived from the SCS survey and other published data. Slope, texture, types, drainage, erosion potential, and structural suitability were described in the coastal inventory (Pacific Rim Planners, 1980).

There are three ecological communities on the Makah Reservation: upland, freshwater, and marine (Figure 3.43). The upland ecological communities of the Olympic Peninsula fall into the Sitka spruce zone that extends into southeast Alaska. The dominate plant species of the coniferous forest is the western hemlock. The freshwater communities forge the link between the uplands and the marine environments. There are two types of freshwater communities: forested swamps and peat bogs. These are discussed with the associated wildlife. Particular attention is paid to the salmonid use because of the socioeconomic importance of salmon to the Makahs (Pacific Rim Planners, 1980).

The Makah Reservation is bordered on the north by the Strait of Juan de Fuca and on the west by the Pacific Ocean. The types of shoreline (rocky, sandy, and mixed-sediment) are summarized in Table 3.4 and shown in Figure 3.44. Each of these marine environments is explained in the

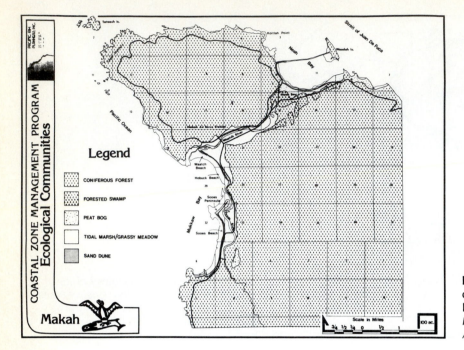

FIGURE 3.43 Ecological communities of the Makah Reservation. *(Source: Pacific Rim Planners, 1980, courtesy of Olympic Associates Co., Seattle, Washington)*

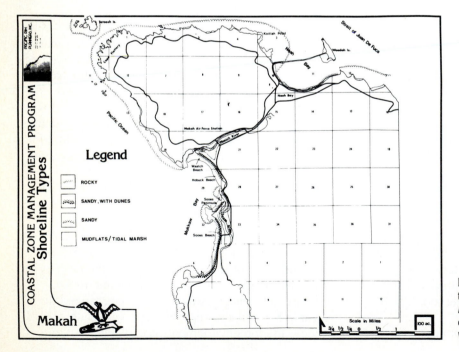

FIGURE 3.44 Shoreline types on the Makah Reservation. *(Source: Pacific Rim Planners, 1980, courtesy of Olympic Associates Co., Seattle, Washington)*

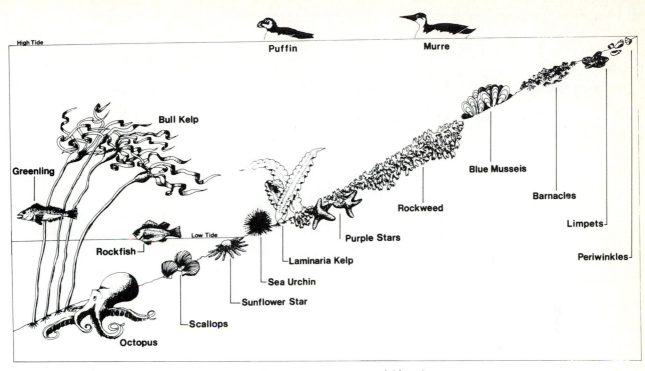

FIGURE 3.45 Rocky shore. *(Source: Pacific Rim Planners, 1980, courtesy of Olympic Associates Co., Seattle, Washington)*

management plan inventory. Schematic drawings (Figures 3.45 and 3.46) illustrate rocky shores and sandy shores and estuaries.

The inventory of ecological processes for planning is a relatively new art. These two examples, the Pinelands and the Makah Reservation, were published in 1980. Both differ from conventional planning processes in the scope of biophysical information collected and analyzed. In both cases, a slice of time was taken of the interacting elements of the place. This slice represents a momentary glimpse of a continuous process where natural factors and human society are in constant change. The landscape changes accordingly. This concept is illustrated in Figure

TABLE 3.4

APPROXIMATE EXTENT OF SHORELINE TYPES ON THE MAKAH RESERVATION

	Miles of Shoreline
Strait of Juan de Fuca:	
Rock	5.5
Sand (Neah Bay)	2.0
Mixed sediment	2.0
Pacific Ocean:	
Rock	8.0
Sand (Mukkaw Bay)	6.0
Total miles	23.5

SOURCE: Pacific Rim Planners, 1980.

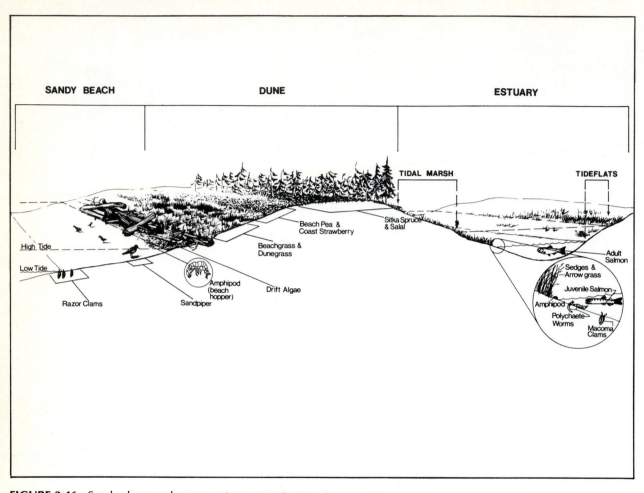

FIGURE 3.46 Sandy shore and estuary. *(Source: Pacific Rim Planners, 1980, courtesy of Olympic Associates Co., Seattle, Washington)*

3.47. Since the landscape is constantly changing, inventories should be viewed as a continuing activity that includes periodic updating and reassessment of information as new data become available.

The landscape is a result of the interaction of natural factors and human activities. The natural factors include both physical, or *abiotic,* elements such as climate, geology, hydrology, and soils as well as the *biotic* elements of plants and animals (Vroom et al., 1980). As noted by the Pinelands Commission:

The present Pinelands landscape and ecosystem have been shaped by natural processes which began millions of years ago and, more recently, by the influence of man. A knowledge of these events is necessary to fully appreciate the region's significance and to plan for its continuing maintenance. (1980, p. 1)

In both the Pinelands and the Makah Reservation such knowledge was directly incorporated into the rest of the planning process. Whereas a more conventional process may have included simple maps or descriptions of selected natural factors, in the Pinelands and on the Makah Reservation a more holistic perspective was taken. In both cases, the relationship of people with nature was carefully considered. For example, the Makah people have traditionally used coastal resources for their livelihood and continue to do so today. As explained by Pacific Rim Planners:

> Some of those resources are strictly coastal: the fish of the ocean, and the shellfish from the shore, but there are other resources which are intimately connected with those of the marine environment, even though not in . . . proximity to the shoreline. Small streams high in the hills and miles from saltwater provide critical spawning habitat for the salmon which are caught offshore, while the tideflats . . . produce food for the young salmon. Even vegetation near the streams is an important contributor to . . . productivity. . . . The streams serve to connect the resources of land with those of the sea, transporting not merely water, but nutrients, sediments, plants, and animals. (1980, p. 15)

Berger and Sinton (1985) provide similar descriptions of how people of the Pine Barrens are linked to natural factors. Human interaction with these factors is more complex than the use of the land. The next chapter explores the elements needed to be collected to understand the human ecology of a place.

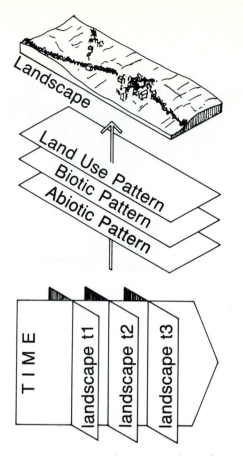

FIGURE 3.47 Landscape in a slice of time. *(Source: Vroom et al., 1980)*

4

HUMAN COMMUNITY INVENTORY AND ANALYSIS

Conventional approaches to planning have incorporated socioeconomic analyses. Connecting such studies to biophysical information for planning is relatively new. In this chapter, those population and economic studies familiar to planners will be reviewed. In addition, a framework for integrating information about people and nature will be presented. Planners use a variety of types of social information, and, basically, these materials fall into three categories: existing data, new information from existing data, and original information. These data include quantitative information, such as the number of people living in an area as counted by a census. Data also may be more qualitative, such as the perceptions of people about the visual impacts of a new roadway or dam.

Planning projects and programs require different types of social information. For example, a growth management plan requires an estimate of future population, economic, and development trends. This information can be derived from existing sources and is quantitative. Conversely, for the placement of a new electric transmission line, planners need to collect original, qualitative information about perceptions and reactions through interviews with affected residents. Because of the variety of possible planning projects and programs, a blanket prescription cannot be given for the specific social inventories that should be conducted. The issues that have stimulated the planning process as well as the goals that have been identified to resolve those problems and opportunities will determine the types of data to be collected and analyzed.

An understanding of current and possible future population trends and characteristics will probably be essential for a community to achieve many of its goals. In Oregon, for instance, local governments are required to address specific goals concerning agriculture and housing. As a result, planners must inventory and analyze information concerning trends in farm population (such as is it growing or declining) and characteristics of the agricultural community (such as what is the average age of farmers). Planners must also analyze population trends and characteristics and forecast future possibilities to make recommendations about housing needs.

To accomplish this, planners need to understand local economies. For agriculture, the percentage that farming contributes to the economic base of a community is important to know, as are the most important commodities and their markets. Through an analysis of the local agricultural economy, planners can determine how healthy it is, whether or not it is worth protecting, and if intervention is necessary to improve local farming systems. The economic base of the community helps planners analyze community needs. If the economic base comprises primary industries (such as farming, fishing, mining, and logging) rather than those of the tertiary sector (such as retail, wholesale, and services), then demands for housing, for instance, will be different. Where primary industries are involved, it may be necessary for houses to be relatively close to farmland, the ocean, the mountains, or forests. With tertiary industries, the linkage between home and workplace may be less spatially bound.

Conventional planning processes have considered and incorporated population and economic studies. But the social characteristics have not been related to the landscape, a major difference between conventional approaches and ecological planning. Through an ecological approach, social processes are connected to landscape features. For instance, agriculture can be related to specific combinations of biophysical elements that vary with crops. Wheat requires different climate, water, and soil characteristics than cranberries. Rural housing has different needs than high-rise apartments. Different users of the land—cranberry farmers or high-rise apartment dwellers—place different demands on the landscape as well.

Each human community must be viewed as having unique characteristics. The population growth of a major Texas city, Dallas, for instance, of 1,000 people per year may not be dramatic or even the source of concern. But in a rural west Texas county the same growth may be quite significant and have consequences for several land uses, especially agriculture and housing. Although ranching may have great symbolic value in Dallas, the number of real cowboys may be few. While in a west Texas county, people actively engaged in ranching may constitute the most important economic sector. Certainly, the landscape and the biophysical processes that created it are different in Dallas than in west Texas. As a result, each place, whether in Texas, Oregon, or New Jersey, must be inventoried and analyzed for its special qualities.

Planners can use many existing sources of information to conduct social inventories. After these sources are summarized, a discussion will follow about how such existing data can be used to generate new information about population, future development, and land users. Some planning efforts may require the generation of original information. Three ways of collecting new information are surveys, interviews, and participant observation. Once information has been collected, there is a need to analyze it. Ecological frameworks for analysis include identifying landscape patterns, social interactions, and relationships between people and nature. The inventory and analysis should lead to an assessment of community needs. Two examples of social inventories and analyses are presented from the New Jersey Pinelands and the Makah Indian Reservation.

(Frederick Steiner)

SOURCES OF EXISTING INFORMATION

Before discussing inventory and analysis methods, the major sources of social information must be identified. Major information sources include maps, histories, census data, newspapers, phone books, community organizations, universities, and public agencies (Table 4.1).

Land-Use Maps and Settlement Pattern Diagrams

Land-use and land-user maps and settlement pattern maps were introduced in Chapter 3. Land use and land users are elements of both the biophysical and the sociocultural environments. The best sources include interviews with individuals and associations; observations; the SCS; city, county, and regional planning agencies; and city and county property tax assessors. School districts; public libraries; private engineering, landscape architecture, and planning consulting firms; gas stations; the Library of Congress; election boards; state departments of state and finance; and real estate agents may all be mapping sources. Another good source is aerial photographs, which may be obtained from the SCS, USGS, private pilots, and state highway departments.

Histories

A sense of history is vital to the understanding of a community or region. Many communities have at least one unofficial historian who has compiled an

account of past events. Local histories can be gathered through interviews and discussions. Many public libraries and local historical societies keep unpublished manuscripts about local events in their archives. As oral histories become more popular, often these may be stored in local libraries or historical societies. State libraries, college and university libraries, and the Library of Congress are also good sources, as are community college, college, and university departments of history, folklore, geography, American studies, and anthropology.

Census Data

The Bureau of the Census, administered by the U.S. Department of Commerce, is the finest single source of demographic information in the United States. A national census is undertaken the first year of every decade. These censuses include vital

TABLE 4.1

SUMMARY OF SOURCES OF INFORMATION FOR HUMAN COMMUNITY INVENTORY, ANALYSIS, AND SYNTHESIS

Land-Use Maps and Settlement Pattern Diagrams
1. Interviews with individuals and associations
2. Observation
3. SCS, USGS
4. City, county, and regional planning agencies
5. City and county tax assessors
6. School districts
7. Public libraries
8. Engineering, landscape architecture, and planning consulting firms
9. Gas stations
10. The Library of Congress
11. Election boards
12. State departments of state and finance
13. Real estate agents
14. Chambers of commerce

Histories
1. Public libraries
2. Interviews
3. Local and state historical societies
4. College and university libraries
5. Community college, college, and university departments of history, folklore, geography, and anthropology
6. The Library of Congress
7. Local used bookshops
8. Genealogical societies

Census Data
1. U.S. Bureau of the Census, U.S. Department of Commerce
2. Agricultural Census, U.S. Department of Agriculture
3. Public utilities
4. Telephone companies
5. Hospital and newspaper birth and death records
6. College and university departments of sociology and geography

Newspapers and Periodicals
1. Local newspapers
2. City, regional, or state magazines (for example, *Philadelphia, Boston, New York, Cincinnati, Sunset, Southern Living, New West, Rocky Mountain, Washington, California*)
3. Public libraries

Phone Books
The numerous private-advertising phone directories

Community Clubs and Organizations
1. Chambers of commerce
2. League of Women Voters
3. Service clubs
4. Educational organizations
5. Garden clubs
6. Political parties
7. Community or neighborhood associations
8. Fraternal organizations
9. Labor unions and guilds
10. Business and professional associations
11. Scouts and other youth groups
12. Arts associations
13. Churches and synagogues
14. Farmers organizations (for example, the Grange, the Farm Bureau, commodity groups)
15. Nature and conservancy groups
16. Sports clubs
17. Volunteer firemen
18. United Way and Community Chest

Colleges and Universities

Government and Public Agencies
1. City, township, county, and regional agencies
   a. Planning commissions and/or staffs
   b. Councils of government
   c. School boards and administrators
   d. County extension agents
   e. Utility companies
   f. Special-use districts
   g. County offices that record land tenure, titles, sales, marriages, divorces, deaths, criminal offenses, and employment
   h. Hospital registers and files
   i. Fire department and emergency services
   j. Police and sheriff offices
   k. Welfare agencies
   l. Health departments
   m. Water and sewer departments, departments of public works
   n. Juvenile deliquency centers
   o. Park and recreation departments
   p. Drug and alcohol counseling centers
   q. Councils on aging
   r. City and/or county prosecutors
   s. Public transit authorities
   t. Recycling centers
2. State (or provincial) agencies
   a. Elected officials and their staffs
   b. Departments of planning, education, health, safety, welfare, natural resources, environmental protection, commerce, agriculture, transportation, and energy
3. Federal (or national) agencies
   a. Elected officials and their staffs
   b. U.S. Department of Housing and Urban Development
   c. U.S. Department of Energy
   d. U.S. Department of Education
   e. U.S. Department of Health and Human Services
   f. U.S. Department of Commerce
   g. U.S. Department of Agriculture
   h. U.S. Department of Transportation
   i. Environmental Protection Agency
   j. The Library of Congress
4. International organizations. The United Nations has several programs that may provide helpful information which might be used to put local communities into a global perspective.

information about age and sex composition, birth and death statistics, ethnic composition, rural-urban distribution, migration, general population characteristics, housing data, and general social and economic characteristics. There is more thorough information available for standard metropolitan statistical areas (MSA) than for rural regions.*

A review of specialized census information, *Census Catalog and Guide,* is published annually by the Bureau of the Census. Additional census data may be obtained from the agricultural census of the USDA and college university departments of sociology and geography. The use of census data will be discussed later in this chapter.

Newspapers and Periodicals

Local newspapers and regional magazines can reveal much about a community or region. Both daily and weekly newspapers can be rich sources of information about local happenings. Some of the information that can be found in local newspapers includes different perspectives on local issues, employment opportunities, the availability of real estate, and the activities of voluntary organizations and civic groups. By reading past newspaper articles and keeping an ongoing clipping file, a planner can track opinion about issues and learn something about trends in employment and real estate.

An ever-growing number of magazines may help to establish the vernacular character of regions. Some of these magazines focus on an individual city, such as *Philadelphia, New York, Boston,* and *Cincinnati.* Others address a broader region like *Sunset, Southern Living, New West,* and *Rocky Mountain* or states like *California* and *Washington.* If a planner is new to a region or is a consultant from some other place, then this type of magazine can provide some information about the character of the planning area.

* See metropolitan statistical area (MSA) in the Glossary for a fuller discussion of this term.

Phone Books

The yellow, white, and blue pages of phone books each reveal information about a community. The yellow pages provide an index of industry, commerce, and services in the area. The white pages provide a source for family names, which may reveal information about ethnic heritage. The location of ethnic neighborhoods may also be identified. The blue pages, which include government listings, often include a map of the area served by the phone book and a brief history of the area. In addition, local place and street names can be learned from phone books.

Community Organizations and Clubs

People usually join an organization or a club to associate with people of similar interests. Community clubs and organizations display much about how people spend their leisure time, their political and religious beliefs, and their employment. In addition to the phone book, two good sources of lists of community organizations and clubs are usually the local chamber of commerce and the League of Women Voters. A list of community organizations and clubs with names and addresses may be useful if the planner is developing a mailing list to send newsletters or other information about the planning program. Such a list can offer information about the scope of community activities in the planning area. For some planning programs and projects, it may be necessary to interview representatives from these groups, which is discussed later in this chapter.

Colleges and Universities

The two main sources of cultural information in community colleges, colleges, and universities are their libraries and individual faculty members. Faculty in departments of sociology, anthropology, economics, planning, geography, business, Afro-American studies, ethnic studies, education, home economics, history, political science, and law should be able to provide information about the sociocultural characteristics of an area. Other members of academic communities, such as librarians and registrars, may be helpful additional information sources. The extension services of land-grant and sea-grant universities often publish bulletins with socioeconomic profiles of counties and cities.

Government and Public Agencies

Government and public agencies collect and store a wealth of material about communities. Usually, however, there is a lack of coordination between agencies, which means information must be collected, analyzed, and put into a format with meaning for the particular studies. All levels of government are good sources: local, regional, state, and national. International organizations may be a useful resource for some planning studies.

Synopsis of Information Sources

Maps, histories, census data, newspapers and periodicals, phone books, community organizations and clubs, colleges and universities, and government agencies can yield much information for inventories of human communities. Maps are important for understanding the spatial organization of the planning area. Planners also may need maps to study the relationship of social systems to natural patterns. Histories inform the planner about the past of the place—when it was settled and why. Newspapers and periodicals can help the planner to confirm or deny the issues that have been identified as well as to learn what individuals or groups have an interest in the issue. Phone books reveal much about who lives and works in the area. Community and government organizations represent the official social structure of the planning area. Universities and colleges provide a bank of information about the place—its history, its social organization, and its culture.

The identification of existing sources of information is just the beginning of a social inventory and analysis. These existing data form the basis for the generation of new information about the people and economy of a community.

USE OF EXISTING DATA TO GENERATE NEW INFORMATION

Population Trends, Characteristics, and Projections

There are three types of population studies important in planning for the future: trends, characteristics, and projections. Population trends include changes in numbers, location, and components of people. Population characteristics include age and gender composition, birth statistics, death statistics, ethnic composition, distribution, migration, and population pyramids. Generally, this information is available from the U.S. Census. Other sources may need to be studied such as the records of county and city governments, hospitals, newspapers, phone companies, public utilities, councils of government, and state agencies. Projection techniques include the cohort-survival model, geometric interpolation, and simulation models. In this section, Whitman County, Washington, where the town of Albion is located, will be used as an example of population studies that were conducted as part of a planning process.

Trends. Planners study population trends to learn how the planning area has changed over time. Whether the population has been growing or declining will be important to know in many planning programs and projects. If a goal of the planning effort is to encourage economic development, then the planner will want to know if the area is growing or declining in order to devise business recruitment strategies. If growth management is a goal, then trends give an indication of how many people have moved to the

TABLE 4.2

WHITMAN COUNTY POPULATION BY DECADE

	1940	1950	% Change	1960	% Change	1970	% Change	1980	% Change
Whitman County	27,221	32,469	19	31,263	−3.7	37,900	21.2	40,103	5.8
% of state population	1.6	1.4		1.1		1.1		0.9	0
Albion	206	206	0.0	291	41.0	687	136.1	631	−8.2
Colfax	2,853	3,057	7.0	2,860	−6.0	2,664	−6.9	2,780	4.4
% of county population	10	9		9		6		6.9	
Colton	262	207	−21.0	253	22.0	279	10.3	307	10.0
Endicott	495	397	−20.0	369	−7.0	333	−9.8	290	−12.9
Farmington	341	239	−30.0	176	−26.0	140	−20.5	176	25.7
Garfield	674	674	0.0	607	−10.0	610	0.5	599	−1.8
LaCrosse	475	457	−4.0	463	1.0	426	−8.0	373	−12.4
Lamont	135	101	−25.0	111	10.0	88	−20.7	101	14.8
Malden	325	332	2.0	292	−12.0	219	−25.0	200	−8.7
Oakesdale	526	590	2.0	474	−20.0	447	−5.7	444	−0.7
Palouse	1,028	1,036	0.7	926	−11.0	948	2.4	1,005	6.0
Pullman	8,432	12,022	172.0	12,957	8.0	20,509	58.3	23,579	15.0
% of population	16	37		41		54		59	
Rosalia	596	660	11.0	585	−11.0	569	−2.7	572	0.5
St. John	526	542	3.0	545	0.6	575	5.5	529	−7.0
Tekoa	1,383	1,189	−14.0	911	−23.0	808	−11.3	854	5.7
Uniontown	332	254	−23.0	242	−5.0	310	28.1	286	−7.7
Asotin County	—	10,878	—	12,909	18.6	13,799	6.9	16,823	21.9
Walla Walla County	—	40,135	—	42,195	5.1	42,176	−0.4	47,435	12.5
State	1,736,200	2,378,963	37.0	2,853,214	19.9	3,409,169	19.5	4,132,156	21.2
WSU*	4,015	5,446	36.0	6,434	18.0	13,150	104.0	16,459	25.0
% of county population	15	17		21		35		41	

* Number of students based on fall enrollment.
SOURCES: U.S. Bureau of the Census, 1970, 1980a; Washington State University, no date; Whitman County Regional Planning Council, no date a.

area and when. If the development of new facilities is involved, for instance, schools and parks, then population trends reveal past demand for these services.

In Whitman County, the issue being addressed was a growing number of people seeking to build homes in the countryside. The demand for new housing in rural areas was negatively impacting agriculture. Table 4.2 illustrates population trends in Whitman County from 1940 to 1980, as interpreted from the 1980 U.S. Census. This table includes all the towns and cities in the county, Washington State University, the total of two neighboring counties (Asotin and Walla Walla), and the state as a whole. Comparisons with neighboring jurisdictions, in this case counties, and with a larger entity, in this case the state, help to show how the planning area relates to other places.

The table shows an overall growth of the county that totally parallels that of Washington State University. Most of the small towns in the county have lost population. This was due to the mechanization of agriculture, the decline of railroads, and the construction of highways that bypassed the small towns. For instance, Albion lost 8.2 percent of its population from 1970 to 1980.

Population trends may also show shifts in the location of people from urban to rural or from rural to urban areas. These changes have been dramatic in the past three decades. As demographers have noted, continued suburbanization, regional redistribution, and rural repopulation are the three major trends shaping population settlement in the United States and other developed nations during the last quarter of the century (Long, 1981; Wardwell & Gilchrist, 1980). Whereas Whitman County only grew by 5.8 percent between 1970 and 1980, rural population growth was 65.8 percent, while urban areas declined by 10.9 percent (Table 4.3). The redistribution of people in nonmetropolitan areas has a dramatic impact on energy use, the conversion of important farmland, coastal management, and the protection of environmentally sensitive areas. In Whitman County, these shifts have been uneven. The city of Pullman has experienced growth, while Albion and other rural communities have had population decreases.

Another element of population trends is the components of change. Components of change include changing birth, death, and migration rates. Birth and death rates are natural trends, while migration rates are due to factors such as changes in employment opportunities. Table 4.4 shows components of change in Whitman County from 1950 to 1980.

Characteristics. Planners study population characteristics to learn about who is living in the planning area. If the planning issue involves economic development, then the planner will want to know about the labor force. If growth management is a goal of the process, then population density becomes important. Age distribution is crucial to know if the planning issue relates to schools or parks.

Density, population distribution, dependency ratios, and labor force participation were important in Whitman County planning. Density is one charac-

TABLE 4.3
URBAN AND RURAL POPULATION, 1950–1980

	Whitman County			Asotin County			Walla Walla County			State		
	Total	Urban	Rural	Total	Urban	Rural	Total	Urban	Rural	Total	Urban	Rural
1950	32,469	15,079	17,390	10,878	5,617	5,621	40,135	27,276	12,859	2,378,963	1,503,166	875,797
% of total	100	46	54	100	50	50	100	70	30	100	63	37
1960	31,263	15,817	15,446	12,909	6,060	3,849	42,195	28,567	13,628	2,853,214	1,943,249	909,965
% change	−3.7	4.8	−11.1	18.6	61.2	−31.5	5.1	4.7	5.9	19.9	29.3	3.9
% of total	100	51	49	100	70.2	29.8	100	67.7	32.3	100	68	32
1970	37,900	23,173	14,727	13,799	10,109	3,690	42,176	30,969	11,207	3,409,169	2,501,051	908,118
% change	21.2	46.5	−4.6	6	11.5	−4.1	−0.5	8.4	−17.7	19.4	28.7	−0.2
% of total	100	61	31	100	73	27	100	73	27	100	73.3	26.7
1980	40,103	26,359	13,744	16,823	10,586	6,237	47,435	34,674	12,761	4,132,156	3,037,014	1,095,145
% change	5.8	13.7	−6.7	21.9	52.3	−8.9	12.5	12.0	13.9	21.2	21.4	20.6
% of total	100	65.7	34.3	100	62.9	37.1	100	73.1	26.9	100	73.5	26.5

SOURCE: U.S. Bureau of the Census, 1980a.

TABLE 4.4
COMPONENTS OF POPULATION CHANGE IN WHITMAN COUNTY, 1950–1980

		Net Population Change		Components of Change			
		Number	%	Natural Increase*	Rate†	Net Migration	Rate†
1950	32,469						
1960	31,263	−1,206	−3.7	4,584	14.1	−5,790	−17.8
1970	37,900	6,637	21.2	3,356	10.7	3,281	10.5
1980	40,103	2,203	5.8	2,424	6.4	−102	−0.3

* Natural increase = births − deaths.
† Rate per 1,000.
SOURCES: U.S. Bureau of Census, 1950, 1960, 1970, 1980a and Whitman County Regional Planning Council, no date a.

teristic of population. It is determined by dividing the total population by the total area. Table 4.5 compares the density of Whitman County with that of Asotin and Walla Walla counties. The Whitman County population density of 18.6 persons per square mile (7.2 per square kilometer) can be contrasted to that of the Netherlands (1,062 people per square mile, or 415 per square kilometer) or Alaska (0.5 people per square mile, or 0.2 per square kilometer).

Age and gender distribution is a characteristic of population. A popular method of displaying this information is the population pyramid, such as Figure 4.1. Racial and ethnic distribution are those characteristics that reveal how many and where minority people live. Special care should be taken

to get an accurate count of minorities, since they have been traditionally undercounted in the U.S. Census. Some racial and minority categories used by the Bureau of the Census include white (excluding Spanish surname), white (Spanish surname), black, American Indian, Asian, mixed ethnic background, and other.

Dependency ratios refer to those portions of the population outside the wage-earning range group. Such ratios are determined by dividing the sum of those in the 0 to 19 age group and those over 64 years old by those from 20 to 64. Table 4.6 illustrates dependency ratios for Whitman, Asotin, and Walla Walla counties and Washington State. Whitman County has a low dependency ratio because of the large proportion of university

TABLE 4.5
POPULATION DENSITY, 1980

	Population	Area		Density	
		mi²	km²	Persons/mi²	Persons/km²
Whitman	40,103	2,153	5,576.3	18.6	7.2
Asotin	16,823	633	1,639.5	26.6	10.3
Walla Walla	47,435	1,262	3,268.6	37.6	14.5
STATE	4,132,156	66,570	172,416.3	62.1	24.0

SOURCE: U.S. Bureau of the Census, 1980a.

Group	Total	Male	Female
75+	1,210	491	719
70–74	813	400	412
65–69	1,073	492	581
60–64	1,161	564	597
55–59	1,376	680	696
50–54	1,285	634	651
45–49	1,263	620	643
40–44	1,374	722	652
35–39	1,861	927	934
30–34	2,449	1,275	1,174
25–29	3,534	1,889	1,645
20–24	6,826	3,793	3,033
15–19	2,518	1,247	1,271
10–14	1,937	983	954
5–9	1,956	993	963
0–4	2,178	1,120	1,058
Total	32,814	16,831	15,983

FIGURE 4.1 Whitman County population distribution by age and gender, 1980. *(Adapted from U.S. Census information)*

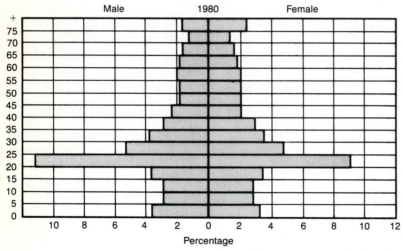

Total 32,814

students relative to the working-age population (Whitman County Regional Planning Council, no date a).

Another characteristic of population is the labor force participation rate. Information about the labor force is useful to understand how many people are employed. This is determined by dividing the number of people in the labor force by the total population. Again Whitman County is an atypical county. Because of Washington State University, many individuals in the 18 to 24 age group who would be in the work force elsewhere are excluded (Table 4.7). It may also help to show age and sex distributions in the work force (Table 4.8).

Projections. Planners make projections to forecast who will be living in the area. As an employee of a municipal, county, or state agency, the planner may be responsible for making the projections. Planning consultants may rely on these projections or, depending on the project or program, make new forecasts. If there is an economic development goal, then it is crucial to know if new people are likely to move to the planning area. Growth management involves allocating places for new residents to live. The number of new people will determine how many new schools and parks are necessary. Conversely, if population projections indicate decline, then different economic development and facility planning strategies will be necessary.

There are several methods for projecting population. Those methods most familiar to planners include the cohort-survival model, multiple regression, and simulation models (Chapin & Kaiser,

TABLE 4.6
DEPENDENCY RATIOS, 1980

	Dependency Ratios*
Whitman County	0.63
Asotin County	0.87
Walla Walla County	0.78
STATE	0.72

* Dependency ratios = population of 0 to 19 age group + population of those over 64 years divided by population of 20 to 64 age group.

SOURCE: U.S. Bureau of the Census, 1970 and 1980a.

TABLE 4.7
POPULATION IN THE LABOR FORCE (16 YEARS AND OLDER) BY CENSUS COUNTY DIVISIONS, 1970

Census County Divisions	Labor Force	Population	Labor Force Participation Rate
Whitman County	14,346	29,470	49
1	305	791	51
2	476	999	48
3	125	334	37
4	405	852	48
5	182	357	51
6	367	674	54
7	415	737	56
8	556	1,097	51
9	360	700	51
10	231	480	48
11	373	766	49
12	131	304	43
13	994	1,628	61
14	457	802	57
Colfax	1,107	2,012	55
Pullman	7,862	17,127	46
Asotin County	5,139	9,555	54
Walla Walla County	17,012	30,952	55
STATE	1,410,000	2,061,146	68

SOURCES: U.S. Bureau of the Census, 1970; Washington Office of Program Planning and Fiscal Management, 1976; Whitman County Regional Planning Council, no date a.

TABLE 4.8
PERCENTAGE IN LABOR FORCE BY SEX AND AGE, 1980

Age Group	Whitman Number in Labor Force	%	Asotin Number in Labor Force	%	Walla Walla Number in Labor Force	%	Washington State Number in Labor Force	%
Male:								
16–19 years	2,710	8.1	579	4.6	1,938	5.2	154,849	4.9
20–24	5,692	17.0	651	5.2	2,604	7.0	206,105	6.6
25–54	6,325	18.9	3,008	24.0	8,995	24.2	818,601	26.1
55–64	1,257	3.8	675	5.4	2,319	6.2	184,570	5.9
65 +	1,467	4.4	1,013	8.1	2,719	7.3	180,207	5.7
Female:								
16–19 years	2,926	8.7	573	4.6	2,105	5.7	145,633	4.6
20–24	4,202	12.5	719	5.7	2,358	6.3	194,149	6.2
25–54	5,751	17.2	3,074	24.5	7,881	21.2	805,654	25.7
55–64	1,355	4.0	837	6.6	2,527	6.8	199,176	6.3
65 +	1,815	5.4	1,385	11.0	3,747	10.1	251,209	8.0
	33,500	100.0	12,550	100.0	37,193	100.0	3,140,153	100.0

SOURCE: U.S. Bureau of the Census, 1980a and Whitman County Regional Planning Council, no date a.

1979; Hightower, 1968). There are three main components to be considered for the *cohort-survival methods:* (1) fertility, (2) mortality, and (3) net migration (Figure 4.2). The natural-increase segment of cohort survival determines the number of births by applying fertility rates to the female population of childbearing age. Each population group, then, is survived; that is, an appropriate mortality rate is applied to each 5-year period. This method provides an estimate of population if it were to grow by natural increase alone with no in-or-out migration. Net migration rate is then considered, usually based on past trends. Multiple regression has been used primarily as a supplement to cohort-survival models. Statistical simulation models involve the use of a sample to project larger trends.

Depending on the project or program, a planning team may make its own projections or may use existing projections from various sources. Whitman County planners used three separate projections to paint different scenarios about potential growth (Table 4.9). The first set of projections had been made by the Bonneville

Power Administration (BPA), the large Pacific northwest federal utility agency. The BPA used cohort-survival techniques to make their projections. The second projection was made by Pacific Northwest Bell (PNB). These estimates were based on the projected growth of the labor force. The final projections had been developed by the Washington Office of Program Planning and Fiscal Management (OPP & FM) and used net rates of migration by age and sex (Whitman County Regional Planning Council, no date b).

Development Projections

For many situations, it is necessary for planners to make development projections based on population studies. If a community is preparing a growth management plan, for instance, then local officials will want to know how much new housing and commercial building will be needed to accommodate the new people. Projections can be made for future development needs based on the relationship

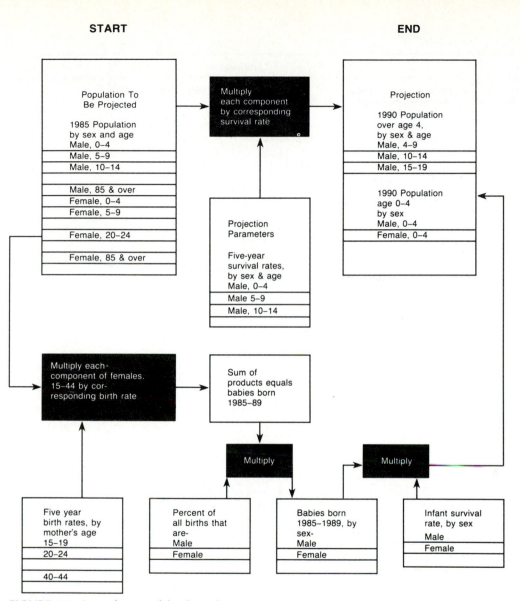

FIGURE 4.2 Procedure used for the cohort-survival method. *(Source: Adapted from Hightower, 1968)*

between population increase and residential building permits.

For example, according to the records of a county for the past 10 years, the population increase for each building permit issued has remained between two and four people per permit. To project the number of additional building permits in future years, a ratio of three people to each permit may be chosen. An assumption is made that the additional building permits

TABLE 4.9
POPULATION PROJECTIONS, 1980–2000*

County	Actual	Estimates					
	1970	1975	1980	1985	1990	1995	2000
BPA							
Whitman	37,900	39,000	40,225	41,425	42,525	43,550	44,521
Asotin	13,799	12,725	13,950	15,850	17,625	18,900	
Walla Walla	42,176	42,425	43,175	44,225	44,175	46,100	
STATE	3,409,169	3,511,800	3,776,400	4,054,800	4,333,800	4,583,200	
PNB							
Whitman	37,900	38,800	40,100	43,000	45,600		
Asotin	13,799	14,300	14,700	15,400	15,900		
Walla Walla	42,176	42,300	42,300	41,700	43,000		
STATE	3,409,169	3,507,600	3,779,100	4,052,400	4,303,100		
OPP & FM							
Whitman	37,900	38,654	43,617	42,248	46,832	48,381	49,734
WSU†	13,150	16,184	16,500	16,500	16,500	16,500	

* These estimates were compiled in 1977 by Whitman County planners as part of the comprehensive planning process. The actual 1980 populations were 40,103 for Whitman County, 16,823 for Asotin, 47,435 for Walla Walla, and 4,132,156 for Washington State. Contrary to the OPP & FM estimates, the WSU enrollment declined slightly in the 1980s and was 15,186 in the 1989 spring semester.

† Average of preceding fall and spring semester enrollments.

SOURCES: Bonneville Power Administration, 1976; Pacific Northwest Bell, 1976; Washington OPP & FM, 1977; Whitman County Regional Planning Council, no date b.

correspond with the number of additional housing units. The ratio of three people per building permit then can be divided by the population increase projected from one period to the next.

The population projections from Whitman County can be used for illustration (Table 4.9). Two population increases for the period 1980 to 2000 are made: 4,296 and 6,117. If these estimates are divided by 3, then a range of between 1,432 and 2,039 new houses is necessary in Whitman County for the 20-year period, or an average of 1,735.5 new houses.

The number of new houses needed then can be used to determine the amount of land needed. If 1,735.5 new houses are needed in Whitman County by 2000, then 289.25 acres (117.1

hectares) will be needed with a density of six houses per acre. If the density is decreased to one house per acre, then 1,735.5 acres (702.9 hectares) will be needed. The amount of land needed then can be compared with the areas suitable for residential use in the planning area.

Land is only one resource to consider. Especially in the western United States, water availability is a crucial consideration when making development projections. There may be enough land available and suitable for new development but not enough water to supply to new residents. In some areas other public services, such as sewer capacity or road budgets, might constrain development.

The example given here focused on housing

TABLE 4.10
COMMON SOURCES OF ECONOMIC INFORMATION

U.S. Government

Bureau of the Census
  Census of Population (printed copies and summary tape files)
  Current Population Report
  Census of Housing
  Annual Housing Survey
  Census of Retail Trade (years ending on 2 and 7)
  Census of Manufactures (years ending on 2 and 7)
  Census of Wholesale Trade (years ending on 2 and 7)
  Census of Service Industries (years ending on 2 and 7)
  Census of Mineral Industries (years ending on 2 and 7)
  Census of Transportation (years ending on 2 and 7)
  Census of Construction Industries (years ending on 2 and 7)
  Survey of Minority Owned Businesses
  Survey of Women Owned Businesses
  Census of Governments
  County Business Pattern
  Bureau of Census Catalog (annual: describes all reports and data files issued during the year)
Internal Revenue Service
  Statistics of Income: Individual Income Tax Returns
Bureau of Economic Analysis (BEA)
  Survey of Current Business (Magazine containing information about national income, federal deficit, and other economic news. Periodic changes in how national income is defined are also published in this magazine.)
  BEA Regional Projections
  Local Area Personal Income

National Center for Health Statistics
  Vital and Health Statistics
Social Security Administration
  Earnings Distribution in the United States
National Institute of Education
  Tax Wealth in Fifty States
Energy Information Administration
  Monthly Energy Review
  Annual Energy Review
Office for Civil Rights
  Directory of Elementary and Secondary School Districts, and Schools in Selected School Districts
U.S. Department of Labor
  Monthly Labor Review
  Survey of Consumer Expenditures
USDA
Federal Bureau of Investigation
Federal Reserve Board
Immigration and Naturalization Service
Federal Trade Commission

Nongovernmental Sources

American Bus Association
American Public Transit Association
Association of American Railroads
Dun and Bradstreet, Inc.
Motor Vehicle Manufacturers Association
National Education Association (teachers' salaries)
Transportation Association of America
Editor and Publisher Company, Inc.
  Market Guide
International Council of Shopping Centers
Communication Channels, Inc.
  Shopping Center World (monthly)
Lebhar-Friedman, Inc.
  Chain Store Age Executive (monthly)

Urban Land Institute
  Dollars and Cents of Shopping Centers (updated periodically)
  Various development handbooks (such as the Industrial Development Handbook)
The National Research Bureau, Inc., Chicago
  Directory of Shopping Centers in the United States (annually)
National Retail Merchants Association
  Stores (monthly)
  Sales and Marketing Management (Annual Survey of Buying Power)
Northeast-Midwest Institute, Washington, D.C.
  The YEAR Guide to Government Resources for Economic Development

SOURCE: Adapted from unpublished class handout of Peter Schaeffer, Program in Urban and Regional Planning, University of Colorado at Denver.

TABLE 4.11
EMPLOYMENT BY INDUSTRY IN WASHINGTON STATE AND WHITMAN COUNTY

	A Washington State, %	B Whitman County, %	$\frac{B}{A}$, Location Quotient*
Agriculture, forestry, and fisheries	4.24	16.82	3.97
Mining	0.17	0.03	0.17
Construction	5.7	3.5	0.61
Manufacturing	20.7	3.1	0.15
Transportation, communications, and other public utilities	7.21	3.15	0.44
Wholesale and retail trade	20.37	15.68	0.77
Finance, insurance, and real estate	5.3	2.41	0.45
Business and repair service	2.96	1.17	0.40
Personal services	4.22	4.7	1.11
Entertainment and recreation	0.83	0.67	0.81
Professional and related services[†]	18.0	44.88	2.50
Public administration	3.75	2.94	0.78
Industry not reported	4.87	0.95	
TOTAL EMPLOYMENT	1,250,270	13,778	

SOURCE: U.S. Bureau of the Census, 1970; Whitman County Regional Planning Council, no date b.

* See Table 4.12 for explanation of this technique.
[†] Includes public education (Washington State University).

development. A similar process can be used to project the need for new commercial development as well as new public services such as schools and roads. As with housing, the demand for such development will need to be compared with the land suitable for such use as well as the availability of water and services.

Economic Analyses

The first step in an economic study is to determine the economic base of the planning area. Some of the common sources of economic information are listed in Table 4.10. An economic base survey may be necessary where such data are not described in existing sources. A survey may be a preferred source if published information is out of date or more detailed data are needed. If a new

economic survey is conducted, then existing information will provide the initial data base.

Lay Gibson suggested the following outline for conducting an economic base survey:

1. *The base area.* Determine the base area. For a planning study this would follow the boundaries for the established planning area.
2. *The measure of magnitude.* Use existing employment figures to show where the area's economy is based. Dollar value of sales, income, or some other measure may also be used.
3. *The labor force.* All public and private sector employers should be surveyed. Additionally, it is probably wise to interview at least the largest employers outside the study area if they provide substantial employment opportunities for

residents of the planning area. It may be assumed that they are, functionally if not physically, part of the local economic base.

4. *The questionnaire.* Questions must be designed (a) to produce a full-time equivalent employment figure—one that is a standard expression of employment magnitude, and (b) to determine the local and nonlocal sales. For an economic base survey, it is enough to determine the portion of total sales made to local and nonlocal customers (adapted from Gibson, 1975, pp. 4–6).

After existing or new information is collected, it is often useful to divide the local economy into sectors, that is, classify employment into different industry types. A general breakdown is:

Primary sector: Industries that use raw materials; extractive industries such as farming, fishing, mining, and logging.

Secondary sector: Industries that assemble products or parts of products from raw materials. This can range from steel mills to clothing manufacturers to makers of calculators. It may be defined to include such local types of manufacture as bakeries, which sometimes causes confusion.

Tertiary sector: Industries and services that primarily survive on the needs of the resident population—internally linked activities that rest on the base of primary- and secondary-sector income: retail, wholesale, and trade; financial services such as banks, real estate, and insurance firms; business services such as lawyers and accountants; repair services; personal services such as barbers and dry cleaners; and recreation and entertainment.

Economic information may be summarized in tables and figures. As with population data, it may be helpful to compare and contrast the planning area with similar areas and place it in a larger context. Table 4.11 illustrates employment by industry in Whitman County and Washington State. Figure 4.3 compares broad employment patterns in Whitman, Asotin, and Walla Walla counties. As has been previously indicated, Washington State University and farming have a strong impact on the Whitman County population. The same is true with the economic base. This is illustrated in Figure 4.4. Figure 4.5 illustrates nongovernment and nonfarm employment patterns in 1973 for the same three Washington counties in addition to the state as a whole and Latah County, Idaho.

Next it is important to provide a measure of the impact of new economic growth (such as new jobs) on the planning areas. Two common methods include economic base analysis and input-output analysis. Economic-base analysis is a generic term covering several techniques such as location quotient, shift-and-share analysis, and minimum-requirement analysis. Each builds on data that may be collected from a survey or census. Jack Kartez (1981) has summarized these techniques, showing how they may be used, the data requirements, and the level of detail that may be expected (Table 4.12).

User Groups

A planning area will probably be used by a variety of people. User groups are often important to identify to clarify who will be impacted by a project or program. Sometimes a goal of the planning effort is to protect what already exists, the status quo. For instance, a community may be seeking to preserve a wetlands, a historic building, or prime farmland. In such cases, it will be crucial to know who uses these areas. On the other hand, an economic development plan may involve enticing new users into an area. In such cases, it may be helpful to identify current users to

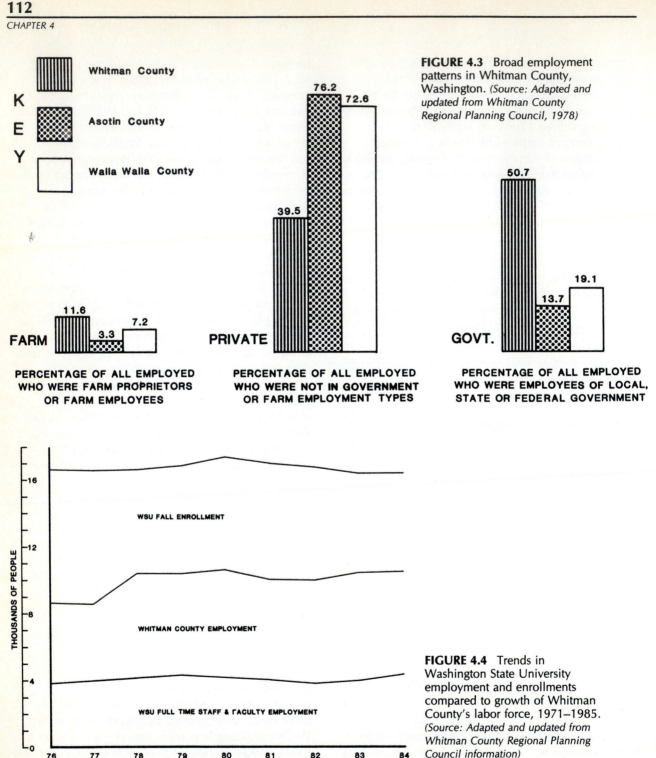

KEY

Whitman County

Asotin County

Walla Walla County

FIGURE 4.3 Broad employment patterns in Whitman County, Washington. *(Source: Adapted and updated from Whitman County Regional Planning Council, 1978)*

FARM
11.6   3.3   7.2

PERCENTAGE OF ALL EMPLOYED
WHO WERE FARM PROPRIETORS
OR FARM EMPLOYEES

PRIVATE
39.5   76.2   72.6

PERCENTAGE OF ALL EMPLOYED
WHO WERE NOT IN GOVERNMENT
OR FARM EMPLOYMENT TYPES

GOVT.
50.7   13.7   19.1

PERCENTAGE OF ALL EMPLOYED
WHO WERE EMPLOYEES OF LOCAL,
STATE OR FEDERAL GOVERNMENT

THOUSANDS OF PEOPLE

WSU FALL ENROLLMENT

WHITMAN COUNTY EMPLOYMENT

WSU FULL TIME STAFF & FACULTY EMPLOYMENT

76 77 78 79 80 81 82 83 84

FIGURE 4.4 Trends in Washington State University employment and enrollments compared to growth of Whitman County's labor force, 1971–1985. *(Source: Adapted and updated from Whitman County Regional Planning Council information)*

Distribution of Employment

FIGURE 4.5 Nongovernment and nonfarm employment patterns. *(Source: Adapted and updated from Whitman County Regional Planning Council information)*

ensure that efforts are made to protect their interests while new users are being invited to the area.

Preliminary user-group categories may be based on land use. The Land-Use and Land-Cover Classification System devised by the USGS for remote sensing (see Table 1.2) provides standard categories. But land use is only the beginning in the establishment of user groups. Land-use classification is relatively straightforward in comparison to land-user classification. User-group identification is much more difficult, especially for those users whose livelihood is not directly related to the landscape.

User activities are actions performed in the landscape—specific categories of people engaged in certain types of activities in particular places. These diverse actions may be triggered by seasonal cycles and are likely to be affected by population and economic trends. Land uses occur spatially and are organized around specific resources. Any person who passes through a region is a consumer of that place's resources.

In early stages of an inventory, land-use and land-user classifications may be general. At the beginning, it may be possible only to identify those users who are most directly associated with the

TABLE 4.12
SUMMARY OF TECHNIQUES FOR ECONOMIC-BASE ANALYSIS AND INPUT-OUTPUT ANALYSIS

Technique	Use	Data Needs	Detail
Location Quotient	Identifies those local sectors or activities which have "comparative advantage" when compared to the same activities in a larger economy (state, region).	Employment data can be collected from the Decennial Census or elsewhere.	Very general. Only a *descriptive* tool. Identifies "basic" industry only vaguely.
Shift-and-Share Analysis	Identifies how local economic change compares to change by sector or industry in a larger economy. Helps summarize employment data in a format that reveals how employment change locally *may* have been due to either (1) the fact that the locality has a large percentage of employment in nationally growing or declining industries, or (2) because the locality had particularly low or high growth in an industry compared to a larger economy.	As above. Secondary data.	Only descriptive. Useful in understanding trends in employment data. Can help identify "basic" activities.
Minimum-Requirements Analysis	Identifies that portion of employment for each industry type which is believed to be "basic" when compared to areas of similar size. Somewhat better basis than location quotients in that it explains why a percentage of employment is defined as being *basic* employment for a particular industry in a particular size range of communities.	Again, secondary data can be collected from the Census.	Provides a method of determining overall multipliers for basic activity in a locality. Cannot determine industry-specific data.
Input-Output Analysis	Provides a very detailed economic accounting of the linkages between each type of industry or activity. Provides the basis for developing industry-specific multipliers. This means that it provides an accurate basis for tracing the probable changes in other industries' employment or sales due to an initial change in another industry type in the local economy.	Requires that original data be collected from individual firms in the area.	Provides highly accurate information on how a change in employment affects other types of activities.

SOURCE: Kartez, 1981.

land (such as farmers). It may be helpful to regard land users in a fashion similar to that used by ecologists in their community studies (see Ricklefs, 1973, pp. 589–775, for instance). It is not difficult to see how the concept of food chains can be expanded to form land chains and the explanation

User group identification is simplified when livelihood is directly related to the landscape. *(Philip Maechling)*

of primary production can be used as the basis to explain primary land users.

As the inventory and analysis proceeds and user groups are identified, their recognized view of the landscape and adaptive strategies will become apparent as will the linkages between user groups. Tables 4.13 and 4.14 were developed for the Kennett region of southeastern Pennsylvania to show user groups there. It must be pointed out that the class, religious, and ethnic distinctions were those that the people of the area used to describe themselves and each other. They were not imposed by the planning team.

The unfortunate thing is that humans do make distinctions concerning the groups with which they identify based on skin color, class and occupation, ethnicity or nationality, and religious or political beliefs. The question that must be asked is: Do planners meet the needs of all people by recognizing these distinctions or by pretending they do not exist?

GENERATION OF NEW INFORMATION

Often planners will need to conduct original research to understand the community where they are working. Sometimes existing information may reveal opinions or attitudes about the issues being addressed by the planning effort, but other times more information will be necessary. For example, what do people think about new housing development? Newspaper articles may indicate that local residents support new housing. If they do indeed favor it, then are they willing to pay the taxes for the necessary services to support the new housing? What do people feel about new industrial development? If they are opposed, then are they aware of the possible implications for the tax base of the community? How is the community organized—formally and informally? Who are the community leaders? Such questions can be posed through mail and telephone surveys, face-to-face interviews, and participant observation.

TABLE 4.13
KENNETT, PENNSYLVANIA, USER GROUP LOCATION

Groups			Farmstead/ Estate Tenent Dispersed	Farmstead/ Estate Tenent Contiguous	Cross- roads Town	Strip Development			Subdivision			Mushroom Complex	Borough
Class*	Religion	Ethnicity				High	Moderate	Low	High	Moderate	Low		
UC	Epis.	Anglo		X									
UC	Quaker	Anglo		X									
UC	Cath.	Ital.		X			X		X				
UMC	Epis.	Anglo		X			X						
UMC	Quaker	Anglo	X	X				X				X	
UMC	Cath.	Ital.		X				X				X	X
MC	Quaker	Anglo	X	X	X	X	X					X	
MC	Pres.	Anglo	X	X	X	X	X		X				X
MC	Meth.	Anglo	X	X	X	X	X		X				X
MC	Bapt.	Anglo	X	X	X		X						X
MC	Jewish	Jewish		X									X
MC	Cath.	Ital.			X			X			X		X
MC	AME	Black		X									X
WC	Pres.	Anglo	X	X	X		X	X			X		X
WC	Meth.	Anglo	X	X	X		X	X			X		X
WC	Bapt.	Anglo	X	X	X		X	X			X		X
WC	Cath.	Ital.		X	X		X	X				X	X
WC	Bapt.	South						X			X	X	
WC	AME	Black	X		X			X					X
WC	Cath.	Hispanic										X	

* UC, upper class; UMC, upper middle class; MC, middle class; WC, working class.
SOURCE: Rose, Steiner, & Jackson, 1978/1979, and Jackson & Steiner, 1985.

Mail and Telephone Surveys

In Chapter 2, surveys were introduced as a means to help establish community goals. Surveys can also be used to inventory community characteristics and as a basis for analysis of the attitudes of citizens. The major ways to conduct surveys are by mail and telephone, although interactive television may also be an option. No one needs to respond to yet another bad survey. Before intruding on people's privacy, planners should ask if the information is truly necessary for the planning effort. If a survey is indeed necessary, then it should be written by someone practiced in the art and science of preparing questionnaires. A sociologist should be retained through a consulting company or university, or, if the budget and scope of the project is appropriate, a social scientist with survey experience should be included on the planning team. If the budget or the scope of the project is more limited, then the planning team should obtain a copy of a standard survey text such as Dillman (1978) or Sudman and Bradburn (1983).

Don Dillman's total design method (TDM) has two parts. First, he suggests that each aspect of the survey process that may affect the quality or quantity of the response be identified. Each aspect should then be designed in such a way that "the best possible responses are obtained" (Dillman, 1978, p. 12). Second, Dillman suggests an administrative plan "guided by a theoretical view about why people respond to questionnaires. It provides the rationale for deciding how each aspect, even the seemingly minute ones, should

TABLE 4.14
DISTRIBUTION OF USERS IN THE CONTROLLING INSTITUTIONS OF THE KENNETT, PENNSYLVANIA, REGION

Class	Religion	Ethnicity	Agriculture					Extraction (Quarry)	Finance (Banking)	Commerce and Industry		Land Development		Government			
			Horse	Dairy	Hort.	Mush.	Beef			Retail	Textiles/ Electronics	Real Estate	Developer/ Builder	Twp.	Co.	St.	Fed.
UC	Epis.	Anglo	O/W				O		O	O	O		O		A		A
UC	Quak.	Anglo	O/W	O/W			O		O	O	O		O	E	A	E	
UC	Cath.	Ital.	O/W														
UMC	Epis.	Anglo	W	O/W		O	W			O	E	O	A				
UMC	Quak.	Anglo		O/W	O/W	O											
UMC	Cath.	Ital.			O/W	O							O				
MC	Quak.	Anglo			O/W	O				W/O				E			
MC	Pres.	Anglo			W	W	W/O			W/O				E	A	E	
MC	Meth.	Anglo			W	W	W/O		W	W/O		W/O	O	E		E	
MC	Bapt.	Anglo			W	W			W	W/O				A			
MC	Jewish	Jewish				O			W	W/O							
MC	Cath.	Ital.		W		O/W		O	W	W/O		W	W/O	E			
MC	AME	Black								W/O				A			
WC	Pres.	Anglo	W		W	W				W/O	W		W				
WC	Meth.	Anglo	W		W	W				W/O	W		W				
WC	Bapt.	Anglo	W	W	W	W				W/O	W		W				
WC	Cath.	Ital.		W	O/W	O/W				W/O	W						
WC	Bapt.	South			O/W	O/W	W/O	O/W			W/O		W				
WC	AME	Black	W		W	W				W/O	W		W				
WC	Cath.	Hisp.			W	W				W/O							

O, owner; W, worker; E, elected; A, appointed.
SOURCE: Rose, Steiner, & Jackson, 1978/1979 and Jackson & Steiner, 1985.

117

be shaped'' (1978, p. 12). The purpose of the administrative plan is ''to ensure implementation of the survey in accordance with design intentions'' (Dillman, 1978, p. 12).

According to Dillman, the essence of the administrative plan is to:

- Identify all the tasks to be accomplished
- Determine how each task is dependent on the others
- Determine in what order the tasks must be performed
- Decide the means by which each task is to be accomplished (1978, p. 20)

Dillman provides clear guidelines and suggestions for realizing these principles. He also reports a high response rate to surveys which use the TDM. Essentially, there are eight steps in conducting a survey:

1. Define the purpose of the survey
2. Choose the study design
3. Select the sample
4. Construct and pretest the questionnaire
5. Implement the questionnaire by mail, over the telephone, or in person (mail surveys may require a follow-up step)
6. Code the interviews
7. Tabulate and analyze the results
8. Write a report (adapted from Survey Research Center, 1976)

The Survey Research Center of the University of Michigan's Institute for Social Research has prepared a manual to follow these eight steps for interviews (Survey Research Center, 1976). A good questionnaire is dependent on the quality of the questions asked. The text by Sudman and Bradburn (1983) provides especially helpful suggestions about how to ask questions. Together,

the Dillman, Sudman and Bradburn, and Survey Research Center books provide much guidance for the preparation of surveys. When designing a survey to provide inventory information, it is useful to remember other steps of the planning process. Synchronized surveys, introduced in Chapter 2 and discussed again in Chapter 6, may be used throughout the process to integrate the steps. Integrated, synchronized surveys can assist planners to identify issues, establish goals, collect information, and select options for realizing planning goals.

Face-to-Face Interviews

Face-to-face interviews are a personal alternative to the mail and telephone. Such interviews may be conducted at random or individuals may be preselected, depending on the nature of the planning project or program. For random interviews, it will be important to select representative neighborhoods of the planning area. Interviews should be conducted in a variety of settlement types and with people of various income levels and ethnic backgrounds. At a minimum the planner should record the date, time, and place of the interview and ask questions about the age of the resident; the size of the family; the occupations of the husband, wife, and children; the place of work; and the length of residence in the planning area (Berger et al., 1977).

If interviewees are selected at random, then there is the possibility that the person may not be a resident. In such cases, it is important to ask why the individual is visiting the planning area. For planning efforts with tourism and recreation issues involved, visitors may be targeted for interviews. Planners may interview people at rest stops or gas stations to learn more about why visitors are attracted to the area.

Interviews can also be conducted with what ethnographers call *key informants*. A list of organizations and clubs can be compiled (see Table

4.1). Officers of these associations can then be contacted and interviewed. In addition to recording the date, time, and place of the meeting, the planner should note the name of the organization and of the person being interviewed. The planner should try to obtain an official statement of the purpose of the group, an organizational chart, and a written biography of the association. The planner should try to learn about the committee structure, scheduled meetings, membership, and dues and funds.

The specific questions asked during the interview will depend on the planning effort. Face-to-face interviews with association officers should yield information about community leadership, how issues are perceived in the planning area, and the use of natural resources by various groups of people.

Participant Observation

Participant observation involves living in a community, being involved in its activities, and carefully recording events. Many agency staff planners live in the community where they work and are participants in its affairs; however this technique for generating new information about a community goes beyond living in a place. Participant observation is used by ethnographers in their fieldwork. The technique involves active listening, supplemented by taking careful field notes. A journal can be used to record observations. Such observations should be carefully recorded and include the date and the places and people involved.

If a team of planners is involved, then they will meet to discuss their observations. One approach is to place individual planning team members in areas and homes of representative individuals from various segments of the community. For instance, one planner may live in a neighborhood with a high-income family; another, a middle-income

family; and a third, a low-income family. One person could live in a neighborhood of an ethnic minority, another in a majority neighborhood. In this way a cross section of observations can be compiled.

Allan Jacobs (1985) suggests a framework for organizing observations about the built environment. He recommends that the planner first walk the entire planning area. A checklist can be prepared prior to such a walk to help with note taking and observation. The checklist should include spaces for visit-specific information such as the date, time of day, and weather as well as detailed information about streets, sidewalks, curbs, street trees, maintenance, building arrangement, and topography (Morrell, 1989). A map that can be written on should also be taken so that the planner can record the route and mark points of interest. Sketches can also be made during the first visit, but a camera should be left in the office. Sketching encourages looking closely, whereas when taking pictures details may be overlooked.

A second site visit can then be made with a camera, photographing the area and verifying initial observations (Jacobs, 1985; Morrell, 1989). A third visit can then be made with a local expert, a key informant in ethnographic terms. The observations from these visits can be recorded in the journal and compared with published information about the study area. During such observation, Jacobs urges planners "to constantly question what one sees as well as the conclusions one comes to" (1985, p. 28). Because planners bring their own cultural values to any observation, it is, according to Jacobs, "necessary to constantly question and refine one's definition of what is really being seen" (1985, p. 28).

Reading the landscape is an art. Planners can learn to look for visual clues that can reveal much about a human community. For instance, some buildings may have the date they were constructed displayed on their facades. By looking at a place, a planner can start to understand something about the history of a community and the people who dwell there. Participant observation can yield rich, personal insights about communities that cannot be gained by reading existing information or by collecting new data through surveys and interviews.

The observation of the built environment is only part of what a planner should study. Planners should also attend meetings of community organizations and clubs to learn more about the people who live in the planning area. These meetings may be with the same associations whose officers have been interviewed. Agenda and membership lists should be collected. In this way, active members of the community can be identified and issues confirmed and denied as being impor-tant to local citizens. A mailing list can be compiled, which can assist planners to begin to form a network to distribute information about the planning process.

ANALYSIS AND SYNTHESIS OF SOCIAL INFORMATION

After new and existing information is collected, it is then necessary to pull it together and determine what it reveals about the area. Combined with the information about biophysical processes, planners can identify patterns that occur on the landscape. Planners can also determine interactions and relationships that occur among groups of people and between social and biophysical processes.

Establish Visual and Landscape Patterns

Ecological processes tend to reveal themselves in certain visual and landscape patterns. Landscape ecologists have explored the spatial arrangement of communities and are studying landscape patterns

and functions (Forman & Godron, 1986). The use of ecological concepts such as patches, corridors, matrices, and networks can help planners understand the patterns of human interaction that occur in the landscape.

Visual analysis is a complex art. NEPA required that "presently unquantified environmental amenities and values" be considered in decision making and that "the environmental design arts" be used when assessing the impacts of projects and programs (U.S. Congress, 1969).

In response, landscape architects have developed several approaches for incorporating visual considerations into decision making. R. Burton Litton, a University of California, Berkeley, landscape architecture professor, worked closely with the USFS and was especially influential (Litton, 1968; U.S. Forest Service, 1973, 1974). Litton's work was influenced by others who had proposed ways of reading the landscape, including Donald Appleyard and Kevin Lynch. Many planning projects and programs will require a detailed visual analysis. In such cases, a landscape architect who specializes in visual resource assessment should be included in the planning team. Landscape architects, who have experience assessing visual characteristics, are included, or direct, many USFS and NPS management planning programs.

In the context of human community analysis, some of the techniques developed for visual resource assessment can be adapted to help identify landscape patterns. Many of these approaches to assess the visual attributes of a place have been developed from the perspective of an outsider, an expert. Viewing the landscape from the road, areas are mapped and evaluated. Such an approach can be helpful in the determination of visual sensitivity to change. (See Tables 10.3 and 10.10 for examples of how this type of information can be used in classifying environmentally sensitive areas.)

The view-from-the-road approach is an

outgrowth of windshield surveys. These surveys are conducted of a planning area from a car. The planning researcher takes photographs, draws sketches, and writes notes about her or his observations. Another general approach to visual analysis is to try to learn the insider, or land-user, view of the landscape. There have been several techniques developed to attempt to gain such a perspective. Photographs are a common tool. One option is to give land users in the planning area cameras and ask them to take pictures of things that they like and do not like about their landscape. These photographs are then collected, compared, and analyzed.

Another option is for the researcher to take photographs. These photographs can then be used to conduct preference surveys. Preferences can be determined by showing the photographs at public meetings, through one-on-one interviews, or by mail surveys. Visual surveys from either the expert or user perspective can be integrated with the participant-observation efforts.

The visual and participant-observation findings should enable the planner or the planning team to identify visual patterns that reflect cultural values. Such patterns can be rather simple land-use types: agricultural, commercial, residential, industrial, and natural. Ideally, the patterns should reveal more complex relationships between biophysical and sociocultural processes that are visually apparent and that are specific to the area: for example, rolling wheatland, old town center, lakeshore suburb, old stream-bank industry, and valley conifer woodland.

The terms that have been developed by Burton Litton and others to describe visual patterns are actually similar to those used by landscape ecologists. For instance, where Kevin Lynch (1960) used *node, path,* and *district,* Forman and Godron (1986) use *patch, corridor,* and *matrix* (Hirschman, 1988, after Steinitz, 1988). Such terms are helpful for describing the visual and cultural patterns observed in a place.

Identification of Interactions and Relationships

Building on the visual and landscape patterns, overlay and computer maps, matrices, and systems diagrams can be used to identify interactions and relationships. The specific technique chosen will be determined, in large measure, by the issues that have been identified and the goals established for the planning effort. Matrices will be used here to illustrate how sociocultural interactions can be analyzed.

Although biophysical and sociocultural factors must be viewed together, it may be useful to consider them separately before putting them together in a synthesis chart. Figure 4.6 demonstrates a way to establish biophysical factor interaction that builds on the bivariate diagram discussed in Chapter 3. Symbols, letters, or numbers can be used in the boxes to indicate if a relationship exists and the relative importance of that relationship. Written descriptions can be used to elaborate and explain the relationships.

In a matrix, land users can be classified in at least two ways, either by their use of the land or by the terms the local people use to classify themselves and each other. As with biophysical factors (see Figure 4.7), a numbered matrix can be constructed so that relationships can be explained in writing. (In Figure 4.7 simple land-use designations are used for illustration, such as industrial. Certainly, more descriptive visual and cultural landscape patterns, like old stream-bank-corridor industry or industrial node can be used as well.)

After classifying land users, it is possible to examine user-group demands. Some of these demands are quite basic: skiers need snow, foresters need timber, farmers need productive soil and ample water, and hunters need game. The relationship between user-group demands and biophysical factors can be illustrated and summarized in a matrix (Figure 4.8) (Jackson and Steiner, 1985).

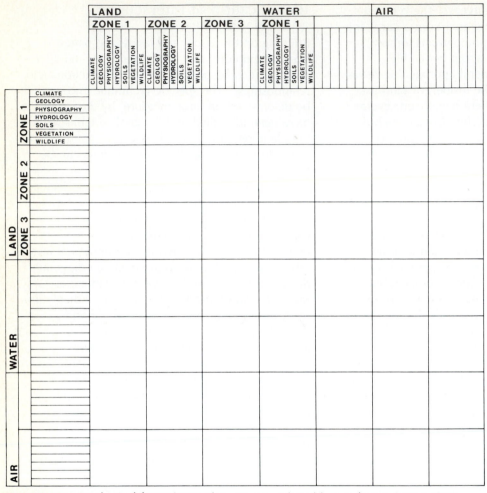

FIGURE 4.6 Biophysical factor interaction. *(Source: Adapted from Jackson & Steiner, 1985)*

Community Needs Assessment

The preceding inventory and analysis of population and economic characteristics as well as the synthesis of human community information should lead to an assessment of needs. These needs should relate to the issues and goals being addressed by the planning effort. These studies, however, may reveal the necessity to amend or establish new goals and may raise new issues. Take, for instance, once again, two of the Oregon statewide goals: agriculture and housing. The agricultural goal is to preserve and maintain agricultural lands, while the housing goal is to

	RESIDENTIAL	COMMERCIAL	INDUSTRIAL	TRANSPORTATION	RECREATION	AGRICULTURE	EXTRACTION
RESIDENTIAL							
COMMERCIAL							
INDUSTRIAL							
TRANSPORTATION							
RECREATION							
AGRICULTURE							
EXTRACTION							

FIGURE 4.7 User-group interaction. *(Source: Adapted from Jackson & Steiner, 1985)*

	RESIDENTIAL	COMMERCIAL	INDUSTRIAL	TRANSPORTATION	RECREATION	AGRICULTURE	EXTRACTION
CLIMATE							
GEOLOGY							
PHISIOGRAPHY							
HYDROLOGY							
SOILS							
VEGETATION							
WILDLIFE							

FIGURE 4.8 User demands. *(Source: Adapted from Jackson & Steiner, 1985)*

provide for housing needs of the citizens of the state (Land Conservation and Development Commission, 1980).

What are the social, economic, and political needs for agriculture in a planning area? And how do those needs relate to the biophysical environment? The answers for the first question should lie in the studies described in this chapter. Through an ecological analysis, linkages should start to be made between the human community and the biophysical environment. Population and economic studies should reveal trends in the agricultural sector and what the needs are to continue to support farming in the planning area. These needs can be quantified. For instance, one can determine the number of cows, farmers, and land needed to support a milk-processing plant. These numbers may vary if the cows graze on the farm or if feed is imported. They may also vary if

technology, such as milking machines or the cost of energy, changes the labor required to maintain a dairy.

As outlined in the Oregon statewide goal, housing needs may be affected by (1) the amount of buildable land; (2) the distribution of existing population by income compared with the distribution of available housing units by costs; (3) a determination of vacancy rates, both overall and at varying rent ranges and cost levels; (4) a determination of expected housing demands at varying rent ranges and cost levels; (5) an analysis of a variety of densities and types of residences; and (6) the amount of sound housing units capable of being rehabilitated (Land Conservation and Development Commission, 1980). Some obvious conflicts exist between the needs for agriculture and housing. Chapter 5 will address how to determine the potential allocation of land uses.

TWO EXAMPLES OF HUMAN COMMUNITY INVENTORY AND ANALYSIS

New Jersey Pinelands Comprehensive Management Plan

The human community inventory and analysis of the Pinelands was accomplished in the same manner as the biophysical studies (see Chapter 3), that is, through the use of consultants. The management plan first reviewed prehistorical, historical, and cultural resources and then land use. The Pinelands has been inhabited and used by humans for approximately 10,000 years. The management plan provides a synopsis of what is known about the prehistory of the region. There is an inventory of sites of archaeological significance and a historical review, beginning with the people who called themselves the "Lenape" who inhabited the area at the time of the initial European contact. The historic activities of Europeans and their American descendants are described in the plan, which include forestry; shipbuilding and seafaring; hunting, gathering, trapping, and fishing; agriculture; iron production; glassmaking; and tourism and recreation (Pinelands Commission, 1980).

Berger and Sinton interviewed 300 Pineland residents and analyzed the cultural resources and attitudes of the Pinelands. They found settlement of the Pinelands taking place in three general patterns and grouped these into three major cultural regions: forest, agricultural and rural suburban, and coastal. Then they identified a number of distinct cultural and ethnic groups including baymen, blacks, Germans, Italians, Jews, mixed urbanizing, Puerto Ricans, Quakers, rural residents, and Russians. Based on this work a number of culturally significant areas were identified (Pinelands Commission, 1980; Berger & Sinton, 1985). These areas contributed to the development of the plan for the Pinelands (see Chapter 7).

Based on the sociocultural study, varied perceptions of the future were drawn, and potential land-use conflicts for the area were foreseen. These conflicts are listed in Table 4.15. This analysis was followed by a description of land use that was linked to the ethnic and cultural groups of the area. Current land uses included land in national reserve, forest and wetland, agricultural land, and built-up land (Table 4.16). This information was linked with future and current demands for agriculture (Table 4.17), sewage systems and wastewater disposal, water supply and water use, solid waste generation and disposal, transportation, government facilities, resource extraction, and recreation.

In addition to the work of Berger and Sinton, other landscape planners led by Ricki L.

TABLE 4.15
POTENTIAL LAND-USE CONFLICTS IN THE PINELANDS

- Public ownership versus lost municipal tax revenues
- Land-use restrictions versus private property rights
- State and federal regulatory power versus home rule
- Extensive versus intensive land uses
- Preservation of lifestyle indigenous to the Pines versus wish for technological improvement
- Preservation of traditional lifestyles versus suburbanization
- Preservation of open space versus need for housing of long-time residents
- Preservation of open space for residents versus preservation of open space for nonresidents
- Intensive recreational use versus light recreational use
- Development of recreation fisheries versus development of commercial fisheries
- Free and unlimited public access versus access for wilderness needs and research
- Preservation of historic sites versus development for recreation
- Preservation of present landscapes versus needs for resource use and habitat restoration

SOURCE: Pinelands Commission, 1980.

TABLE 4.16
ESTIMATED LAND USES IN THE PINELANDS, IN THOUSANDS
OF ACRES (Pinelands National Reserve = 1,082,816 total acres)

County	Land Area in National Reserve	Forest and Wetland	Agricultural Land	Developed Land
Atlantic	243.6	201.6	16.5	25.4
Burlington	346.6	295.6	24.8	26.2
Camden	54.6	39.5	6.5	8.6
Cape May	85.6	78.7	2.3	4.6
Cumberland	55.7	52.4	1.0	2.3
Gloucester	33.2	23.5	5.9	3.8
Ocean	263.5	235.3	1.0	27.2

SOURCE: Pinelands Commission, 1980.

McKenzie of the U.S. Department of Interior analyzed scenic resources. They identified fifty-three visual types (Figure 4.9) that were divided into twenty-seven natural types, "landscapes that are mostly green with few human structures," and twenty-six cultural types, "landscapes dominated by buildings and paving" (McKenzie, no date, p. 5). There are three types, one woodland and two farmland, included in both sets, so there are actually only fifty types.

Each visual type was illustrated with a transparent color photograph that was projected at nine public meetings involving about 155 people to collect preference votes. The fifty visual types were scored and ranked for preference (Figure 4.10). Certain patterns, the forested lake type, were clearly liked by the people who participated in the meetings. Other images, such as the nuclear power plant, were "actively disliked" (McKenzie no date; Pinelands Commission, 1980).

The management plan then put the Pinelands into a regional perspective, using population and economic studies. The population of the Pinelands study area was 394,154 and growing steadily (Table 4.18). The economic activities in the management plan included development activity and land transactions that were reviewed for the region as a whole and each county in the Pinelands. Development regions and trends were determined.

Two development phenomena in New Jersey especially impact the Pinelands: the proliferation of retirement communities and the advent of casino gambling in nearby Atlantic City. From these studies, population and housing demand projections were made for each county to the year 2000 (Table 4.19) and different growth scenarios of development.

Makah Coastal Zone Management Plan

Within the Makah Reservation, the population, economy, and resource use are closely interrelated. The number of people in the Makah nation is about the same as it was a century ago, but it has experienced much fluctuation during that time. In 1855, when the Makah people signed a treaty with the United States, the total population was about 800. Afterward, the population dwindled as the people's prosperous maritime economy was curtailed by restrictions of fur trade, halibut fishing, and whaling. After leveling off for a number of years, the population has grown since the 1940s. In 1980, about 1,020 Indians and 461 non-Indians lived on the Makah Reservation (Pacific Rim Planners, 1980).

Analysis of population data reveals a major distinction between Indian and non-Indians.

TABLE 4.17
PINELANDS AGRICULTURE

Crop	Pinelands Area Acres (100) (x .4047 ha)	Pinelands Area Income ($1,000)	Seven Counties Acres (100) (x .4047 ha)	Seven Counties Income ($1,000)	New Jersey Acres (100) (x .4047 ha)	New Jersey Income ($1,000)
TOTAL	578.2	61,041.82	—	—	6,116.2*	359,590
Field crops	268.2	3,859.61	1,369	—	5,290	102,720
Corn and grain	55.3	746.18	236	5,084.8	950	19,884
Hay	58.2	478.35	210	5,190.0	1,119	23,250
Soybeans	123.4	2,484.95	715	14,527.5	2,060	42,333
Others	31.3	132.13	208	—	1,090	17,253
Ornamentals	32.9	9,863.31	—	—	—	—
Nursery	—	—	37	—	111	—
Sod	17.9	3,131.09	—	—	—	—
Trees and shrubs	9.9	2,413.98	—	—	—	—
Others	5.0	4,318.24	—	—	—	—
Fruits and berries	152.2	27,350.60	—	—	257	48,779
Apples	14.5	2,645.25	33	6,022.9	56	10,170
Blueberry	77.0	13,897.49	78	14,074.0	78	14,074
Cranberries	28.8	4,643.45	30	4,839.0	30	4,839
Peaches	27.7	5,523.79	73	14,561.2	83	16,520
Strawberries and grapes	4.2	640.62	7	1,270.5	10	1,768
Vegetables	121.6	13,477.03	—	—	711	78,762
Asparagus	1.8	172.03	11	1,103.6	19	1,789
Corn (sweet)	29.9	1,785.63	66	3,946.8	100	5,978
Peppers	8.4	914.17	39	4,128.1	60	5,709
Potatoes (white)	8.9	886.10	26	2,519.4	82	8,155
Potatoes (sweet)	17.1	2,749.47	24	3,825.2	26	4,176
Tomatoes	12.4	1,479.70	77	8,717.9	138	16,384
Others	43.0	5,489.47	—	—	286	36,562
Livestock (head)						
Cattle (dairy)	13.2	1,796.07	79	10,721.3	470	60,998
Chicken (layers)	2,251.7	2,425.97	—	6,604.2	17,160	18,488
Swine	71.3	701.16	630	5,982.4	760	6,592
Turkeys	308.8	389.15	—	—	580	762

* Total agricultural land in New Jersey is 1,058,600 acres (428,415 ha).
SOURCE: Pinelands Commission, 1980.

Generally, the Indian people experience significantly higher birth and death rates as well as having a shorter life expectancy. The birth rates are especially high, and, as a result, the Indian population is expected to grow. Pacific Rim Planners, the company responsible for the Makah coastal management plan, analyzed this trend as well as considered migration patterns for both the Makahs and non-Indians who live on the reservation. From this analysis, they were able to make a number of population projections that are shown in Table 4.20.

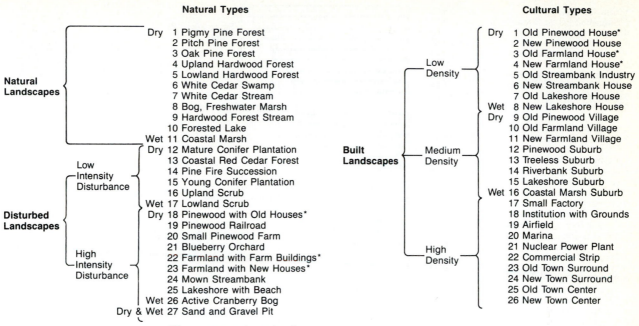

Natural Types

Natural Landscapes
Dry
1 Pigmy Pine Forest
2 Pitch Pine Forest
3 Oak Pine Forest
4 Upland Hardwood Forest
5 Lowland Hardwood Forest
6 White Cedar Swamp
7 White Cedar Stream
8 Bog, Freshwater Marsh
9 Hardwood Forest Stream
10 Forested Lake
Wet 11 Coastal Marsh

Disturbed Landscapes

Low Intensity Disturbance
Dry 12 Mature Conifer Plantation
13 Coastal Red Cedar Forest
14 Pine Fire Succession
15 Young Conifer Plantation
16 Upland Scrub
Wet 17 Lowland Scrub

High Intensity Disturbance
Dry 18 Pinewood with Old Houses*
19 Pinewood Railroad
20 Small Pinewood Farm
21 Blueberry Orchard
22 Farmland with Farm Buildings*
23 Farmland with New Houses*
24 Mown Streambank
25 Lakeshore with Beach
Wet 26 Active Cranberry Bog
Dry & Wet 27 Sand and Gravel Pit

*Types common to each set

Cultural Types

Built Landscapes

Low Density
Dry
1 Old Pinewood House*
2 New Pinewood House
3 Old Farmland House*
4 New Farmland House*
5 Old Streambank Industry
6 New Streambank House
7 Old Lakeshore House
Wet 8 New Lakeshore House
Dry 9 Old Pinewood Village
10 Old Farmland Village
11 New Pinewood Village

Medium Density
12 Pinewood Suburb
13 Treeless Suburb
14 Riverbank Suburb
15 Lakeshore Suburb
Wet 16 Coastal Marsh Suburb
17 Small Factory
18 Institution with Grounds
19 Airfield
20 Marina

High Density
21 Nuclear Power Plant
22 Commercial Strip
23 Old Town Surround
24 New Town Surround
25 Old Town Center
26 New Town Center

FIGURE 4.9 Pinelands visual types. *(Pinelands Commission, 1980)*

The economy of the Makah was traditionally dominated by natural resources—fish, timber, and wildlife. The conservation of these resources for future generations was highly valued in the Makah culture. Natural resources, especially fishing and timber harvesting, remain the foundation on which the Makahs base their livelihood (Pacific Rim Planners, 1980). The Makahs were actively engaged in commerce long before contact with Europeans. Through regular trading expeditions along the Pacific coast, they traded dried halibut, herring eggs, and whale blubber and oil for timber products for housing and canoe building. Because of the importance of this trade, the Makahs placed a high value on individual ownership rights of resource areas. For instance, as noted by Pacific Rim Planners:

> Individuals or families owned sections of the halibut banks, the salmon streams, shellfish beds, and stretches of coastline where usable items might be washed up on the shore. Cranberry bogs and stands of cedar were also under this type of ownership. (1980, p. 51)

The historical settlement patterns of the Makah were concentrated along the coastal beaches, adjacent uplands, and the major rivers. From these areas the people were able to exploit both fish and forest resources. The historical settlement and use patterns, as well as traditional ownership of resources, were major factors considered by Pacific Rim Planners and the Makah Tribal Council in their development of a coastal management plan.

The Makah people historically looked to the sea for their living. Yet, the maintenance of this relationship had become increasingly difficult because of the intervention of outside forces. The recognition of their interdependence with the coastal environment led the Makah Tribal Council to develop a plan to manage those resources and to

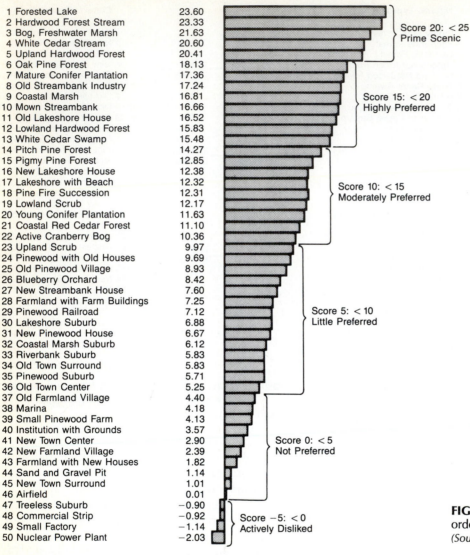

1 Forested Lake	23.60	
2 Hardwood Forest Stream	23.33	Score 20: < 25
3 Bog, Freshwater Marsh	21.63	Prime Scenic
4 White Cedar Stream	20.60	
5 Upland Hardwood Forest	20.41	
6 Oak Pine Forest	18.13	
7 Mature Conifer Plantation	17.36	Score 15: < 20
8 Old Streambank Industry	17.24	Highly Preferred
9 Coastal Marsh	16.81	
10 Mown Streambank	16.66	
11 Old Lakeshore House	16.52	
12 Lowland Hardwood Forest	15.83	
13 White Cedar Swamp	15.48	
14 Pitch Pine Forest	14.27	
15 Pigmy Pine Forest	12.85	
16 New Lakeshore House	12.38	Score 10: < 15
17 Lakeshore with Beach	12.32	Moderately Preferred
18 Pine Fire Succession	12.31	
19 Lowland Scrub	12.17	
20 Young Conifer Plantation	11.63	
21 Coastal Red Cedar Forest	11.10	
22 Active Cranberry Bog	10.36	
23 Upland Scrub	9.97	
24 Pinewood with Old Houses	9.69	
25 Old Pinewood Village	8.93	
26 Blueberry Orchard	8.42	
27 New Streambank House	7.60	
28 Farmland with Farm Buildings	7.25	
29 Pinewood Railroad	7.12	Score 5: < 10
30 Lakeshore Suburb	6.88	Little Preferred
31 New Pinewood House	6.67	
32 Coastal Marsh Suburb	6.12	
33 Riverbank Suburb	5.83	
34 Old Town Surround	5.83	
35 Pinewood Suburb	5.71	
36 Old Town Center	5.25	
37 Old Farmland Village	4.40	
38 Marina	4.18	
39 Small Pinewood Farm	4.13	
40 Institution with Grounds	3.57	
41 New Town Center	2.90	Score 0: < 5
42 New Farmland Village	2.39	Not Preferred
43 Farmland with New Houses	1.82	
44 Sand and Gravel Pit	1.14	
45 New Town Surround	1.01	
46 Airfield	0.01	
47 Treeless Suburb	−0.90	
48 Commercial Strip	−0.92	Score −5: < 0
49 Small Factory	−1.14	Actively Disliked
50 Nuclear Power Plant	−2.03	

FIGURE 4.10 Final scores and order of preference of visual types. *(Source: Pinelands Commission, 1980)*

mitigate the negative influences from outside forces.

This recognition of the intricate interrelationship between people and nature distinguishes the Makah and Pinelands plans from more conventional efforts. Furthermore, Berger and Sinton (1985) have provided lively sketches of people from the Pine Barrens who spend their days and nights clamming, crabbing, trapping, oystering, fishing, hunting, farming cranberries and blueberries, truck farming fruits and vegetables, and controlling the fires that are much a part of the ecosystem. Such knowledge about how people live and relate to their environment is too often absent from the information-collection phase of planning processes. This information is crucial if the planning process is to be humanized.

TABLE 4.18
PINELANDS POPULATION AND POPULATION INCREASE, 1950–1978

	Pinelands Population	Population Change	Population Change, %	Average Annual Change, %
1950	118,400	—	—	—
1950–1960	—	+ 72,731	+61.4	+4.9
1960	191,131	—	—	—
1960–1970	—	+ 77,613	+40.6	+3.5
1970	268,744	—	—	—
1970–1978	—	+125,410	+46.7	+4.9

SOURCE: Pinelands Commission, 1980.

TABLE 4.19
HOUSEHOLD INCREASE PROJECTIONS FOR
PINELANDS SECTION OF EACH COUNTY TO 2000

	1980–1990	1990–2000
Atlantic	38,700	14,600
Burlington	19,700	18,800
Camden	16,100	6,800
Cape May	4,500	2,800
Cumberland	1,300	800
Gloucester	9,000	8,700
Ocean	52,000	31,000
TOTAL	141,300	83,500

SOURCE: Pinelands Commission, 1980.

TABLE 4.20
PRESENT AND PROJECTED POPULATION, MAKAH INDIAN RESERVATION

Year	Low Projection			Most Probable Projection			High Projection		
	Indian	Non-Indian	Total	Indian	Non-Indian	Total	Indian	Non-Indian	Total
1977	1,020	461	1,481	1,020	461	1,481	1,020	461	1,481
1978	1,052	464	1,516	1,067	467	1,534	1,081	469	1,550
1979	1,084	467	1,551	1,116	472	1,588	1,146	478	1,624
1980	1,118	469	1,587	1,167	478	1,645	1,215	486	1,701
1985	1,271	484	1,755	1,475	507	1,982	1,688	532	2,220
1990	1,438	498	1,936	1,856	538	2,394	2,324	581	2,905
1995	1,619	513	2,132	2,313	571	2,884	3,169	636	3,805
2000	1,814	529	2,343	2,814	607	3,421	4,280	695	4,975

SOURCES: 1977 figures from the 1977 Makah Tribal Demographic Survey. All other figures from Pacific Rim Planners, Inc., estimates.

5

SUITABILITY ANALYSIS

Once an ecological inventory of a place has been conducted, and some understanding of the interrelationships between people and nature achieved, it is then necessary to make more detailed studies of these interactions to present options for future use. One such type of detailed study is a suitability analysis. "Consult the Genius of the place in all," Alexander Pope suggested, and this is an apt definition of *suitability analysis*.

There are several more recent, and rather more wordy and cumbersome, definitions. Often, *capability* and *suitability* are two words that are used interchangeably; however, there is enough subtle variation in how these terms have been adapted for the purpose of land classification that it would be useful to define each. To be capable is to have the ability or strength to be qualified or fitted for or to be susceptible or open to the influence or effect of. To be suitable is to be appropriate, fitting, or becoming (Barnhart, 1953). Various definitions for land-capability analysis have been proposed. Land-capability classification has been defined by soil scientists as a grouping of kinds of soil into special units, subclasses, and classes according to their potential uses and the treatments required for their sustained use (Brady, 1974). An alternate definition is evaluation based on an inherent, natural, or intrinsic ability of the resource to provide for use, which includes abilities that result from past alterations or current management practices.

A third definition has been suggested by the U.S. Geological Survey that relies solely on geologic and hydrologic information. According to this definition, land-capability analysis measures the ability of land to support different types of development with a given level of geologic and hydrologic costs (Laird et al., 1979, p. 2). A fourth definition has been developed by the U.S. Forest Service to implement the Forest and Rangeland Renewable Resources Planning Act of 1974. According to the USFS, capability is "the potential of an area of land to produce resources, supply goods and services and allow resource uses under an assumed set of management practices and at a given level of management intensity" (U.S. Congress, 1979, p. 53984).

Land suitability may be defined as the fitness of a given tract of land for a defined use (Food and Agriculture Organization of the United Nations, 1977). Differences in the degree of suitability are determined by the relationship, actual or anticipated, between benefits and the required changes associated with the use on the tract in question (Brinkman & Smyth, 1973). Another definition for suitability analysis provided by the USFS, is "the resource management practices to a particular area of land, as determined by an analysis of the economic and environmental consequences" (U.S. Congress, 1979, p. 53985). For this chapter, suitability analysis is considered to be the process of determining the fitness, or the appropriateness, of a given tract of land for a specified use.

Approaches to suitability analysis that merit closer review include (1) several SCS systems, (2) the McHarg suitability analysis method, and (3) suitability analysis methods that have been developed in the Netherlands. In addition, in this chapter computer applications and the carrying-capacity concept are briefly reviewed and two applications

of suitability analysis are discussed as examples: Medford Township, New Jersey, and Whitman County, Washington.

APPROACHES TO SUITABILITY ANALYSIS–METHODS

Soil Conservation Service Systems

The oldest, most established system for defining the ability of soil to support various uses is the U.S. Soil Conservation Service capability classification. As a result of the disastrous effects of the dust bowl era, the Soil Erosion Service was established in 1933 by the Franklin Roosevelt administration. The agency was reorganized and named the Soil Conservation Service in 1935. The SCS works closely with a system of locally elected conservation district boards responsible for soil and water conservation policy in almost every county of the United States. The conservation districts receive technical assistance locally from professional soil conservationists.

The capability classification is one of several interpretive groupings made by the SCS in standard soil surveys. Capability classes are based on soil types as mapped and interpreted by the SCS. They were developed to assist farmers with agricultural management practices. While there are other systems that have also been developed to classify soils for agriculture (Donahue et al., 1977; Reganold & Singer, 1978, 1979), the SCS system is the most common in the United States. Groupings are made according to the limitations of the soils when they are used for field crops, the risk of damage when they are used, and the manner in which they respond to management. The classification does not take into account major construction activity that would alter slope, soil depth, or other soil characteristics. Nor does it take into account reclamation projects or apply to rice, cranberries, horticultural crops, or other crops requiring special management (Davis et al., 1976).

In the capability system, all kinds of soils are grouped at three levels: the capability class, the subclass, and the unit (Soil Conservation Service, 1975; Soil Survey Staff, 1951, 1975a, and 1975b). The following description of three major categories of capability classification was adopted from Singer et al. (1979) and Davis et al. (1976). Capability classes are the broadest groups and are designated by Roman numerals I to VIII. The numerals indicate progressively greater limitations and narrower choices for practical agricultural use, defined as follows: Class I soils have few limitations that restrict their use. Class II soils have moderate limitations that reduce the choice of plants which can be grown or which require moderate conservation practices. Class III soils have severe limitations that reduce the choice of plants which can be grown, require special conservation practices, or both. Class IV soils have very severe limitations that reduce the choice of plants which can be grown, require very careful management, or both. Class V soils are not likely to erode but have other limitations that limit their use mainly to pasture or range, woodland, or wildlife habitat. Class VI soils have severe limitations that make them generally unsuited to cultivation and limit their use mainly to pasture or range, woodland, or wildlife habitat. Class VII soils have very severe limitations that make them unsuited for commercial crop production and restrict their use to recreation, wildlife habitat, water supply, or aesthetic purposes. Class VIII soils and landforms have limitations that preclude their use for commercial plant production and restrict their use to recreation, wildlife habitat, water supply, or aesthetic uses (Singer, et al., 1979; Davis et al., 1976).

Capability subclasses are soil groups within one class. They are identified by adding the lowercase letters *e, w, s,* or *c* to the Roman numeral, for example, IIe. The letter *e* indicates that the chief limitation is risk of erosion unless close-growing plant cover is maintained. The letter *w* indicates that water in or on the soil interferes with plant growth or cultivation. The letter *s* shows that the soil is limited primarily because it is shallow, droughty, or stony, while *c* shows that the major limitation is that the climate is too cold or too dry. In class I there are no subclasses because there are no limitations on this class. On the other hand, subsequent classes may contain several subclasses (Singer et al., 1979; Davis et al., 1976).

Capability units are further distinctions of soil groups within the subclasses. The soils in one capability unit are sufficiently similar to be suited to the same crops and pasture plants, to require similar management, and to have similar productivity and other responses to management. Capability units are identified by the addition of an Arabic numeral to the subclass symbol, for example, IIe-2 or IIIe-3 (Singer et al., 1979; Davis et al., 1976).

In addition to capability classification, soil surveys also include interpretation of limitations for such land uses as septic tanks, sewage lagoons, home sites, lawns, streets and parking lots, athletic fields, parks and play areas, campsites, sanitary landfills, and cemeteries. Soil conservationists have long stressed that the main purpose of soil survey information is for agriculture and that capability classes were developed specifically for row crops. Nevertheless, soil survey information has been increasingly utilized by planners, landscape architects, and civil engineers, because it is the most ubiquitous standard source of information about the natural environment in the United States available on the local level.

Soil surveys are seen to be useful for community and regional planning by their authors. Take, for example, this statement from the Montgomery County (Dayton), Ohio, soil survey:

The expansion of nonfarm uses of land can remove many acres from farming in a short time. Freeways and super highways can displace up to about 50 acres per mile [20.25 hectares per mile, or 50 acres per 1.6 kilometers]. A shopping center can easily replace 50 to 100 acres of farmland [20.25 to 40.5 hectares]. These uses tend to permanently remove land from farm use.

The rapid suburban expansion has emphasized soil-related problems that builders must deal with. For example, some of the soils have severe limitations for use as septic tank disposal fields, some are shallow to hard limestone bedrock, some are underlain by a porous substratum and are droughty, some are easily eroded, and a few soils have no serious limitations. Two of the most serious concerns in community development are the limitations of the soils for septic tank disposal fields and the erosion hazard. Improperly functioning septic tank systems are a threat to health in areas where the soils have severe limitations for this use. Erosion losses in developing areas are commonly much higher than on comparable farmland, particularly during periods of construction. Erosion control practices, therefore, become very important in areas undergoing development. Specific erosion control practices for use in rural-fringe areas have been developed by the Soil Conservation Service. City officials and developers interested in these practices can obtain information about them from the office of the Montgomery Soil and Water Conservation District. (Davis et al., 1976, pp. 34–35)

Several researchers have illustrated how soil survey information can be applied to planning and resource management (Bartelli et al., 1966; Lynch, 1971; McCormack, 1974; Meyers et al., 1979; & Lynch & Hack, 1984). Miller (1978) has described how soil surveys have been criticized because of the limitations of information for urban land-use planning. According to the research of Gordon & Gordon (1981), soil survey information was found to be accurate for septic tank limitations but very inconsistent for home sites and roads. They warn that "this implies that planners must use these published ratings with extreme caution in making environmental and land-use planning decisions and

that consultation with state and local soil experts should be sought" (1981, p. 301).

As a result of the shortcomings of the soil surveys, a dilemma is faced by conservationists and planners alike. Soil conservationists have done an excellent job mapping and classifying land in the United States and have generated the most uniformly available source of physical science information. Planners faced with tight budgets must use soil survey information because they lack the time and/or money to generate original data.

The SCS has met the growing demand for its products with new systems to assist planners and resource managers. One such effort is the SCS important farmland mapping program. This classification system identifies two major categories of farmland of national importance, prime and unique lands, and two other categories, farmlands of statewide and of local importance. There are national criteria for the first two categories, while the latter have criteria established on the state level (Dideriksen, 1984).

The important farmland mapping program [coupled with the publication of the National Agricultural Lands Study (1981) that documented a loss in the prime cropland base of the nation] presented new problems for both planners and soil conservationists. For instance, in DeKalb County, Illinois, 97 percent of the land is prime farmland. Obviously not all this land can be preempted for agricultural use, because there are demands for other uses also. On the other hand, in Whitman County, Washington, only 2.8 percent of the land is prime. Most of the land is excluded from the prime category because of steep slopes and high erosion potential. Yet it is the most productive winter white wheat county in the nation, and most of the land in the county is under cultivation. A new system was needed to weigh the agricultural capability of land against its demands for other uses. In 1981, a pilot program for such a system was launched (Wright, 1981; Wright et al., 1982; & Steiner et al., 1987; Steiner, 1987).

Lloyd E. Wright of the SCS office of land use in Washington, D.C., along with planners and soil conservationists from twelve selected counties across the United States, is responsible for the new system. The system is divided into two phases: establishing an agricultural land evaluation (LE) and establishing an agricultural site assessment (SA). Together the LE and SA are known as the Agricultural Land Evaluation and Site Assessment (LESA) System.

Land Evaluation Value. Agricultural land evaluation (LE) is a process of rating soils of a given area and placing them into ten groups ranging from the best-suited to the poorest-suited for a specific agricultural use. A relative value is determined for each group, with the best group being assigned a value of 100 and all other groups assigned a lower relative value. The LE is based on soil survey information (U.S. Department of Agriculture, 1983).

Land evaluation rates the quality of soil for agricultural use by incorporating four rating systems: land-capability classification, important farmland classification, soil productivity, and soil potential. SCS recommends that one of the last two ratings (soil potential being preferred) be used in conjunction with the first two ratings. The land-use staff of SCS has explained the method for combining these four systems in the *National Agricultural Land Evaluation and Site Assessment Handbook* as given below:

- *Land capability classification* identifies degrees of agricultural limitations that are inherent in the soils of a given area. It enables state and regional planners to use the system for planning and program implementation at regional and state levels.
- *Soil productivity* relates the LE score to the local agricultural industry based on productivity of the soils for a specified indicator crop. The use of both soil productivity and land capability

The process of land evaluation rates soils in an area from best to worst for a specific agricultural use. *(Philip Maechling)*

classification should provide some indication of relative net income expected from each category of soils.
- *Soil potentials* for specified indicator crops are preferred in place of soil productivity in the LE system. Soil potential ratings classify soils based on a standard of performance and recognition of the costs of overcoming soil limitations, plus the cost of continuing limitations if any exist. These classes enable planners to understand the local agricultural industry.
- *Important farmland classification* enables planners to identify prime and other important farmlands at the local level. Use of the national criteria for definition of prime farmland provides a consistent basis for comparison of local farmland with farmland in other areas. (Adapted from U.S. Department of Agriculture, 1983)

The SCS recommends that soils be arrayed into ten groups ranging from the best- to the worst-suited for the agricultural use considered (cropland, rangeland, forest). Each group should contain approximately 10 percent of the total planning area (U.S. Department of Agriculture, 1983). Three evaluation systems are used in the ranking to prevent the possibility that any one method would have an undue effect on the final outcome. For example, soil productivity may be used to establish the initial groupings. These groupings are then modified based upon the other evaluation systems. Specifically, two soils may have the same productivity rating but different land capability ratings. In this case, the soil type with the better land capability rating would be placed in a higher grouping. Similarly, prime soils (according to the important farmland classification) would be placed in a higher grouping than soils of statewide importance even though both soils may have the same productivity rating.

A relative value is determined for each agricultural grouping based on adjusted average yields. That is, a weighted-average yield is calculated for each soil type within the grouping.

The weighted-average yield for each grouping is then expressed as a percentage of the highest weighted-average yield. This percentage becomes the relative value for each agricultural grouping, and the relative value is the LE value that is combined with the site assessment value (U.S. Department of Agriculture, 1983). Table 5.1 gives an example of the worksheet from which the LE relative values are determined.

Site Assessment Value. Although the value from the LE system provides a good indication of the relative quality of a soil for a particular agricultural use, it does not take into account the effect of location, distance to market, adjacent land uses, zoning, and other considerations that determine land suitability. In other words, relative agricultural value is only one of many site attributes which may be considered by planners and land-use decision makers. Consequently, SCS has created the site assessment (SA) system to incorporate some of these other attributes into the decision-making process.

The attributes that are included in the SA system form seven groups: agricultural land use; agri-

TABLE 5.1

AGRICULTURAL LAND-EVALUATION WORKSHEET SHOWING CRITERIA FOR DELINEATING THE TEN BASIC GROUPS OF SOIL

1 Agricultural Group	2 Land Capability	3 Important Farmland Determination	4 Potential or Productivity	5 Percentage of Total Area	6 Acres	7 Relative Value
1	I	Prime	95–100	18.8	76,270	100
2	IIw	Prime	95–100	31.3	127,470	94
3	I	Prime	94	5.4	21,975	88
4	II	Prime	90–94	9.6	39,365	84
5	II	Prime	80–89	21.0	85,635	81
6	II	Prime	70–79	3.5	14,570	75
7	II	Prime	69	7.1	28,695	44
8	II/IIIw	Statewide	All	2.1	8,275	31
9	IIIe/IV/V	Statewide	All	0.9	3,410	28
10	Others	All	All	0.3	1,375	0

SOURCE: Steiner et al., 1987 adapted from U.S. Department of Agriculture, 1983.

cultural viability factors; land-use regulations and tax concessions; options to proposed use; impact of proposed use; compatibility with, and importance to, comprehensive development plans; and urban infrastructure. The factors listed below have been identified in the LESA handbook for use in site assessment procedures:

Agricultural land use
- Percentage of area in agriculture use within 1 mile
- Percentage of site farmed in two of the last 10 years
- Land use adjacent to site

Agricultural viability factors
- Size of farm
- Agricultural support system
- Land ownership
- On-site investments (barns, storage, and conservation measures)
- Impact of this conversion on retention of other farmland and the agricultural support system
- Conservation plan

Land-use regulations and tax concessions
- Zoning for site
- Zoning for area around site
- Use of agricultural value assessment or other tax benefits
- Agricultural districts or right-to-farm legislation

Options to proposed use
- Unique siting needs for proposed use
- Suitability of site for proposed use
- Availability of less productive lands with similar attributes for proposed use
- Number of undeveloped and suitable alternative sites and need for additional land

Impact of proposed use
- Compatibility of proposed use with existing land use
- Impact on flooding
- Impact on wetlands
- Impact on historical areas
- Impact on recreation and open spaces
- Impact on cultural features

- Impact on unique vegetation

Compatibility with comprehensive development plans
- Local
- Regional
- Degree of socioeconomic importance of proposed use to the community

Urban infrastructure
- Distance to urban area
- Central water distribution system (within x miles)
- Central sanitary sewage system (within x miles)
- Investment for urban development
- Transportation
- Distance to other urban infrastructure (job centers, schools, and shopping)
- Emergency services (U.S. Department of Agriculture, 1983)

Local communities may identify other factors. Any of the factors noted in the list may or may not be needed, or used, in the design of any local LESA system. Once specific factors have been chosen for the SA evaluation, each factor must be stratified into a range of possible points. The SCS recommends that a maximum of 10 points be given for each factor. In general, the maximum points are assigned when on-site conditions are most favorable to the continuation of agriculture. For example, suppose that the factor "percentage of area in agriculture" is included in the SA evaluation. If 90 to 100 percent of the area in proximity to a site is in agricultural use, then the maximum of 10 points would be given. Alternatively, if only about one-third of the surrounding area is in agriculture, then a lower number of points (such as 4) would be given.

After points have been assigned for all factors, weights ranging from 1 to 10 can be considered for each factor. Those factors considered most important would be given the highest weights, while factors of lesser importance would be given lower weights. The weights are multiplied by the assigned points for each factor, and the resulting products are then summed. Finally, the total is converted to a scale having a maximum of 200 points. Thus, the final SA value, as recommended in the LESA handbook, can range from 0 to 200 (U.S. Department of Agriculture, 1983).

Combining the LE and SA Systems. Although the LE and SA systems can be used separately, they are most useful when combined. Table 5.2 shows one method that was tested to combine these systems in a county in Washington State. For each site, the acreage of each soil unit is multiplied by its relative value (LE value). These products are summed over all units, and the sum is divided by the total acreage of the site to get an average LE value. In this example, ten SA factors were selected, with each having a maximum of 20 points. The sum of the points assigned for each factor results in the SA value, which can be a maximum of 200 points. Finally, the LE value is added to the SA value for the total LESA value. The maximum LESA value is 300. The SA system tested in this Washington county deviated from the one recommended by the SCS in the LESA handbook. Instead of the more complicated weighting system for obtaining an SA score, a more straightforward addition approach was used.

In the example in Table 5.2, site 1 has the greatest LESA value, indicating that it is more suitable for agricultural use than site 2. Consequently, site 2 would be favored for the residential development.

In addition to being useful for judging the agricultural suitability of alternative sites, the LESA system can also be used to help decide whether a single parcel should be converted to a nonfarmland use. Local decision makers would have to specify a cutoff LESA value out of 300 points (or other maximum value). Parcels with a LESA value below the cutoff could be considered for conversion.

Use of LESA at Federal Level. The importance of LESA was enhanced by the regulations implementing the Farmland Protection Policy Act (FPPA) of 1981. These federal rules were adopted in 1984 (U.S Department of Agriculture, 1984). The FPPA was amended and strengthened somewhat by Congress in the passage of the Conservation Title in the Food Security Act of 1985. The FPPA requires federal agencies to identify and take into account the adverse effects of federal programs on farmland protection, to consider alternative actions, as appropriate, that could lessen such adverse effects, and to ensure that such federal programs, to the extent practical, are compatible with state, local, and private programs and policies to protect farmland.

For the purposes of the FPPA, farmland includes land identified under the important farmland program. However, prime farmland that a state or local government has designated through planning or zoning for commercial, industrial, or residential use is excluded from the provision of the FPPA. Federal programs under this act include activities or responsibilities that involve undertaking, financing, or assisting construction or improvement projects as well as acquiring, disposing, or managing of federal lands and facilities. Some activities are not subject to the act, such as licensing activities, the granting of permits, and national defense projects.

The SCS has been given a prominent role in the implementation of the FPPA. In particular, the SCS is responsible for developing the criteria that federal agencies must use in assessing the effects of their programs on farmland; providing information to states, local governments, individuals, organizations, and other federal agencies useful in farmland protection; and providing technical assistance to states, local governments, and nonprofit-making organizations wanting to develop farmland protection programs.

Regarding criteria for assessing farmland effects, the SCS has mandated that federal agencies use LESA. The LE value is determined by the SCS on the form shown in Figure 5.1. Federal agencies must then determine the SA value and combine it with the LE value as specified in the regulations implementing the FPPA. As can be seen from

TABLE 5.2

HYPOTHETICAL EXAMPLE DEMONSTRATING A POSSIBLE USE OF THE COMBINED LE AND SA SYSTEMS IN A WASHINGTON STATE COUNTY

Proposed land use: single-family residential development
  Site 1: 23 acres of Palouse silt loam, 7–25% slope with LE of 87
        37 acres of Anders silt loam, 3–15% slope with LE of 48

  Site 2: 32 acres of Cheney silt loam, 0–7% slope with LE of 80
        23 acres of Staley silt loam, 7–25% slope with LE of 63

Land evaluation:

Site 1
$23 \times 87 = 2,001$
$37 \times 48 = \underline{1,776}$
$3,777$

Site 2
$32 \times 80 = 2,560$
$23 \times 63 = \underline{1,449}$
$4,009$

Average LE rating $= \dfrac{3,777}{23 + 37} = 63$ Average LE rating $= \dfrac{4,009}{32 + 23} = 73$

Site Assessment Factors	Max. Pts.	Site 1	Site 2
1. Percentage of area in agriculture within 1 mile	20	20	10
2. Land use adjacent to site	20	20	10
3. Wasting agricultural land	20	20	15
4. Availability of non-agricultural land for proposal	20	20	15
5. Compatibility with comprehensive plan and zoning	20	17	15
6. Availability of public services	20	15	10
7. Compatibility of proposed use with surrounding use	20	20	15
8. Environmental factors	20	20	15
9. Open-space taxation	20	15	10
10. Other factors unique to the site	20	15	13
Total site assessment points	200	182	128
Average land evaluation rating	100	63	73
Total points (total of previous two lines)	300	245	201

Choice for development: Site 2

SOURCE: Steiner et al., 1987

Figure 5.1, the SCS chose not to use the more complex weighting system that it had recommended for SA in its handbook. In addition, the maximum SA value that can be obtained by federal agencies is 160 from the twelve SA factors rather than the 200 maximum which the SCS recommends in its LESA handbook. Thus, the maximum LESA value is 260. In cases where a state or local government has adopted a LESA system and this system has been certified by the SCS state conservationist, it is recommended that the federal agencies use that system to make their evaluation of the farmland conversion effects on their programs.

U.S. Department of Agriculture

FARMLAND CONVERSION IMPACT RATING

PART I *(To be completed by Federal Agency)*	Date Of Land Evaluation Request
Name Of Project	Federal Agency Involved
Proposed Land Use	County And State

PART II *(To be completed by SCS)* | Date Request Received By SCS

	Yes	No	Acres Irrigated	Average Farm Size
Does the site contain prime, unique, statewide or local important farmland? *(If no, the FPPA does not apply — do not complete additional parts of this form).*	☐	☐		

Major Crop(s)	Farmable Land In Govt. Jurisdiction Acres: %	Amount Of Farmland As Defined in FPPA Acres: %
Name Of Land Evaluation System Used	Name Of Local Site Assessment System	Date Land Evaluation Returned By SCS

		Alternative Site Rating			
PART III *(To be completed by Federal Agency)*		Site A	Site B	Site C	Site D
A.	Total Acres To Be Converted Directly				
B.	Total Acres To Be Converted Indirectly				
C.	Total Acres In Site				
PART IV *(To be completed by SCS)* Land Evaluation Information					
A.	Total Acres Prime And Unique Farmland				
B.	Total Acres Statewide And Local Important Farmland				
C.	Percentage Of Farmland In County Or Local Govt. Unit To Be Converted				
D.	Percentage Of Farmland In Govt. Jurisdiction With Same Or Higher Relative Value				
PART V *(To be completed by SCS)* Land Evaluation Criterion Relative Value Of Farmland To Be Converted *(Scale of 0 to 100 Points)*					

PART VI *(To be completed by Federal Agency)* Site Assessment Criteria *(These criteria are explained in 7 CFR 658.5(b)*	Maximum Points				
1. Area In Nonurban Use					
2. Perimeter In Nonurban Use					
3. Percent Of Site Being Farmed					
4. Protection Provided By State And Local Government					
5. Distance From Urban Builtup Area					
6. Distance To Urban Support Services					
7. Size Of Present Farm Unit Compared To Average					
8. Creation Of Nonfarmable Farmland					
9. Availability Of Farm Support Services					
10. On-Farm Investments					
11. Effects Of Conversion On Farm Support Services					
12. Compatibility With Existing Agricultural Use					
TOTAL SITE ASSESSMENT POINTS	160				

PART VII *(To be completed by Federal Agency)*					
Relative Value Of Farmland *(From Part V)*	100				
Total Site Assessment *(From Part VI above or a local site assessment)*	160				
TOTAL POINTS *(Total of above 2 lines)*	260				

Site Selected:	Date Of Selection	Was A Local Site Assessment Used? Yes ☐ No ☐

Reason For Selection:

FIGURE 5.1

The McHarg, or University of Pennsylvania, Suitability Analysis Method

The seminal explanation of suitability analysis was provided by McHarg (1969), based on his work with colleagues and students at the University of Pennsylvania. This method has been compared to those approaches of the Canadian forester G. Angus Hills and the University of Wisconsin landscape architect Philip Lewis (Belknap & Furtado, 1967, 1968). The Hills method (1961) has been influential in the development of the Canadian Land Inventory System (Coombs & Thie, 1979). Professor McHarg has also been influential as a teacher. Many of his colleagues and former students have contributed to his suitability analysis method, so it may be considered the "University of Pennsylvania method."

In *Design with Nature*, McHarg explained suitability analysis in the following manner:

> In essence, the method consists of identifying the area of concern as consisting of certain processes, in land, water, and air—which represent values. These can be ranked—the most valuable land and the least, the most valuable water resources and the least, the most and least productive agricultural land, the richest wildlife habitats and those of no value, the areas of great or little scenic beauty, historic buildings and their absence, and so on. (1969, p. 34)

Lewis Hopkins has explained this method in the following manner:

> The output of land suitability analysis is a set of maps, one for each land use, showing which level of suitability characterizes each parcel of land. This output requirement leads directly to two necessary components of any method: (1) a procedure for identifying parcels of land that are homogeneous and (2) a procedure for rating these parcels with respect to suitability for each land use. (1977, pp. 386–387)

A simplified illustration of how the suitability analysis procedure works is provided in Figure 5.2.

TABLE 5.3
STEPS IN SUITABILITY ANALYSIS

1. Identify land users and define the needs for each use.
2. Relate land-use needs to natural factors.
3. Identify the relationship between specific mapped phenomena concerning the biophysical environment and land-use needs.
4. Map the congruences of desired phenomena and formulate rules of combination to express a gradient of suitability. This step should result in maps of land-use opportunities.
5. Identify the constraints between potential land uses and biophysical processes.
6. Overlay maps of constraints and opportunities, and through rules of combination develop a map of intrinsic suitabilities for various land uses.
7. Develop a composite map of the highest suitabilities of the various land uses.

SOURCE: Adapted from Berger et al., 1977.

Berger et al. (1977) have developed an outline of the method, which is summarized in Table 5.3. These seven steps are dependent on a detailed ecological inventory and analysis. Step 1 is to identify potential land uses and define the needs for each. Berger and his colleagues have suggested the use of matrices for the first and other steps. Figure 5.2 and the following matrices used for illustration were taken from an ecological inventory and land-use suitability analysis of Asotin County, Washington (Beach et al., 1978). These matrices were the working documents of a student project and so contain a few imperfections. However, they illustrate the process by which this method was thought through. Figure 5.3 illustrates the land-use needs for agricultural, recreational, residential, commercial, and industrial uses.

Step 2 covers the relationship of these land-use needs to natural factors (Figure 5.4). Next, in step 3, specific mapped phenomena must be related to the land-use needs (Figure 5.5). Step 4 is to map the congruences of desired phenomena and formulate rules of combination to express a gradient of suitability. *Rules of combination* are the rankings used to weight the relative importance of

STEP 1
MAP DATA FACTORS BY TYPE

Example 1

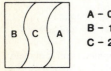

A – 0 – 10%
B – 10 – 20%
C – 20 – 40%

SLOPE MAP

Example 2

A – SLIGHTLY ERODED
B – SLIGHT TO MODERATE
C – MODERATE
D – EXTREMELY ERODED

EROSION MAP

STEP 2
RATE EACH TYPE OF EACH FACTOR FOR EACH LAND USE

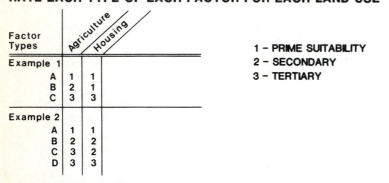

Factor Types	Agriculture	Housing
Example 1		
A	1	1
B	2	1
C	3	3
Example 2		
A	1	1
B	2	2
C	3	2
D	3	3

1 – PRIME SUITABILITY
2 – SECONDARY
3 – TERTIARY

STEP 3
MAP RATINGS FOR EACH AND USE ONE SET OF MAPS FOR EACH LAND USE

Example 1   Example 2   Example 1   Example 2

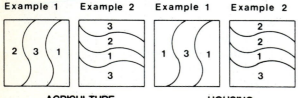

AGRICULTURE   HOUSING

STEP 4
OVERLAY SINGLE FACTOR SUITABILITY MAPS TO OBTAIN COMPOSITES. ONE MAP FOR EACH LAND USE

AGRICULTURE   HOUSING

LOWEST NUMBERS ARE BEST SUITED FOR LAND USE

HIGHEST NUMBERS ARE LEAST SUITED FOR LAND USE

FIGURE 5.2 Suitability analysis procedure.

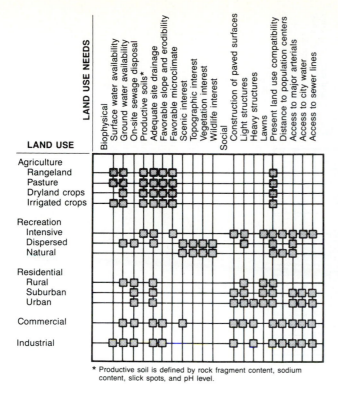
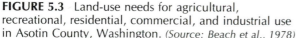

* Productive soil is defined by rock fragment content, sodium content, slick spots, and pH level.

FIGURE 5.3 Land-use needs for agricultural, recreational, residential, commercial, and industrial use in Asotin County, Washington. *(Source: Beach et al., 1978)*

physical (for instance, an earthquake hazard), biological (endangered species), or cultural (a historic site) reasons. Such areas may pose a threat to human health, safety, or welfare and/or contain rare or unique natural attributes. In step 6 these constraints are mapped and then overlaid with those areas showing opportunities for various land uses. Finally, in step 7 a composite map of the highest suitabilities of the various land uses is developed (Berger et al., 1977; University of Pennsylvania, 1985).

One of the most attractive features of the Pennsylvania method is that it can be used for both the conservation and development of resources. One of the goals of the World Conservation Strategy (International Union for the Conservation

mapped phenomena. Rules of combination assign suitabilities to sets of criteria rather than to single criterion and are expressed "in terms of verbal logic rather than in terms of numbers and arithmetic" (Hopkins, 1977, pp. 394–395). The result of this step should be a series of maps of opportunities for various land uses.

Step 5 involves an identification of constraints between potential land uses and biophysical processes (Figure 5.6). Constraints are environmentally sensitive, or critical, areas that should be preempted from development because of

FIGURE 5.4 Relationship of land-use needs to natural factors in Asotin County, Washington. *(Source: Beach et al., 1978)*

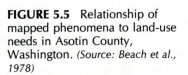

URBAN RESIDENTIAL

- ▣ compatible
- ☐ not compatible
- * more heavily weighted

LAND USE NEEDS

Biophysical:
- Surface water availability
- Ground water availability
- On-site sewage disposal
- Productive soils
- Adequate site drainage
- Favorable slope and erodibility
- Favorable microclimate
- Scenic interest
- Topographic interest
- Vegetation interest
- Wildlife interest

Social:
- Construction of paved surfaces
- Light structures*
- Heavy structures
- Lawns
- Present land use compatibility*
- Distance to population center
- Access to major arterials
- Access to city water
- Access to sewer lines*

PHENOMENA

Slope
- 0–3%
- 3–8%
- 8–15%
- 15–25%
- 25% and greater

Soil
- Asotin silt loam
- Asotin silt loam deep
- Asotin silt loam shallow
- Beverly gravelly silt loam
- Beverly loam fine sand
- Chard silt loam 3–7%
- Chard silt loam 7–25%
- Chard silt loam 25–40%
- Chard fn sandy loam 7–25%
- Chard fn sandy loam 25–40%
- Chard grav. fn sand loam
- Pataha stony silt loam
- Patit Creek silt loam
- Patit Creek sty silt loam
- Riverwash
- Basalt rock outcrop

Drainage
- Poor
- Good

Erosion Hazard
- High
- Medium
- Low

Flood Hazard
- Flood plain
- Intermittent/perennial

Existing Land Use
- Single-family residential
- Multifamily residential
- Public and quasi-public
- Commercial
- Industrial
- Cropland/orchard/pasture
- Rangeland
- Vacant or undeveloped

Distance to Population Cntr
- 0–1/2 mile
- 1/2–1 mile
- 1 mile and greater

Proximity to Arterials
- 0–1,000 feet
- 1,000–2,000 feet
- 2,000 feet and greater

Proximity to water/sewer
- 0–1,000 feet
- 1,000–3,000 feet
- 3,000 feet and greater

FIGURE 5.5 Relationship of mapped phenomena to land-use needs in Asotin County, Washington. *(Source: Beach et al., 1978)*

of Nature and Natural Resources, 1980) is to encourage planning that balances conservation and development. The authors of the strategy defined *conservation* as the management of human use of the biosphere to yield the greatest sustainable benefit to present generations while maintaining its potential to meet the needs and aspirations of future generations. *Development* was defined as the modification of the biosphere and the application of human, financial, living, and nonliving resources to satisfy human needs and improve the quality of human life. The Pennsylvania suitability analysis method is consistent with both definitions.

Dutch Suitability Analysis

The present Dutch landscape has resulted largely from human intervention in natural processes and represents an eloquent equilibrium between people and their environment. This balance has resulted in an elaborate system of physical planning. One component of this system is a sophisticated set of suitability analysis methods. A. P. A. Vink, a Dutch professor of physical geography and soil science at the University of Amsterdam, has made the distinction between actual land suitability, soil suitability, and potential land suitability. (See also Brinkman & Smyth, 1973; Food and Agriculture Organization of the United Nations, 1977; and Beek, 1978, for additional discussions from a Dutch perspective.) Vink's actual land suitability is analogous to McHarg's intrinsic suitability. According to Vink, actual land suitability is "an indication of the possibility of using the land within a particular land utilization type without the application of land improvements which require major capital investments" (1975, p. 238).

Vink defines soil suitability as "physical suitability of soil and climate for production of a crop or group or sequence of crops, or for other defined uses or benefits, within a specified socio-economic context but not considering economic factors specific to areas of land" (Vink, 1975, p. 249). This would be analogous to the SCS capability classification system. Finally, potential land suitability "relates the suitability of land units for the use in question at some future date after 'major improvements' have been effected where necessary, suitability being assessed in terms of expected future benefits in relation to future recurrent and minor capital expenditure" (Vink, 1975, p. 254; Brinkman & Smyth, 1973).

It is this final category, potential land suitability, that distinguishes the Dutch approaches. It has been necessary for the Dutch to reclaim wet, low-lying land in order to prosper. One example of the application of potential land suitability is the polders built on the former Zuider Zee (Southern Sea) (Figure 5.7). The Zuider Zee was an extension of the North Sea into the heart of the Netherlands. According to the accounts of Roman historians, it was, at one time, a large inland lake. As early as 1667 the Dutch speculated about damming the Zuider Zee and reclaiming it, but the technology of the seventeenth century was not advanced enough to tame the tempestuous inland sea of nearly 400,000 hectares (approximately 1 million acres). However, by the late nineteenth century serious plans were developed by the engineer Cornelis Lely (Ministry of Transport and Public Works, no date).

The Zuider Zee reclamation plan that Cornelis Lely developed essentially was one based on the potential suitability of an area for agriculture. Soil surveys were conducted on soil samples taken from the sea. Using these surveys, Lely proposed that those areas with predominantly clay soils be made polders after the Zuider Zee was transformed into a lake and renamed IJsselmeer (Figure 5.8). The success of the Zuider Zee project is well-documented (see, for example, Steiner, 1981, & van Lier & Steiner, 1982).

COMPUTER APPLICATIONS

Several techniques may be used to accomplish suitability analysis. Ian McHarg popularized the

LAND USES	Unique Geological Features	Slopes Greater than 25%	Problem Drainage Areas	High Potential Erosion Areas	High Elevation Recharge Areas	Shorelines under S.M.A. 1971 and Other Significant Waters	Hudsonian Life Zone	Botanically Noteworthy Habitats	Zoologically Noteworthy Habitats	Cultural and Historical Landmarks	Existing Significant Recreation Areas
Pasture		6		6			6 7	3	6	5 8	5 8
Rangeland		6		6			6	6	6	5 8	5 8
Cropland	7 8	2 6	6	6			6 7	3 4	3 4	5 8	5 8
Intensive Recreation	7	6 8	6	6	6		6 7	3 4	3 4	5 8	
Dispersed Recreation		6 8	6	6			6 7	3 4	3 4		
Natural Recreation							6	6	6		
Urban Residential	7 8	1 2 6 8	6	6	5 6	1 3 4 5 6	3 6 7 8	3 4	3 4	5 8	5 8
Suburban Residential	7 8	1 2 6 8	6	6	5 6	1 3 4 6	3 6 7 8	3 4	3 4	5 8	5 8
Rural Residential	7 8	1 2 6 8	6	6	6	1 3 6	3 6 7 8	3 4	3 4	5 8	5 8
Commercial	7 8	1 2 6 8	6	6	5 6	1 3 4 5 6	3 6 7 8	3 4	3 4	3 4	3 4
Industrial	7 8	1 2 6 8	6	6	5 6	1 3 4 5 6	3 6 7 8	3 4	3 4	3 4	3 4

Key:

1 = hazard or potential danger to human life, quality, or health
2 = hazard or potential danger to human life, quality, or health through specific human action
3 = modification of habitat and/or ground cover
4 = endangering or reducing species
5 = depletion of natural or social resources
6 = vulnerable area that requires further regulation to avoid social or environmental costs
7 = alteration of unique, scarce, or rare attribute
8 = general incompatibility with land feature or present land use

FIGURE 5.6 Identification of constraints between land uses and biophysical processes in Asotin County, Washington. *(Source: Beach et al., 1978)*

"overlay technique" (1969). Transparent maps with information about landscape elements are placed on top of each other to reveal areas of opportunity and constraints. This technique is used to develop the opportunities maps of step 4, the constraints map in step 5, the intrinsic suitability maps of step 6, and the composite map of step 7 in Table 5.3. MacDougall (1975)

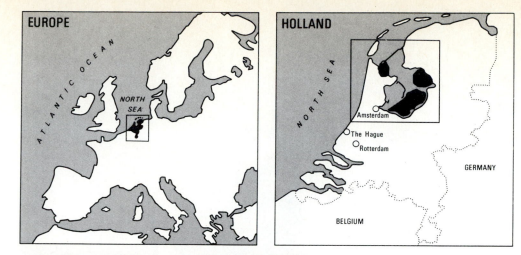

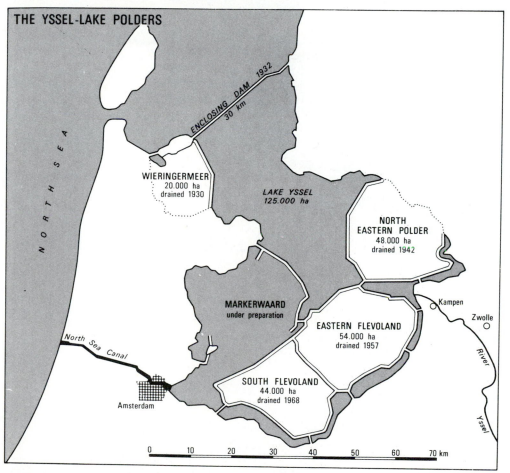

FIGURE 5.7 Location of Zuider Zee polders in the Netherlands. *(Source: IJsselmeer Polders Development Authority)*

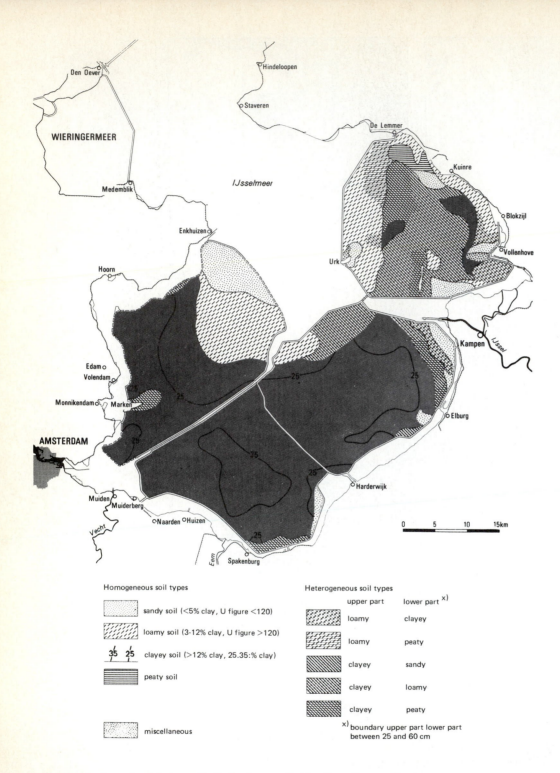

FIGURE 5.8 Location of clay soils in the former Zuider Zee. *(Source: IJsselmeer Polders Development Authority)*

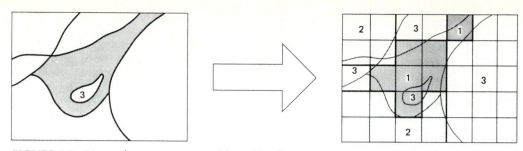

FIGURE 5.9 Mapped areas represented by grid cells. *(Source: Laird et al., 1979)*

criticized the accuracy of map overlays and made suggestions for improved accuracy.

Although there has been a general tendency away from hand-drawn overlays, there are still occasions on which they may be useful. For instance, they may be helpful at small study sites within a larger region for project planning. However, it is important to realize the limitations of hand-drawn overlays. For instance, if there are more than three or four overlays, the map may appear opaque; there are accuracy questions raised by MacDougall (1975) and others that are especially pressing with hand-drawn maps; and there are limitations for weighting various values represented by map units. Computer technology has helped to overcome these limitations.

There have been numerous computer program systems developed that can replace the technique for overlaying information by hand. Some of these

programs are intended to model only positions of environmental processes or phenomena, while others are designed as comprehensive information storage, retrieval, and evaluation systems. These systems are intended to improve efficiency and economy in information handling, especially for large or complex planning projects (Meyers, 1971; Fabos & Caswell, 1977; Beeman, 1978; & Killpack, 1981).

Biophysical information for planning use can be represented in three ways: grid cells, polygons, and image processing. Figure 5.9 illustrates how mapped areas are represented with grid cells. These areas may be soil types or capabilities, slope angles, vegetation associations, and so on. The disadvantage of grid-cell representation is that details can be missed unless the cell size is made very small. Smaller grids necessitate more data collection. Also, the world does not fit a square or

FIGURE 5.10 Mapped areas represented by polygon system. *(Source: Laird et al., 1979)*

rectangular grid pattern. This forces data to be compromised in order to fit into the grid format. Mapped areas in a polygon system are represented by enclosed spaces (Figure 5.10). A polygon system can show curved lines, thus making it potentially more accurate than grid cells (Laird et al., 1979). The third approach to computer mapping is digital-image processing. This is a sophisticated grid approach, where the cell size is very small, similar to those cells on a television screen. Maps are created directly from photo-imagery such as that from satellite or aerial photographs. Simply put, "a digital computer processes information in discrete numerical units: digits" (Cannon & Hunt, 1981, p. 214). Because of the level of detail that can be achieved, digital-image processing overcomes many of the short-comings inherent in the simpler grid and polygon approaches. Advancements in hardware and software technologies will continue to make computers increasingly effective tools for landscape inventory, analysis, synthesis, monitoring, and administration.

For example, Wisconsin law requires counties to prepare erosion control plans. These plans are to specify the maximum acceptable rates of erosion, identify parcels where erosion standards are not being met, identify land-use changes and man-agement practices that would bring each area into compliance standards, specify procedures for assisting landowners and land users to control erosion, and establish priorities for controlling erosion. To achieve these goals in Dane County, an interdisciplinary team of planners and researchers from the University of Wisconsin-Madison, Dane County, the state and federal government, the Madison Area Surveyors Council, and the Wisconsin Power and Light formed the Dane County Land Records Project (Ventura, 1988).

The Dane County Land Records Project developed a geographic information system (GIS). This GIS enabled the planners to collect, store,

"Environments are finite; users and uses multiply and compete." *(Philip Maechling)*

analyze, and disseminate information about the Dane County landscape. An inventory of biophysical and land-use information was undertaken. From that inventory, highly erodible lands were identified (Ventura, 1988). These areas are unsuited for agriculture or need specific management practices to maintain productivity. The Dane County Land Records Project is but one example of the use of computer technology to determine land-use suitability.

THE CARRYING-CAPACITY CONCEPT

In essence, suitability analysis helps determine the carrying capacity of the planning area. William Catton, a sociologist, has observed that "environ-ments are finite; users and uses multiply and com-pete. Carrying capacity means the extent to which an environment can tolerate a given kind of use by a given type of user" (1983, p. 270).

In ecology, *carrying capacity* has been defined as the number of individuals that the resources of a habitat can support without significant deterioration. In wildlife ecology, the definition used is a bit more specific: the maximum number of animals an area can support during a given period of the year. In recreation planning and management, carrying capacity has been defined as the amount of use a recreation area can sustain without deterioration of the experience provided or of the resource base. According to Schneider et al.:

> Carrying-capacity analysis, as a planning tool, studies the effects of growth—amount, type, location, quality—on the natural and man-made environments in order to identify critical thresholds beyond which public health, safety, or welfare will be threatened by serious environmental problems unless changes are made in public investment, government regulation, or human behavior. (1978, p. 1)

Several planners, especially those in outdoor recreation management and planning, have discussed the utilization of the carrying-capacity concept (Lime & Stankey, 1971; Stankey & Lime, 1973; Van Lier, 1973, 1980; Wagner, 1974; Pfister & Frankel, 1975; Lime, 1979; & Meester & Van der Voet, 1980). The outdoor recreation specialists' interest in this concept may be traced to two sources. First, they have been historically involved with forest and range ecologists, and are thus familiar with ecological terms. Second, they work within discrete boundaries where there are clear demands on and conflicts over resources. The public patronage of state and federal parks in the United States has increased dramatically since the Second World War, partly because of the interstate highway system and the increase in automobile ownership and also because of population shifts from the eastern to western states and from metropolitan to nonmetropolitan regions.

Lime and Stankey (1971) distinguished three aspects of outdoor recreational carrying capacity: management objectives, visitor attitudes, and impact on biophysical resources. The three aspects are viewed as interdependent, no one being necessarily more important than others. Suitability analysis offers a framework to study in detail these three aspects.

While the concept has enjoyed relatively wide application in outdoor recreation, carrying capacity has had more limited use by community and regional planning agencies. One exception is the Tahoe Regional Planning Agency that has adopted an environmental threshold approach based on carrying capacities. The Tahoe Regional Planning Agency has defined these threshold carrying capacities as "an environmental standard necessary to maintain a significant scenic, recreational, educational, scientific, or natural value of the region or to maintain public health and safety within the region" (1982, p. vii).

Thomas Dickert and Andrea Tuttle of the University of California, Berkeley, have advocated the use of thresholds, such as those developed by the Tahoe Regional Planning Agency, as a means to control cumulative environmental impacts. Such thresholds would be based on "an assumed acceptable amount of land-use change over time" (Dickert & Tuttle, 1985, p. 38). They observe a problem with conventional planning is that it is often incremental, and, thus, does not address cumulative impacts. In the words of Dickert and Tuttle, "Cumulative impacts are those that result from the interactions of many incremental activities, each of which may have an insignificant effect when viewed alone, but which become cumulatively significant when seen in the aggregate" (1985, p. 39). They suggest an alternative approach whereby the "rate or total amount of development is managed to stay below prestated threshold levels, and halted when such thresholds are reached" (1985, p. 39). Such thresholds can be determined by an analysis of the suitability of resources for various uses.

TWO APPLICATIONS OF
SUITABILITY ANALYSIS

The Development of Performance Requirements in Medford Township, New Jersey

The officials of Medford Township, New Jersey, sought to develop an alternative system to traditional zoning. A study exploring the use of performance requirements was undertaken for Medford by the Center for Ecological Research in Planning and Design at the University of Pennsylvania under the direction of Ian McHarg and Narendra Juneja. The performance requirements were based on the social values and natural environment of the township. (For a comprehensive description of the planning process in Medford Township, see Palmer, 1981).

Medford Township is located on the edge of the New Jersey Pinelands within commuting distance of Philadelphia, Trenton, and Camden (Figure 5.11). This is an area that, on the one hand, grew from the great suburban explosion of the 1950s and 1960s, but, on the other, is part of one of the few remaining natural ecosystems in the eastern United States.

After a detailed ecological inventory of the township, the planning team related the biophysical phenomena to their values to society and individuals. Juneja explained this in the following manner:

> The values assigned vary depending upon the individual's interest. For example, a farmer is concerned about sustained productivity from his land; a homeowner seeks a healthy delightful setting; and a developer searches for sites where he can build to get the most return for his money. The operative value system employed by individuals are as likely to be discrete and mutually exclusive as to be competitive and conflicting. To deal with the latter exigency and to ensure sustained health, welfare, and prosperity for all, it is important to identify those values which are common to all present and future residents of the

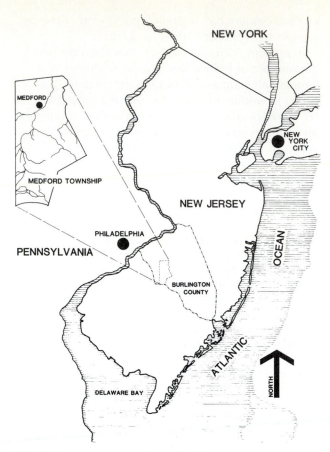

FIGURE 5.11 Location of Medford Township, New Jersey.

township. This can best be accomplished by interpreting the available understanding of the extant phenomena and processes in terms which are clearly definable and about which agreement can be reached by all those affected. (1974, p. 11)

Juneja and colleagues accomplished this by a system of matrices linked to mapped phenomenon. Figure 5.12 is an example of one such matrix for vegetation. Along the horizontal axis, the values of society and individuals, as determined by the residents of the township, are listed. The land-cover classifications are listed as mapped on the

Phenomenon	Value to Society				Value to Individuals: High Productivity for: Extract		Agriculture					Forest			Minimum On-site Costs for: Foundations			Maintenance				Water Supply			Maximum Desirabilty for: Location								Activity			
VEGETATION 1 See page 13 2, 3, 4, 5, 6, 12, 13 See page 20 7, 8, 9, 10, 11 See page 31	Inherently Hazardous to Human Life	Hazardous to Human Life and Health by Specific Human Actions	Irreplaceable Unique or Scarce Resource	Vulnerable Resource Requiring Regulation to Avoid Social Costs	Sand	Gravel	High Value Crops	General Crops	Pasture	Fruits	Special Produce	Timber	Pulp	Firewood	Paved Surfaces	Light Structures	Heavy Structures	Site Drainage	Paved Surfaces	Lawns, Playgrounds, etc.	On-Site Sewage Disposal	Domestic Use	Industrial Use	Irrigation	Favorable Microclimate	Topographic Interest	Long Views	Sense of Enclosure	Water-related Views	Vegetation Diversity	Wildlife Diversity	Historic Association	Educational	Fishing	Swimming	Canoeing Boating
Cropland																																				
Pasture																																				
Orchard																																				
Successional Meadow				●8																																
Successional Forest (Inner CP)				●8								P		P																						
Pine-Oak Forest	●1			●7								●	●	●																						
Oak-Pine Forest	●1			●7								●	●	●																						
Oak Forest Complex	●1			●7								●		●																						
Mixed Deciduous Forest				●7								●		●																						
Bog	●1		●2	●11							C																					●				
Shrub Woodland	●1		●3	●9								P																				●	●			
Successional Forest (Outer CP)	●			●8								P	P	P																						
Pine Forest	●1			●7								●	●	●																						
Deciduous-Comf. Mixed Forest	●1			●7								●		●																						
Deciduous Lowland Forest	●			●7										●																						
Flood Plain Forest				●7, 10								●		●																						
Cedar Swamp	●1		●5	●7, 10								●																				●				
Urban: Open																																				
Urban: Wooded																																				
Pine Barrens	●1		●4	●12																													●			
Old Mature Specimen Trees			●6	●13																												●	●			

1 Subject to forest fires endemic to the Pine Barrens ecology.
2 Scarce resource of historic value.
3 Unique herbaceous flora of educational, scientific, and recreational value.
4 Ecological association of unique national value.
5 Scarce resource of scientific and historic value.
6 Unique and scarce resource of historic and recreational value.
7 Deforestation will lead to loss of mature forest resource.
8 Other development of these areas will prevent these developing into mature forest resources.
9 Other development on these areas will pre-empt potential sites for growth of cedar.
10 Alteration of vegetation cover will result in disruption of stream balance and pollution.
11 Vulnerable to pollution locally and from adjacent areas.
12 Unregulated and incompatible development will degrade the unique value of this national resource.
13 Any disruption of existing conditions within the crown area will result in loss of these unique specimens.

C Cranberries only
P Potential resource

FIGURE 5.12 Matrix of vegetation values to society and individuals in Medford Township, New Jersey. *(Source: Juneja 1974)* vertical axis. Each of the categories—cropland, pasture, orchard, and so on—is explained in a technical report. The occurrence of a dot in the matrix indicates a relationship; some explanations of these relationships accompany the matrix. For instance, a dot with the number 4 indicates an ecological association of unique national value. Similar matrices were developed for geology, aquifers, microclimate, physiography, hydrology, limnology, soil types, water runoff, the depth to water table, nutrient retention, potential soil loss, recreational values of vegetation, wildlife habitats, historic sites, and scenic units (Juneja, 1974).

The matrixed value-to-society relationships were used to develop constraints to various land uses. The value-to-individuals relationships were used to establish opportunities for land uses. Again, matrices and maps were used to illustrate this process. Figure 5.13 shows such a matrix listing suitability criteria for recreation and urbanization. In the translation of this information to maps, rules of combination were used. Table 5.4 lists those for recreation, while Table 5.5 is an explanation of the rules of combination for one type of urbanization (clustered suburban). Similar rules were developed for other forms of urbanization.

Suitabilities were established for forest production and agricultural production. Intrinsic suitabilities or composite suitabilities were not developed at this stage for Medford Township. Juneja and colleagues instead developed a framework for establishing performance requirements based on constraints and opportunities for specific land uses. These were proposed to then become a part of the township plan and zoning ordinance (Juneja, 1974).

FIGURE 5.13 Matrix of suitability criteria for recreation and urbanization in Medford Township, New Jersey. *(Source: Juneja, 1974)*

Development Type	Cost-Savings for: FOUNDATIONS — Paved Surfaces	Light Structures	Heavy Structures	MAINTENANCE — Site Drainage	Paved Surfaces	Lawns, Playgrounds, etc.	On-Site Sewage Disposal	WATER SUPPLY — Domestic Use	Industrial Use	Irrigational Use	Maximum Desirability for: LOCATION — Favorable Microclimate	Topographic Interest	Long Views	Sense of Enclosure	Water-related Views	Vegetation Diversity	Wildlife Diversity	Historic Association	ACTIVITY — Educational	Fishing	Swimming	Canoeing	Boating
URBANIZATION																							
Rural Urban		◩					◩	○			◩	◩	◩	◩	◩	◩	●	◩					
Suburban	○	◩		◩		◩	●	○			○	○	○	○	○	●	●	◩					
Clustered Suburban	◩	◩		◩	◩	○		○			○	●	●	●	●	○	○	●					
Urban	◩		◩	○	○					○		●			●			●					
RECREATION																							
Intensive				◩	○	◩					○												
General				○		○					●	◩	◩	◩	◩	●	●	●					
Natural											◩	◩	◩	◩	◩	◩	◩	◩					
Cultural and Historic																	◩	◩					
Water-Related																				○	○	○	○

◩ Critical   ◩ Preferred/Compatible
● Optional   ● Preferred/Partially Compatible
○ Desirable   ○ Desirable

TABLE 5.4
RULES OF COMBINATION FOR RECREATION IN MEDFORD TOWNSHIP, NEW JERSEY

Suitability criteria: Recreation cost savings for intensive recreation

A. Concurrence of 4 acceptable factors = prime suitability (1)
Concurrence of 3 acceptable factors = secondary suitability (2)
Concurrence of 2 acceptable factors = tertiary suitability (3)
Presence of only 1 acceptable factor = unsuitable

Factor	Acceptable Limit
Maintenance: site drainage	Somewhat poorly drained soils
Maintenance: site drainage and lawns, playgrounds, etc.	Minimum 1–3 in. (2.54–7.62 cm) depth to the seasonal high water table
Maintenance: Lawns, playgrounds, etc.	Concurrence of at least two of the following: a. Moderate available soil mixture b. Fair nutrient retention c. Moderate shrink-swell potential
Maintenance: Lawns, playgrounds, etc.	Maximum 100 tons/acre/year potential soil loss (100 tons/ 0.405 ha/year)

B. Suitability categories derived from step A are modified by the following site factors:

Factor	Location	Suitability Modified
Lack of gradient (site drainage cost)	Inner lowland: plain;	1 becomes 2
		2 becomes 3
	Outer lowland: plain	3 becomes 4
Excessive runoff (site drainage cost)	*	1 becomes 2
		2 becomes 3
		3 becomes 4
		4 becomes 5

Desirable locations for general, natural, and cultural-historic-educational recreation

Type	Location
Water related	Stream, artificial lakes, enclosure with view of water, view of water
Scenic interest	Enclosure, regional and local prominence, terrain interest, agriculture
Vegetation and wildlife interest	Cedar swamp, bog, shrub woodland, upland successional meadow, floodplain, mixed deciduous, coniferous-deciduous mixed, pine, pine-oak, oak pine, upland successional oak, lowland successional, deciduous lowland forests, urban forested
Scenic, educational, and scientific interest	Ironstone, old mature specimen trees
Historic, cultural, and educational interest	Historic sites, land routes, water routes and lakes

* Assumed acceptable limit is that no more than 5% of site area is required to infiltrate within 3 hours the excess runoff generated over that site during the 10-year recurrent 24-hour storm, most intense hour.

SOURCE: Adapted from Juneja, 1974.

Locating Areas for Rural Housing in Whitman County, Washington

In July 1978, the Whitman County, Washington, Board of Commissioners adopted a revised comprehensive plan that assigned high priorities to agricultural and residential land-use issues (Whitman County Regional Planning Council,

1978). The commissioners' goal was to preserve productive agricultural land and the family farm as the prime economic and social resource of the county. They felt that goal could be met by preventing land from being taken out of production by indiscriminate or excessive land-use changes.

In the case of residential land use, the com-

TABLE 5.5
RULES OF COMBINATION FOR CLUSTER SUBURBAN DEVELOPMENT IN MEDFORD TOWNSHIP, NEW JERSEY

Suitability criteria: Cost savings for clustered suburban

A. Concurrence of 5 acceptable factors = prime suitability (1)
   Concurrence of 4 acceptable factors = secondary suitability (2)
   Concurrence of 3 acceptable factors = tertiary suitability (3)
   Concurrence of fewer than 3 acceptable factors = unsuitable

Factor	Acceptable Limit
Foundations: Light structure	Fair subsoil shear strength
Foundations: Paved structures	Concurrence of at least two of the following: a. Fair subsoil shear strength b. Moderate shrink-swell potential c. Moderate frost-heave susceptibility
Maintenance: Paved surfaces	Concurrence of acceptable foundation conditions for paved surfaces and maximum 100 tons/acre/year potential soil loss (100 tons/0.405 ha/year)
Maintenance: Site drainage	Somewhat poorly drained soils
Maintenance: Site drainage	Minimum 1–3 in. (2.54–7.62 cm) depth to seasonal high water table

* Assumed acceptable limit is that no more than 5% of site area is required to infiltrate within 3 hours the excess runoff generated over that site during the 10-year recurrent 24-hour storm, most intense hour.

SOURCE: Adapted from Juneja, 1974.

B. Suitability categories derived from step A are modified by the following site factors:

Factor	Location	Suitability Modified
Sloping terrain (paved surfaces)	Inner lowland terrace: slope, scarp, stream dissection; inner lowland: stream dissection; inner upland: hill, slope, scarp, stream dissection; inner and outer lowland plains are also included because the saving in construction cost is negated by increased drainage cost resulting from lack of gradient	1 becomes 2 2 becomes 3 3 becomes 4
Excessive runoff (site drainage cost)	*	1 becomes 2 2 becomes 3 3 becomes 4 4 becomes 5

Desirable location
Presence of 1 desirable factor = tertiary suitability (A)

Factor	Desirable Element
Scenic interest	Regional prominence, terrain interest, view of water, field

missioners' goal was to provide limited, low-density housing on unincorporated land with the lowest potential for agricultural use. This measure would attempt to satisfy those desiring a rural living environment while protecting farmland from residential encroachment.

The commissioners realized that preserving productive agricultural land while providing limited, low-density living opportunities is not a simple process, so their revised comprehensive plan includes a number of guidelines identifying those areas suitable for rural housing. These guidelines state that areas to be considered for rural housing must be adjacent to a state or county road and also meet at least two of the following criteria:

• Land whose near-surface geology consists of basalt or alluvium or, on slopes of greater than 20 percent, crystalline rock, all as defined by Water Supply Bulletin No. 26 of the Washington Department of Ecology, *Reconnaissance of*

Geology and of Ground-Water Occurrence in Whitman County, or any updated version of this document. (Walters & Glancy, 1969)

- Land that is not normally cultivated, used for production of forage, or for commercial grazing of livestock.
- Distinct areas of land 15 acres [6.08 hectares] or less that are of insufficient size, quality, and/or accessibility to be efficiently used for agricultural production for income. "Distinct" means that the area is substantially bounded by natural or man-made features that buffer this land from agricultural lands, such as wooded areas, steep canyon walls, railroads, surface water, or public roads. (Whitman County Regional Planning Council, 1978)

Parcel size needs to be sufficient to meet health regulations for on-site sewage disposal while providing adequate acreage for productive use of rural residential land. Productive uses include small numbers of livestock and large gardens. Further guidelines for rural housing include a minimum of 200 feet (61 meters) of frontage from perennial surface water passing through or along the property lines of the acreage and less than 50 percent of the acreage in a designated flood hazard area, as defined by the federal flood insurance program.

During public hearings on the plan, several local residents, including realtors and builders, questioned whether there was any land in the county that could meet these guidelines and, if so, how much? To mitigate the suspicion that these lands were inordinately scarce, a planning team was formed to investigate the potential for rural housing using these guidelines in conjunction with actual land use throughout the county.

The planning team (Steiner & Theilacker, 1979) chose a 150 square mile (388.35 square kilometer) demonstration area adjacent to the city of Pullman for the feasibility study and including the town of Albion, which was used as an example in Chapters 3 and 4. The demand for rural housing is greater in this area than in other parts of the county. This area is close to the cities of Pullman, location of Washington State University, and Moscow, Idaho, location of the University of Idaho. These two cities contain most of the people in the region. Many of the faculty from the two universities seek a rural-living situation.

The planning team inventoried uncultivated "scablands" adjacent to improved county and state roads, estimating and demarcating the total area suitable for rural housing development. Scablands, as commonly defined by local farmers, are those areas not suitable for commercial cultivation.

Scientific definitions of these lands are somewhat similar. The SCS, for example, identifies scabgrounds as those consisting of Gwin-Linvill and Gwin-Tucannon soils. These areas differ from the channel scabland identified by geologists that resulted from the Spokane, or Missoula, Flood of the Pleistocene Era.

Because the farmers' scablands definition is more readily understood by decision makers, this is the definition that was used. However, the work of scientists was not ignored. It formed the basis for the inventory process and was crucial to the selection of feasible areas.

The planning team used the principles of suitability analysis, as defined by McHarg (1969), to determine those areas feasible for rural housing. Instead of overlaying inventory information to find intrinsically suitable areas, the team overlaid information to identify areas meeting the established policy guidelines for rocky and agriculturally unproductive lands, or scablands. The team then subtracted constraint areas, leaving the areas feasible for housing (Steiner & Theilacker, 1979).

The study began with an extensive inventory and mapping of the demonstration area. The team collected information at two scales: 1:2,000 for the overall demonstration area and 1:100 for two more specific sites. The information collected included bedrock geology, elevation, basalt outcrops and steep slopes, soil series, surface water, wildlife habitat, transportation, property ownership,

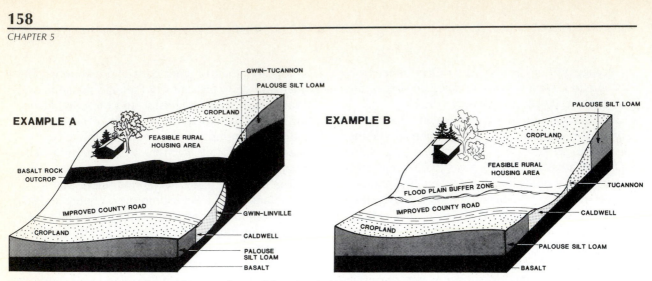

FIGURE 5.14 Generalized feasible areas for rural housing in Whitman County, Washington.

scablands, and generalized areas feasible for rural housing. The team related all this material directly to the criteria established in the comprehensive plan revision for rural housing.

The team identified scabland areas by inventorying the physical features that prevent dryland farming. Areas of basalt outcroppings and steep slopes were considered scablands, along with several soil types identified by the SCS. These generally thin or gravelly soils, which are poor for agricultural purposes, often occur on steep slopes. Such soil types are also found in floodplains, adjacent to or deposited within basalt outcroppings.

The generalized areas feasible for rural housing were next located on maps by a process of elimination (Figure 5.14). Once the scablands were identified, conditions considered unsuitable for rural housing were addressed and such lands eliminated. These conditions included floodplain areas, valuable wildlife habitats, exposed basalt rocks, areas with slopes greater than 40 percent, lack of frontage on improved state and county roads, and soil characteristics unsuited for structures or for on-site water supply and sewage disposal.

The planning team estimated about 12,443 acres

(5,039.42 hectares) of scablands in the 150 square mile (388.35 square kilometer) demonstration area. In the two more specific study sites, which together totaled 76 square miles, 1,734 acres were identified with a potential for rural housing development (196.76 square kilometers, or 702.27 hectares). These findings enabled the county commissioners to respond affirmatively to the many earlier questions about whether there was land that met the guidelines in the county comprehensive plan revision. The findings also established a procedure for identifying such land. This procedure was supplemented with a suggested environmental checklist for rural housing that can be used when developers make specific requests. The checklist helped to ensure the environmental quality sought by the commissioners by incorporating specific siting criteria into zoning and building code requirements (see Chapter 10). Since 1979, these criteria have successfully been used in Whitman County to protect good farmland, promote the siting of rural housing in suitable areas, and to concentrate urban development within the city of Pullman.

The suitability analyses conducted in Whitman County and Medford Township considered a wide range of information about nature and people. This breadth distinguishes these examples from detailed studies undertaken in more conventional planning processes. Human values were considered in both examples. In Whitman County, the study was responding to values expressed in the comprehensive plan goals. Farmers' values were considered in the identification of scablands. The

feelings of the community as expressed through public hearings was a major reason the study was conducted. In Medford Township, suitability criteria were developed for each land use based on values to society and to individuals. Values were important in determining rules of combination as well. Suitability analyses for several land uses will result in a number of choices for the future.

6

PLANNING OPTIONS AND CHOICES

To a large extent, every step in the planning process requires that choices be made. Planning may be viewed as a "process for determining appropriate future action through a sequence of choices" (Davidoff & Reiner, 1962, p. 103). Throughout this sequence, questions arise. What goals should a community adopt? What information about biophysical and sociocultural processes of a planning area should be collected? What are the boundaries of the planning area and at what scale or in what format should information be collected and presented? In ecological planning, once detailed studies such as suitability analyses have been performed, the community will have a number of choices. The planning area may be faced with a growing population. Several specific parcels of land may be intrinsically suited for several uses—possibly agriculture, housing, and recreation. Which use should the community encourage?

The purpose of this step in the process is to attempt to answer such questions by presenting a series of options to the people of the area. Conceptual visions should be presented which link planning decisions to actions and then actions to impacts in the landscape. Such visions can be presented in a series of models or scenarios that depict the future possibilities for the planning area.

Many techniques can assist a community in making choices among planning options. The techniques are similar to those used to identify issues and to establish planning goals. A few of the more popular include the charrette, task forces, citizens advisory committees, technical advisory committees, public hearings, citizen referendum and synchronized surveys, and goals-achievement matrices. Two good examples of selecting preferences include the Walworth County, Wisconsin, options to protect farmland and the land-use alternatives for the Portland, Oregon, comprehensive plan. The Wisconsin example illustrates how inventory information was used to help make choices, while the Oregon case shows how options were derived from existing goals.

OPTIONAL PLANS

Suitability analyses may present a number of choices to a community. For instance, a community may have established goals both to provide for housing and to protect prime farmland. A parcel of land may be highly suited for both uses. To assist elected and appointed officials in decision making, it can be helpful to develop a number of optional landscape plans that would enable officials to see the spatial impacts of their decisions.

The Albion example will be used to illustrate optional plans. The first option (Figure 6.1) is based on agricultural protection and enhancement. This conceptual option for Albion involves the protection of prime farmland from conversion to other uses. Productive farmland, which is also highly erodible, would be managed with maximum soil conservation practices. Marginal farmland would be retired from cultivation and used for rural housing or open space.

The second option (Figure 6.2) would encourage industrial development. This concept includes expanding gravel pits and rock-crushing facilities.

(The basalt of the region has a number of commercial uses.) The industrial development option identifies land that could be used for agricultural industry and business. Roads, railroads, and sewer and water facilities need to be improved. New housing in and around Albion would be built. In other areas, the same uses as in the first option (prime agricultural land, farmlands managed for soil conservation, rural housing, and open space) would be encouraged.

In the third option (Figure 6.3), Albion would be developed as a bedroom community for nearby Pullman. This option would involve expanding areas for business and low-density and high-density housing in or adjacent to Albion. Highways, sewers, and water lines would again need to be improved. As in the second option, the areas not impacted by these uses would retain the same purposes as in the first option.

A number of conflicting uses are readily apparent. Prime agricultural lands are also good for housing. Areas that are suitable for rock crushing can be used for rural housing as well. Rural housing areas are suitable for higher-density housing. Lands that should be withdrawn from cultivation and used for open space are currently in active agricultural use. The techniques that follow can be used to resolve such conflicts.

TECHNIQUES FOR SELECTING PREFERENCES

The Charrette

The *charrette* (from the French word for cart) technique is derived from its original usage in the École des Beaux-Arts. The École des Beaux-Arts, the French academy of fine arts, was founded in Paris in 1617, incorporating several older art schools. The purpose was to give instruction in drawing, painting, sculpture, architecture, and engraving to a fixed number of students selected by a highly competitive examination. The training

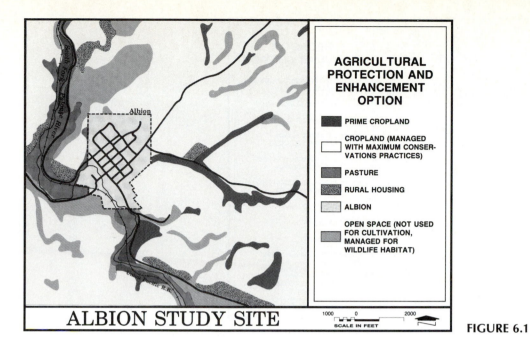

AGRICULTURAL PROTECTION AND ENHANCEMENT OPTION

- PRIME CROPLAND
- CROPLAND (MANAGED WITH MAXIMUM CONSERVATIONS PRACTICES)
- PASTURE
- RURAL HOUSING
- ALBION
- OPEN SPACE (NOT USED FOR CULTIVATION, MANAGED FOR WILDLIFE HABITAT)

ALBION STUDY SITE

1000   0   2000
SCALE IN FEET

FIGURE 6.1

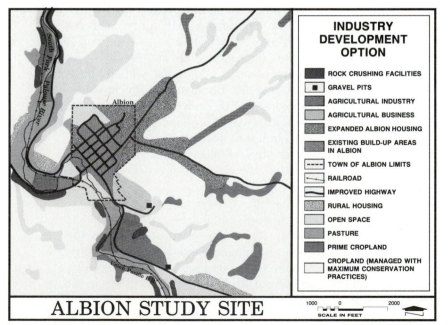

INDUSTRY DEVELOPMENT OPTION

- ROCK CRUSHING FACILITIES
- GRAVEL PITS
- AGRICULTURAL INDUSTRY
- AGRICULTURAL BUSINESS
- EXPANDED ALBION HOUSING
- EXISTING BUILD-UP AREAS IN ALBION
- TOWN OF ALBION LIMITS
- RAILROAD
- IMPROVED HIGHWAY
- RURAL HOUSING
- OPEN SPACE
- PASTURE
- PRIME CROPLAND
- CROPLAND (MANAGED WITH MAXIMUM CONSERVATION PRACTICES)

ALBION STUDY SITE

1000   0   2000
SCALE IN FEET

FIGURE 6.2

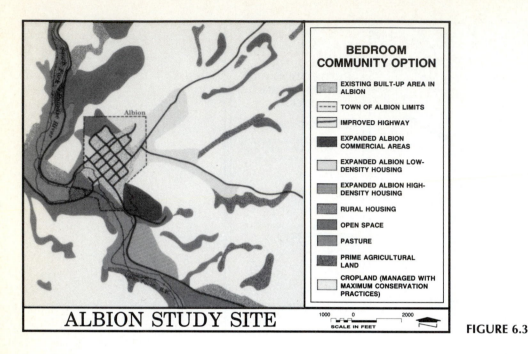

ALBION STUDY SITE

FIGURE 6.3

process consisted of lectures on diverse subjects, such as anatomy and history, and practice in studios under the direction of eminent master artists. Charrettes were the carts on which students of the École des Beaux-Arts carried their paintings. The paintings were criticized by those who watched the carts pass. This method of criticism was institutionalized first by the French school and later in American art, design, and planning education.

A charrette may be used to present a series of conceptual plans based on suitability analyses for various land uses. Much preparation is necessary before a session is held. Each of the plans may involve different organizations of the planning areas with each optimizing a different use, such as agriculture, recreation, housing, nature conservation, and industry. The participants may also represent groups advocating various uses. The emphasis is placed on discussing the merits of each plan.

One way of organizing a charrette is to present each option in an illustrated format, often on a map or aerial photograph, with a brief written description. Each illustration is then placed in the front of the room where the session is being held. A map or aerial photograph without illustrated options is also displayed on which consensus opinions may be drawn. It is important to have technical experts on hand to answer questions on such topics as floodplain boundaries, soil capabilities, wildlife habitat locations, housing demand, the potential direction of emissions from industry, and so on.

Charrettes have been proven especially effective for choosing preferences among different physical plans. It is a way for participants to visualize the merits of different land-use plans. Charrettes require time, often several months, before a consensus may be reached and hence may be expensive.

One way to present land-use options is on a map or on an aerial photograph placed in the front of the room where the planning session is being held. *(Whitman County Regional Planning Council)*

Task Forces, Citizens Advisory Committees, and Technical Advisory Committees

Task forces, citizens advisory committees (CACs), and technical advisory committees (TACs) were described in Chapter 2. A sagacious strategy is to involve the same people in determining planning preferences who established the original goals. Such involvement may be accomplished several ways. After the goals are established, task forces, CACs, or TACs may not meet until a staff completes technical studies. Alternatively, these groups may assist a staff with the collection of information or may collect data themselves. If there is a period when such groups are not directly involved, then it is important to keep the participants informed about the planning activities through newsletters or other written reports.

An option may be to split the CAC or TAC into task forces after the planning goals are established. Data are next collected and each task force given the same information. It may then be the responsibility of each task force to complete a

suitability analysis for one land use. The larger CAC or TAC then may reconvene in a charrette to reach a consensus about a desired composite scheme. This approach is especially useful with a technical advisory committee that has different areas of special expertise.

Citizen Referendum and Synchronized Surveys

To establish a preference among several choices, it may be helpful to return to two other techniques used to set goals: voting and surveying. If, for instance, a goal was established by an election, then a referendum may be held on proposed options to achieve that goal. An advantage of an official vote is that the selected preference might have greater popular support, which may make implementation easier.*

An alternative to an official vote is an unofficial tally. Such a poll may be conducted through local newspapers. For instance, different plans may be published in local newspapers with relevant background data. Television can also be employed to conduct an unofficial vote. Different plans with background data can be presented on television with a poll taken afterward. Interactive cable systems greatly increase the possibilities for presenting options and for receiving indications of preferences.

---

* A referendum may occur at any stage in the planning process. For instance, Oregon statewide planning laws have faced referenda four times. In 1970, prior to Senate Bill 100, a measure to repeal all state land-use laws failed by a margin of 55 to 45 percent. In 1976, an initiative sought to repeal the Land Conservation and Development Commission. It was defeated 57 to 43 percent. Another initiative was launched in 1978 and was defeated 61 to 39 percent (Pease, 1984). Finally, in 1983, a final initiative to repeal several aspects of the bill was voted down. There has been a gradual increase of support for planning in Oregon at the ballot box. Of course, a referendum can go the other way. For instance, in a rural western county, an ill-conceived zoning ordinance was put to a vote and was overwhelmingly defeated. The defeat was interpreted as evidence of the community's opposition to planning.

Synchronized surveys proposed by Don Dillman (1977) also present possibilities to keep people involved through the planning process. Dillman believes synchronized surveys, handled correctly, may help to overcome the weakness of standard surveys described in Chapter 2. (See Figure 2.2 for an illustration of the differences between standard and synchronized surveys.) A standard model is a one-step procedure: the survey response leads directly to the policy decision, be it the establishment of goals or the selection of a preferred option. With the synchronized survey, a goal can be established with the help of a survey. Data may then be collected and options explored through another survey. A third survey then may be used to select the preferred option. This technique allows interaction between citizens and planners throughout the process.

Goals-Achievement Matrix

Often a planning team will be asked to identify the option that achieves the established goals. The goals-achievement matrix, proposed by Morris Hill (1968), is one technique that can be used to establish relationships between means and ends. Hill explained that the evaluation of various courses of action requires the determination for each option of whether or not the benefits outweigh the costs, measured in terms of the total array of ends. He proposed a procedure for cost-benefit accounting. Depending on the goal statements, the cost and benefits are expressed as:

1. Tangible costs and benefits expressed in monetary terms
2. Tangible costs and benefits which cannot be expressed in monetary terms but can be expressed quantitatively, usually in terms derived from the definition of the goal
3. Intangible costs and benefits (Hill, 1968, p. 22)

This procedure is summarized in Figure 6.4. According to Hill, for each goal and for each

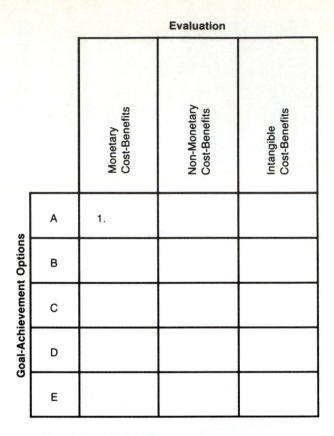

1. Keys in the matrix refer to explanations.

FIGURE 6.4 Summary goals-achievement matrix. *(Source: Adapted from Hill, 1968)*

option, costs and benefits can then be compared, aggregated when possible, and reported separately. Planners are then in a position to weigh the various courses of action against each other. Hill stressed that it is necessary to identify those sections of the public who are affected by each option. He admitted the tasks involved for such analysis are complex, but "its complexity is no excuse for abandoning the attempt" (1968, p. 28). Goals-achievement matrices provide a rational procedure for comparing options.

Donald Miller of the University of Washington provides an example of the use of the goals-achievement method in the evaluation of selecting neighborhoods for rehabilitation loan associations (1980). Miller evaluated different neighborhoods in the city of Everett, Washington, in terms of their relative potential for successful rehabilitation should the loan program and other public improvements be implemented. In this case consultants worked with the local planning agency, a citizens advisory committee, and the city council. According to Miller, "these groups appreciated having empirical evidence in an understandable form, were able to follow . . . the methodology, and were convinced the analysis was valid" (1980, p. 204).

Scenario Writing

Another technique of selecting choices is scenario writing. Larry Hirschhorn has explained that scenario writing "encompasses a broad range of approaches, assumptions, and techniques, but all share in common an attempt to describe or write a history of the future" (1980, p. 172). Scenarios can be developed for the various conceptual options designed to achieve planning goals.

Hirschhorn (1980) distinguishes between state scenarios and process scenarios. *State scenarios* describe what the planning area will be like at some date in the future without explaining how that situation is achieved. *Process scenarios* discuss the events that may lead to a future situation. Both can be used to explain the potential consequences of various planning options.

Hirschhorn (1980) furthermore examines four types of process scenarios. The first is the *idealization* process, whereby ideal scenarios are envisioned. The second are the *prophecy* scenarios, in which Hirschhorn notes "the prophet has a compelling vision of how the world will and must be in the future" (p. 174). The third type is *simulation,* which Hirschhorn describes as "state driven, process based, and used for predictive purposes" (p. 174). The final type is the *developmental* scenario, which begins "with an initial state and describes a process through which

a particular social system can arrive at one or a series of end states that are not specified prior to the construction of the scenario itself" (p. 175).

Hirschhorn makes a compelling argument for the benefits of developmental scenario writing and explains how such a scenario can be constructed in an article in the *Journal of the American Planning Association* (1980). Scenario writing presents a useful way to create a framework to discuss the consequences of various planning options by a planning commission or staff, CAC, TAC, or task force.

Public Hearings

Public hearings will probably be a legal requirement for making planning choices. Those who have been involved in public hearings will attest that such events are not noted for their rationality. As a result, it is essential for planners to make clear, thorough presentations of the various options available to achieve community goals. Summaries of inventories, suitability analyses, surveys, and goal-achievement matrices can be presented. It is also good to involve citizens who have participated in advisory committees and task forces, as well as expert testimony.

For example, the Yakima County, Washington, planning commission and staff worked for over a year exploring ways to slow down the conversion of prime farmland to urban uses and direct growth near existing cities and towns. The effort had been well-publicized and involved hundreds of people. Yet, at the first public hearing where the options were presented, several individuals claimed they had heard nothing about the program and that only a few citizens had been involved in developing the various choices.

At the second hearing the planning staff posted the numerous newspaper accounts of the program along the long hallway leading to the meeting room. All those who attended the hearing passed by this extensive account. In addition, the many people who had been involved in the process were asked to attend the hearing to testify concerning their involvement. As a result, no one raised the issue that they knew nothing about the program, and there was substantial testimony about citizen involvement. This format continued through subsequent hearings, and debate was focused on the merits of the various options available to the community to achieve its goals.

TWO EXAMPLES OF SELECTING PREFERENCES

The Walworth County, Wisconsin, Farmland Protection Program

Walworth County, Wisconsin, is located near the cities of Chicago, Milwaukee, and Madison (Figure 6.5). The county is within 1½ hours driving distance of 9 million people. There are many clean, glaciated lakes in the county, including Lake Geneva, which attract many urban visitors and retirees to the area. In addition, the majority of Walworth County's soils fall into SCS capability classes I and II, those best for agricultural pro-

FIGURE 6.5 Location of Walworth County, Wisconsin.

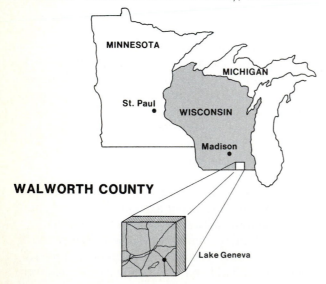

duction. About 69 percent of the total area of the county is in these two classes, and, if class III is added, this figure rises to 86 percent (Manuwoto et al., 1978).

Walworth County is a member of the Southwestern Wisconsin Regional Planning Commission. The regional plan establishes the basis for county planning and provides the goals and policies that create the framework for land-use programs and ordinances. The major goals of Walworth County's planning include (1) the preservation of prime agricultural lands, (2) the preservation of environmentally sensitive corridors, (3) the concentration of urban development of growth centers, and (4) the maintenance of agriculture and recreation as strong components of the county's economy. The plan followed state-mandated policy requiring shoreline, floodplain, subdivision, and forestry regulations (Johnson, 1984).

Between the establishment of these policies and the implementation of measures to achieve them were several steps. These steps included the inventory of resource information and a review of the various land areas to be affected by implementation measures. The implementation was accomplished by a two-tier zoning ordinance. An overall ordinance was developed for the county, and then sixteen individual ordinances were adopted for each of the county's townships (Johnson, 1984).

The team that collected resource information included the county planning staff, the University of Wisconsin-Extension, and the SCS. The zoning ordinance seeks to balance the need to protect the rich agricultural base in the county while preserving its natural beauty. To address this balancing, the county ordinance includes a total of twenty-six separate zoning districts grouped into six major land-use categories: agriculture, resource conservation, park and recreation, residential, business, and industry (Johnson, 1984).

The selection of areas for these districts was accomplished on the township level. The townships were also responsible for adopting the ordinance. An extensive process was undertaken that eventually involved 500 public meetings. The purpose of these meetings was to describe the general scheme of the ordinance and to work with individual townships to develop specific zones. During these meetings, the planning team worked closely with an advisory group of local farmers concerned about the amount of farmland being lost to urbanization. Called the Farm Council, this group comprised representatives of the Grange, Farm Bureau, the Pure Milk Association, and other active farm groups (Johnson, 1984).

Much of the effort was focused on the mapping of areas for the various districts. The planning team presented the inventory information on maps and aerial photographs. In the words of one official involved, these maps "were not cast in concrete, they were cast in felt tip pen" (West, 1978). As a result, changes could be made in the charrette sessions of public meetings. The areas eventually chosen for the agricultural zones closely followed those determined by the SCS to be the best farmland in the county. However, the areas were chosen by the people of the county rather than the professionals. Eventually all sixteen townships adopted zoning ordinances, and Walworth County provided the model for a statewide farmland protection law.

Portland, Oregon, Alternative Land-Use Plans

With the adoption of Oregon's statewide goals, the cities and counties set about revising and updating their comprehensive plans to comply with the new requirements. Among the municipalities involved in this process was the state's largest city, Portland. After detailed population, economic, and environmental studies by the city planning staff, a report entitled *The City Planner Handbook* (Portland Bureau of Planning, 1977) was published. This report contained summarized background information, three alternative land-use plans, and a technical appendix. The handbook was used as a starting point for the process of selecting options for the city's future.

The centerpiece of *The City Planner Handbook* was the three staff-prepared, land-use planning alternatives. These three options included a description of the number and types of housing units, people, and jobs each future vision might support. Each option was analyzed to assess how it addressed a list of thirty-two goals. The thirty-two goals were developed by the planning staff and related to the fourteen statewide goals Portland was to meet. (Of Oregon's nineteen goals, five are applicable to only coastal counties and municipalities.) The purpose of the Portland alternatives was to indicate the choices necessary to accomplish each goal and to seek advice from citizens (Portland Bureau of Planning, 1980).

The list of goals provided a wide range of choices to Portland residents. The choices addressed neighborhood quality, city economy, housing, water and sewer systems, transportation, air and water quality, and energy conservation. Each of these choices was linked to maps that illustrated the impact of the decision on commercial, residential, agricultural and forestry, and industrial land uses in the city. Portland citizens were asked to respond by mail to the alternatives.

Community organizations, neighborhood associations, individuals, and government agencies were also asked to review and comment upon the choices presented in the handbook. Some 150 special interest groups were contacted. Meetings were held with each including construction, business, ethnic, fraternal, health and education, legal, religious, social, service, transportation, trade, political, and union groups. Portland is divided into ten districts. In each district, neighborhood associations were organized. These associations were asked by the city planning staff to review the three alternatives and to determine if an additional alternative was necessary to expand the range of choice for public discussion. The neighborhood associations were also asked to write scenarios about the implication of each alternative (Portland Bureau of Planning, 1980).

There was a strong emphasis placed on neighborhood review of the options. The process of planning in Portland was used to strengthen its neighborhoods. According to a former planning commission president, Joan Smith, "if the planning process did nothing else for this city, it made many of the neighborhoods more articulate and better organized" (Sistrom, 1979, p. 1).

From this process each planning district developed a new alternative. Ten town meetings were then held in the evening in each district where testimony was heard on the scenarios developed for each option. Two citywide meetings, one during the day and one at night, were also held downtown to discuss the four alternatives.

Next the city hired a consulting firm to conduct a random survey consisting of 450 in-home interviews during April and May 1978. Those interviewed were asked to evaluate each of the options. At the same time all the alternatives, including those developed by the ten planning districts, were distributed to over 33,000 people. Again citizens were asked to review each alternative and rank the list of thirty-two goals (Portland Bureau of Planning, 1980). In a sense, this was a form of a goals-achievement matrix combined with synchronized survey.

These surveys and the testimony from the town hall meetings were analyzed and tabulated by the Center for Population Research at Portland State University. The results of this analysis were incorporated into the first draft of a comprehensive plan, called a *discussion draft*. The publication of this discussion draft initiated another round of citizen review lasting 6 months (Portland Bureau of Planning, 1980).

During this period, over eighty neighborhood association meetings, many business and service group meetings, two citywide conferences, and nine planning district town hall meetings were held, as concurrently the planning staff conducted

additional surveys. Over 800 suggestions were received, of which 65 percent were used in a second draft called the *proposed comprehensive plan*. This proposed plan was taken to the city planning commission in September 1979. The planning commission held eight public hearings during the next 2 months. At the same time, the proposed plan was distributed to neighborhood associations; civic, environmental and business groups; and other government agencies. In addition, a total of 10,000 proposed plan maps were mailed out to groups and individuals (Portland Bureau of Planning, 1980).

Responses to the mailing and testimony from the hearings were compiled in summary notebooks. These notebooks were used by the planning commission and staff to write a third draft, the *recommended comprehensive plan*. The recommended plan was submitted to the city council in January 1980. At this time nearly 14,000 recommended plans were mailed to groups and individuals. The city council then held a series of thirty-three more public hearings during which time about 400 amendments were made.

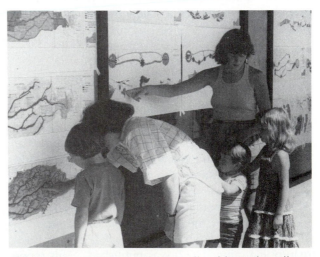

Effective planning programs are well publicized to allow residents time to discuss and select available options. *(Frederick Steiner)*

On August 21, 1980, the city council adopted the plan (Portland Bureau of Planning, 1980).

This was a lengthy process of reviewing planning options. In the end, Portland adopted its first comprehensive plan. In 1981, the Oregon Land Conservation and Development Commission acknowledged that the plan was in compliance with the fourteen statewide planning goals.

In both examples a combination of techniques was used to select planning options. In Wisconsin, public meetings, charrettes, an advisory committee, and hearings were employed. All these were applied in Portland, as were preference surveys, interviews, and scenario writing. There are other common characteristics in both cases. In Walworth County and Portland, planners allotted ample time to discuss and select the available options. The Wisconsin program took 7 years, while the Portland plan took 4 years. Each program was well-publicized with an effort to reach all people in the planning area. As well, both local programs were linked to state policy. The Walworth County program was related to statewide policy for shorelines, floodplains, forestry, and subdivisions. The Walworth County effort influenced the development of the Wisconsin farmland protection policy. Portland's program fit within Oregon statewide goals.

As compared with more conventional planning examples, planners in both Walworth County and Portland relied heavily on information about environmental resources that had been collected through inventories. Information about geology and soils as well as surface water and forest vegetation was central to the effort of Walworth County. The values of Walworth County citizens influenced how this information was interpreted and used. Likewise, the values of the people of Portland were reflected in how information about their environment would be employed to implement their plan.

7

LANDSCAPE PLANS

Plans can take many forms. Early American plans were quite specific about the layout of cities and towns—the location of streets and the division of land—from colonial times through the nineteenth century. These early plans were utilitarian when used as part of a land speculation venture or utopian when developed for settlement by religious sects. City planning practitioners of the late nineteenth and early twentieth centuries produced master plans that reflected the influence of landscape architecture, architecture, and engineering. In master plans, uses were prescribed for each place in the city or town. Comprehensive plans in cities and multiple-use plans in national forests, both advocated beginning in the early twentieth century, attempt to address competing demands for land and other resources. Beginning in the 1960s, policy plans became popular. Rather than specify uses of space, policies are established for the planning area that address the goals and aspirations of its inhabitants and/or users. During the 1970s, management plans began to appear. Management plans present guidelines for administrators to consider when making decisions.

Landscape plans combine elements of all these other types of plans. Like master and comprehensive plans, they consider the physical ordering of space, a feature often not addressed in policy plans. Landscape plans also reflect policy and management strategies. More than a land-use plan, a landscape plan recognizes the overlap and integration of land uses. Landscape plans provide a flexible framework for ordering the physical elements of a place. Such a plan is one product of the planning process.

Federal land management agencies and some state governments have specific standards for plans, which vary in what the plans are called and what they are to contain, but include common elements. The National Park Service calls the major planning document for all parks a general management plan. Like other federal land resource agencies—the USFS and the BLM—the NPS combines its plan with the environmental document, either an environmental impact statement or an environmental assessment, which is required by the NEPA (see Chapter 11). Every NPS general management plan contains:

- *Purpose and need for the plan:* a discussion of planning issues, park purpose, legislative mandates, and management objectives
- *Management zoning:* prescribed land classifications to designate where various strategies for management and use will best fulfill management objectives and achieve park purposes
- *Proposal:* interrelated proposals for preservation of resources, land protection, interpretation, visitor use, carrying capacities, park operations, and a general indication of location, size, capacity, and function of physical development
- *Alternatives to the proposal:* different management approaches for dealing with issues, including no action and minimum requirements
- *Plan implementation schedule and cost estimates*
- *Description of the affected environment:* background inventory information
- *Environmental consequences:* Discussion of the proposal and alternatives (adapted from deFranceaux 1987, pp. 15–16)

According to deFranceaux (1987), there are several other elements that may be included in a NPS general management plan. These other components include land suitability analyses, visitor carrying-capacity analyses, a land protection component, discussion of necessary legislative actions, a transportation-access-circulation component, and wilderness studies. Although historically most national park land has been publicly owned, park planners have long had to consider inholdings and adjacent lands. Increasingly, the NPS is responsible for places that include large areas of privately owned lands. As a result, it is important for park service planners to understand traditional city and county planning. There is also much that city and county planners can learn from the long-standing planning efforts of the NPS and other federal land management agencies.

The contents of local government plans and the procedures for adopting them vary from state to state. State enabling legislation defines the scope of local plans and the adoption process. As with many other elements of planning, the state of Oregon has been quite clear about what constitutes a comprehensive plan.

A comprehensive plan is a set of public decisions dealing with how the land, air, and water resources of an area are to be used or not used. These decisions are reached after considering the present and future of an area.

Being comprehensive in scope, the plan provides for all of the resources, uses, public facilities and services in an area. It also incorporates the plans and programs of various governmental units into a single management tool for the planning area. (Land Conservation and Development Commission, 1980, p. 1)

In Oregon, land-use plans are to include an "identification of issues and problems, inventories and other factual information for each . . . goal, evaluation of alternative courses of action and ultimate policy choices, taking into consideration social, economic, energy and environmental needs" (Land Conservation and Development Commission, 1980, p. 4). The guidelines for the contents of the plan are quite specific. First, they are to include the factual basis for the plan: the natural resources, their capabilities and limitations; human-made structures and utilities, their location and conditions; population and economic characteristics; and the roles and responsibilities. Second, the elements of the plan are to be included: the applicable statewide goals, any critical geographic area designated by the state legislature, elements that address any special needs and desires of the people, and the temporal phasing of the plan. These elements are to "fit together and relate to one another to form a consistent whole at all times" (Land Conservation and Development Commission, 1980, p. 4).

Once these findings and elements are compiled in Oregon, the plan and its implementing ordinances are to be adopted by the county or city after a public hearing. Oregon law requires that the plans be filed with the county recorder and that they be approved by the state. The state recognizes the impermanent nature of plans and requires that they be revised periodically.

Whether the planners are addressing private or public lands or both in a federal agency or for a local government, a landscape plan should include at least four key elements: the formal recognition and adoption of the previous steps in the planning process, a statement of policies, the identification of strategies to achieve those policies, and some indication of the physical realization of those policies and strategies. These components will be illustrated by using parts of the Whitman County comprehensive plan and the erosion control plan for the Missouri Flat Creek watershed. At the end of the chapter, the plans of the New Jersey Pinelands and Teller County, Colorado, will be used as examples.

RECOGNITION AND ADOPTION OF PLAN

A key component of the plan is the formal recognition of the findings of the previous steps of the process. The legislative body—the county commission or the city council—adopts a statement summarizing the issues facing the area. Policies are adopted that include the goals to address the problems and opportunities which have been detailed through the process. The biophysical and sociocultural elements are documented in the plan, as are the detailed studies.

The 1978 Whitman County plan, introduced earlier, was actually a revision of the 1970 comprehensive plan. As a result, the plan documented and acknowledged conditions that had changed during the intervening years. The plan recognized three phases in the revision process: broad information gathering, goal setting, and policy-making (Whitman County Regional Planning Council, 1978).

Since 1978 other plans have been developed in Whitman County to address specific issues. Soil erosion has been a vexing problem in the Palouse region. It has been recognized as an issue by governments at all levels for many years, but in spite of many federal programs, the Palouse continues to be one of the most highly erodible regions in the nation. In 1985, a planning effort was undertaken in the Missouri Flat Creek watershed (Figure 7.1) that closely parallels the one being described in this book (Steiner & Osterman, 1988). The Missouri Flat Creek plan took advantage of a new federal law for erosion control (the Food Security Act of 1985) as well as state water quality legislation. Erosion is a major source of water pollution, so the dual goals of soil conservation and water quality could be addressed in the plan.

The plan includes comprehensive descriptions of the biophysical and sociocultural environments of the Missouri Flat Creek watershed. The plan documents erosion and sedimentation problems and the perceptions of farmers about what lands

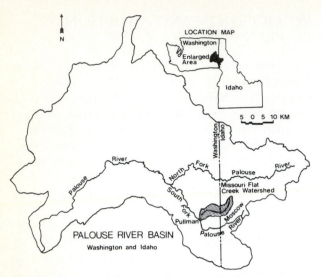

FIGURE 7.1 Location of Missouri Flat Creek watershed. *(Source: Steiner & Osterman, 1988)*

are erodible. Much of the planning effort in the watershed involved getting farmers to recognize that soil erosion and sedimentation were indeed problems and that each farmer was a major contributor to the problem (Osterman, 1988). The plan was the responsibility of the local conservation district, a special-purpose governmental entity.

STATEMENT OF POLICIES

After the documentation and adoption of findings, plans include a statement of policies. These policies may be organized in a variety of ways. Commonly, formal goals and objectives are adopted by the appropriate legislative or administrative body. According to Verburg and Coon, "goals provide statements of the condition that a plan is designed to achieve. A goal is usually not quantifiable and may not have a specific date of accomplishment. Comparatively, objectives focus on measurable results that need to be achieved" (1987, p. 22). A *goal* is a statement of purpose that gives direction for accomplishing

the aspirations of the community, while an *objective* is a statement of the measurable and desired ends that a community will achieve to accomplish its aspirations. Often the terms goal and objective are used interchangeably, but they are different. Whatever terms are used in a plan, it is important to link broad policies with specific strategies to achieve the goals.

The Whitman County comprehensive plan includes six elements: land use, transportation, economic development, environmental quality and natural conservation, parks and recreation, and implementation. In each element, there is a statement of purpose for the element, goal(s), goal rationale, planning guidelines, and implementation guidelines. In comparison, the Missouri Flat Creek plan has a single goal, three objectives, and four strategies to achieve the objectives.

The Whitman County goals and policies are designed to guide the decision making of the planning commissions and the county commissioners. The *purpose of the element* explains its context as part of the plan and the role of the planning commission in carrying out the element. The *goals* are broad statements of community direction. The *goal rationale* explains the specific reasons for including it in the plan. The *planning and implementation guidelines* are the official policies of the county for the development of standards, procedures, and cooperation for implementing the plan (Whitman County Regional Planning Council, 1978).

The Whitman County land-use element includes goals and guidelines for agricultural, rural residential, suburban and urban residential, industrial, commercial, and public facilities uses as well as for unincorporated rural communities. One reason for including the land-use element is that it is required by the Washington law that enables planning and zoning. The purpose of the land-use element is "to serve directly as a basis for local policies on land-use changes" (Whitman County Regional Planning Council, 1978, p. 25).

A system of parallel level terraces controls sheet erosion on this land. *(USDA—Soil Conservation Service)*

The agricultural and rural residential portions of the land-use elements were discussed in Chapter 5. Here, suburban and urban residential land use will be described. It is the county's goal to "discourage urban and suburban development outside incorporated areas in Whitman County, except within designated unincorporated communities" (Whitman County Regional Planning Council, 1978, p. 28). This policy was based on four factors identified during the planning process. First, concentrations of residential units adjacent to farmland were a condition that resulted in land-use conflicts. Second, land users at suburban densities had expectations of public service levels that were not and could not be provided by a rural county. Third, suburban development adjacent to city boundaries was seldom annexed, because rural subdivisions were often constructed to standards different than those of the potentially annexing city.

Fourth, growth was occurring slowly and, as a result, could be absorbed by the cities and towns in the county (Whitman County Regional Planning Council, 1978). The Whitman County policy for suburban and urban land use was adopted in response to these tendencies and the resulting issues that were created for local officials.

The Missouri Flat Creek watershed plan, developed a decade later in Whitman County, was the result of a collaborative effort among several groups, including the Palouse Conservation District, the Washington Conservation Commission, the Washington Department of Ecology, SCS, and the Program in Environmental Science and Regional Planning at Washington State University. People from these organizations formed a planning team whose work was funded by the state through its Agricultural Wastes Grant Program, approved by voters in a 1980 referendum. This state law authorizes funding for agricultural waste management purposes to control agricultural non-point-source pollution. *Non-point-source pollutants* are those that derive from a broad area rather than a single place. Soil erosion is a major non-point source of pollution.

The Missouri Flat Creek watershed plan seeks to control non-point-source pollution through the compliance provisions of the federal Food Security Act. Thus, the plan will help farmers comply with these provisions, assist SCS in preparing federally required conservation plans, and address broader resource management concerns, including water quality.

The Missouri Flat Creek watershed is near Albion and covers 17,530 acres (7,100 hectares) in parts of Whitman County, Washington, and Latah County, Idaho. The creek arises on the slopes of the Palouse Range north of Moscow, Idaho. From there, it flows southwesterly to the heart of Pullman, where it empties into the South Fork of the Palouse River. The watershed is part of the larger Palouse River drainage basin, a 2 million acre (810,000 hectare) catchment in Washington and Idaho. The Palouse region is famous for its beauty, agricultural productivity, and severe erosion.

The dual problems of soil erosion and degraded water quality in the Palouse region have been identified in numerous studies. Goals to address these interrelated problems have been established at the federal level through non-point-source pollution control laws and at the local level through policies of both the Palouse Conservation District and Whitman County in its 1978 comprehensive plan. A specific sediment-reduction goal was indited in the watershed plan.

The goal of the Missouri Flat Creek watershed plan to reduce and ultimately to eliminate sediment in Missouri Flat Creek resulted in an action-oriented plan with the three policy objectives of problem awareness, providing awareness of solutions, and implementing solutions (Osterman et al., 1989). Creating problem awareness, objective one, relied on farmer and agency interaction. Through watershed evaluations, surveys, meetings, workshops, and one-on-one communication, the idea was to move farmers from awareness to action. By approaching this awareness at a watershed level, the farmers felt they were part of a community and recognized the landscape dynamics occurring in the watershed. This encouraged cooperation and the flow of information among them.

Problem awareness was followed by a program that provided farmers with solutions, objective two, tailored to the natural and social systems of the watershed. Individual conservation plans were used to create awareness of solutions. Policy objective three, implementation of solutions, provided a framework for putting soil conservation practices on the ground. Economic incentives and technical expertise were used to encourage farmers to adopt these practices. Information and education activities seek to give farmers reasons to implement permanent soil conservation practices.

STRATEGIES TO ACHIEVE POLICIES

Strategies outline the approach and/or methods through which problems are solved or minimized and objectives are achieved (Verburg & Coon, 1987). A *strategy* is the broadly stated means of deploying resources to achieve the community's goals and objectives. The plan should specify what actions are necessary to achieve its objectives. For each planning element, there should be clear definitions of terms so that there is no confusion between light or heavy industrial use or low-density or high-density residential use. Each strategy should contain specific actions, for instance, "the county or city shall adopt land-use ordinances to implement its policies." There should also be target dates associated with specific actions, for instance, "soil erosion shall be reduced to tolerable levels by the year 2010." Thus, strategies should be linked to *outcome measures* that are specific means of determining if goals and objectives are being accomplished.

In the 1978 Whitman County plan, the planning and implementation guidelines were intended to give guidance for the development of local ordinances. The first goal for industrial land use was to "provide a basis for public and private decisions concerning the siting of new light industrial land use as a means of supporting the long-term economic health" of the county (Whitman County Regional Planning Council, 1978, p. 29). Light industrial land use was defined as small manufacturing establishments. Planning guidelines were provided for determining the site suitability for light industrial use. In addition, several "light industrial opportunity areas" were identified as places to encourage such use. The implementation guidelines specified that approvals for light industrial use would only be granted in those opportunity areas. A second goal stated that only sites along the Snake River would be used for heavy industrial use. The idea was to encourage the further development of port sites along the Snake River.

For the Missouri Flat Creek plan, the strategies for achieving the three objectives are (1) to plan and implement actions on a watershed basis, taking into consideration the social, political, economic, institutional, and biophysical processes of the area; (2) to implement farm conservation plans on all the cropland in the watershed; (3) to stabilize the stream bank and channel of the creek; and (4) to supplement all actions with areawide education and information programs (Osterman et al., 1989).

The first strategy attempts to link individual actions to the processes occurring throughout the watershed. The mechanism to effect individual actions is farm conservation plans, the second strategy. One reason for the watershed approach is that soil movement and stream sedimentation transcend individual properties. The third strategy to stabilize the stream bank and the channel of the

Missouri Flat Creek benefits farmers in the watershed and people downstream including urban residents and fishers. Another reason for the watershed approach is to make the dissemination of information about erosion and sedimentation control easier. By bringing groups of farmers together at the watershed level, education programs can be conducted more effectively, and the opportunity for neighbors to positively influence neighbors about land-use practices is enhanced.

The implementation of the Missouri Flat Creek watershed plan included the use of educational and technical assistance, cost-sharing programs, and the conservation provisions of the Food Security Act, as well as the consideration of other options. Educational and technical assistance under this program concentrated on three problem areas. First, in some cases farmers do not recognize that erosion is occurring on their land, or, even if they do, they do not realize the rate at which it is happening. Second, farmers often do not understand erosion's damaging effects, both on-farm, such as lost productivity, and off-farm, such as impaired water quality. Unaware of these problems, the farm operators may see no reason to implement soil conservation measures. Third, even if they are aware of these two facts, they may not be sure of the best systems for controlling erosion or have misconceptions about those systems. Additional educational and technical assistance in these three areas was viewed by planners as critical. Successful implementation depends upon farmers understanding and believing in the goals of the program.

Solutions for controlling erosion were implemented through various cost-sharing programs that have attempted to encourage the adoption of soil conservation measures for a long time. However, with the enactment of the Food Security Act, cost sharing is no longer the only economic incentive that encourages the adoption of soil conservation measures. The conservation compliance provision of the act requires that farm operators with highly

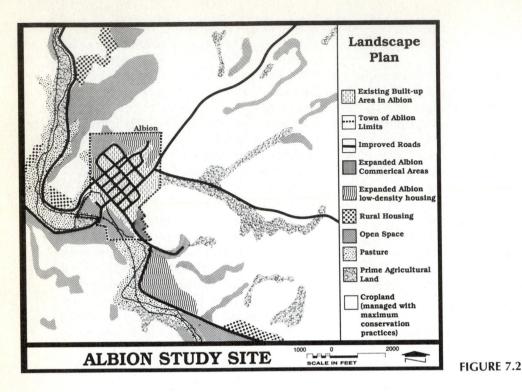

ALBION STUDY SITE

Landscape Plan

Existing Built-up Area in Albion

Town of Albion Limits

Improved Roads

Expanded Albion Commerical Areas

Expanded Albion low-density housing

Rural Housing

Open Space

Pasture

Prime Agricultural Land

Cropland (managed with maximum conservation practices)

SCALE IN FEET

FIGURE 7.2

erodible land (97 percent of the watershed) practice approved soil conservation measures to remain eligible for federal agricultural programs.   Additionally, a large percentage of the land area in the watershed is eligible for the conservation reserve program, which pays farmers not to farm highly erodible cropland.   Other options that were explored to implement the plan included long-term contracts, public purchase, and additional research.

LANDSCAPE PLAN MAP

The landscape plan map should attempt to physically represent information collected and decisions reached in the previous steps in the planning process.   It should reflect existing land uses and land users.   The plan should also consider potential land users, who can be identified

through population projections.   Their impact on the land can be analyzed by making development projections for various uses.   Environmentally sensitive or constraint areas that present a concern because of health, safety, or welfare considerations should be mapped.   Composite suitabilities should be included in the landscape plan map as should preferred concepts or options considered for the area.

Figure 7.2 is a landscape plan for Albion. Population projections for the area indicate that relatively little growth can be expected for the near future.   There is ample land within the city limits to accommodate future housing needs.   Whitman County policy encourages growth in existing cities; it also seeks to provide opportunities for rural housing and to protect agricultural land.   The landscape plan reflects both goals.   Some land adjacent to Albion has been identified for future commercial and limited low-density residential use. These areas would be annexed to Albion.   The plan identifies environmentally sensitive areas—flood-plains and steep slopes—where development should not occur and the land used as open space. Most of the Palouse is highly erodible land. As a result, these lands are identified because farming in these areas should be undertaken using conservation practices.

The landscape plan is based largely on the options developed previously in the process (see Chapter 6). Because of county policies and implementation measures, the agricultural protection and enhancement options (Figure 6.1) are reflected most strongly in the map. The bedroom community option (Figure 6.3) also had an impact on the spatial organization represented on the map.

The four key elements of a landscape plan (the recognition and adoption of the findings of the process, policy statements, strategies, and a map) can be organized as follows.

OUTLINE OF LANDSCAPE PLAN ELEMENTS
1. Summary of major recommendations
2. Recognition and adoption of findings
   a. Purpose and need of the plan
      (1) Problems and/or opportunities
      (2) Planning issue(s)
      (3) Enabling legislation
   b. Affected environment
      (1) Biophysical environment
      (2) Sociocultural environment
   c. Detailed studies
      (1) Population and development projections
      (2) Suitability analysis: opportunities and constraints for development and conservation
3. Policy statements
   a. Residential land use
      (1) Goal(s) and objective(s)
      (2) Goal rationale
   b. Commercial land use
      (1) Goal(s) and objective(s)
      (2) Goal rationale
   c. Industrial land use
      (1) Goal(s) and objective(s)
      (2) Goal rationale
   d. Agricultural land use
      (1) Goal(s) and objective(s)
      (2) Goal rationale
   e. Public facilities land use
      (1) Goal(s) and objective(s)
      (2) Goal rationale
   f. Parks and recreation
      (1) Goal(s) and objective(s)
      (2) Goal rationale
   g. Transportation
      (1) Goal(s) and objective(s)
      (2) Goal rationale
   h. Environmental quality
      (1) Goal(s) and objective(s)
      (2) Goal rationale
   i. Economic development
      (1) Goal(s) and objective(s)
      (2) Goal rationale
4. Implementation strategies
   a. Residential land use
      (1) Definitions
      (2) Implementation actions
      (3) Enforcement provisions
      (4) Compliance dates
   b. Commercial land use
      (1) Definitions
      (2) Implementation actions
      (3) Enforcement provisions
      (4) Compliance dates
   c. Industrial land use
      (1) Definitions
      (2) Implementation actions
      (3) Enforcement provisions
      (4) Compliance dates
   d. Agricultural land use
      (1) Definitions
      (2) Implementation actions
      (3) Enforcement provisions
      (4) Compliance dates
   e. Public facilities land use
      (1) Definitions

(2) Implementation actions

(3) Enforcement provisions

(4) Compliance dates

f. Parks and recreation

(1) Definitions

(2) Implementation actions

(3) Enforcement provisions

(4) Compliance dates

g. Transportation

(1) Definitions

(2) Implementation actions

(3) Enforcement provisions

(4) Compliance dates

h. Environmental quality

(1) Definitions

(2) Implementation actions

(3) Enforcement provisions

(4) Compliance dates

i. Economic development

(1) Definitions

(2) Implementation actions

(3) Enforcement provisions

(4) Compliance dates

5. Landscape plan map

Bibliography

Glossary

TWO EXAMPLES OF PLANS

Comprehensive Management Plan for the New Jersey Pinelands

The comprehensive management plan for the New Jersey Pinelands has been used in earlier chapters as an example of establishing planning goals (Chapter 2) and inventory and analysis (Chapters 3 and 4). The process undertaken by state, federal, and local officials resulted in an exemplary plan. The plan is divided into two parts. The first part documents the natural and human history of the Pine Barrens, describes regional growth factors, identifies ecologically critical areas, establishes goals and policies, lays out the structure for

intergovernmental coordination, and establishes the financial and public participation programs. The second part contains the legal, substantive land-use programs and development standards that implement the plan. This part sets forth the procedures under which the Pinelands Commission certifies that county and local master plans and implementing ordinances are consistent with the plan (Pinelands Commission, 1980). Like in Oregon, all county and local plans in the Pinelands region must be consistent with the goals for the larger area.

The heart of the Pinelands plan is its resource goals and policies. The goals in Table 2.1 were established by the Pinelands Commission based on its analysis and on provisions of state and federal legislation. These goals and policies also reflect the land capability of the area. The land capability map identifies those areas which are most suited for preservation, forestry, agriculture, rural development and growth as well as existing towns and villages and military and federal installations. From the capabilities for these uses, eight allocation areas are defined in the plan as follows:

The *Preservation Area District* represents that area found by the New Jersey Legislature to be "especially vulnerable to the environmental degradation of surface and ground waters which would be [negatively impacted] by the improper development or use thereof;" and "which constitutes an extensive and contiguous area of land in its natural state."

The *Agricultural Production Areas,* occurring in both the Preservation and Protection Areas, represent those areas that are primarily devoted to field agricultural uses, and adjoining lands with soil conditions suitable for those farming activities.

The *Special Agricultural Production Areas,* occurring in the Preservation Area, represent those areas devoted to berry agricultural and native horticultural uses, and the adjoining lands utilized for watershed protection, to be designated at the option of the municipality.

The *Military and Federal Installation Area,* occurring in both the Preservation and Protection Areas, represents major federal landholdings with an established land-use pattern and providing significant benefits to the people of the Pinelands.

The *Forest Areas* of the Protection Area represent largely undisturbed forest and coastal wetland areas adjoining the Preservation Area and extending into the southern section of the Pinelands. The Commission has determined that these areas possess "the essential character of the existing Pinelands environment," which the Legislature said was the Commission's responsibility to "preserve and maintain."

The *Rural Development Areas* in the Protection Area represent those transitional areas that generally separate growth areas from the less developed, predominantly forested areas of the Pinelands. These areas are somewhat fragmented by existing development and serve a dual purpose as buffers and reserves for future development.

The *Regional Growth Areas* represent those land areas that are (1) in or adjacent to existing developed areas, (2) experiencing growth demands and pressure for development, and (3) capable of accommodating development without jeopardizing the most critical elements of the Pinelands environment.

Pinelands Towns and Villages are spatially discrete existing developed areas. Most of these settlements have cultural, historical, and commercial ties to the Pinelands environment, while others represent areas of concentrated residential, commercial, and industrial development. (Pinelands Commission, 1980, pp. 195–196)

These allocation areas formed the basis for a

FIGURE 7.3 New Jersey Pinelands preservation areas and protection area. *(Source: Pinelands Commission, 1980)*

planning map that designated preservation and protection areas in the national reserve (Figure 7.3). The Pinelands plan is based, first, on state and federal law, then, second, on the five resource and use goals and the twenty-five related policies (Table 2.1). These goals and policies then led to the spatial description of the region and the allocation of appropriate land uses among the different areas. From this allocation, programs were developed "to ensure that activities allowed within different areas are compatible with the characteristics of particular sites" (Pinelands Commission, 1980, p. 193).

There were seventeen programs developed plus strategies for areas adjacent to the Pinelands that are important for water management or cultural viability. The seventeen programs address development credits; land acquisition; surface and ground water resources; vegetation and wildlife; wetlands; fire management; forestry; air quality; cultural resources; natural scenic resources; agriculture; waste management; resource extraction; recreation; housing; capital improvements; and data management.

The Pinelands development credit program is one of the more innovative elements of the plan. The Pinelands Comprehensive Management Plan establishes a land-use regulatory system that limits residential development in environmentally sensitive regions. Concurrently, the plan seeks to direct growth toward designated areas in a more compact pattern. The development credit program supplements land-use regulations. Development credits are provided to landowners in preservation and agricultural areas where residential uses are limited or prohibited. The credits can be sold by the landowners from these restricted areas to individuals in growth areas. The landowners in the growth areas use the credits to gain bonus residential densities. According to Pinelands planners, the credits "thus provide a mechanism for landowners in the [restricted] areas to participate in any increase in development values which is realized in growth areas" (Pinelands Commission, 1980, p. 210). (For more discussion about the transfer-of-development-rights concept, see Chapter 10.)

Teller County/City of Woodland Park, Colorado, Growth Management Plan

The city of Woodland Park in Teller County, Colorado, is located 20 miles (32 kilometers) west of Colorado Springs, which has a metropolitan population of nearly 400,000 (Figure 7.4). This proximity to Colorado Springs is a source of both opportunity and problems for Woodland Park and Teller County. The scenic Rocky Mountain location makes the city and county attractive places for growth. The growth, in turn, has the potential to destroy the very natural and scenic qualities that attract people in the first place.

Gold mining created boomtown settlement in the late nineteenth century. With the demise of mining, the population declined until the 1960s. Teller County's population had peaked in 1900 at around 30,000* and bottomed out at 2,495 persons in 1960 (Ansbro et al., 1988; Steiner et al., 1989). Between 1970 and 1980, the population increased 142.3 percent to 8,024. This growth has continued, and the population is expected to double between 1980 and 2000. Most of these people have settled in and around Woodland Park, which has become a "bedroom community" for Colorado Springs. The majority of Woodland Park residents commute over 30 minutes to work, which emphasizes the economic linkage to Colorado Springs (U.S. Bureau of the Census, 1983).

The continued growth of Teller County and Woodland Park raises several specific issues that need to be addressed by local officials and planners. A primary concern of local residents is that new development should not be a burden on taxpayers. A second important issue involves the quality of new development. It is felt that there should be policies and guidelines that ensure quality development. A third concern is that new development be timed and sequenced with the ability of local governments to provide services and facilities. These three issues have been identified by local residents through an ongoing public participation process initiated by local citizens. Once the concerns were publicly identified, there was a desire that the issues generated by growth be addressed.

As a result, planners and citizens of Woodland Park and Teller County initiated a growth management process in cooperation with the

---

* Although transient populations during the nineteenth century gold rush as high as 160,000 have been reported, somewhere around 30,000 people appears to have been the peak resident population.

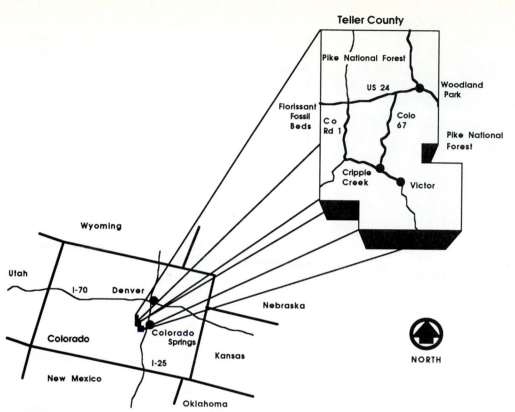

FIGURE 7.4 Location of Teller County and Woodland Park, Colorado.

School of Architecture and Planning, University of Colorado at Denver. Through the School of Architecture and Planning, Teller County and the city of Woodland Park involved two planning studios in the development of a growth management plan. The first phase of the work involved research and data collection in the fall of 1988. Students from the planning studio inventoried and analyzed natural and social conditions of the Woodland Park growth management area as well as the whole county (Ansbro et al., 1988; Bowie et al., 1988). There were two teams of students, one working on Teller County and the second on Woodland Park. The teams collected and interpreted, in reports and on maps, information about natural resources, including the funda-mental geologic, hydrologic, and bioclimatic proc-esses that form the landscape. They also collected information about the socioeconomic and built en-vironments of Teller County. They conducted sur-veys about the public attitudes concerning growth. This information was presented to county and city officials and planners to provide a basis for under-standing environmentally sensitive areas and oppor-tunities and constraints for development. Suitabil-ity analyses were conducted for several land uses at both the city and the county levels.

The second phase was undertaken during the spring of 1989. Again there were two teams of students: one each for Teller County and Woodland Park. These two teams made detailed population and development projections for the county.

(Frederick Steiner)

Essentially, because of its proximity to Colorado Springs and its scenic mountain location, the county's population has been growing and is expected to continue to grow. The students developed visions and concepts for the county and the city as well as landscape plans and development design guides. Detailed designs were completed for specific areas in the region (see Chapter 9). The students analyzed options to implement the growth management plan. In addition, they developed a point system for development review that recognized environmentally sensitive areas and set performance criteria for various land uses.

The plan is one that attempts to direct new growth to suitable areas and away from environmentally sensitive places. The Teller County and Woodland Park landscape plans prepared by the students influenced the growth management plan adopted by county and city officials (Petersen et al., 1989). The Teller County landscape plan (Figure 7.5) was based on the landscape patterns plus the opportunities and constraints for development that were derived from the ecological inventory and analysis. Several conceptual visions were used to formulate the plan. The concepts for Teller County were to preserve and enhance its

rural and historic character, its scenic views, its economic base including outdoor recreation and tourism, and its identity and sense of community. Additional Teller County concepts included the integration of development into the landscape, the interpretation and protection of the county's rich history, the creation of a tourism circulation system using existing roads, and the protection of environmentally sensitive areas (Bell et al., 1989).

The resulting landscape plan is an attempt to order the physical elements of the county in response to these concepts. The Teller County plan (Figure 7.5) comprises the following components of land use: residential, urban, historic mining district, water recreation, scenic roadways, entryways, public lands, and rangeland (Bell et al., 1989). Three categories of future residential development indicate primary, secondary, and tertiary locations for new housing. Urban centers are represented on the plan as three unincorporated communities, two towns, and the city of Woodland Park (which was addressed in a separate landscape plan). Within these centers, the land uses are a combination of commercial, office, industrial, recreational, and residential. Two of the centers—Cripple Creek and Victor—are further recognized for their historic value. The two towns are part of a historic district listed on the National Register of Historic Places (Bell et al., 1989).

Eight areas are designated in the plan for future water recreation use, currently an underutilized resource in the county. The plan also suggested the creation of a scenic tourism circulation system that would include improving the quality of entryways into the county. These scenic roadways would take advantage of the stunning visual resources in the area. Since public lands constitute almost half the county, the lands managed by the state and federal government provide an additional resource for tourism and recreation. Finally, the landscape plan designated rangeland areas that are important as open space and as a reminder of the cowboy heritage of the county (Bell et al., 1989).

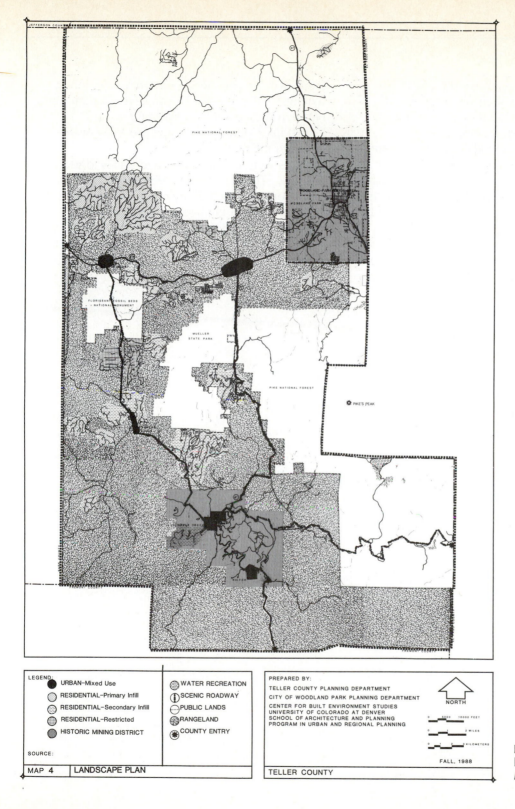

FIGURE 7.5 Teller County landscape plan. *(Source: Bell et al., 1989)*

187

The Pinelands and Teller County plans differ from conventional comprehensive plans in the recognition of landscape ecology. In the Pine Barrens, where it is called a comprehensive management plan, critical landscape features are documented, recognized, and protected. In the Pinelands plan, the goal is established to "preserve, protect, and enhance the overall ecological values of the Pinelands." This goal is backed up both by specific policies and detailed implementation strategies. These policies and programs are concerned with soil, water, biotic, air, and human elements. The areas most suited for protection and for growth are identified both on a map and in writing. The plan seeks to achieve a balance between preservation and development.

In Teller County, landscape processes were linked to the planning process. Landscape analyses were conducted at two scales to reveal patterns. These patterns were recognized first in a set of concepts for Teller County and Woodland Park and then in landscape plans for each. The landscape plans differ from conventional land-use plans in their recognition of integrated, rather than separated, uses.

8

CONTINUING CITIZEN INVOLVEMENT AND COMMUNITY EDUCATION

Education is a lifelong process that should seek to achieve awareness, balanced perception, learning, and decision making. To accomplish these goals, individuals must develop a functional understanding of their cultural inheritance as well as the ability to contribute in a positive manner to society. Education occurs through the traditional institutions identified for that purpose, through continuing involvement in a discipline, through community programs, and, in the broadest sense, through popular culture.

Many planners have urged that public education and involvement efforts be integrated thoroughly into each step of the planning process. For instance, according to Lassey:

If planning is to be successful, a major reordering of public education, involvement, and communication processes may be necessary. Existing scientific knowledge about effective communication processes, and knowledge about human learning provide vastly increased potential for public understanding, appreciation, and involvement in significant societal decisions. Formal education methods for diffusing information and internalizing knowledge are archaic compared with potential learning capability of the human population. It is increasingly clear that lifelong educational processes are essential for adequate human adjustment to changing job requirements and life-styles, but effective communication of knowledge crucial to public decision making is equally important if the planet is to survive. (1977, p. 74)

As a result, education must be both future-oriented and ongoing. Continuing education should assist people in making linkages between their individual skills and interests and larger public issues. Without such linkages, the rules and regulations developed to protect people's health, safety, and welfare will be treated with suspicion by those whom they were meant to protect. Although education and citizen involvement should be considered central and integral to each step in the planning process as indicated by Figure 1.1, it is placed here in the process as a reminder that even after a landscape plan has been developed, continued explanation about the plan is often necessary before it is implemented.

Citizen involvement techniques can be classified as information dissemination, information collection, initiative planning, reactive planning, decision making, and participation process support. Community organization, publications, and television and radio can be used in a community education program. Two examples of planning efforts that have included an educational element include the University of Wisconsin community development program and the Davis, California, energy planning program.

CITIZEN INVOLVEMENT

One of the major purposes of planning is to involve citizens in their government. A program should be developed that seeks to involve all citizens in each step of the planning process. There is no formula as to how to involve citizens in all phases of planning. The characteristics of such an open planning process are easy to identify. According to the U.S. Department of Transportation, "Openness means that the purpose and the content of the process as well as the schedule for doing it, are described as clearly and concretely as possible—the decisions that have to be made, the information that will be used to make them, the choices which are and are not open for consideration and why, and the time when different steps are necessary and desirable" (1976, p. 8).

Many state laws and legislation for federal land management agencies mandate such involvement. In Oregon, for instance, county and city governments, which are responsible for preparing and adopting comprehensive plans, must have a program that involves the public in an iterative way. The Oregon citizen involvement program has six components:

1. Citizen involvement
2. Communication
3. Citizen influence
4. Technical information
5. Feedback mechanisms
6. Financial support (Land Conservation and Development Commission 1980, p. 3)

The guidelines for the citizen involvement component stipulate that the program should use a range of media, including television, radio, newspapers, mailings, and meetings. Oregon universities, colleges, community colleges, high schools, and grade schools are to provide information and courses about land-use planning. The program is also to include an officially recognized citizens advisory committee or committees. This committee is responsible for assisting the county commission or city council in the involvement effort (Land Conservation and Development Commission, 1980).

Two-way communication between the governing

body and the public is to be assured in Oregon cities and counties. Mechanisms such as newsletters, mailings, posters, and mail-back questionnaires are recommended. The purpose of the involvement and the communication is to give Oregon citizens direct influence in the planning process. Citizens are to be involved in data collection, plan preparation, the adoption process, implementation, evaluation, and revision (Land Conservation and Development Commission, 1980).

Planners in Oregon are responsible to "assure that technical information is available in an understandable form." There is also a requirement that "feedback mechanisms" exist to "assure that citizens will receive a response" from policymakers. Finally, Oregon law requires that there be adequate financial support to ensure "funding for the citizen involvement program" (Land Conservation and Development Commission, 1980, p. 3).

All federal land management agencies have guidelines for public participation, but the requirements vary. For instance, the intent of public participation in the National Forest System is to:

- Ensure that the U.S. Forest Service understands the needs and concerns of the public
- Inform the public of U.S. Forest Service land and resource planning activities
- Provide the public with an understanding of U.S. Forest Service programs and proposed actions
- Broaden the information base upon which land and resource management planning decisions are made
- Demonstrate that public issues and inputs are considered and evaluated in reaching planning decisions (adapted from U.S. Congress, 1979)

One of the reasons why federal land management agencies have public participation programs is to comply with NEPA requirements and regulations (see Chapter 11). As a result of NEPA, federal land planning activities are subject to environ-

One of the major purposes of an open planning process is to involve residents in their government. *(Washington State University College of Agriculture and Home Economics)*

mental impact reviews. USFS public participation efforts include keeping the news media informed of planning actions. Other activities include "requests for written comments, meetings, conferences, seminars, workshops, tours, and similar events designed to foster public review and participation" (U.S. Congress, 1979, p. 53988). To increase information about its plans, the USFS is supposed to coordinate its planning activities among all levels of government, including other federal agencies, state and local governments, and Indian nations.

CLASSIFICATION OF CITIZEN PARTICIPATION TECHNIQUES

The U.S. Department of Transportation (1976) has classified citizen participation techniques, such as those described in Chapters 2 and 6, on the basis of their function, as follows:

- Information dissemination
- Information collection
- Initiative planning
- Reactive planning
- Decision making
- Participation process support

Although a technique may have more than one function, the classification is based on its primary purpose. The information dissemination class "contains techniques which inform the public of any steps the agency is taking, any opportunities the public has to [influence] the process, and the proposed plans that have been brought forward" (U.S. Department of Transportation, 1976, p. 18). Various community education and information programs and open meetings are examples of this technique classification.

Information collection techniques are used to identify the major issues facing a community or to assess the attitudes which that community may have regarding the issues. These techniques can also be used to determine the public support for planning goals, policies, and strategies as well as to collect inventory information. Surveys, public opinion polls, Delphi, community sponsored meetings, public hearings, and participant observation are some ways information is collected (see Chapter 4).

In initiative planning, the responsibility for producing proposals and structuring options is assigned to the community or its representatives. Planning agencies, meanwhile, supply information and technical assistance. Conversely, in reactive planning, it is the agency that makes the proposals and the community that reacts. Advocacy planning, task forces, workshops, and charrettes are examples of initiative planning. Citizens advisory committees are an example of reactive planning (U.S. Department of Transportation, 1976).

Decision-making techniques are designed to help a community develop a consensus on an issue, a goal, an option, or a plan. Such techniques do not replace the responsibilities of elected or appointed officials but are intended to augment them. Referenda, which may in fact be binding, and citizen review boards are two decision-making techniques (U.S. Department of Transportation 1976).

The final classification is participation process support techniques. According to the Department of Transportation (1976), these methods serve to make other types of techniques more effective and cut across all the other categories. Citizen honoraria may be used, for instance, to compensate people for being involved in the process. Such payment may permit people to become active who would not be able to otherwise. But paying people to be citizens raises important ethical questions about the responsibilities of people in a democracy. Another technique is citizen training, where individuals are taught leadership and planning skills (U.S. Department of Transportation, 1976).

CONTINUING COMMUNITY EDUCATION

Public participation is concerned with both involving people in the process and then continuing to inform citizens about changes and adjustments to the plan and its implementation and administration. Once a community is organized for the process, some form of that organization can continue. For example, in the New Jersey Pinelands a commission was established that is responsible for involving people in the planning process and establishing a continuing information effort. The public participation program included activities like workshops and conferences, public workshops on specific topics, personal communications and meetings, and the use of knowledgeable private individuals for guidance in research areas of interests to the Pinelands Commission (Pinelands Commission, 1980). Means to keep people involved include publications such as newsletters, television, and radio.

Information and Education

In addition to being a means for the establishment of goals and for the selection of preferences, community organizations can provide information and education and can keep people involved. As reviewed in Chapters 2 and 6, there are various

Here, a film is being produced to explain a planning program. *(Frederick Steiner)*

types of organizations that can be used in a community, including task forces, advisory committees, and neighborhood councils. Such groups might sponsor a lecture by an expert and/or the showing of a film or a slide presentation. Other meetings may take the form of a workshop where the group interacts with facilitators or with a two-way television connected with an individual or individuals or another group or groups.

Information can also be presented to communities through conferences and symposia. Community colleges, universities, or the Cooperative Extension Service may be used to help organize such gatherings. Professional and academic associations may be contacted for involvement as well. Since many members of associations are required to receive a certain number of hours of continuing education credit annually, conference organizers may want to arrange to offer credit when appropriate. The content of conferences and symposia may range from that of a general nature to very advanced. For example in the Pinelands, conferences and workshops have been organized ranging from rather simple question and answer sessions to academic conferences on the ecology and culture of the Pine Barrens.

Planners are often invited to community organizations and clubs, such as those listed in

Table 4.1, to make presentations. These are good opportunities to explain the planning process. Youth groups, such as the Scouts and 4-H, also often invite speakers to their meetings.

The Pinelands Commission developed a continuing program based on providing information to the public, creating awareness through education, and involving people in the implementation of the plan. According to the Pinelands Commission:

> The public has to be kept informed of the Commission's activities and the purpose of the Comprehensive Management Plan. Public information efforts must reach as wide and diverse an audience as possible. Educational materials have to be provided, emphasizing the sensitive nature of the Pinelands' resources and detailing critical issues related to their protection. Points at which public involvement is most meaningful have to be highlighted, with a range of opportunities provided for both active and passive involvement. The overall program must be visible, continuous, and responsive. (1980, p. 330)

Pinelands planners recognized that overlap would necessarily occur among the information, education, and involvement: "All information is educational in nature, and education requires involvement" (Pinelands Commission, 1980, p. 330). Publications such as newsletters and interaction with reporters from the print and electronic media are crucial elements of the public information program in the Pinelands.

In the view of the commission, the Pinelands are "a living laboratory" for education. Similarly, any place, any landscape can be considered a classroom to study natural, physical, and cultural processes. In the Pinelands, state and regional resources have been utilized to develop curriculum material for students and teachers at both the primary and secondary school levels. Bibliographic and library resources have been created as part of the process and have been made available to teachers and researchers. With the NPS, interpretation programs about recreational areas and historic sites have been developed. A speakers bureau was created to match experts on various topics with community groups. In addition, the commission developed ongoing educational activities with private nonprofit and public organizations like 4-H, the Boy and Girl Scouts, garden clubs, and environmental groups (Pinelands Commission, 1980).

The Pinelands Commission attempts to keep the public involved in a number of ways. There are the meetings of the commission and its subcommittees. Advisory committees established during the planning process remain intact. The commission also maintains its liaison with county and municipal governments (Pinelands Commission, 1980). Planning depends on the involvement of people. To keep people involved, planners must provide timely and accurate information and create educational opportunities. There are several media that can be utilized for information and education.

Publications

Many types of publications are helpful educational tools: newspapers, popular magazines, extension bulletins, planning agency reports and manuals, and professional journals. Newspapers are, of course, quite interested in planning issues at stages of controversy. Often the passage of a new plan or regulation can hinge on how it is reported in local newspapers and the ebb and flow of letters to the editor. Concise press releases are helpful to brief reporters during periods of controversy. Press releases should include the name, address, and phone number of the chief contact on the planning staff as well as a succinct summary of the debate. It may also be necessary to include dates and places of meetings and hearings.

Equally important, journalists should be informed during less heated times. Ecological inventory information makes interesting copy for Sunday supplements or series by nature reporters. A rare plant or animal species can arouse much public interest. Popular magazines may be used in much the same way. Regional and city magazines are a

good forum. *Southern Living,* for instance, has published especially good articles on planning issues such as historic preservation, energy conservation, and farmlands protection. In addition, *Southern Living* is an advocate of regional natural and cultural ecology. Articles about flora and fauna mixed with vernacular architecture and rich southern literary comment are common.

One nationwide educational organization with an extensive publication program is the Cooperative Extension Service. As its name indicates, the extension service is a cooperative organization that involves federal, state, and local governments as well as state land-grant universities. The mission of the Cooperative Extension Service is to foster the transfer of technological and scientific knowledge generated from land-grant university research to the citizens of each state and to encourage adoption of that knowledge. Although the extension service is active in urban areas, its traditional clientele is rural people. Broadly the subject matter to be addressed by the extension service is to be related to agriculture and home economics. Publications are the major device that the extension service has used to disseminate information. The Cooperative Extension Service works with both local officials and the public. While the extension service vigorously promotes the transfer of knowledge and information, it does not take positions on political issues. In several areas, the extension service has collaborated with local agencies to provide and to distribute publications about planning.

The Cooperative Extension Service prints helpful planning-related reports and bulletins in many states. They cannot print advocacy publications. However, the extension service can provide information helpful for citizens to gain a better understanding about planning issues and techniques. One noteworthy example is the "Coping with Growth" series published by the Western Rural Development Center, a consortium of western land-grant universities. This informative series addresses topics such as community needs assessment, population studies, fiscal and social impacts, and citizen involvement and is available through the Western Rural Development Center, Oregon State University, Corvallis, Oregon. Similar rural development consortia of land-grant universities exist in the east, south, and midwest.

Planning agency reports and manuals are important educational tools. Some of these reports must be technical and thus will have a limited readership; others, however, should be written for a broader audience. Manuals in simple English that explain regulatory procedures are especially helpful for real estate agents, home builders, and developers. Packets explaining a community comprehensive plan, zoning ordinance, subdivision regulations, public services, cultural activities, and natural and social histories are interesting to new residents of an area.

Professional and academic journals address a narrower audience. Such publications are invaluable forums for sharing experiences. But planners should not be constricted by disciplinary territorialism. They should read, and publish in, journals of the many related disciplines. This is a way to build needed linkages among people trained or educated in various fields.

Television and Radio

Television is a ubiquitous part of American life, while radio provides an ongoing narration of public events. Commercial television and radio news are interested in controversial local issues in the same way as newspapers. Relations with television and radio reporters can be approached in the same way as print journalists, although commercial stations will seldom explore issues in much depth during news programs. Television "magazine" and talk-show programs offer opportunities to explore issues in greater detail.

Public television and radio may even devote more time to certain issues than their newsprint colleagues. Many planners cooperate with public broadcast journalists to develop in-depth analysis of issues and explanations of legislation. The Cooper-

ative Extension Service frequently works with public broadcasting stations and provides similar background information through television and radio as in its printed bulletins and reports.

The continued extension of cable television systems offers expanded opportunities for conveying planning information. Because of the increase in the number of channels, there is a need for programming to fill the time. Planning commission meetings and hearings can be broadcast live. Interactive arrangements between individual homes and government offices can be made so that interested citizens can provide their views to elected and appointed officials. Public opinion polls and preference surveys can be conducted via television. Cable systems also offer opportunities for continuing education courses through community colleges and universities. These can be flexible short courses or an extended series targeted at the public, elected and appointed officials, or professional planners.

TWO EXAMPLES OF EDUCATION PROGRAMS

University of Wisconsin-Extension Community Development Program

The University of Wisconsin-Extension initiated a long-term relationship with a number of small towns in Dane County as a part of the extension service's community development program. In each town, a similar community development strategy was employed (Figure 8.1) and a similar format for reports was used (Figure 8.2). The county extension agent coordinated and involved various academic departments at the University of Wisconsin. These departments included city planning, economics, rural sociology, landscape architecture, and architecture. The extension service was able to bring to these small towns information that was not readily available to citizens and leaders. The extension service was

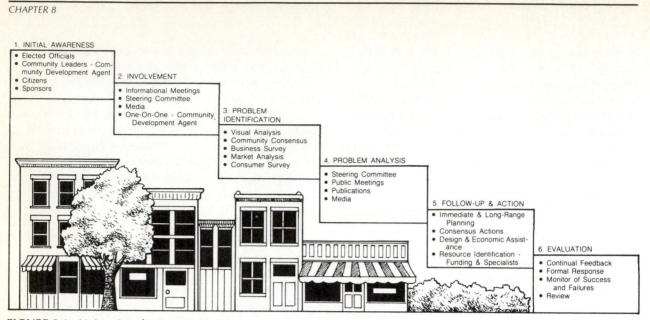

FIGURE 8.1 University of Wisconsin-Extension community development strategy. *(Source: Domack, 1981)*

then able to demonstrate to the citizens how this information could be useful (Domack, 1981).

A common set of studies was undertaken in each Dane County town. These studies included a community-consensus study, a visual analysis, a trade area survey, a survey of business owners/managers and building owners, a threshold-level analysis, and a report concerning the design options for the main business district. The

community-consensus study was essentially a preference survey. Three categories of people were surveyed: elected officials, nonelected community leaders, and citizens in general. These groups were asked to rank potential problems facing the community (Domack, 1981).

The community-consensus survey consisted of five steps. First, a survey was developed, designed specifically for each small town. Second, the

FIGURE 8.2 University of Wisconsin-Extension community development report format. *(Source: Domack, 1981)*

 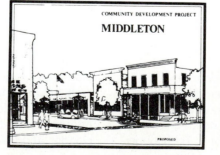 

people to be surveyed in the three categories were identified. The third step was to conduct the interviews, which were done by University of Wisconsin students meeting directly with the identified individuals. The survey generally included seventeen topic categories, plus "other" (Table 8.1) (Domack, 1981).

Compiling and analyzing the survey information was the fourth step in the community-consensus study. Results were reported back through community meetings, local news media, and publications. After about 10 weeks, once the survey results were reported, the fifth step occurred. This involved again surveying the elected officials, community leaders, and the sampling of citizens to ascertain if any change may have occurred as a result or a reaction to the original survey (Domack, 1981).

The downtowns of smaller towns deteriorate slowly, often unnoticed by local residents. The

purpose of the visual analysis portion of the University of Wisconsin-Extension program was to help the community see how their town looked to outsiders. This was accomplished through an extensive photographic effort, in which between 600 and 800 slides were taken. The effort concentrated on important gathering areas such as the downtown, parks, schools, and churches. The results of the visual analysis were presented to community meetings (Domack, 1981).

According to the University of Wisconsin-Extension, a *trade area* is the economic region from which community businesses draw their customers. It comprised both rural and built-up areas. In the University of Wisconsin-Extension trade area survey, a consumer questionnaire was utilized to provide local businesses information about their current and potential customers. In this survey the following information was sought from those interviewed:

- Where they shop (what towns and shopping centers)
- What influence media advertising (newspapers, radio, television, and/or direct mail fliers) has on their shopping decisions
- What are their main consideration (price, quality, and/or brand name) when they purchase a particular product
- Where they purchase specialized goods and services most often
- Whether existing store hours are compatible with their schedules
- What additional services and facilities they think the community needs
- How government officials can better serve the needs of downtown business people (Domack, 1981, p. 12)

The survey of business owners/managers and building owners was used to determine what these people thought about potential economic development in their downtown area. The survey helped to gauge the willingness of the business

TABLE 8.1
TOPIC CATEGORIES USED IN THE UNIVERSITY OF WISCONSIN-EXTENSION COMMUNITY CONSENSUS STUDY

Topic Categories

1. Parking
2. Traffic
3. Streets and Roads
4. Public Transportation
5. Community Growth and Planning
6. Economic Growth
7. Shopping for Goods and Services
8. Condition and Appearance of Downtown
9. Crime and Law Enforcement
10. Public Utilities
11. Local Government Officials and City Service
12. Health Care
13. Education
14. Recreation and Leisure-Time Activities
15. Local Environment
16. Housing
17. Human Relations
18. Other

SOURCE: Domack, 1981.

community to participate in change. This survey also provided an overview about how the business people viewed economic opportunities and problems in their towns (Domack, 1981).

The final survey used in the extension program was the threshold-level analysis. This was a market survey used to determine whether a particular type of new business could be a success in the town. According to the University of Wisconsin-Extension, a *threshold* is the minimum number of people needed to support one business of a particular type. The extension service has developed thresholds through the study of 100 small Wisconsin communities. Table 8.2 illustrates threshold populations, hierarchical marginal goods, and the rank of selected central functions for central place hierarchy in Wisconsin. Figure 8.3 illustrates the relationship between community size and the number of businesses that can be supported, while Table 8.3 shows the number of people required to support various businesses in Wisconsin. Threshold-level analysis helps local businesspeople and investors paint an accurate picture of the economic potential of their town (Domack, 1981).

The purpose of all these studies—the community consensus, visual analysis, trade-area survey, survey of business owners/managers and building owners, threshold-level analysis—was to help small-town residents better understand their community, particularly its limitations and potentials (Figure 8.4). The program integrated community education with citizen participation.

The Davis, California, Energy Planning Program

The city of Davis, California, has undertaken an ambitious energy planning program that has been successful, in large part, because of the emphasis placed on community involvement and education. Some of this effort resulted because of a grant from the U.S. Department of Housing and Urban Development (HUD). The HUD grant financed, among other things, a workbook demonstrating how to use the city's new building code, prototype designs for demonstration low-cost passive solar housing, and creative exploration concerning energy conservation (McGregor, 1984).

The workbook produced from the HUD grant was written by the Living Systems Company and entitled *Practical Use of the Sun* (1977). This workbook was written so that the new building code could be understood by the whole community. More technical seminars explaining the code were held for builders and other interested people, such as the city building inspectors.

As a result of the prototype designs in the workbook, an unexpected educational opportunity occurred. A small local builder named Mike Corbett built a neighborhood demonstrating the new energy conservation policies of Davis. According to Gloria Shepard McGregor, the past planning director of Davis, "this new solar neighborhood provided valuable demonstration homes for Davis citizens and for many visitors outside the city. It began to cause change in the focus of the Davis programs from energy conservation to use of solar energy systems" (1984, p. 206; see also Thayer, 1989).

From the Davis example one can see how government policy, community education, individual initiative, and the wise use of resources can be influenced by each other. According to McGregor (1984), in Davis there are several examples of such interactions. She cites how the League of Women Voters made energy conservation a study item and monitored the implications of proposed actions. The two Davis daily newspapers attempted to keep themselves and the city informed about energy conservation. Civic organizations, such as the Rotary Club and the chamber of commerce, carefully examined the impact of conservation policies in the Davis public schools, while teachers gave lectures about energy conservation (McGregor, 1984).

TABLE 8.2

THRESHOLD POPULATIONS, HIERARCHIAL MARGINAL GOODS, AND RANK OF SELECTED CENTRAL FUNCTIONS FOR THE CENTRAL PLACE HIERARCHY IN WISCONSIN

Hierarchical Level	Central Functions		Mean Population
Hamlet	Taverns Grocery stores	Service stations	200
Minimum Convenience	Post office Bank Elementary and secondary school Beauty shop Hardware stores Farm supplies Motor vehicle dealer Lumber and building materials Insurance agent Dentist Farm machinery and equipment Physician Barber shop Auto repair	Drugstore Auto parts and supplies Legal services Hotel or motel Bowling alley Public golf course Furniture store Bakery Women's clothing store Laundry and cleaning service Variety store Petroleum bulk station Real estate agent Liquor store	800
Full Convenience	Funeral home Radio and television store Accounting, auditing, and book- keeping services Optometrists Shoe store Movie theater	Jewelry store Florists Billiard hall Sheet metal works Men's clothing Photographer	2,000
Partial Shopping Centers	Nursing home Sporting goods and bike shops Labor unions	Fire and casualty insurance brokers Civic, social, and fraternal associations Engineering and surveying services	3,800
Complete Shopping Centers	Amusement and recreational services Family clothing stores Gift and novelty shop	Auto and home supply store Wholesale beer distributor	11,000
Wholesale-Retail Centers	Telephone office Dairy wholesalers Department stores Chiropractors Business associations Janitorial services Used car dealers (used only) Specialty repair Sports and recreation clubs Fuel oil wholesalers Boat dealers Day care centers Floor covering stores Used merchandise stores Title abstract services	Mobile home dealers Sewing, needlework, and piece goods Industrial equipment and machinery Paint, glass, and wallpaper Meat and fish markets Livestock marketing Welding repair Hospitals Radio stations Lumber, plywood, and millwork Dairy product stores Car washes Stationery stores Household appliance stores	62,000

SOURCE: Domeck, 1981.

SELECTED BUSINESS FUNCTIONS

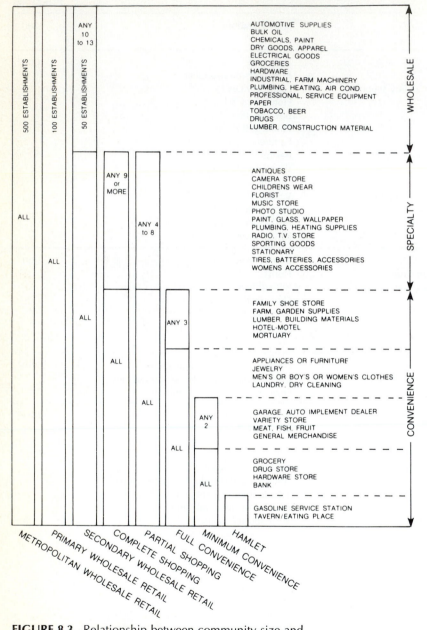

FIGURE 8.3 Relationship between community size and the number of businesses that can be supported. *(Source: Domack, 1981)*

TABLE 8.3
POPULATIONS REQUIRED TO SUPPORT ADDITIONAL ESTABLISHMENTS OF
SELECTED FUNCTIONS IN WISCONSIN

| Function | Number of Establishments | | | |
	1	2	3	4
Taverns	77	244	478	711
Food Stores	92	1,104	4,697	29,119
Fuel Oil Dealers	164	685	1,577	2,850
Filling Stations	186	459	799	1,135
Feed Stores	247	4,895	28,106	97,124
Beauticians	268	851	1,673	2,702
Insurance Agencies	293	666	1,077	1,514
Farm Implements	309	3,426	14,004	38,025
Restaurants	316	754	1,253	1,797
Hardware Stores	372	1,925	5,032	9,949
Auto Repair Shops	375	1,148	2,209	3,517
Motels	384	2,072	5,557	11,189
Real Estate Agencies	418	1,226	2,301	3,597
Auto Dealers	420	1,307	2,937	4,063
Plumbers	468	2,717	7,604	15,780
Physicians	493	1,352	2,436	3,702
Lawyers	497	1,169	1,927	2,748
Radio-TV Sales	521	1,815	3,765	6,316
Drive-in Eating Places	537	4,851	17,572	43,799
Dentists	563	1,744	3,379	5,402
Supermarkets	587	2,968	7,610	14,881
Appliance Stores	607	3,709	10,691	22,659
Liquor Stores	613	4,738	15,669	36,509
Barber Shops	632	5,297	18,372	44,404
Furniture Stores	637	4,833	15,819	36,686
Drugstores	638	4,285	13,053	28,771
Auto Parts Dealers	642	5,496	19,284	46,991
Laundromats	649	5,665	20,114	49,264
Women's Clothing Stores	678	5,471	18,544	44,133
Department Stores	691	5,408	18,012	42,295
Dry Cleaners	692	4,131	11,746	24,655
Shoe Stores	712	7,650	30,670	82,146

SOURCE: Domack, 1981.

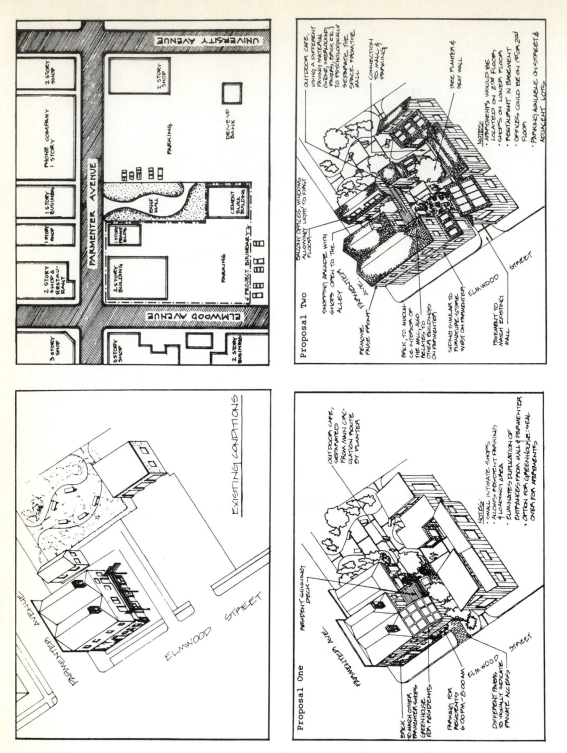

FIGURE 8.4 An example of decision options resulting from a University of Wisconsin-Extension community development program. *(Source: Domack, 1981)*

Another important element in the Davis program was the series of public meetings where ideas were presented and argued. As McGregor stresses, the public meeting, and all the other factors of success in Davis, are present in every American community. Newspapers, public schools, and civic associations are often eager to listen to ideas and work to improve their communities.

In Davis, planners sought to better inform people about alterations in their environment that could better conserve energy. The goal in both Davis and Wisconsin was to illustrate cause-and-effect relationships. The thesis is: If people better understand such relationships, then they will support government actions based on the same understanding. This vigorous pursuit of public education differentiates these examples from more conventional planning processes, where an educational campaign may only be mounted at one or two steps in the process.

9

DETAILED DESIGNS

To design is to give form and to arrange elements spatially. By making specific designs based on the plan and the planning process, landscape planners can help decision makers and citizens visualize the consequences of their policies. By carrying policies through to the arrangement of the physical environment, another dimension is added to the process. The spatial organization of a place is affected through design. Detailed designs represent a synthesis of all the previous steps in the planning process. During the design step, the short-term benefits for the land user or individual citizen have to be combined with the long-term economic and ecological goals for the whole area.

According to Anne Spirn (1989), design should respond to the "deep structure" of the place. She defines *deep structure* as the fundamental geologic, hydrologic, and bioclimatic processes that form the landscape. Spirn's design theory is "based upon an understanding of nature and culture as comprising interwoven processes that exhibit a complex, underlying order that holds across vast scales of space and time" (1988, p. 108). The purpose of making designs as part of planning is to understand these fundamental processes and illuminate the underlying order so that it will be helpful in decision making. Design should make the interrelationships between natural and cultural processes and political choices less abstract. Design should make visible "natural processes and their temporal cycles," according to Spirn (1988, p. 108).

Designs may be presented in various formats. The design may involve individual site or land-user plans that form parts of the overall landscape plan. Examples of such specific designs are the farm conservation plans completed for individual land users by the SCS. A design simulation may be done that compares the existing situation with various scenarios, such as one based on the landscape plan and one with no action. There may be specific designs for new facilities to illustrate the implications of plan implementation. Demonstration projects can be built as prototypes to exemplify the consequences of the plan. Two examples of detailed landscape design will be presented, one from the Connecticut River valley in Massachusetts and the second from Teller County, Colorado.

SITE DESIGN

Site design is concerned with the physical arrangement of the built and natural elements of a specific land parcel. A single house or group of houses, an office park, a commercial shopping center, or a combination of uses may be involved. Kevin Lynch and Gary Hack define *site planning* as "the art of arranging structures on the land and shaping the spacing between, an art linked to architecture, engineering, landscape architecture and city planning" (1984, p. 1). *Site design* may be viewed as the application of the planning process to a specific parcel of land. Kevin Lynch, who wrote the standard text on the topic, identified the eight stages of site planning proper as:

1. Defining the problem
2. Programming and the analysis of site and user

3. Schematic design and the preliminary cost estimate
4. Developed design and detailed costing
5. Contract documents
6. Bidding and contracting
7. Construction
8. Occupation and management (Lynch & Hack, 1984, p. 11)

Lynch recognized this process as a standard organizing tool but one that seldom occurs in a step-by-step fashion. "Reciting these stages makes them sound logical and linear, but the recital is only conventional; the real process is looping and cyclical" (Lynch & Hack, 1984, p. 11). Design, according to Lynch, is the "search for forms" that "deals with particular solutions" (Lynch & Hack, 1984, p. 127). Lynch and Hack observe that "site design deals with three elements: the pattern of activity, the pattern of circulation, and the pattern of sensible form that supports them" (1984, p. 127).

The conventional Lynch site planning process has many strengths, but design is not part of broader planning concerns, except in its response to government restrictions, nor is the site linked to its larger context. Lynch wrote elsewhere about "the sense of the region," and Lynch and Hack mention "contextualism" in the third edition (1984) of Lynch's (1962) classic text on site planning, but the site is not viewed as part of a hierarchical organization.

One approach that does advocate a hierarchical perspective is "diagnosis and design" developed by planner John Raintree for agroforestry work in Africa and other tropical and subtropical places. It is a method for the diagnosis of land management problems and the design of solutions. Raintree bases his approach on a medical analogy, "Diagnosis should precede treatment" (1987, p. 4). The key features of a diagnosis and design, according to Raintree, are its flexibility, speed, and repetition.

In the diagnostic stage, the designer asks, "How does the system work?" (Raintree, 1987, p. 6). Such questions inevitably lead the planner to view the site as part of a larger network of activities. The design stage then focuses on how to improve the system. Raintree's approach includes a regional reconnaissance from which sites are selected for diagnosis and design. When conducting a diagnosis of a place, the planner conducts surveys, makes analyses, and identifies specifications for appropriate interventions. Design at the site level then represents appropriate interventions at the local level.

INDIVIDUAL LAND-USER DESIGNS: FARM CONSERVATION PLANS

Farm conservation plans are an example of site-specific land-user designs with a relatively long tradition in the United States. Farm-level conservation plans were first conceived during the 1930s to help farmers address soil erosion problems. For 50 years, these plans remained voluntary. In the early 1980s, states like Iowa and Wisconsin began to require such plans as prerequisites for certain types of financial benefits. Then, in 1985, the U.S. Congress passed conservation provisions requiring farm plans on highly erodible land in order for landowners to remain eligible for federal agricultural programs.

Farm plans are prepared by SCS conservationists with land users in cooperation with local conservation districts. A conservation plan involves a process parallel to the broader one being described in this book and with similarities to the approaches advocated by Lynch and Raintree. A conservation plan is a collection of information, an identification of erosion and other conservation problems, and the proposal of solutions. The planning principles, the elements of the planning process, and the data to be used in the plans are clearly outlined in the SCS's *National Conservation Planning Manual*. The planning principles include

close personal contact with farmers and ranchers, the use of interdisciplinary resource information, an open-ended planning process, and flexibility to local situations (U.S. Soil Conservation Service, 1978).

According to the SCS approach, site-level planning involves the pooled knowledge and experience of both the planner and the land user. It is stressed that there is "a direct and essential link between effective participation in planning and applying resource management systems on the land" (U.S. Soil Conservation Service, 1978, p. 506-3). To accomplish this linkage, a process is suggested that should sound familiar: establishing goals and objectives, inventorying resources, developing options, making decisions, implementing decisions, and evaluating and updating plans.

Traditionally, the farm has been used as the unit for conservation plans. Sometimes the farms have been a part of a larger watershed planning effort. For instance, in Chapter 7 the Missouri Flat Creek watershed plan was described. A goal of this plan is to reduce and ultimately eliminate sediment in the creek for avoidable soil erosion. One of the strategies to achieve this goal was the preparation of individual farm conservation plans.

For example, the Young family has a 501-acre (203-hectare) farm in the Missouri Flat Creek watershed. The family grows wheat and barley. The erosion rate is about twice the tolerable level. The Palouse Conservation District and the SCS designed a plan for the farm that would reduce the rate to at or below the tolerable level. The plan provided the Young family with an alternative rotation system to the one currently being employed. The plan also identified three farming practices that would reduce erosion. The farmer selected the alternative rotation system and two new agricultural practices. Specific critical erosion areas were identified. These areas were withdrawn from cultivation and planted to grass. As a result of the farm-level plan, the Young family was able to reduce erosion on their farm by one-half.

SIMULATION

Perspective drawings, artist's impressions, photography, and three-dimensional models are some of the techniques that can be used to simulate the consequences of a plan. Drawings are used commonly to describe visual changes. A sequences of sketches can be used to show the existing conditions, the consequences of current trends, and the potential outcomes of various interventions (see the discussion of the Connecticut River valley and Teller County later in this chapter). Computers can be used to produce perspective drawings or to insert a drawing into a photograph. There are various ways to manipulate photographs to illustrate the consequences of an action, including photomontage and photoretouching. Three-dimensional models can be built that graphically display before-and-after situations. Videotape or film may be used to give people a ground-level view of those models (Ortolano, 1984).

In its 1988 state development and redevelopment plan, the New Jersey State Planning Commission used drawings to illustrate its regional design system. The regional design system attempts to link communities into networks by redistributing "regional growth from sprawling settlement patterns into a variety of relatively compact, mixed-use communities" (New Jersey State Planning Commission, 1988, p. 45).

The New Jersey regional design system has three components. The first part is a five-level hierarchy of central places: cities, corridor centers, towns, villages, and hamlets. Transportation corridors form the second component and the land surrounding the central places the third part. The New Jersey State Planning Commission has developed a series of strategies and policies to direct growth to the central places and away from the surrounding areas and to manage the development of transportation corridors. Community design plans, which include site design criteria and design review procedures, are to be used by the state, counties, and municipalities. The consequences of this regional design system were illustrated with drawings simulating existing conditions (Figure 9.1), trends (Figure 9.2), and the implemented plan (Figure 9.3) (New Jersey State Planning Commission, 1988).

CONCEPTUAL DESIGN OF NEW FACILITIES

To illustrate the impact of the plan on the landscape, it may be helpful to design new

FIGURE 9.1 Simulated existing conditions. *(Source: New Jersey State Planning Commission,* Communities of Place: The Preliminary State Development and Redevelopment Plan for the State of New Jersey, 1988, Vol. 2)*

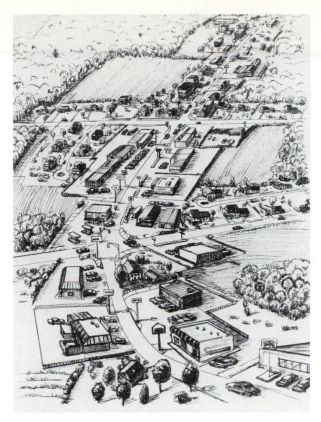

FIGURE 9.2 Simulated trends. *(Source: New Jersey State Planning Commission,* Communities of Place: The Preliminary State Development and Redevelopment Plan for the State of New Jersey, 1988, Vol. 2)

FIGURE 9.3 Simulated consequences of the regional design system. *(Source: New Jersey State Planning Commission,* Communities of Place: The Preliminary State Development and Redevelopment Plan for the State of New Jersey, 1988, Vol. 2)

facilities. Returning to Whitman County and the Palouse region, the area between Pullman and Moscow had been recognized as a "light industrial opportunity area" in the 1978 county comprehensive plan. Because Washington State University was located in Pullman and the University of Idaho in Moscow, there were also strong demands on the 10-mile (16.09-kilometer) corridor for transportation and recreational use. There are also established goals in the region and state for the conservation of soil and water resources as well as the protection of envi-

ronmentally sensitive areas. The design of a new facility—a recreational path—was used to show how all these conflicting goals could be achieved. Planner Dennis Canty and landscape architect Christine Carlson from the National Park Service cooperated with local citizens, elected officials, and county, city, and university planners in 1986 to prepare such a design.*

* This section has been adapted from Carlson and Canty, 1986, and Carlson et al., 1989.

FIGURE 9.4 Concept plan diagram, phase 1.
(Source: Carlson et al., 1989, drawn by Christine Carlson & Dennis Canty)

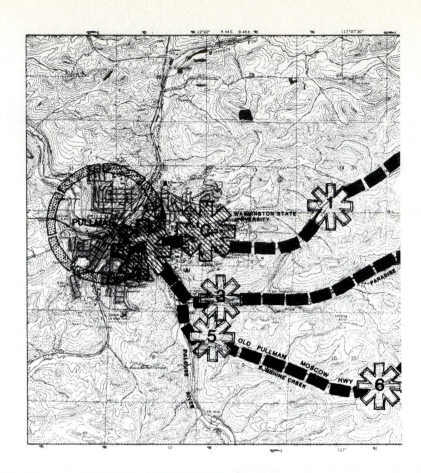

Legend

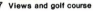 Phase 1 routes

 Existing city bike routes and sidewalks

Existing Sites

A Reaney Park, River Park, City playfields
B Ghormley Park and CBD mall
C Washington State University bikeways, west
    entrance
D University of Idaho bikeways

Potential Sites

1 Access to creek and trees, habitat
2 Location and views
3 Access to creek, riparian vegetation and habitat
4 Access to road and creek, location and views
5 Access to road and trees
6 Location and views
7 Views and golf course

The Concept Design

There were two major interests in the design of the path. The first was to provide a safe, attractive recreational link between the communities of Pullman and Moscow. The second was to conserve the natural and cultural features in the corridor area between the two communities. The concept design that follows was developed by Canty, Carlson, and the local residents directly from these interests.

The central element of the concept is a pathway designed to meet recreation and conservation needs that physically links Pullman and Moscow and is the backbone of a broader enhancement program for the local landscape. The path is a way for the community as a whole to assume responsibility for the shape and quality of the corridor area between Pullman and Moscow.

The basic ingredients of the concept plan are design components of the path—the function, form, and character it manifests as it passes through the landscape. To be successful, any path must flow from place to place, and sometimes back again, in a continuous manner, like a stream or river. It must connect places with each other. And it must begin some place and end somewhere else; it must have a clear origin and destination and provide a strong sense of direction. These characteristics—continuity, connection, and an origin and des-

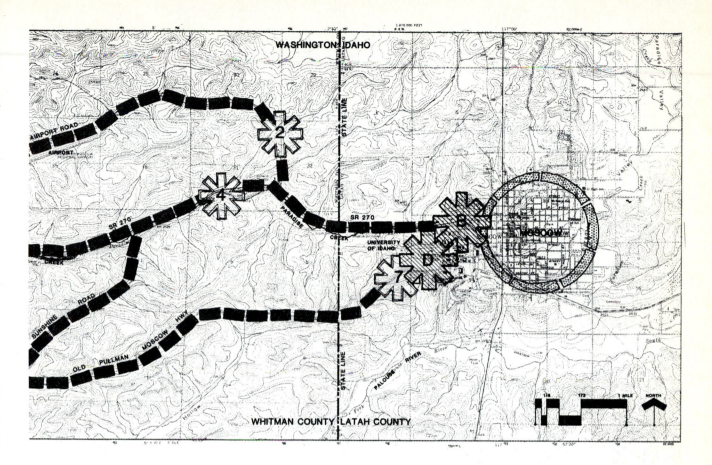

tination—are fundamental to the development of any path.   The function, form, and character of the path are the physical means by which these intrinsic requirements are met (Carlson & Canty, 1986).

The Palouse path was to have a variety of functions. It was to be used for safe transportation and recreation and for understanding the intricate relationships between the natural and cultural resources of the Palouse landscape.   The path was to capture the ambience of the Palouse and present it in ways that are interesting, educational, and satisfying for all who use the Pullman-Moscow corridor.

The implementation of the concept plan is divided into two phases that develop the function, form, and character of the path.   Phase 1 provides a response to the immediate need for safe travel for bicyclists and, consequently, motorists between Pullman and Moscow.   It also establishes a physical and planning framework for future development of the path.   Phase 2 supplements the development actions of phase 1.   It outlines options for more extensive, formalized development and for use by a broader constituency of users. The following sections review how the function, form, and character of the path are developed in each phase.

Phase 1

Important features of phase 1 are the incorporation of the path into existing circulation patterns, the development of roadside recreation sites and conservation areas, and the promotion of safe transportation for bicyclists between Pullman and Moscow by upgrading bicycle use areas.

The emphasis in phase 1 is on upgrading bicycle use on all established routes in the corridor area (Figure 9.4). These roads are an integrated transportation network between Pullman and Moscow that fits the landscape. In general, they wind through lowlands and stream valleys and, with the exception of state highways 270 and 8 (the Pullman-Moscow highway), are narrow and quiet. Because of the location and predominance of agriculture, these roads are also the primary means

of experiencing the landscape. Various wildlife and plant communities populate the roadsides, and long views of distant forests and ridges are often visible from the open-road corridors. Consequently, local roads are used heavily by bicyclists, joggers, and pedestrians for recreation and commuting. However, roads are often unsafe because of narrow shoulders, visual obstructions, and consistently heavy traffic along the Pullman-Moscow highway. Up to 10,000 cars per day use this two-lane highway at peak use times. Improvements to road shoulders and road surfaces, formal designation of bike routes and scenic and/or recreation routes by cities, counties, and state departments of transportation, and frequent placement of signs and pavement markings will be used to ensure safe use of roads by recreationists

FIGURE 9.5 Phase 1 bicycle standards for highway width and traffic controls. *(Source: Carlson et al., 1989, drawn by Christine Carlson)*

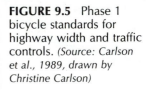

10'-0"
Minimum
paved width

Pavement marking line
bike lane stencil
Bike route guide sign

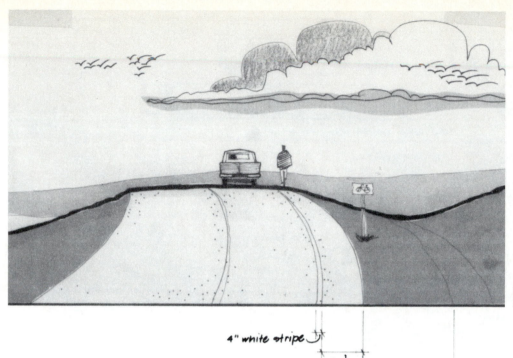

4" white stripe

4'-0" minimum paved shoulder width

bike route guide sign in r.o.w.

FIGURE 9.6 Phase 1 bicycle standards for rural road width and traffic controls. *(Source: Carlson et al., 1989, drawn by Christine Carlson)*

(Figures 9.5 and 9.6). The cities of Pullman and Moscow and Washington State University and the University of Idaho have designated corridors that could unite the Palouse path with city parks and other facilities, schools, and the downtown business districts (Figure 9.4).

Sites 1 through 7 on Figure 9.4 indicate places for potential development as small roadside rest stops, gathering places, safe pull-outs for picnicking, bike maintenance, or relaxation, and conservation areas. Each site is defined by important and interesting natural and cultural features in the corridor area, such as distinct riparian zones, access to Paradise Creek (a tributary of the Palouse River), and pleasant views of attractive farmsteads and distant ridges, that can enhance the recreational and visual character of

the path as it moves between Pullman and Moscow. Each site also provides recreationists with an opportunity to understand complex interrelationships that make up the landscape and the need to protect them. Site designs could combine conservation measures, such as supplemental plantings to buffer existing habitat and plant communities, with other site detailing to protect the resources while simultaneously allowing contact with them (Figure 9.7).

The Pullman-Moscow corridor will come under increasing land-use pressures in the coming years as demand for recreational, agricultural, commercial, industrial, and residential uses increases. Without a concerted effort to resolve the demands of competing users, land-use conflicts will increase, and air and water quality, wildlife

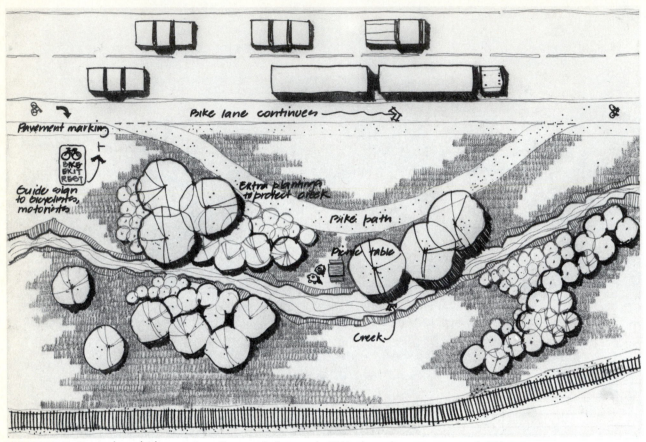

FIGURE 9.7 Typical roadside rest stop. *(Source: Carlson et al., 1989, drawn by Christine Carlson)*

habitat, and the visual character of the corridor will be degraded. The phase 1 path provides an opportunity to establish a program of locally administered design and planning standards to separate and buffer adjacent uses. The standards would emphasize setbacks, vegetative and topographic buffers, provisions for safe vehicle access, and control of noise and water contamination. With sensitive siting and the use of such standards, the continued use and development of the corridor need not be at the expense of its quality (Figures 9.8 to 9.10).

Phase 2

The purpose of phase 2 is to broaden the function, form, and character of the path from a linear transportation corridor to an intensive recreation and conservation greenbelt between Pullman and Moscow. More formalized settings for recreation are developed. Along with bicyclists and joggers, walkers, hikers, motorists, and others use the path for recreation. Upon completion of phase 2, the path will be a highly designed facility that meets all the priorities established by the local task force organized for the project.

Vegetation screen for visual + noise buffer
- 30' - 75 '0' minimum depth
- densely growing mixed trees, shrubs
- several rows planted closely together

FIGURE 9.8 Typical screening of incompatible uses. *(Source: Carlson et al., 1989, drawn by Christine Carlson)*

The concept design diagram for phase 2 (Figure 9.11) and Figures 9.12 to 9.14 present one of many options for intensive path development. Although the same sites are reserved for development in phase 2 as in phase 1, they take on a greater, more developed recreation function. A simple rest stop in phase 1 might become a small streamside park in phase 2 with picnic tables, pathways to and from the creek, and interpretive signs describing small mammal and bird habitats in the park. Sites could be expanded into county or state parks in the corridor area with highly developed facilities. As these sites are developed, the path becomes a means of linking them together, and the sites

themselves become more important components of the concept plan (Figure 9.12).

In phase 2, the path connects a variety of parklike settings. These sites are a backdrop for recreation activities, such as interpretation of physical features or elements belonging to the cultural development of the corridor area. For example, interpretive signs could be located near riparian zones to explain the nature of their habitats and the composition of their plant communities. The site can be arranged to focus views on a historic farm or scenic landscape and can include displays describing its significance. Through its alignment, the path itself can be interpretive,

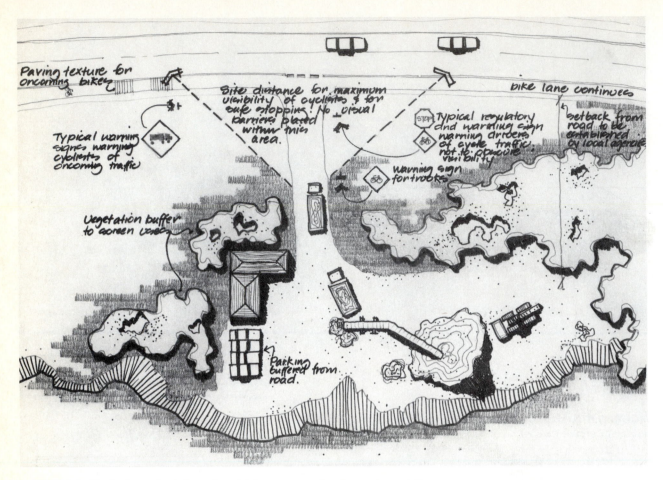

FIGURE 9.9 Typical standards for safe vehicle access, setbacks, and vegetation buffers. *(Source: Carlson et al., 1989, drawn by Christine Carlson)*

directing users to important features or moving them past others (Figure 9.13).

The path moves along and off the road, connecting sites that feature access to Paradise Creek, dense clusters of willow or hawthorn, and wildlife habitats. Flexibility in path alignment and the rich resources available create many opportunities to include conservation as an important path function. The path can move people away from fragile habitats. It can buffer native plant communities and protect stream banks with design features that include special planting schemes and bank fortification measures. In conjunction with the development of interpretive features, it can educate users about the protection of the landscape.

The form of the path in phase 2 is complex. Unlike the simple linear alignment and basic form of the phase 1 path, the phase 2 path alternatively follows roadways, railbeds, and features in the landscape. In shape and materials, it becomes a separate and formal feature in the corridor area.

FIGURE 9.10 Phase 1 path alignments. *(Source: Carlson et al., 1989, drawn by Christine Carlson)*

Finally, it is no longer simply a line between the two communities of Pullman and Moscow but a link between several formal gathering places along the way. The character of phase 2 begins with the best of the natural and cultural features of the corridor area and adds an extra ingredient, that of people entering, using, and enjoying the Palouse landscape (Figure 9.14).

Summary of the Concept Design

Phase 1 of the concept design secures a safe route for commuters and recreationists between Pullman and Moscow. It establishes a recreation route through the corridor area at minimal costs, using the existing planning structure. It provides a practical means for directing changes in land uses that accommodate growth and development and

preserve the visual quality and natural resources of the often politically controversial corridor area. Finally, it sets the stage for more intensive development of the pathway.

Phase 2 completes the concept plan. It supplements the development of phase 1 with highly designed, expanded parks and recreation sites for many user groups. It changes the role of the path from that of a transportation link between Pullman and Moscow to that of a link between the two communities. Along with performance standards, it forms the nucleus for future land uses.

DEMONSTRATION PROJECTS

Conceptual designs may remain just that, paper images illustrating how the plan can be realized.

FIGURE 9.11 Concept plan diagram, phase 2. *(Source: Carlson et al., 1989, drawn by Christine Carlson)*

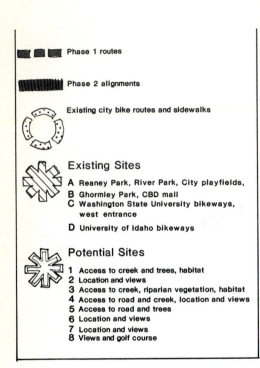

Phase 1 routes

Phase 2 alignments

Existing city bike routes and sidewalks

Existing Sites

A Reaney Park, River Park, City playfields,
B Ghormley Park, CBD mall
C Washington State University bikeways, west entrance
D University of Idaho bikeways

Potential Sites

1 Access to creek and trees, habitat
2 Location and views
3 Access to creek, riparian vegetation, habitat
4 Access to road and creek, location and views
5 Access to road and trees
6 Location and views
7 Location and views
8 Views and golf course

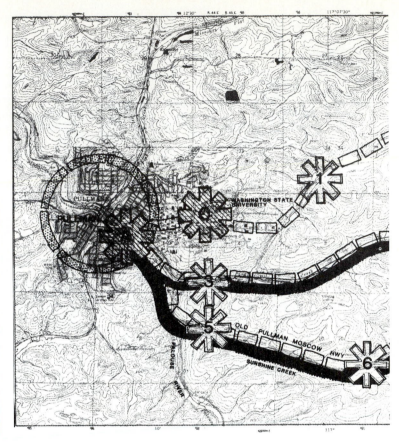

Such designs may or may not actually be built. A more concrete way to show the realization of the plan is to construct a demonstration project. One of the ugliest of America's ugly commercial strips is Colfax Avenue through Aurora, Denver, and Lakewood, Colorado. As a section of U.S. 40, Colfax Avenue was part of one of the major east-west routes in the nation. After the completion of Interstate 70, the road began a steady economic and aesthetic decline.

In 1988, in response to goals established in its comprehensive plan, the city of Lakewood adopted design guidelines for West Colfax Avenue (City of Lakewood, 1988a). The guidelines included design standards for urban and suburban streets (see Figures 9.15 and 9.16). Specific guidelines were included for street trees and other plantations, sidewalks, curbs, and building setbacks. The planners also established standards for building height and scale, building design, pedestrian access, site design, signage, lighting, and parking.

Further, the city with local business leaders undertook the West Colfax Pedestrian Improvement Demonstration Project, which involved a four-block area. The project included both public and private improvements. The city provided street

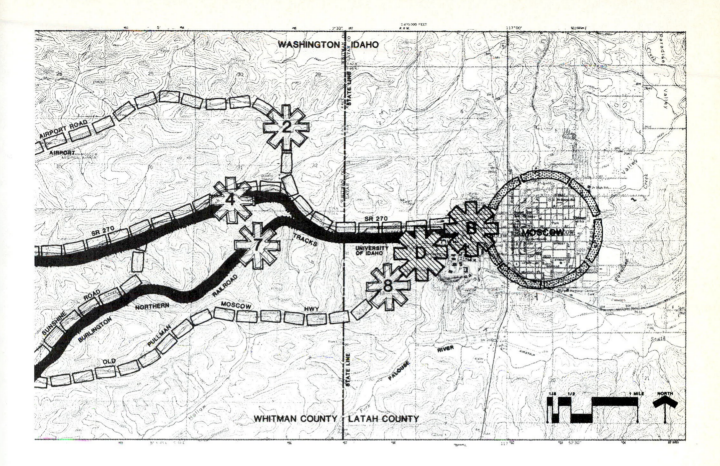

trees and plantations plus improved sidewalks, curbs and gutters, pedestrian seating areas, street furniture, and lighting. Utilities were also relocated underground to reduce the visual clutter of overhead wires. Business owners improved building facades, signage, parking lots, and the general character of the site (City of Lakewood, 1988b). The project was intended to demonstrate the implications of the recommendations in the design guidelines. As a result of the project, Lakewood planners were able to provide before-and-after images of Colfax Avenue (Figure 9.17).

The demonstration project illustrated to business owners, citizens, and local officials the ramifications of the city goals for economic revitalization and for the redevelopment of strip commercial areas.

TWO EXAMPLES OF DETAILED DESIGN

Connecticut River Valley, Massachusetts

The Connecticut River valley provides an example of "greenline" planning, an approach developed

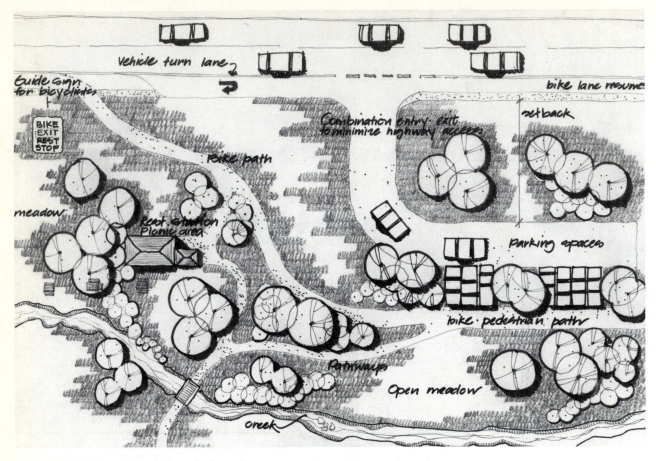

FIGURE 9.12 Phase 2 typical roadside park. *(Source: Carlson et al., 1989, drawn by Christine Carlson)*

and promoted largely by the National Park Service Mid-Atlantic Regional Office in Philadelphia. A greenline park contains a mixture of public and private land, more like a European national park than the traditional American national park. Some land and structures may be acquired by the federal or state governments, but most of an area is protected with scenic easements, local zoning, and other techniques (Corbett, 1983; Alesch, 1987). The greenline planning process involves the cooperation of local, state, and federal officials in analyzing landscape resources, deciding priorities for conservation and development, establishing regulatory measures, and continuing to manage the area according to the plan (Corbett, 1983).

The Connecticut River forms the border between Vermont and New Hampshire as it flows southward through Massachusetts and Connecticut before entering the Atlantic Ocean. In 1984, the Mid-Atlantic Regional Office of the NPS began work on a management plan with state agencies from Massachusetts on the 68-mile (109-kilometer) portion of the river through that state. The NPS is authorized to participate with state and local agencies in such greenline efforts through Section 11 of the Wild and Scenic Rivers Act (Public Law 90-542, as amended). The NPS planning team cooperated with the Massachusetts Department of Environmental Management and three other state agencies, the Audubon Society, the SCS, the regional utilities company, and two local planning and watershed groups.

Based on the problems and opportunities facing the people of the valley, the planning team identified a number of rural resource issues including agricultural land protection (Sutro, 1984), water quality, recreation, natural resource conservation and management, soil and stream-

bank erosion, cultural and historic resources, and economic development. Local landowners were surveyed and township zoning ordinances analyzed (U.S. National Park Service, 1985, 1986). Based on an analysis of the issues and the various options to resolve them, a number of actions were recommended to balance conservation and development.

Among the recommendations was the suggestion that state and local efforts to protect prime farmland be expedited. The Center for Rural Massachusetts of the University of Massachusetts developed this suggestion through the production of a compelling design manual for the valley (Yaro et al., 1988). A series of beautiful drawings were made illustrating specific sites in the valley and

FIGURE 9.13 Phase 2 typical conservation measure and interpretive feature. *(Source: Carlson et al., 1989, drawn by Christine Carlson)*

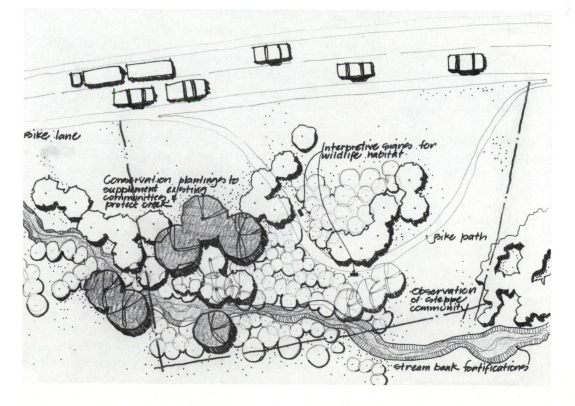

FIGURE 9.14 Conceptual sketch of phase 2 pathway. *(Source: Carlson et al., 1989, drawn by Christine Carlson)*

contrasting conventional development with creative landscape designs. Specific suggestions were made to integrate new development into the rural landscape, review site plans for proposed development, control signs, manage development of land adjacent to rivers and lakes, protect farmland, encourage the preservation of open space, and make rural roadways attractive.

The interdisciplinary team of planners and landscape architects prepared site-specific designs that provided conceptual demonstrations of the options for the valley. Site G, for example, was the Franklin Emery farm. The existing conditions of this site were described—its landform, land use, land cover, utilities, and zoning. The University of Massachusetts landscape planners prepared an aerial view of this site before development (Figure 9.18), a ground-level view before development (Figure 9.19), and a plan of the site before development (Figure 9.20) (Yaro et al., 1988).

The owner of the 200-acre (81-hectare) dairy farm and orchard was a tenth-generation Yankee whose ancestors had settled the land over 200 years ago. Mr. Emery had declined several offers to purchase the farm before he died in 1982. His heirs did not want to continue farming and wished to sell the property for the highest possible price. Because of its proximity to a large university, the conventional development of the property would result in multifamily apartment buildings. There was considerable local opposition to such apartment development because it clashed with the rural character of the town. However, multifamily housing was consistent with the local zoning regulations. The impact of this conventional development scenario was illustrated by the University of Massachusetts landscape planning team by drawing an aerial view of site G after conventional development (Figure 9.21), a ground-level view after conventional development (Figure

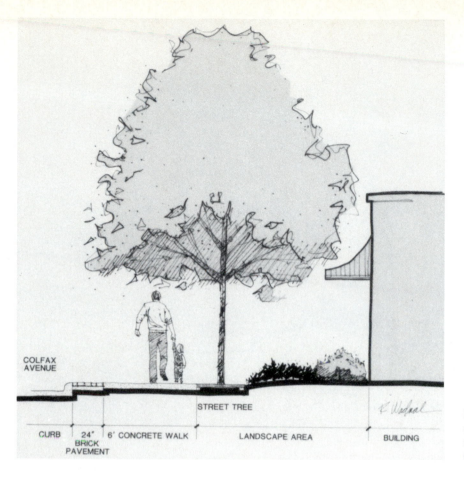

COLFAX
AVENUE

STREET TREE

CURB | 24" BRICK PAVEMENT | 6' CONCRETE WALK | LANDSCAPE AREA | BUILDING

FIGURE 9.15 Typical urban street design for West Colfax Avenue. *(Source: City of Lakewood, 1988a, drawn by Roger Wadnal)*

9.22), and a plan of the site after conventional development (Figure 9.23) (Yaro et al., 1988).

To contrast the conventional scenario, the University of Massachusetts team proposed a creative development scenario. With this design, apartments would be smaller in scale, more varied, and sited in the woodland adjacent to the farmland. The design of the apartments would create a sense of privacy, easy access, and screened parking. The apartment units would have views of the farmland and a pond that would increase their value and marketability. A new road would wind through the woodland and respond to

the topography. The existing eighteenth century farmstead would be restored and sold as a single-family residence (Yaro et al., 1988).

The creative scenario involved siting the new development at the edge of the woodland. To preserve the farmland and orchard, the apartment developer would donate a conservation easement on that part of the land and rent it to a young farmer. In return for the easement, the developer would receive a substantial tax deduction. The landscape architects designed controlled access to the farmland for the new apartment dwellers by fencing and pathway alignment. The design was

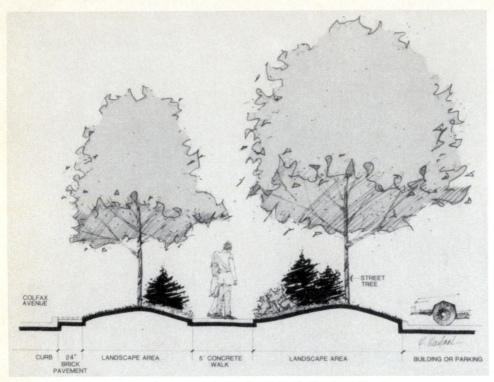

FIGURE 9.16 Typical suburban street design for West Colfax Avenue. *(Source: City of Lakewood, 1988a, drawn by Roger Wadnal)*

illustrated with an aerial view of site G after creative development (Figure 9.24), a ground-level view after creative development (Figure 9.25), and a plan view after creative development (Figure 9.26) (Yaro et al., 1988). This creative scenario for the land involved preserving the farmland and open space and clustering residential development. Thus, a design was presented that fitted the goals and plans to protect the farmland and visual quality of the Connecticut River valley.

Teller County, Colorado

As part of the Teller County growth management process, a team of local planners and students from the University of Colorado at Denver developed detailed designs for housing, village centers, scenic roadways, and the historic mining towns. Scattered residential development is one of the few liabilities of Teller County. Sprawling subdivisions are costly economically, environmentally, and aesthetically. The planning team prepared several conceptual designs to preserve the rural character of the area. Inspired by the drawings of the Connecticut River valley, the Teller County team prepared illustrations of the existing residential landscape (Figure 9.27), of development if conventional suburbanization trends continue (Figure 9.28), and of creative residential siting through growth management (Figure 9.29). The creative approach relies on clustering development,

FIGURE 9.17 West Colfax pedestrian improvement demonstration project: before and after. *(Source: City of Lakewood 1988b)*

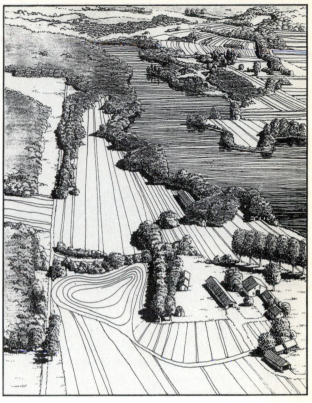

FIGURE 9.18 Aerial view of site before development. *(Source: Yaro et al., 1988, Center for Rural Massachusetts, University of Massachusetts, Amherst, drawn by Kevin Wilson)*

where the topography and vegetation are used to screen new housing and former rangelands are left open as community parkland. To protect the new housing from wildfires, the planning team made design suggestions including the selective thinning of trees and the use of flame-retardant roof materials (Bell et al., 1989).

The villages in Teller County—Florissant, Divide, and Evergreen Station—contain a few Victorian farmhouses, with bay windows and front porches, but the dominant style in these crossroad

settlements is of a utilitarian, commercial highway character. The planning team suggested that there is much potential to encourage mixed infill residential and commercial development in these villages and add to their charm and vitality in the process. The team again prepared illustrations of the existing situation (Figure 9.30), the likely future without planning (Figure 9.31), and a creative design possibility (Figure 9.32). The creative option encourages site design that would maintain the rhythm of existing houses. The team

FIGURE 9.19 Ground view of site before development. *(Source: Yaro et al., 1988, Center for Rural Massachusetts, University of Massachusetts, Amherst, drawn by Kevin Wilson)*

recommended that the design of these rural villages adapt the local vernacular style—a western, mountain Victorian—for the future (Bell et al., 1989).

In the Teller County landscape plan, scenic roadways were designated. Illustrations of potential roadway elements were developed to illustrate the implications of such a designation. One key element is highway pull-offs. The landscape planners suggested upgrading several existing pull-offs. Figure 9.33 shows the typical condition of the pull-offs with panoramic views obstructed by trees and limited opportunities for tourists to view the landscape. The planners suggested a number of improvements, illustrated in Figure 9.34, that included to selectively cut some trees to broaden view angles, provide signage with interpretive information, create seating, demarcate between the viewing and parking areas, add trash receptacles, indicate cliff edges for safety, upgrade parking areas, and build toilet facilities (Bell et al., 1989).

The key components of the design of Cripple Creek and Victor, the towns of the historic mining district, included parking, pedestrian circulation, vacant lots, signage, street furnishings, and the condition of historic structures. Because of the influx of 300,000 to 400,000 tourists annually, parking is especially important. The planning team made specific designs for rearranging parking along the main streets of the town and in a few strategically placed small parking lots. Coupled with the new parking system, sidewalks were widened and improved to allow for better pedestrian circulation (Bell et al., 1989).

Currently, several vacant lots in the downtowns of Cripple Creek and Victor interrupt the visual rhythm of the continuous street-level facade. The planning team proposed locating temporary and permanent pocket parks in these vacant lots. Specific features for these pocket parks include seating areas, planting of coniferous trees native to the area, and lighting (Bell et al., 1989).

Connecticut Valley Design Guidelines

G

Emery Farm

EXISTING CONDITIONS

Landform:	Edge of Valley
Landuse:	Dairy Farm
Landcover:	Pasture, Orchard, Forest, Lake
Utilities:	Town Sewer & Water Available
Zoning:	Multi-family, 12 units/acre

North:

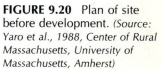

FIGURE 9.20 Plan of site before development. *(Source: Yaro et al., 1988, Center of Rural Massachusetts, University of Massachusetts, Amherst)*

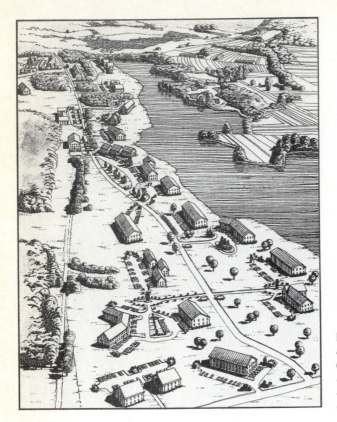

FIGURE 9.21 Aerial view of site after conventional development. *(Source: Yaro et al., 1988, Center for Rural Massachusetts, University of Massachusetts, Amherst, drawn by Kevin Wilson)*

FIGURE 9.22 Ground view of site after conventional development. *(Source: Yaro et al., 1988, Center for Rural Massachusetts, University of Massachusetts, Amherst, drawn by Kevin Wilson)*

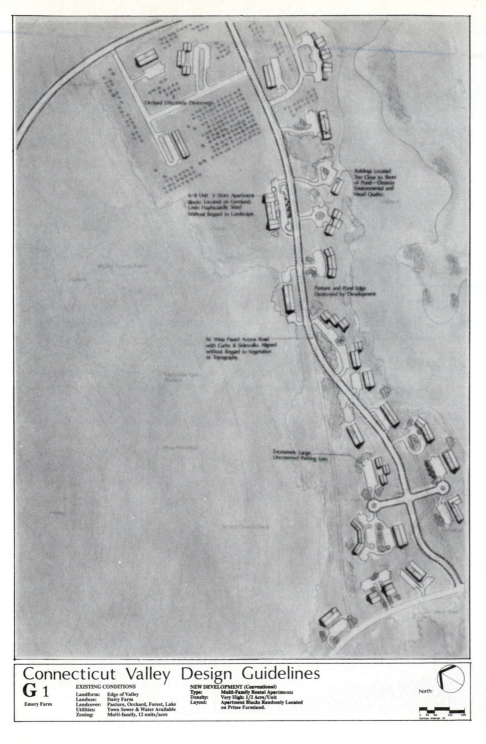

Connecticut Valley Design Guidelines

G 1

Emery Farm

EXISTING CONDITIONS
Landform: Edge of Valley
Landuse: Dairy Farm
Landcover: Pasture, Orchard, Forest, Lake
Utilities: Town Sewer & Water Available
Zoning: Multi-family, 12 units/acre

NEW DEVELOPMENT (Conventional)
Type: Multi-Family Rental Apartments
Density: Very High: 1/2 Acre/Unit
Layout: Apartment Blocks Randomly Located on Prime Farmland.

North:

FIGURE 9.23 Plan of site after conventional development. *(Source: Yaro et al., 1988, Center for Rural Massachusetts, University of Massachusetts, Amherst)*

FIGURE 9.24 Aerial view of site after creative development. *(Source: Yaro et al., 1988, Center for Rural Massachusetts, University of Massachusetts, Amherst, drawn by Kevin Wilson)*

FIGURE 9.25 Ground level view of site after creative development. *(Source: Yaro et al., 1988, Center for Rural Massachusetts, University of Massachusetts, Amherst, drawn by Kevin Wilson)*

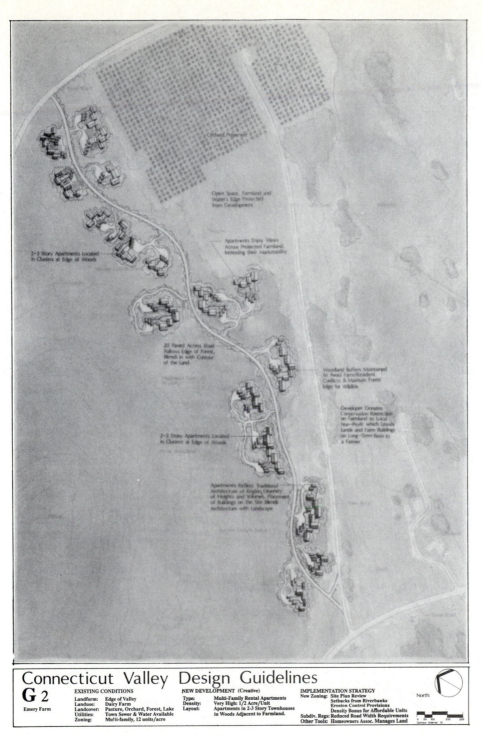

Orchard Preserved

Open Space, Farmland and Water's Edge Protected from Development

Apartments Enjoy Views Across Protected Farmland, Increasing their Marketability

2-3 Story Apartments Located in Clusters at Edge of Woods

20' Paved Access Road Follows Edge of Forest, Blends in with Contour of the Land

Woodland Buffers Maintained to Avoid Farm/Resident Conflicts & Maintain Forest Edge for Wildlife

Developer Donates Conservation Restriction on Farmland to Local Non-Profit which Leases Lands and Farm Buildings on Long-Term Basis to a Farmer

2-3 Story Apartments Located in Clusters at Edge of Woods

Apartments Reflect Traditional Architecture of Region, Diversity of Heights and Volumes, Placement of Buildings on the Site Blends Architecture with Landscape

Connecticut Valley Design Guidelines

G 2

Emery Farm

EXISTING CONDITIONS
Landform: Edge of Valley
Landuse: Dairy Farm
Landcover: Pasture, Orchard, Forest, Lake
Utilities: Town Sewer & Water Available
Zoning: Multi-family, 12 units/acre

NEW DEVELOPMENT (Creative)
Type: Multi-Family Rental Apartments
Density: Very High: 1/2 Acre/Unit
Layout: Apartments in 2-3 Story Townhouses in Woods Adjacent to Farmland.

IMPLEMENTATION STRATEGY
New Zoning: Site Plan Review
　　　　　 Setbacks from Riverbanks
　　　　　 Erosion Control Provisions
　　　　　 Density Bonus for Affordable Units
Subdiv. Regs: Reduced Road Width Requirements
Other Tools: Homeowners Assoc. Manages Land

North:

FIGURE 9.26 Plan of site after creative development. *(Source: Yaro et al., 1988, Center for Rural Massachusetts, University of Massachusetts, Amherst)*

FIGURE 9.27 Existing residential landscape of Teller County, Colorado. *(Source: Bell et al., 1989, drawn by Joseph Bell)*

FIGURE 9.28 Future Teller County, Colorado, residential development with no planning. *(Source: Bell et al., 1989, drawn by Joseph Bell)*

The planning team developed suggestions for signage and street furnishings. The street furnishings for the two towns include benches, paving materials, street lighting, trash containers, and newspaper boxes. The team recommended that the design of signage and street furnishings reflect the Victorian, historic character of Cripple Creek and Victor.

The integrity of that historic character is currently being eroded by the deteriorating condition of many of the buildings in the towns. Painstakingly restored structures provide a sharp contrast with those left to fall apart. The planning team made drawings of inappropriate remodeling with nonconforming materials tacked onto walls and over windows. The planning team recommended design guidelines that would ensure the preservation of the Victorian mining heritage of Cripple Creek and Victor as it is expressed in the architecture of the towns (Bell et al., 1989).

Anne Spirn advocates ecological design that recognizes the deep structure of the place. The detailed designs for the Connecticut River valley in Massachusetts and Teller County, Colorado, are responsive to the natural and cultural processes, the landscape patterns that give each place its

FIGURE 9.29 Creative residential siting design as a result of growth management planning. *(Source: Bell et al., 1989, drawn by Joseph Bell)*

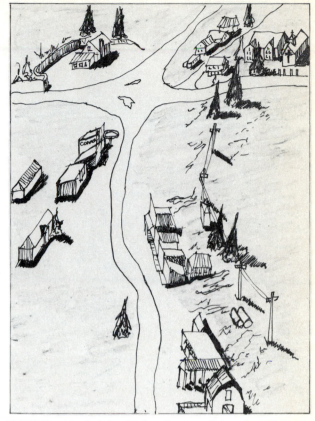

FIGURE 9.30 Existing Teller County, Colorado, village settlement. *(Source: Bell et al., 1989, drawn by Joseph Bell)*

identity and character. The designs differ from more conventional approaches in both their response to landscape ecology and their linkage to a broader planning process.

The Center for Rural Massachusetts design manual for the Connecticut River valley was integrated with the planning efforts undertaken by the state and the NPS. The design manual included specific ways to fit development into the fabric of the landscape through creative design. Site plan review with detailed design guidelines and performance standards were suggested for the towns in the valley. Recommendations were made

to control signage and to manage development on riverfronts and lakefronts and along roadways. Measures to protect farmland and open space were recommended. The landscape planning suggestions were illustrated through a series of designs.

The landscape planners involved in Teller County, Colorado, were familiar with the Connecticut River valley design manual and used it as a model. Through the use of drawings, they were able to illustrate to residents the likely consequences of uncontrolled growth. The planning team also presented visions, through

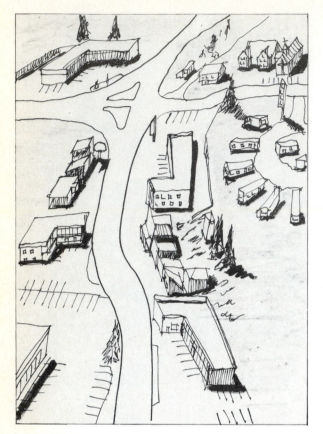

FIGURE 9.31 Likely future of Teller County, Colorado, village without planning. *(Source: Bell et al., 1989, drawn by Joseph Bell)*

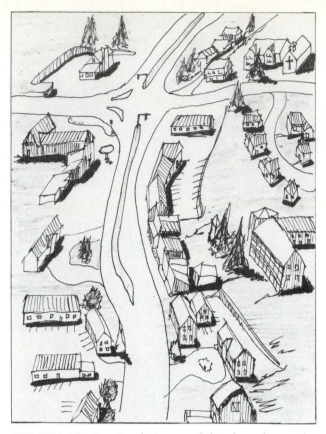

FIGURE 9.32 Creative design possibility through growth management planning for Teller County, Colorado, village. *(Source: Bell et al., 1989, drawn by Joseph Bell)*

conceptual designs, for how the county could develop with planned growth.

The detailed designs completed in the Connecticut River valley and Teller County differ from more conventional approaches in several ways. Many conventional designs are not explicitly linked to the planning process except to the extent they respond to government regulations. Conventional designs are often not connected to scales higher than the site level—the community and the region. The Center for Rural Massachusetts and the University of Colorado at Denver designs were undertaken as part of a

comprehensive landscape planning process.

Both designs seek to respond to the landscape ecology of their regions and to be appropriate to the local culture. Laurie Olin (1988) has identified several elements that are central to thoughtful contemporary landscape design. The subject matter identified by Olin (1988) as important includes ideas of order, ideas of nature, ideas about the arrangement of places, ideas that reveal something about process, and considerations about the history of places. These ideas and considerations are evident in the designs completed for the Connecticut River valley and Teller County.

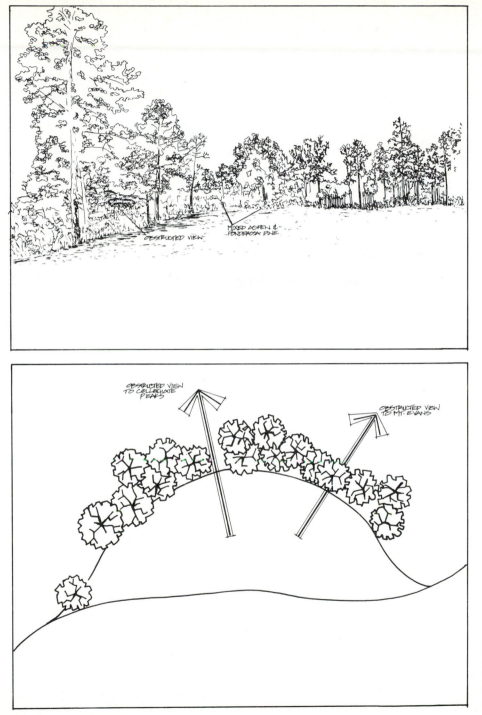

FIGURE 9.33 Existing roadway pull-off in Teller County, Colorado. *(Source: Bell et al., 1989, drawn by Gretchen Schalge)*

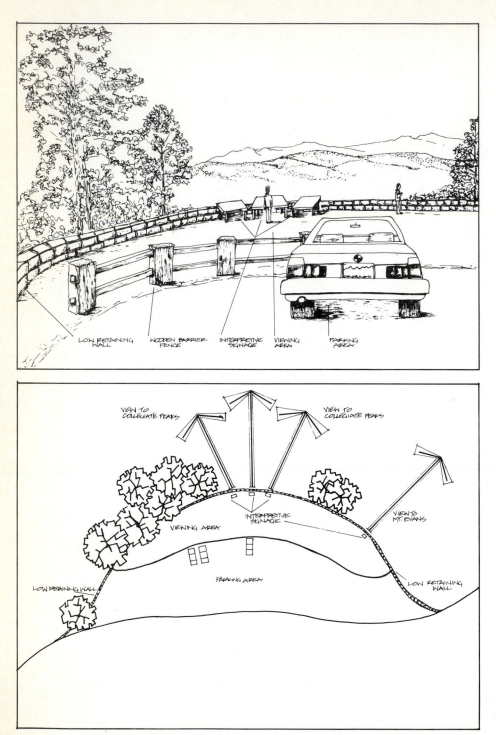

FIGURE 9.34 Design for roadway pull-off in Teller County, Colorado. *(Source: Bell et al., 1989, drawn by Gretchen Schalge)*

10

PLAN AND DESIGN IMPLEMENTATION

American politicians, planners, lawyers, and public administrators have been quite resourceful in developing a wide array of techniques to realize plans. Once a plan has been prepared and adopted, then it is necessary to develop the means for implementation. Often the selection of an implementation strategy coincides with the selection of a preferred option, the development of a landscape plan, and/or the preparation of a detailed design. For this discussion, it is helpful to separate the steps in the planning process to illustrate the intricacies involved in each.

Governments have three general kinds of authority that can be used to implement plans: the power to regulate, the power to spend, and the power to tax. The most popular regulatory technique used in the United States is zoning. Other techniques, which may be used in conjunction with zoning, include planned unit developments (PUDs), performance standards, critical (or environmentally sensitive) areas protection, subdivision regulations, building codes, and covenants.

Governments may spend money in a variety of ways. The

outright, or fee simple, purchase of land is one option. Governments can buy an easement, or partial rights, to a parcel of property. A specific type of easement, development rights, is another possibility. Condemnation can also be used to obtain property. Government may manage its major expenditures through capital improvement programs and through the administration of public lands.

The power to tax is the third general kind of authority. All three powers may be in concert. The activities and programs of agencies can be coordinated to manage growth. In addition to government activities, there are also nongovernment strategies that can be used to implement plans. These nongovernmental strategies can be employed in cooperation with the efforts of governments.

Whatever means is selected to implement community goals, it is helpful to assign responsibilities for the selected measure(s). One device to help organize such responsibilities is an implementation matrix. After presenting an example of this matrix, three examples of planning implementation will be described: the York County, Pennsylvania, sliding-scale zoning; the Black Hawk County, Iowa, agricultural zoning; and the Snohomish County, Washington, growth management plan.

POWER TO REGULATE

Zoning

The planning profession is a fickle friend to zoning. Since the 1960s, there has been a continual stream of criticism about zoning in the planning community. The noted historian John Reps called for a "requiem for zoning" (1964). Such diverse individuals as Herbert Gans and Ada Louise Huxtable joined the chorus of criticism. Much of this criticism was justified; zoning is an imperfect device.

Because of this criticism, the curricula of many university planning programs do not explicitly address zoning. Planning programs are mistaken for not addressing zoning more fully in their curricula for two reasons. First, other professions—law, civil engineering, public administration, and landscape architecture—have continued to incorporate zoning into their education and practice.

Second, zoning has remained an important tool for the practice of planning. With weak comprehensive planning statutes in most states, planners must rely on case law for implementation. Zoning has been upheld continually in the courts. The first zoning ordinances in the United States were adopted in California in the late nineteenth century for repugnant reasons. The purpose was to discriminate against Chinese immigrant businesses, specifically laundries, considered fire risks and a public nuisance. These ordinances were upheld in the California courts.

At about the same time in the Eastern and Great Lake states, similar devices were being used to regulate the height and bulk of buildings. The first comprehensive zoning ordinance was adopted in New York City in 1916, written largely by attorney Edward M. Bassett. Because of the interest in zoning created by Bassett and other lawyers, such as Alfred Bettman, James Metzenbaum, and F. B. Williams, the U.S. Department of Commerce published the Standard Zoning Enabling Act in 1922. Zoning was found to be constitutional in 1926 as a result of the U.S. Supreme Court's landmark decision *Euclid v. Ambler Realty Co.* (272 U.S. 365). As a result, even more local interest was generated as states continued to adopt the standard zoning enabling act.

The purpose of zoning is derived from the police power of government, which is to ensure the welfare of a community. A well-prepared zoning ordinance, based on a plan, seeks to secure the most appropriate use of land and to facilitate adequate but economic provisions of public improvements. The authority for local governments to adopt zoning ordinances is contained in state enabling legislation. Ideally, and as required by law in some states, a comprehensive development plan is a prerequisite for the preparation of a zoning ordinance.

Zoning refers to the land-use controls that limit the use to which land in an area may be put. Zoning includes variances, special-use permits, and other devices that allow regulatory flexibility. According to Leary, "zoning is a means of insuring that the land uses of a community are properly situated in relation to one another, providing adequate space for each type of development" (1968, p. 403).

The basic idea of zoning is to separate potentially conflicting land uses. Zoning ordinances usually include a statement of purpose, definitions, and a description of districts. Zoning districts commonly include specific uses like residential (R), agriculture (A), commercial (C), and industrial (I) as well as areas like floodplains (FP) and open space (OS). Uses are further specified by intensity like R1 (low-density residential) and R3 (high-density residential). Some rural counties have adopted similar hierarchies for agricultural land use: A1 (orchards) to A3 (pasture land). Each zone is regulated by specific provisions, including permitted uses, accessary uses, provisional uses, height restrictions, yard regulations, land-to-building ratio, parking requirements, fencing and screening requirements, sign requirements, and ingress and egress requirements. The districts are designated in a map that is part of the ordinance. Ideally, these zoning districts should relate to the suitability of the land for such use. Ordinances also include provisions for nonconforming uses, variances, platting of land, enforcement, and penalties.

There are a number of requirements that zoning ordinances must follow. They are summarized by Leary:

- While regulations may vary for different zoning districts, they must be uniform within each district for each class and kind of building.
- State legislatures and the courts have insisted that

The basic idea of zoning is to separate potentially conflicting land uses, and the integration of uses to form communities. Here is an example where uses are separated, but the new use is inappropriate and does not fit the landscape. As a result, instead of helping to build a community, the new use disrupts the traditional settlement. *(USDA-Soil Conservation Service)*

there be a reasonable basis for classifying particular areas differently from others.
- The courts have insisted that an ordinance cover the entire jurisdictional area of a city or county, rather than singling out a small area for regulation and leaving the remainder unrestricted.
- The courts insist that the zoning regulations be reasonable in their application to particular properties. In other words, there should be a relationship between the physical character of an area and its zoning classification. (1968, p. 404)

Three common weaknesses of zoning are the inconsistency between the zoning ordinance and planning goals and policies, the relative ease of zone changes or rezoning, and the relative vulnerability of ordinances to ephemeral political changes. From the late 1960s and through the

1980s there have been a number of gradual changes that somewhat ameliorate these past weaknesses. Three court decisions especially important in this regard include:

- *Udell v. Haas* (21 N.Y. 2d 46, 1968), in which the New York Supreme Court in 1968 struck down zoning provisions as contrary to the comprehensive plan
- *Fasano v. Board of County Commissioners of Washington County* (507 P. 2d 23, 1973), in which the Oregon Supreme Court in 1973 determined that zone changes must be in conformance with the local comprehensive plan
- *Baker v. City of Milwaukie* (P. 2d 772, 1975), in which the Oregon Supreme Court in 1975 held zoning decisions must be in accordance with the comprehensive plan (Callies, 1980)

Combined with new planning legislation in several states mandating—rather than enabling— local planning, these three court decisions and many others have resulted in a resurgence of zoning. The renaissance has been strengthened by the growing movement to protect resources such as wetlands, coasts, farmlands, and historic places. In their farmland protection work, for instance, several planners have found zoning to be more acceptable by rural people generally, and farmers specifically, than more complex, innovative land-use controls (Nellis, 1980; Kartez, 1980; Toner, 1981).

Planned Unit Developments (PUDs)

A *planned unit development* (PUD) is comprehensively conceived and contains some mix of residential, commercial, industrial, institutional, and recreational land uses on a single tract of land. Sometimes a PUD ordinance is included as a part of zoning regulations, while at other times it is allowed under separate rules. PUD ordinances offer benefits to both developers and communities.

Often developers are allowed greater design flexibility and greater densities, while communities are able to protect environmentally sensitive areas or enforce design standards. For instance, a tract of land may include areas with steep slopes and unique vegetation. Part of the land may be located inside a floodplain. These steep-sloped, vegetated, flood-prone places could be left in open space, allowing the developer to cluster denser housing or commercial structures in a more suitable location.

PUD ordinances usually require a developer to submit a complete development plan for review. Such a plan includes a combination of maps, drawings, site designs, charts, and supportive narrative material that portray the development to be achieved in the overall project. The PUD documents provide sufficiently detailed information to both illustrate and describe the intended character and configuration of the proposed development. These proposals are reviewed by the city or county staff, the planning commission, and the elected officials.

According to De Chiara and Koppelman (1975), PUDs have three major characteristics:

1. PUDs usually involve areas and undertakings of a relatively large scale at least 100 acres (40.5 hectares) and occasionally smaller, but usually larger, up to 1,000 acres (405 hectares).
2. PUDs usually involve a mixture of land uses and building types.
3. PUDs usually involve stage-by-stage development over a relatively long period of time (5 to 15 years) during which buildings, arrangements, and uses may have to be redesigned to meet changes of requirements, technology, financing, or even design concepts.

Performance Standards

Like many other planning techniques, *performance standards* is a rather broad, generic term that has been defined and applied in several different ways. Basically, the term refers to criteria that are established and must be met before a certain use will be permitted. These criteria, or standards, may be a set of economic, environmental, or social factors or any combination of these factors.

Originally performance standards were used as a means for prescribing specific conditions for observable or scientifically measurable industrial plant emissions. This system was first proposed by the executive director of the American Society of Planning Officials, Dennis O'Harrow in his 1954 study, *Planning Standards in Industrial Zoning*.

More recently, performance standards have been linked to zoning ordinances in various ways. For instance, in some areas that permit septic tanks, a number of environmental factors, such as the depth to water table and soil type, are used to determine whether or not housing will be allowed. Permitting too much housing with septic tanks in many areas will result in environmental degradation that can endanger human health.

In the Whitman County, Washington, zoning ordinance, performance standards were established creating minimum standards for agricultural districts, including requirements for single-family housing. The intent of this district was that agriculture be the primary use and that all other uses be sited so as to minimize their impact on, or conflict with, adjacent agricultural uses (Table 10.1).

Bucks County, Pennsylvania, has also developed a system for performance zoning. This straightforward system is based on a five-step process, outlined in Table 10.2 (Kendig, 1977). Both the Whitman and Bucks County examples rely on accurate technical information concerning an area's resources.

Kirk Wickersham (1978) and Lee Nellis (1981) have developed permit systems to implement performance standards. Permit systems do not rely on conventionally defined (residential, industrial, and agriculture) zoning districts to segregate potentially incompatible uses. Instead, these systems evaluate all development proposals on the basis of their compliance with a checklist of performance standards. The standards are derived from the planning goals and policies. Most permit system checklists include two kinds of policies:

TABLE 10.1

WHITMAN COUNTY ZONING ORDINANCE FOR RURAL HOUSING

Two of the following three conditions must exist:

1. The subject lot is underlain by basaltic or alluvial surface geology, or if it is underlain by crystalline surface geology, the average slope must be no less than one vertical foot in five horizontal feet. These facts must be verified by reference to the geological map contained in Water Supply Bulletin No. 26, *Reconnaisance of Geology and Ground-Water Occurrence in Whitman County, Washington*, published by the State of Washington, Department of Ecology, and dated 1969. Whenever difficulty exists in the verification of surface geological conditions from this map, reference shall also be made to the maps of detailed soil mapping units maintained by the Soil Conservation Service, which maps shall either indicate or not indicate a pattern of specific soil types which is known to be associated with basaltic, alluvial or crystalline surface geological conditions.

2. The subject lot has been cultivated, used for production of commercial forage for sale, commercial grazing of livestock for sale or subjected to any agricultural practice designed to produce a product for sale in the preceding three years.

3. The subject lot is within a distinct area of land 15 acres or less which is of sufficient size, quality and/or accessibility to be efficiently used for agricultural production for income. "Distinct" shall mean that the subject area is substantially bounded by natural or man-made features which buffer this land from agricultural lands, such as: wooded areas, steep canyon walls, railroads, surface waters or public roads.

All the following requirements must be met:

1. The subject lot must have frontage on an improved county or state road of at least 200 feet. "Improved" shall mean a gravel surface or better.

2. If perennial surface water passes through, or along any boundary of the subject lot, there must be at least 200 feet of frontage along such surface water.

3. Less than one-half of the area of the subject lot shall be in an area of special flood hazard and/or a floodway as designated on the flood hazard boundary map of the *Flood Insurance Study for Whitman County*.

4. Construction plans for structures, parking areas and private roads on the subject lot shall leave a maximum amount of existing vegetation undisturbed.

5. The area of the subject lot shall be less than the minimum area required by the Whitman County Department of Environmental Health to safely accommodate approved water supply and on-site sewage disposal systems.

SOURCE: Whitman County Regional Planning Council, 1979.

TABLE 10.2
BUCKS COUNTY, PENNSYLVANIA, PERFORMANCE ZONING

STEP 1. Calculating Base Site Area

Certain portions of tracts may not be usable for the activities proposed for the site. These are subtracted from the site area to determine base site.

	Site A	Site B
1. Site area as determined by actual on-site survey.	20.6 acres	20.6 acres
2. Subtract land within ultimate right-of-way of existing roads, or utility rights-of-way or easements.	−0.6	−0.6
3. Subtract land which is not contiguous: a. A separate parcel which does not abut or adjoin nor share common boundaries with the rest of the development. b. Land which is cut off from the main parcel by a road, railroad, existing land uses, or major stream so as to serve as a major barrier to common use, or so that it is isolated and unavailable for building purposes.	0	0
4. Subtract land which in a previously approved subdivision was reserved for resource reasons such as flooding or recreation.	0	0
5. Subtract land used or zoned for another use (land which is used or to be used for commercial or industrial uses in a residential development, or land in a different zoning district than the primary use).	0	0
	20.0 acres (8.1 ha)	20.0 acres (8.1 ha)

STEP 2. Subtracting Resource Protection Land

Resource	Open Space Ratio	Site A		Site B	
		Acres of Land in Resource	Resource Protection Land (Acres in Resource × Open Space Ratio)	Acres of Land in Resource	Resource Protection Land (Acres in Resource × Open Space Ratio)
Floodplains	1.00	0.5	0.5	4.5	4.5
Floodplain soils	1.00				
Lakes or ponds	1.00				
Wetlands	1.00	0.2	0.2	1.5	1.5
Natural retention area	0.90				
Steep slope (25% or more)	0.85				
Forest	0.80	1.0	0.8	2.3	1.84
Pond shore	0.80				
Lake shore	0.70				
Steep slope (15–25%)	0.70				
Steep slope (8–15%)	0.60				
Total land with resource restrictions		1.7		8.3	
Total resource protection land			1.5		7.84

All land within the base site area shall be mapped and measured for the purpose of determining the amount of open space needed to protect it.

TABLE 10.2 *(continues)*

STEP 3. Allowing for Recreation Land

While some of the open space required by the zoning district may be resource protection land, the intent is to provide for usable public or common open space as near to each unit as possible. Thus, there is a need for specific guidelines ensuring that a minimum amount of land not restricted by 1 or 2 above is retained for this purpose. Therefore:

		Site A	Site B
Take	Base site area	20.0 acres	20.0 acres
Subtract	Total land with resource restriction	− 1.7	− 8.3
Equals	Total unrestricted land	= 18.3	= 11.7
Multiply	Total unrestricted land by 0.2	× 0.2	× 0.2
Total	Recreation land	= 3.66 acres	= 2.34 acres

STEP 4. Determining Site Capacity

Individual site capacity is found by calculating net buildable site area. For single-family, single-family cluster, or performance subdivisions, the number of allowable dwelling units is determined by multiplying the net density by net buildable site area. The calculations are as follows:

		Site A	Site B
Take	Resource protection land	1.5 acres	7.84 acres
Add	Recreation land	+ 3.66	+ 2.34
Equals	Total open space	= 5.16	= 10.18 acres
Take	Base site area	20.0	20.0
Multiply	By open space ratio*	× 0.4	× 0.4
Equals	Minimum required open space	= 8.0 acres	= 8.0 acres
Take	Base site area	20.0 acres	20.0 acres
Subtract	Total open space or minimum required open space, which ever is greater	− 8.0	− 10.18
Equals	Net buildable site area	= 12.0 acres	= 9.82 acres

* Each zoning district has minimum open space requirements as described in its zoning regulations. In this example it is 40% (0.4).

STEP 5. Calculating Permitted Number of Dwelling Units

		Site A	Site B
Take	Net buildable site area	12.0 acres	9.82 acres
Multiply	Net density	× 2.4	2.4
Equals	Number of dwelling units (do not round off)	= 28.0 du/acre	23.568 du/acre

SOURCE: Adapted from Kendig, 1977.

absolute and relative. Absolute policies require or prohibit certain kinds or levels of performance, while the performance of the project on the relative policies is assessed by using a point-scoring system. The total "score" of a project may be used as the basis for density bonuses that reward positive actions on the part of developers.

While permit systems do not use conventional zoning districts, they may make extensive use of mapped environmental information. They may also be implemented on a neighborhood basis, in which a different set of policies applies to each neighborhood, with the neighborhoods being defined by watershed boundaries, visual or historical character, or the presence of a local "sense" of community. The development of a permit system for a particular place usually involves extensive public participation and an emphasis on procedural simplicity. Permit systems have been successfully used in growing rural areas in the Rocky Mountains, Alaska, the Missouri Ozarks, and Kentucky.

An example of a point system used with zoning districts exists in Breckenridge, Colorado (Wickersham, 1978; Humphreys, 1985). The Breckenridge comprehensive plan sets forth the guidance of growth as the town goal to preserve historic buildings in the old mining town and to integrate new buildings. To implement the plan, a land-use guidance system was adopted which establishes forty-two districts with specific standards for uses and architectural character. The guidance system is enforced through the Breckenridge Development Code, a set of two policies covering a range of subjects like air and water quality, the restoration of historic artifacts, and housing (Humphreys, 1985).

The Breckenridge code contains two types of policies: absolute and relative. Projects are analyzed by planners based on a point system to determine how well the proposed development meets both absolute and relative criteria. A proposed project must be approved by the town of Breckenridge when it meets all the absolute

policies or has no negative effect on those policies and when it receives a positive score for its compliance with relative policies. According to Humphreys, the point analysis "is the quantitative backbone of the development code system" (1985, p. 23). He notes that "over the past three years, I have watched over some 1,200 reviews, and, in that time, I have come to believe that the development code has major strengths in flexibility, comprehensiveness, and capacity for negotiation and revision" (Humphreys, 1985, p. 24).

Similar point systems, added on top of traditional zoning regulations, have also been used to help manage growth on a competitive basis in Petaluma, California; Boulder, Colorado; and Ramapo, New York. (See Chapter 11 for more discussion about Boulder). In competitive systems added to zoning ordinances, a fixed number of permitted developments within each zone is allowed each year. Development proposals are measured against a fixed standard and permitted or denied on its merits.

Critical or Environmentally Sensitive Areas

Performance standards are a tool to encourage as well as control development. In contrast, critical or environmentally sensitive areas protection are a way to prohibit development. Critical and environmentally sensitive areas are terms and concepts often used interchangeably. Critical areas were proposed by the American Law Institute's *Model Land Development Code,* which described them as:

- An area significantly affected by, or having an effect upon, an existing or proposed major public facility or other areas of major public investment
- An area containing or having a significant impact upon historical, natural or environmental resources of regional or statewide importance (American Law Institute, 1974)

The Washington State Environmental Policy Act (SEPA) describes environmentally sensitive areas as

> [those that] could have a significant adverse environmental impact, including but not limited to, areas with unstable soils, steep slopes, unusual or unique plants or animals, wetlands, or areas which lie within floodplains. (State of Washington, 1984, section 908)

SEPA provisions in Washington enable city and county governments to designate areas within their jurisdictions which are environmentally sensitive. As a result of SEPA, a procedural review is required for proposed actions that may impact the environment. Some actions, however, are specifically exempt from the environmental review process. Because these actions still may have a significant impact on environmental quality, the SEPA law includes the provision allowing the local designation of environmentally sensitive areas. Within locally designated areas, proposals, programs, and actions are subject to environmental review procedures (Jennings & Reganold, 1988). This Washington provision is consistent with the suggestions of the American Law Institute (1974) that critical area policy be adopted on the state level. On the local level, such an area may be separated by zoning districts or may overlay several zones.

The courts have taken a favorable view to protecting critical or environmentally sensitive areas. For instance, in the 1972 case *Just v. Marinette County* (56 Wisc. 2d 7), the Wisconsin Supreme Court upheld county restrictions on wetlands. According to the Wisconsin court:

> [Marinette County's] ordinance that requires a wetland owner to obtain a permit before filling, draining, or dredging is constitutional, since restrictions on use of privately owned wetlands serve to protect the state's natural resources and constitute reasonable application of police power. (Wisconsin Supreme Court, 1972)

In this case, wetlands were clearly identified through state policy and local ordinance.

According to the Marinette County shorelines ordinance, such wetlands needed protection because "uncontrolled use of shorelines and pollution of navigable waters adversely affect public health, safety, convenience, general welfare, and impair the tax base" (Wisconsin Supreme Court, 1972).

George Newman (1982) suggested a system for classifying environmentally sensitive areas adapted from those developed by the New Jersey Pinelands Commission and the Smithsonian Institution (Table 10.3). The Pinelands Commission divides environmentally sensitive areas into four categories: ecologically critical areas, perceptually and culturally critical areas, economically critical areas, and natural hazard critical areas. Newman renamed economically critical areas "resource production critical areas" and developed the following four definitions:

1. *Ecological critical areas* contain one or more significant natural resources that could be degraded or lost as a result of uncontrolled or incompatible development. They are based on resource quality, scarcity, or the role the resource plays in the ecosystem. These areas can provide many amenities and services to the public and to private landowners. Maintaining the natural system helps to provide flood control, water purification, water supply, pollution abatement, wildlife habitat, and a pleasing and visually diversified landscape. Ecological areas provide sites for outdoor education, scientific study, or habitat for the spawning and rearing of anadromous fish. Such areas also have the psychological or philosophical value to those who gain comfort from knowing that open semiwilderness areas and rare and endangered species and habitats still exist.

2. *Perceptual and cultural critical areas* contain one or more significant scenic, recreational, archeological, historical, or cultural resources that could be degraded or lost as a result of

TABLE 10.3
ENVIRONMENTALLY SENSITIVE AREA CLASSIFICATION SYSTEM

Class	Subclass
Ecologically critical areas	1. Natural wildlife habitat areas
	2. Natural ecological areas
	3. Scientific areas
Perceptual and cultural critical areas	4. Scenic areas
	5. Wilderness recreation areas
	6. Historic, archeological, and cultural areas
Resource production critical areas	7. Agricultural lands
	8. Water quality areas
	9. Mineral extraction areas
Natural hazard critical areas	10. Flood prone areas
	11. Fire hazard areas
	12. Geologic hazard areas
	13. Air pollution areas

SOURCES: Column 1 is adapted from Pinelands Commission, 1980; column 2 is adapted from Center for Natural Areas, Smithsonian Institution, 1974.

uncontrolled or incompatible development. They have features such as access and proximity to water, special recreation sites, or buildings possessing significant historic or archaeologic values.

3. *Resource production critical areas* provide essential products supporting either the local economy or economies of a larger scale. The significant resources can be either the essential products—such as agricultural crops, timber products, or sand and gravel—or the resources necessary for the production of such essential products—such as soil and water. These resources are primarily economically valuable; however, secondary values may include recreational values or cultural or life support values associated with local communities. These resources can be renewable, like timber, or nonrenewable, like mineral resources.

4. *Natural hazard critical areas* may result in the loss of life and property due to incompatible development. These areas include earth-slide, flood-prone, earthquake, avalanche, or fire hazard areas. (Adapted from the Pinelands Commission, 1980; Newman, 1982)

Newman suggested the use of the definitions developed by the Smithsonian Institution for use in the subclasses of his system:

1. *Natural wildlife habitat areas* are essential to the preservation of either game species or unique, rare, or endangered species. They provide food, shelter, and breeding areas and may be areas where animals seasonally concentrate, such as, deer yards, migratory stop-over areas, aquatic spawning areas, and nesting areas for birds. The size of the area must be large enough to fulfill the species' needs. It is important that the area is inherently stable, which is more likely if it contains a high diversity of flora or fauna. Additionally, a greater variety of animal species is associated with a diversity of vegetation types. The uses of these areas will vary according to wildlife. Habitats of endangered species may have to be strictly protected while recreational hunting can be allowed in areas supporting game species.

2. *Natural ecological areas* have ecosystem units that are either superlative examples of their type or locations that perform a vital function in maintaining the ecological integrity and environmental quality of a larger region. Furthermore, natural areas may be an important component of the human life-support system.

3. *Scientific areas* are of geological interest or present ecological processes warranting study. Most of these areas have been studied, and they can be identified by experts within the local scientific and academic community. Scarcity on regional, state, and national levels is an important factor.

4. *Wilderness recreation areas* are isolated tracts of land large enough to support recreational

(Frederick Steiner)

activities like camping, hiking, and canoeing. Isolated wilderness areas close to population centers are the most valuable.

5. *Scenic areas* contain natural features of sufficient aesthetic quality to warrant their preservation. Several methods have been developed for determining scenic values, but the determination of aesthetic quality remains subjective. Some methods attempt to survey the public's values of various landscapes and geological formations, while other methods review such factors as vegetative type, composition, and texture; topography; and geographic features. The scarcity and location of these areas is often an important consideration.

6. *Historic, archaeological, and cultural areas* are important to the heritage of the community, region, state, or nation. These areas may contain structures or artifacts, or they may be associated with an important historic event. The sites may be considered by archaeologists as likely to yield important information. These

areas are listed by state historical and heritage agencies or societies, although most of these organizations do not rate the sites according to their importance.

7. *Agricultural lands* are used for crop or animal production or for silviculture. A reason for including these lands in the subclassification is that the private market is unable to adequately incorporate long-term or future agricultural demands so as to ensure prime lands will remain in farm use. Soils for agriculture and forest for timber production are renewable resources when properly managed. However, development of these areas may cause irreversible damage to the resources. Soil productivity (generally based on the SCS land-capability or productivity ratings) and the availability of water are the factors important for crop production. The LESA system, described in Chapter 5, can be used to help identify important agricultural areas. State agriculture departments have production-yield figures, and the USFS maintains a forest growth

potential rating system to determine timber production areas.

8. *Water quality areas* ensure the maintenance of sources of high-quality water. These areas are generally aquifer recharge areas, headwaters, stream corridors, and wetlands that function as a natural filter for surface waters.

9. *Mineral extraction areas* contain sufficient quantities of high-quality minerals to warrant their protection from development that would exclude the possibility of extraction. These areas contain minerals or materials of commercial quality and quantity and include, but are not limited to, sand, gravel, clay, peat, rock, and ores.

10. *Flood-prone areas* are identified on the basis of the frequency of flooding. They may be either floodplain areas adjacent to rivers or coastal areas within the hurricane zone. The U.S. Army Corps of Engineers can help to identify the frequency of flooding in these areas.

11. *Fire hazard areas* are identified by the USFS and state wildfire management agencies as being particularly susceptible to forest fires. The important factors are the type and quantity of fuel accumulation and weather.

12. *Geological hazard areas* are characterized by a high frequency of earthquake shaking, landslides, fault displacements, volcanic activity, subsidence, or severe erosion.

13. *Air pollution areas* require restraints on air pollution emissions due to periods of poor vertical air mixing and the subsequent entrapment of polluting substances. Topographic features and meterological conditions are the most important factors in their identification (Center for Natural Areas, Smithsonian Institution, 1974; Pinelands Commission, 1980, Newman, 1982)

The identification of critical areas in the Pinelands was based on the work of the Philadelphia-based consulting firm of Rogers, Golden, and Halpern. Areas for consideration as

critical were nominated and ranked. Table 10.4 illustrates how mapped areas were ranked, while Table 10.5 shows the criteria used for ranking ecological critical areas in the Pinelands.

Subdivision Regulations

In contrast to performance standards and critical areas, subdivision regulations and building codes are much older forms of land-use controls. In the Old Testament there is a description of the proposals made by Ezekiel for the building of Jerusalem. The first recorded regulations on the division of land in the Western Hemisphere were the Laws of the Indies of 1573 used in Spanish colonization. According to John Reps, "in 1573, Philip II proclaimed the Laws of the Indies to establish uniform standards and procedures for planning of towns and their surrounding lands as well as for all other details of colonial settlement" (1970, p. 41). The Laws of the Indies were based on older European laws dating back to the time of the Romans. Modern American subdivision regulations are, according to Green,

> locally adopted laws governing the process of converting raw land into building sites. They normally accomplish this through plat approval procedures, under which a developer is not permitted to make improvements or to divide and sell [the] land until the planning commission has approved a plat (map) of the proposed design of [the] subdivision. The approval or disapproval of the commission is based upon compliance or noncompliance of the proposal set forth in the subdivision regulations. In the event that the developer attempts to record an unapproved plat in the local registry of deeds (or county record's office) or sell lots by reference to such a plat, [the developer] may be subject to various civil and criminal penalties. (1968, p. 445)

Obviously, from this description, there is a strong enforcement capability in such regulations. The purpose of subdivision regulations is to protect the public interest during the laying out of land and

TABLE 10.4
SAMPLE OF FORM USED TO RANK ECOLOGICALLY CRITICAL AREAS IN THE NEW JERSEY PINELANDS

CEDAR CREEK WATERSHED

Critical Area Mapping Units	Linkage Corridors	Unique or Exceptional Ecosystems	Pristine Aquatic Communities	Headwaters	Nationally Endangered Animal Species	Diversity of Vegetation Types within a Given Area	Nationally Proposed or under Review Plant or Animal Species	State Endangered, Threatened, Declining, or Undetermined Plant or Animal Species	Representative Vegetation Types	Outlier, Disjunct, or Relict Species	Species at the Limits of Their Range	Restricted and Endemic Species	Breeding Areas (Nesting and Spawning)	Overwintering Concentrations	Migratory Stopover Areas	Areas of Scientific Interest and Research	Oldest, Largest, or Exceptional Specimen Trees
Cedar Creek (1)			•	•		•	•	3		•	3	•	•	•	•		
Cedar Creek (2)			•	•		•	•			•							
Factory Branch			•	•		•	•	•	•	•	•						
Newbolds Branch		•	•	•		•	•	•		•	•						
Daniels Branch		•	•	•		•	•	•	•	•	•						
Bamber Lake			•	•		•		•	•	•	•			•			
Chamberlain Branch			•	•		•		•	•	•				•			
Webbs Mill Branch		•	•	•		•	•	3		2	2			•		•	

Legend

• The criterion applies to the critical area.

2 Two species from the criterion are found in the critical area.

3 Three species from the criterion are found in the critical area.

SOURCE: Pinelands Commission, 1980.

253

TABLE 10.5

RANKING CRITERIA FOR ECOLOGICALLY CRITICAL AREAS IN THE NEW JERSEY PINELANDS

Critical Areas Criteria	Group and Sample Size (*n*)				
	Staff, Scientists and Consultants (*n* = 17)	Burlington County Public Meeting (*n* = 31)	Atlantic County Public Meeting (*n* = 22)	Ocean County Public Meeting (*n* = 29)	Average (*n* = 99)
Pristine aquatic communities	1	1	1	2	1
Headwaters	2	2	2	1	2
Unique or exceptional ecosystems	3	3	3	3	3
Nationally endangered species	5	5	5	7–8	6
Linkage corridors	4	4	7	4	4
State endangered, threatened, declining, or undetermined species	7	9	6	5–6	5
Breeding areas (nesting or spawning)	6	6	4	5–6	5
Species proposed or under review for national list	8	12–13	10	10	11
Diversity of vegetation types within a given area	9	7	11	9	8
Outlier, disjunct, or relict species	11	16	14	15	15
Migratory stopover areas	12	8	8	12	9
Restricted and endemic species	10	11	12	14	13
Overwintering concentrations	14	10	9	11	10
Representative vegetation types	13	12–13	13	7–8	12
Species at limits of their geographic range	15	15	16	16	16
Areas of scientific interest and research	16	14	15	13	14
Oldest, largest, or exceptional tree specimens	17	17	17	17	17

SOURCE: Pinelands Commission, 1980.

the construction of public improvements. Like comprehensive or general plans and zoning ordinances, local governments have the authority to enact subdivision regulations through state enabling legislation. Subdivision regulations usually have strong enforcement provisions: deeds to subdivided land may not be recorded or registered, and consequently land may not be sold until the planning commission forwards an approved copy of a final plat to the county clerk or auditor (Kleymeyer, no date)

Subdivision regulations often require a six-step process:

1. A *preapplication stage* where the developer and planning staff discuss the proposed development to check if all the requirements are met
2. A *preliminary plat,* often prepared by a landscape architect, registered surveyor, or engineer, is submitted to the planning agency
3. The planning commission and/or agency *reviews* the preliminary plat and approves or denies it
4. Most subdivision regulations next require that the developer *construct the improvements* specified in the preliminary plat
5. A *final plat,* which is sometimes two documents: an engineering plat and a plat of record, is submitted for approval
6. The *approved plat* is recorded

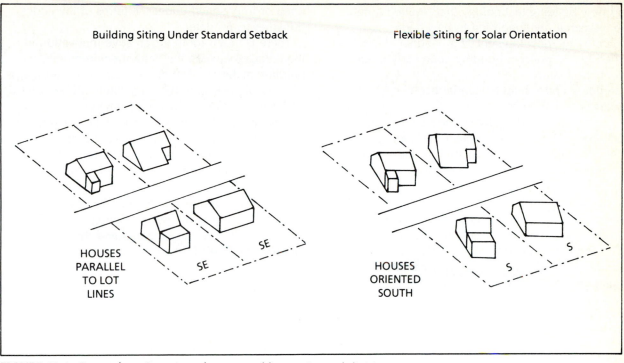

FIGURE 10.1 Poor solar orientation of streets and houses in a subdivision compared with good solar orientation. *(Source: Jaffee & Erley, no date)*

Like performance standards and critical areas protection, subdivision regulations are often connected to zoning ordinances. Much innovation occurred in the drafting of subdivision regulations during the 1970s largely as a result of the energy crisis. These innovations rely heavily on natural science information: regional climate, slope (aspect and steepness), microclimate, and vegetation. For instance, Figure 10.1 compares poor solar orientation of streets and houses in a subdivision with good solar orientation.

Building Codes

Building codes have a long history. The code of the Babylonian King Hammurabi is the first written reference to building codes. The code of Hammurabi sets forth the principle of compensatory justice for damages and punishment for faulty construction. There are biblical references to building specifications that were used to construct the ark and the temple. The poor natural conditions and overcrowding in Rome necessitated the development of tenement codes that were adopted in Roman new towns. There are numerous examples of codes in European cities after the Renaissance, such as those in Munich, Kiev, and London.

Building codes in North America began in Boston in 1629 and continued with English colonial activity in the middle Atlantic and southern states. After the American Revolution, height limitations were imposed on the new federal capital in Washington, D.C. The overcrowding and new building technology that resulted during the industrial revolution led to new codes, including the development of a national electrical code and uniform building code early in the twentieth century.

Building codes help to standardize construction practices and augment the spread of new materials and practices. Codes specify the size and use of materials as well as help protect the safety of the public through ensuring structural soundness and fire prevention and control. Health is protected through water and sewage systems. Building codes are often used with zoning ordinances and subdivision regulations to control population density. The purpose of building and other codes is to secure the general public safety, health, and welfare through structure strength, stability, sanitation, adequate light, and ventilation. Codes also ensure safety to life and property from fire hazards incident to the construction, alteration, repair, removal, demolition, use, and occupancy of buildings or premises. As with zoning ordinances and subdivision regulations, the authority for codes is derived from state enabling legislation with local governmental adoption (Kleymeyer, no date).

The major codes include the uniform building code (Table 10.6) and plumbing, electrical, mechanical, fire, and, recently, solar codes. These codes are usually enforced through a permit process. Plans are approved by inspection of new construction and remodeling. Continuing inspections are made during construction by the building, fire, plumbing, electrical, or elevator inspectors as well as other specialists employed by the building or health department of the jurisdiction. Violations are noted by these inspectors and are written as "building orders" against the owners of the properties in violation. Owners are given a specified time to correct the deficiencies or face a court action. A building official checks the structure to ensure it complies to the codes before an occupancy permit is granted. Those not making the necessary corrections are cited to court where they may be

fined or imprisoned under the terms of the codes (Kleymeyer, no date).

There is much room for creative innovation in the linkage between the natural environment, new building materials, and codes. Davis, California, is an example of a city that completely revised and updated its codes to encourage energy conservation. The revised codes take into account the climate, hydrology, and vegetation of Davis. For instance, it was hypothesized that light-colored roofing materials might serve to reflect heat in the intense summer climate of central California and therefore keep buildings cooler. Davis officials experimented with numerous roofing materials and found their theory substantiated and then incorporated their findings into the building code.

Covenants

Covenants are agreements, usually voluntary, that restrict what can be done with private property. Generally, for a covenant to be imposed, property has to change hands, at which time these agreements appear in the property deed. Typically, covenants are placed on a property by an owner prior to sale. Usually it is private parties, rather than governments, who impose covenants. They are usually backed up by government authority and may be called *voluntary covenants,* *restrictive covenants,* or *deed restrictions.* The purpose of covenants is to place additional rules, regulations, and/or restrictions upon the use of land over and above, or not capable of being implemented, those in the zoning ordinances, subdivision regulations or building codes; or in the absence of such ordinances, regulations, or codes. The authority for covenants is derived from real estate laws that have been codified by the various states, based upon English common law and additionally interpreted by the state and federal courts (Kleymeyer, no date).

Often all lots within a subdivision will have covenants attached to the land title that describe and design limitations on houses or other structures

TABLE 10.6
UNIFORM BUILDING CODE (SUMMARY OF COMPONENTS)

1. Location on the lot
2. Light, ventilation, and sanitation
   a. Windows and ventilation
   b. Ceiling heights
   c. Room size
   d. Sanitation
   e. Fire warning system
3. Private garages and carports
4. Foundations, retaining walls, and drainage
5. Chimneys, fireplace, and barbecues
   a. Reinforcing and seismic anchorage
   b. Flue area
   c. Height
   d. Inlets
   e. Loads on chimney
6. Masonry Chimneys
   a. Lining
   b. Wall thickness
   c. Support
   d. Clearance
   e. Factory-built chimneys
7. Fireplaces
   a. Fireplace walls
   b. Lintel
   c. Hearth
   d. Hearth extensions
   e. Combustible materials
   f. Imitation fireplaces
8. Framing
   a. Workmanship
   b. Spacing and penetration of nails
   c. Columns or posts
   d. Wood and earth separation
   e. Headers
9. Floor construction
   a. Foundation ventilation
10. Roof framing
    a. Design
11. Wall construction—wood
    a. Wall and partition framing
    b. Bracing
    c. Foundation cripple studs
    d. Fire-stops
12. Weather protection
    a. Flashing
    b. Exterior wall covering
       (1) Siding
       (2) Plywood
       (3) Shingles or shakes
       (4) Nailing
    c. Exterior plastering
13. Wall construction—masonry
    a. General
       (1) Height
       (2) Chases
       (3) Supported members
       (4) Support
       (5) Anchorage
       (6) Piers
       (7) Openings
    b. Solid masonry
       (1) Construction
       (2) Corbeling
    c. Grouted masonry
    d. Reinforced grouted masonry
    e. Hollow-unit masonry
    f. Cavity-wall masonry
    g. Stone masonry
    h. Veneered walls
14. Exits
    a. Doors
    b. Door landings
    c. Emergency exits
15. Stairs
    a. Rise and run
    b. Winders
    c. Spiral stairs
    d. Handrails
    e. Headroom
    f. Guardrails
16. Plastering and installation of wallboard lathing
    a. Application
    b. Gypsum lath
    c. Stripping
    d. Cornerite
    e. Metal plaster bases
    f. Exterior surfaces
    g. Building paper
17. Plastering
    a. Interior
    b. Exterior
18. Wallboard
    a. Gypsum wallboard
19. Softwood plywood paneling
20. Roof covering
    a. General
    b. Wood shingles
    c. Hand-split shakes
    d. Asphalt shingles
21. Valley flashing
    a. Wood shingles and wood shakes
    b. Asphalt shingles
22. Glass and glazing

such as outbuildings and fences. The same principle has been used to a limited extent to control the use of land in the larger community. For instance, a local government may choose to implement its land-use plan through covenants rather than zoning. Another example may be the use of covenants by a citizens group to implement a plan. Farmers in a watershed could agree to keep their land in agricultural production rather than convert it to urban or industrial use.

If a covenant is broken, then other landowners affected by the action can bring suit to restore the original covenant-specified condition or receive compensation for damages. Covenants specify who can bring suit, including local municipalities. Traditionally, courts have upheld suits regarding covenants only if it can be demonstrated that a certain party is not adhering to all agreements stated. Since neighbors find it very difficult to bring suit against each other, often covenants are not enforced. Therefore, the use of voluntary covenants would only be a reasonable means to control the use of land as long as the parties affected by the covenants are willing to see that they are enforced. One way covenants could be made more efficient in land-use control is if a nonpartisan entity, such as a local government, were employed to enforce voluntary agreements. Another way is for a homeowners' or watershed association to be formed so that complaints are a result of a collective, rather than individual, action.

POWER TO SPEND

The most direct way that a government may exert its power to spend is by purchasing land fee simple. This can be an expensive option in terms of both the initial price and the long-term management. Other options available include easements and development rights purchases and transfers. The government has the power to gain ownership, for compensation and for a public purpose, through condemnation. Governments can implement plans through capital expenditures and through public property management.

Easements

An *easement* is the purchase of partial rights to a piece of land. It is enacted through an agreement between two parties for the purpose of a specific use. The most common form of easement occurs when a property owner agrees to let a utility company cross the land with a service line. Easements can also be made to provide access across one property to another. The right to the limited use specified in the easement is usually purchased for a specified period of time, which can be indefinite.

Governments have purchased easements for scenic or aesthetic purposes. In this case, the seller of the easement agrees not to alter the land in a way that would change its scenic value. For example, a grove of trees may be of sufficient historic, aesthetic, or ecologic value to warrant a local, state, or federal government purchase of an easement that would prohibit the removal of the grove.

Similarly, it is possible for the government or a nonprofit organization to purchase an easement that would limit the use of land for conservation purposes. This limitation could be for a specified period of time or be perpetual and paid for at a mutually agreeable price. The purchase controls and limits use of the land for a specified period, a number of years or in perpetuity. However, the land and all its associated rights ultimately rest with the property owner. Therefore, such a conservation easement, especially if it is donated, might make the property owner eligible for certain tax benefits.

According to the Land Trust Exchange, in 1985 more than 500 government agencies and nonprofit organizations were using conservation easements. These easements, both purchased and donated, protect more than 1.7 million acres (688,500 hectares) of land in the United States (Emory,

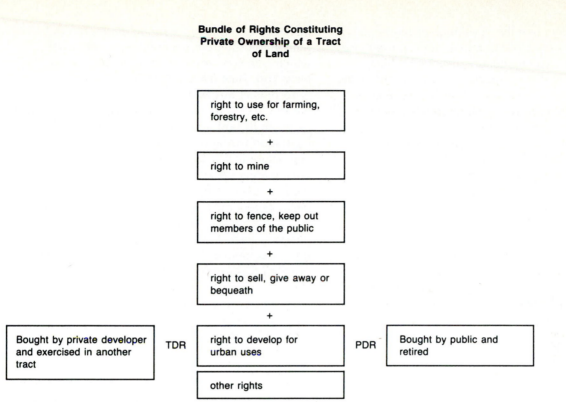

**Bundle of Rights Constituting
Private Ownership of a Tract
of Land**

right to use for farming, forestry, etc.

+

right to mine

+

right to fence, keep out members of the public

+

right to sell, give away or bequeath

+

Bought by private developer and exercised in another tract — TDR — right to develop for urban uses — PDR — Bought by public and retired

other rights

FIGURE 10.2 How the bundle of ownership rights is affected by purchase of development rights and transfer of development rights. *(Source: Adapted from Coughlin & Keene, 1981)*

1985). Easements have been used in all but four states. The major public goals implemented by these easements include:

- Permanent protection of beautiful scenery visible from a public road or waterway
- Protection of pure drinking water in urban areas
- Preservation of the rural character of a town
- Maintenance of critical wildlife habitat
- Conservation of a farm, forest, or grazing land (Emory, 1985)

Development Rights Purchase and Transfers

Some local and state governments separate property ownership and the rights to the development of

property. One person can own the land while another can own the right to develop the same parcel of land. In essence, development rights are among those rights that can be controlled by easements.

Through the *purchase of development rights* (PDR), the property owner's development interests are relinquished to the purchaser of the development rights, who will control the use of the land. The idea is to guarantee the rights associated with private property (Figure 10.2). In most cases, a public government entity purchases the development rights and holds them in trust, thereby withdrawing them from use. The rights may also be donated to nonprofit organizations, who then control the use.

This land-use management concept is viewed as

a means of divesting the developmental potential of the property so that it will remain in its present use (e.g., natural area, agriculture, historic building or site). PDR would be especially useful when zoning mechanisms or voluntary controls like covenants are limited either through inappropriateness or by lack of authoritative control.

Suffolk County, New York, and King County, Washington, are two examples of local governments that have adopted PDR programs. State programs exist in Connecticut, New Hampshire, New Jersey, New York, Maryland, Massachusetts, and Rhode Island. The oldest of these programs is that of Suffolk County. Suffolk County is the easternmost county on Long Island, bounded to the north, east, and south by water and to the west by Nassau County, which is adjacent to New York City (Figure 10.3). Because of this proximity to the nation's largest city, Suffolk County has been under intense development pressure for decades. Still, during the 1970s county farmers

managed to produce an annual cash crop of $100 million (mostly from potatoes and cauliflower), which is the greatest cash crop of any county in New York State (Fletcher, 1978).

To protect this threatened resource, the county has developed a program to purchase development rights on its best agricultural land. The initial legislation was approved by the Suffolk County Legislature in 1974. In September of 1976, the county approved a $21 million bond issue to begin the first phase of the program, the purchase of development rights on approximately 3,800 acres (1,539 hectares) of farmland. In 1977, the first contracts were signed with two farmers to purchase their development rights. The ultimate goal of this program was to purchase development rights to about 12,000 to 15,000 acres (4,860 to 6,075 hectares) of the best farmland, or between 30 and 38 percent of the existing agricultural base at an estimated cost of $55 million (Fletcher, 1978).

One variation on easement and development

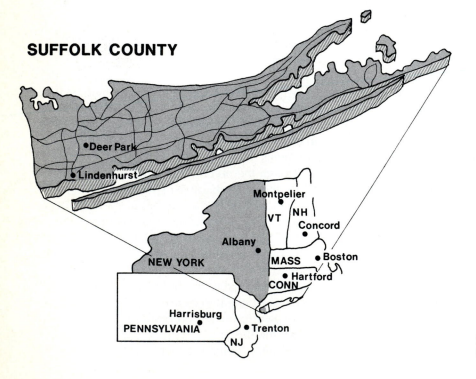

FIGURE 10.3 Location of Suffolk County, New York.

rights programs is to simply purchase the land outright, then lease it for a specified use. This is a strategy used by several public-interest trusts. A criticism used against easements or development rights and fee simple purchases is that they are expensive.

A related implementation technique is the *transfer of development rights* (TDR). This technique involves the same development rights as PDR. However, in this case the development rights are purchased to be used in another location rather than to be retired. Development rights are sold in a sending or preservation zone to be used in a receiving or development zone. Generally, the private market is the transfer mechanism.

The TDR concept was developed to help mitigate the problem of zoning windfalls and wipeouts. For example, the rezoning of an owner's property from agricultural to an urban use could cause an increase in value that could financially benefit the landowner, thus creating a windfall. However, a property owner whose land remains in an agricultural zone may be deprived of the increased value that may be derived from an urban use zone. This could cause the property owner economic hardship, a wipeout situation. The transfer of development rights attempts to distribute economic gains created by development from all property owners in an area, not just those who receive a windfall from a favorable zoning decision (Barron, 1975).

One of the first examples of this concept was provided in the Wallace-McHarg Plan for the Valleys, described by McHarg in *Design with Nature* (1969). Developed in 1963 for an area northwest of Baltimore, Maryland, the plan addressed the issue of how to compensate owners whose land was proposed for a less intensive use. McHarg and David Wallace proposed a syndicate to both develop and preserve the land involved. Through this scheme, the profits from land transactions and developments would be used to compensate landowners whose property was not planned for development (McHarg, 1969).

TDR can be described through the following example. A county commission designates two 100-acre (40.5-hectare) parcels of land, A and B. Each parcel is zoned for residential development at one unit per acre. The commissioners later decide that parcel A should remain in its current agricultural use. As a result, to ensure the continued agricultural use, the county permits the transferring of the one unit per acre development rights to parcel B. The property owner can then use those rights to develop parcel B at one unit per ½ acre (0.203 hectare), which amounts to the original one unit per acre plus the transferred unit per acre (Figure 10.4).

As noted in Chapter 7, a TDR approach has been used to implement part of the Pinelands plan. A land-use regulatory system was established "which limits residential development in the undisturbed, environmentally sensitive parts of the Pinelands and seeks to direct growth into a more compact pattern within designated growth areas" (Pinelands Commission, 1980, p. 210). To augment the regulatory elements of the plan, a development rights program was established. Property owners in preservation and agriculture zones receive rights, known as *development credits,* that they can sell for use in growth areas. The sales of such credits are recorded on the property deeds, which acts as a controlling and monitoring device.

Property Acquisition

As previously mentioned, the government can directly purchase private property. If property is needed for a public purpose and the owner is unwilling to sell it, then it may be obtained through condemnation. The Fifth Amendment to the U.S. Constitution states "nor shall private property be taken for public use without just compensation." *Condemnation* is the process of legally appropriating property for public use. To condemn property in the United States, the public purpose must be clearly defined and "just compensation" must be awarded the property owner. Through

FIGURE 10.4 Illustration of the transfer of development rights concept.

condemnation, the public entity acquires full ownership of the property. The use of condemnation in the United States is referred to as *eminent domain*.

There are obvious benefits to owning the property outright from a government point of view. The government has a freer reign on the possibilities for its use. A highway, hydroelectric plant, or flood-control project can be more easily constructed. Conversely, the fiscal, social, and political costs can be high. People value their property highly and resist its taking, even for a clearly defined public use. This resistance can result in financial costs because of project delays and lawsuits. Social costs can be caused by the destruction of established neighborhoods, even if the larger community benefits. Political costs may result from the emotional and bitter struggles that

accompany many projects involving condemnation.

Capital Improvement Programming

Capital improvements are major projects that require the expenditure of public funds over and above annual operating expenses (Meyer, 1980). Some examples of such projects include airports, jails, courthouses, fire and police stations, parks, bridges, streets and roads, sidewalks, sewer and water lines, sewage treatment plants, traffic and street signs and lights, and fire hydrants. According to the National Council on Government Accounting, a *capital improvement program* is

a plan for capital expenditures to be incurred each year over a fixed period of years to meet capital needs arising from the long-term work program or otherwise. It sets forth each project or other contemplated expenditure in which the local government is to have a part and specifies the full resources estimated to be available to finance the projected expenditures. (1968, p. 155)

A capital improvement program then is a means to implement plans by directing public expenditures into areas suitable for needed projects. Roads, sewers, water lines, and other structural elements of community development can be directed to those areas identified though suitability analysis.

The major steps in developing a capital improvement program include:

1. Submission of project proposals to a review team or coordinator
2. Evaluation of each project and selection and ranking of projects of inclusion in the program
3. Financial analysis of the jurisdiction's ability to pay for the projects and selection of the means to be used in financing them
4. Preparation of a proposed capital improvement program
5. Consideration and final approval of the program by the responsible governing body
6. Public approval of financing arrangements for individual projects
7. Annual review and revision of the program (adapted from Meyer 1980)

Public Property Management

About 40 percent of the land in the United States is owned by federal, state, and local governments (Lewis, 1980). The federal government alone administers 32 percent of the 2.3 billion acres (932 million hectares) of land in the nation (U.S. Bureau of Land Management, 1988). Most the federal land is in the western states and includes national parks, forests, resource lands, wildlife refuges, designated wildernesses, wild and scenic rivers, and national trails. All federal land management

agencies are subject to environmental planning laws, notably NEPA. Agencies that are especially large and important landholders include USFS, NPS, and BLM. Each federal agency has its own planning procedures. Many federal agencies use planning processes with similarities to the one described in this book. In relationship to implementation, in some cases communities can influence federal and state property management to achieve their goals.

One way that communities can influence the use of public property is by encouraging federal and state agencies to adopt plans consistent with local goals. Conversely, federal and state agencies can encourage local governments to do the same. This may require that plans be amended or modified. Cooperation can be accomplished between governments through memorandums of understanding or agreement.

Government can also set an example through the management of its property. If a state government seeks to encourage energy conservation, then it can start with the design of its own buildings. The design of government buildings can be used to demonstrate the realization of planning policies. Governments can locate its buildings out of floodplains and other environmentally sensitive areas. Through property management, governments can provide a model for the rest of the community.

POWER TO TAX

Taxes may be used as an incentive for implementing a plan. Two examples are the various tax benefits offered for farmland, and often for open space owners too, in all states and the incentives given to businesses and industries to locate in certain areas. Enterprise zones are another means that may be considered to encourage business development.

All states have adopted some form of legislation providing tax relief for owners to keep their land in

TABLE 10.7
STATE PROPERTY TAX RELIEF PROGRAMS BY TYPE OF PROGRAM

States	Preferential Assessment	Deferred Taxation	Voluntary Restrictive Agreements	Mandatory Zoning or Planning
Alabama		X		
Alaska		X		
Arizona	X			
Arkansas	X			
California			X	
Colorado	X			
Connecticut	X			
Delaware	X			
Florida	X			
Georgia		X		
Hawaii		X		X
Idaho	X			
Illinois		X		
Indiana	X			
Iowa	X			
Kansas	X			
Kentucky		X		
Louisiana	X			
Maine		X		
Maryland		X		
Massachusetts		X		
Michigan*			X	
Minnesota		X		
Mississippi	X			
Missouri	X			

* Property tax relief is achieved using circuit-breaker tax credits instead of preferential assessment.
† Land within agricultural districts is automatically eligible, while other land must meet certain eligibility criteria.
SOURCE: Adapted from Dunford, 1984.

agricultural and/or open space use (Table 10.7). Richard Dunford (1984), an economist, has explained the three types of tax relief used: preferential assessment, deferred taxation, and voluntary restrictive agreements. With the *preferential assessment* system, land is taxed on its use rather than its market value. *Deferred taxation* programs provide for preferential assessment, but some or all of the property tax relief becomes due when the land is converted to a nonpermitted use. Under *voluntary restrictive agreement* programs, eligible landowners agree to restrict the use of their land for a number of years. In exchange, their property taxes are based on current-use assessments (Dunford, 1984).

The criticisms levied against such programs are many. The programs are often abused by speculators and developers to avoid taxes. Even

TABLE 10.7 *(continues)*
STATE PROPERTY TAX RELIEF PROGRAMS BY TYPE OF PROGRAM

States	Preferential Assessment	Deferred Taxation	Voluntary Restrictive Agreements	Mandatory Zoning or Planning
Montana		X		
Nebraska		X		
Nevada		X		
New Hampshire			X	
New Jersey		X		
New Mexico	X			
New York†		X		
North Carolina		X		
North Dakota	X			
Ohio		X		
Oklahoma	X			
Oregon		X		
Pennsylvania		X		
Rhode Island		X		
South Carolina		X		
South Dakota	X			
Tennessee		X		
Texas		X		
Utah		X		
Vermont		X		
Virginia†		X		
Washington		X		
West Virginia	X			
Wisconsin*			X	X
Wyoming	X			

penalties under deferred taxation programs may be minor when compared to inflated land values. Another criticism is that unequal tax shifts, or perceived inequalities, occur as a result of such programs. A final weakness is that, except in a few states, there is no connection between state tax-relief programs and local planning and zoning.

Another type of tax program involves incentives offered to businesses and industries to locate in certain areas. One such type of program is tax-increment financing. Wisconsin has a typical program (Huddleston, 1981) that permits incorporated cities and villages to create tax-increment districts to eliminate blight, rehabilitate declining areas, and promote industrial growth.

In these districts, for a period of time, all the increase in tax revenue from the property will go only to the municipality involved. The property owners will be free of taxes on such increases from various other local taxing entities, such as school districts and the county. All the increased revenue must be spent for public facilities in the district: roads, sidewalks, parking areas, sewers, water lines, street trees, and so on. Bonds may be sold first in order to rebuild an area to make it more attractive to investors. The dedicated revenue from the tax-increment district in turn is used to repay the bonds.

Another approach, originated by the British Conservative Party, is the enterprise zone concept. The underlying thesis is that the incentive for entrepreneurship must be restored in the inner city. Stuart M. Butler, a proponent of the concept, explained it in the following manner:

> Small businesses would be encouraged to start up by drastic cuts in regulation and taxes (e.g., abating property taxes, reducing Social Security taxes, and changing depreciation schedules). Mixing land uses would be facilitated by relaxing zoning. In short, a climate for enterprise would be established by cutting the cost and complexity of going into business and by allowing entrepreneurs to make do with whatever is available. No grants, no special loans, no expensive plans. It would be an exercise in *unplanning*. (1981, p. 6)

The enterprise zone concept is based on the opinion that the costs of government inhibit small business. An alternative view is that private-sector costs such as interest on loans and fees for services (legal, insurance, health care, and so on) inhibit small businesses. An opposing concept to enterprise zones is that new businesses and industries should pay their share of the services they need—sewer, water, transportation, and so on—and that businesses and industries are responsible for the health, safety, and welfare of their neighbors. Indeed, in some communities growth impact fees are assessed on new developments for certain public services.

INTERAGENCY COORDINATION FOR GROWTH MANAGEMENT

Government agencies can coordinate their activities to implement plans and manage growth. To manage growth, it may be necessary to use some or all of the implementation strategies discussed thus far. A central feature in the concept of growth management in plan implementation is the coordination of various responsible groups. Often this involves different government agencies at the local, state, regional, and federal levels.

Ronald Canham (1979) defines *interagency coordination* as a process in which two or more organizations come together to solve a specific problem or meet a specific need. Interagency coordination implies that by working together, agencies will increase their effectiveness, resource availability, and decision-making capabilities. As a result, the agencies will more effectively assist in the resolution of a community need or problem that could not be met by any single agency acting alone. Interagency coordination is often essential to implement a plan.

Bruce Weber and Richard Beck (1979) provide an example of interagency coordination for coordinated growth management. The location, density, and site design of residential developments have a direct effect on the costs of installing public facilities and providing services, as well as their varying potential impacts on the natural environment. As illustrated in Figure 10.5, proposed subdivision A would require a considerable length of sewer and water pipes across vacant land and consequently would result in higher costs to the taxpayer than subdivision B (Weber & Beck, 1979).

To encourage subdivision B over subdivision A, it will be necessary for the city and the county (or possibly the township) to cooperate. The cooperation of agencies within each jurisdiction may include combinations of zoning ordinances, performance standards, capital improvement programming, and taxing programs. Inter-jurisdictional agreements and the establishment of spheres of influence may also be necessary.

Interjurisdictional agreements can involve growth management techniques other than zoning, budgeting, and taxing programs like service districts, annexation, moratoriums, and impact

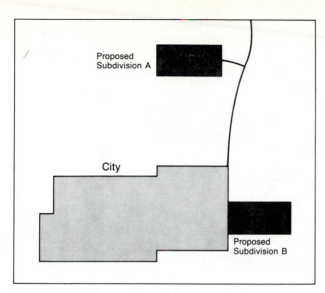

FIGURE 10.5 Comparison of distances for the extension of services to two subdivisions. *(Source: Weber & Beck, 1979)*

fees. States like Oregon and Vermont permit local governments to divide their jurisdictions into urban and rural service districts with different tax rates. According to Harris, services "are not extended to a rural service district until the area is reclassified as an urban service district, at [a] higher tax rate, which takes place at the time the district is developed for commercial, industrial, or urban residential use" (Harris, 1988, p. 469). Such a change from rural to urban use can be coupled with annexation. The determination of urban and rural service districts as well as the coordination of annexations require the cooperation among several jurisdictions.

Moratoriums involve the prevention of the issuance of building permits until urban service capacity levels are attained or until plans and ordinances are completed (Harris, 1988). Impact fees are imposed to require developers to pay for new public services necessary for new growth. Florida state law, for instance, requires "that

growth be accommodated and that localities find ways to provide the necessary facilities and services while minimizing the negative effects of growth" (Harris, 1988, p. 470). Impact fees can be linked to local policy related to low- and moderate-income housing, recreation facilities, or open space protection.

PROGRAM LINKAGE AND CROSS COMPLIANCE

Certain government benefits (the "carrots") can be linked to requirements (the "sticks") for specific actions. For instance, in order to receive preferential property taxation, the land may need to be zoned for a specific use. For a landowner to receive property taxes at current use rates, like for open space or agriculture, a county may require that the land be zoned for open space or agricultural use.

The U.S. government has adopted such a linkage strategy to implement soil conservation goals. As a result of the 1985 Food Security Act, landowners are required to have a conservation plan, prepared by the SCS, for highly erodible lands in order to remain eligible for federal agricultural benefits. The federal programs affected include price support payments, storage facility loans, crop insurance, disaster payments, and other loans and subsidies. Many farmers participate in these programs, so there is a strong incentive to comply with the requirement. The concept of cross compliance among various programs is that private citizens should not receive windfalls or support from the government without taking actions that promote public objectives.

NONGOVERNMENT STRATEGIES

Implementation need not rest on the actions of government alone. Nongovernment organizations can use some of the same implementation strategies that have been described in this chapter. There are several national organizations active in land planning, such as the National Trust for Historic Preservation, the American Farmland Trust, the National Audubon Society, the Nature Conservancy, and the Trust for Public Land. There are numerous local land trusts and conservancies that make fee simple purchases of land. Such groups buy and receive donated easements. They may be involved in developing or overseeing restrictive covenants. Nongovernment organizations consult with citizens about the tax aspects of land use. Nongovernment organizations can play an important role in community education (see Chapter 8). They can also be watchdogs, monitoring government agencies to ensure that plans are followed.

One example of a local nongovernment organization is the Brandywine Valley Association in eastern Pennsylvania. The Brandywine Valley Association is a local group organized in 1945 in Chester County, Pennsylvania. Its dues-paying members are interested in improving, conserving, and restoring the natural resources of the Brandywine River valley. This group is a model of a locally based group with a long-term commitment to preserving their rural heritage. With a small professional staff, it urges and helps the people of Chester County unite their efforts to make the Brandywine valley a more pleasant and profitable place in which to work and live. The Brandywine Valley Association accomplishes this goal through a variety of educational programs and through lobbying with local governments. Many such local groups are active in neighborhoods and at the community or watershed level.

The 1000 Friends of Oregon is an example of a statewide, nongovernment organization that has been extremely instrumental in planning implementation. The group was organized to ensure that local government complied with the Oregon land-use law (see Chapters 2 and 6 as well as the case study section of this chapter). The 1000 Friends of Oregon has been active in ensuring implementation by providing continuing citizen support for planning. The 1000 Friends of Oregon,

with its dedicated, professional staff, has taken numerous cities and counties to court over noncompliance with the statewide goals. The organization has had an excellent success rate with these suits. The result is that Oregon not only has a good planning enabling act and well-defined statewide goals but a record of case law that supports plan implementation.

IMPLEMENTATION MATRIX

Often a community will select more than one means to implement its goals. Because of the potential complexity and confusion in overlapping or conflicting responsibilities, it is helpful to clarify roles of involved groups. One way to assist in such organization is an implementation matrix. Such a matrix can be illustrated by returning to the Albion example.

The Whitman County commissioners adopted a number of goals that potentially impact Albion. A sample of these goals is listed in Figure 10.6. Each goal has a different implementation measure and different groups responsible for its administration. To protect agriculture, exclusive farm-use zoning was enacted. The primary responsibility for this zoning rests with the planning commission. Variances from the zoning requirements are handled by a special review board, called the board of adjustment in Washington State. The county commissioners provide the backup power for enforcing the ordinance. The planning department administers the ordinance. (The roles of planning commissions, review boards, and planning agencies are discussed in more detail in Chapter 11.) The goal to provide for rural housing is handled in a similar manner to that of agricultural protection. The major difference is that the building department, instead of the planning agency, is responsible for administration.

The other two example goals in Figure 10.6 are addressed differently. The quality of surface water in the Palouse has been negatively impacted by eroding soils. Soil erosion is a major source of

IMPLEMENTATION MATRIX

Planning Goal	Implementation Measure	Primary Responsibility	Secondary Responsibility	Back-up Power	Administration Responsibility
Protect Agriculture	Exclusive Farm-Use Zoning	Planning Commission	Board of Adjustment	County Commissioners	Planning Staff
Improve Water Quality	Best Management Practices	Water Quality Commission	Conservation District	Washington Department of Ecology	U.S. Soil Conservation Service
Preserve Environmentally Sensitive Areas	Environmental Impact Assessment	Planning Commission	Washington Department of Ecology	County Commissioners	Planning Staff
Provide for Rural Housing	Performance Zoning	Planning Commission	Board of Adjustment	County Commissioners	Building Department

FIGURE 10.6 Implementation matrix.

sediment in water. Best-management practices have been identified that farmers can use to reduce erosion. The areawide water quality commission and local conservation district are responsible for encouraging farmers to use these practices. The Washington Department of Ecology provides backup power and can fine farmers for water-polluting activities. The SCS provides staff to the water quality commission and the conservation district as well as giving technical assistance to farmers about conservation practices.

The environmental impact assessment process is to be used to protect sensitive areas. Such areas were defined in the county comprehensive plan. The planning commission and the Washington Department of Ecology are responsible for impact statements. The county commissioners provide backup power, and the process is administered by the planning agency. These sample goals illustrate how responsibilities for implementation can be delineated.

THREE EXAMPLES OF PLANNING IMPLEMENTATION

Innovative Zoning for Agricultural Land Protection in York County, Pennsylvania, and Black Hawk County, Iowa

The concern about the conversion of agricultural land to other uses was an emergent issue during the 1970s. The National Agricultural Lands Study, an interagency study, was initiated by President Jimmy Carter in 1979 to address the issue. A conclusion of the study was that the problem was a "crisis in the making." One of the suggestions made by the participants in the study was that farmland protection was best addressed by state and local governments (National Agricultural Lands Study, 1981). Two local governments that have developed innovative programs include York

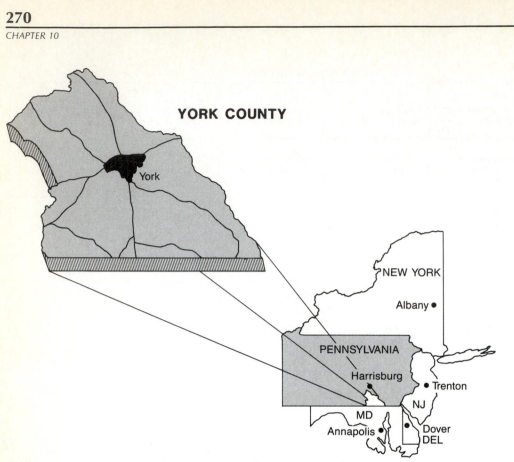

FIGURE 10.7   Location of York County, Pennsylvania.

County, Pennsylvania, and Black Hawk County, Iowa.*

York County is located in south-central Pennsylvania, 25 miles (40.225 kilometers) south of Harrisburg (Figure 10.7).   The county had a population of just under 313,000 people living on 911 square miles (2,358.58 square kilometers) in 1980.   The county is in one of the richest, nonirrigated regions in the United States yet is within a half-hour's drive to Harrisburg, an hour to Baltimore, and an hour and a half to Philadelphia.

*More complete descriptions of both the York and Black Hawk county examples are provided by officials from those counties in Steiner and Theilacker (1984).

According to planner William Conn (1984), the York County Planning Commission became concerned about the problem of declining farmland in 1975.   The commission reviewed various options to reverse this trend.   Among the techniques reviewed were the transfer and purchase of development rights, easements, and tax benefits. The planning commission selected zoning as the best way to protect the farmland in the county.

The majority of the county municipalities using zoning adopted a novel sliding-scale approach.   As described by William Toner, under sliding-scale zoning "each landowner is entitled to a certain number of buildable lots according to the size of the parcel—permitted density varies inversely with the size of the parcel. Thus, small landowners are permitted to develop a higher percentage of their property than are large landowners" (1978, p. 15).

According to Toner (1978), the rationale supporting this inverse relationship between size of a parcel and permitted density is that large landholdings must be retained in agricultural use if the community is to retain its agricultural base. Officials in Peach Bottom Township of York County decided to use the sliding-scale approach in their zoning ordinance. Table 10.8 is an excerpt from that ordinance. Single-family housing is regulated in the township in the agricultural zone on a sliding scale through a conditional-use procedure. In Peach Bottom Township, a minimum lot size of 1 acre (0.405 hectare) is permitted, and a maximum of 1 acre is also established unless it is determined that the additional land desired is either on poor soil or it cannot feasibly be farmed because of size, shape, or topographical considerations (Conn, 1984).

Black Hawk County, Iowa, has taken a different approach to protect farmland but has also used zoning. The county is located in northeastern Iowa (Figure 10.8). The two largest cities in the county, Waterloo and Cedar Falls, adjoin each other and are the largest places of employment. It is a metropolitan county with over 100,000 people (Daniels & Reed, 1988). John Deere and Company has major manufacturing facilities in the metropolitan area of the two cities. Both growing cities were expanded into the fertile cornfields of Black Hawk County.

In 1971, county officials working with the Iowa Northland Regional Council of Governments began to address the issue of the conversion of farmlands. After 2 years of planning, the county officials decided to implement their farmland protection policy through zoning. The unique feature of this 1973 ordinance was a system for rating soil types for their relative long-term ability to produce corn and other crops. This system was named the Crop Suitability Rating (CSR), although it is more popularly known as the "Corn" Suitability Rating.

The CSR scale ranges from 5 to 100. County officials decided those soil types receiving a ranking of 70 or better would be considered "prime." The soils will yield an approximate average of 115 bushels or higher of corn per acre. Using this criteria, 68 percent of the county has prime soils. For those soils with a CSR above 70, there is a 35-acre (14.2-hectare) minimum on development.

Black Hawk County also addressed the issue of allowing some people the opportunity to live in the country and completed a rural living study. Planners discovered fifteen soil types with a CSR of 70 and below that also had very few limitations for development. A zoning ordinance was then developed to allow rural housing on these soils with a minimum 3-acre (1.2-hectare) lot size (Iowa Northland Regional Council of Governments, 1975).

This system is working well, and the regional council has expanded its use to the other five counties in its jurisdiction. In the years since the implementation of their zoning ordinance, a major redirection in land use has occurred within Black Hawk County. As the late planner Janice Clark (one of the principal individuals responsible for the ordinance) observed:

> The rate of residential development within the unincorporated areas has remained fairly steady, but this development is now occurring on soils deemed suitable for such land use, while the vast majority of land in the county remains in agricultural production. (Clark, 1977, p. 154)

Sonia Johannsen and Larry Larsen (1984) report that from 1979 through 1981, 680 acres (275.4 hectares) was requested to be rezoned from the "A-1" Agricultural District to another district. Only 72 acres (29.2 hectares) was approved, of which only 42 acres (17 hectares) was on lands that had a majority of its soils rated prime by the CSR process. The lands that were approved for rezoning had already been committed to other uses by subdivision approval or were difficult sites to

TABLE 10.8
PEACH BOTTOM TOWNSHIP SLIDING SCALE

1. There shall be permitted on each tract of land the following number of single-family dwelling units:

Size of Tract of Land, Acres	Number of Single-Family Dwelling Units Permitted
0–7	1
7–30	2
30–80	3
80–130	4
130–180	5
180–230	6
230–280	7
280–330	8
330–380	9
380–430	10
430–480	11
480–530	12
530–580	13
580–630	14
630–680	15
680–730	16
730–780	17
780–830	18
830 and over	19

2. New single-family dwelling units shall be located on lots in soil capability units IIIe-3 through VIIs-2, as classified by the *Soil Survey of York County, Pennsylvania,* Series 1959, No. 23 issued May 1963, or on lots of lands, which cannot feasibly be farmed; (a) due to existing features of the site such as rock outcropping, swamps, the fact that the area is heavily wooded, or the fact that the slope of the area exceeds fifteen (15) percent or (b) due to the fact that the size or shape of the area suitable for farming is insufficient to permit efficient use of farm machinery. Where such location is not feasible, permits shall be issued to enable dwelling units to be located on lots containing higher quality soils. However, in all cases such residential lots shall be located on the least agriculturally productive land feasible, and so as to minimize interference with agricultural production.

3. A lot on which a new dwelling is to be located shall not contain more than one (1) acre, unless it is determined from the subdivision plan submitted by the property owner that the property owner has sufficient land of the type described in paragraph 5 of this section to justify using more than one (1) acre for the location of the proposed dwelling unit, or that the physical characteristics of the land itself requires a lot size in excess of one (1) acre.

4. A property owner submitting a subdivision plan will be required to specify on his plan which lot or lots shall carry with them the right to erect or place any unused quota of dwelling units his tract may have.

5. Lots for the location of single-family dwelling units in addition to those authorized by subparagraph (1) and all the additional new dwelling units are located on lots which are located:
   a. On land in soil capability units IVe-5 through VIIs-2 as classified by the *Soil Survey of York County, Pennsylvania,* Series 1959, No. 23 issued May 1963; or
   b. On lands which cannot feasibly be farmed:
      (1) Due to the existing features of the site such as rock outcropping, rock too close to the surface to permit plowing, swamps, the fact that the area is heavily wooded, or the fact that the slope of the area exceeds fifteen (15) percent; or
      (2) Due to the fact that the size or shape of the area suitable for farming is insufficient to permit efficient use of farm machinery.

   Such additional lots must meet all the requirements of the ordinance, the Township Subdivision Ordinance and all requirements of the Pennsylvania Department of Environmental Resources.

6. The applicant shall have the burden of providing that the land he seeks to subdivide meets the criteria set forth in this section.

7. Any landowner who disagrees with the classification of his farm or any part of it by the *Soil Survey of York County, Pennsylvania,* Series 1959, No. 23 issued May 1963, may submit an engineering analysis of the soils on the portion of the farm which he seeks to have reclassified, and if the Board of Township Supervisors finds his study correct, it shall alter the township soil map to reflect the results of such analysis.

SOURCE: Conn, 1984.

farm. Johannsen and Larsen concluded that the CRS is working and that "many potential requests for rezoning of farmland have been discouraged by the county's reputation for preserving these lands" (1984, p. 124).

An analysis of zoning decisions between 1975

BLACK HAWK COUNTY

FIGURE 10.8 Location of Black Hawk County, Iowa.

and 1985 by Daniels and Reed (1988) indicates that the administration of the Black Hawk County program has continued to improve. Relatively little farmland has been rezoned in the county "for nonfarm uses, and several proposals for nonfarm uses have been denied" (Daniels & Reed, 1988, p. 303). According to Daniels and Reed, the "local farm economy appears stable, given the slight decline both in the number of farms and the amount of farmland. The large majority of non-farmland transfers have occurred near urban boundaries. About one-quarter of the farmland transfers have also occurred near cities. These figures suggest urban sprawl is being fairly well contained" (1988, p. 303). They also observe that the best farmland in the county is in quite stable ownership and is not likely to be developed.

One unique aspect about both York and Black Hawk counties is the use of information about nature in implementation ordinances. Most zoning ordinances before the 1970s were based primarily on economic determinants. In York and Black Hawk counties, information about the physical suitability for a specific use (agriculture) and natural limitations of the land were used to implement a community goal.

The Snohomish County, Washington, Growth Management Strategy

Nestled between Puget Sound and the Cascade Mountains, Snohomish County is located in northwestern Washington (Figure 10.9). Because of the spectacular natural beauty and the location of the prosperous city of Seattle to the south, the county is experiencing pressure from rapid growth. Snohomish County has experienced skyrocketing population increases: the county has grown by 225,436 people from 111,580 in 1950 to 337,016 in 1980, an increase of 202 percent. The

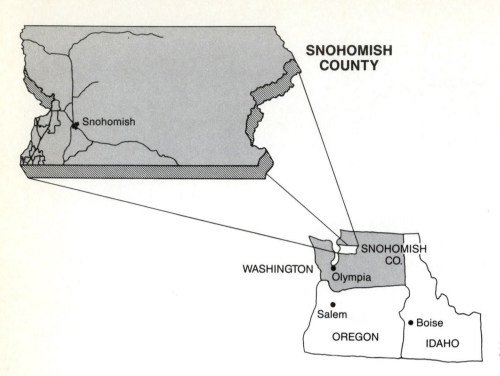

FIGURE 10.9 Location of Snohomish County, Washington.

projected growth through the year 2000 will put the county population at 568,959, or 410 percent above the 1950 population (Snohomish County Office of Community Planning, 1981).

The Snohomish County regional development strategy is a combination of implementation techniques. The key element is the clear distinction between the urban, suburban, and rural areas of the county. The county policy is to confine growth to areas contiguous with already existing cities and towns. This policy is to be implemented through comprehensive planning in divisions of the county known as subareas, city or county sphere-of-influence planning, capital improvement programming, road system capital improvement programming, and park system capital improvement programming (Snohomish County Office of Community Planning, 1981).

The coordination of comprehensive planning

means that the subareas would develop plans consistent with the growth policies of the county. Another form of the intergovernment cooperation embodied in the strategy is the sphere-of-influence concept. Spheres of influence for each jurisdiction in the county are established, and proposed growth is contained within recognized boundaries. Capital improvement programming links the policies of the county to the extension of services (Snohomish County Office of Community Planning, 1981).

A novel (and controversial) element of the Snohomish County growth management strategy was a proposed growth impact fee schedule. This fee schedule directly addresses the capital costs associated with the new growth. Fees would be levied on all new development in the county. These fees are summarized in Table 10.9. Public services, such as parks, fire protection, and

TABLE 10.9
GROWTH MANAGEMENT FEE MATRIX FOR SNOHOMISH COUNTY, WASHINGTON

Public Service	Single-Family Detached	Multiple	Mobile Home Sep. Lot	Mobile Home Park	Commercial or Industrial
Parks	$ 445	$ 311	$ 445	$ 311	
Fire	75	75	25	25	$1/$1,000 av × $1.00 × 1.5
County government	135	95	46	46	$1/$1,000 av × $1.80 × 1.5
Roads	1,250	1,250	1,250	1,250	$125 per VTE
Subtotals	$1,950	$1,731	$1,766	$1,632	Variable
Schools	938	442	938	442	
TOTAL	$2,843	$2,173	$2,704	$2,074	

SOURCE: Snohomish County Department of Community Planning, 1981.

county government, are connected to types of development, such as single-family detached housing, multiple-family housing, mobile homes, and commercial or industrial development (Snohomish County Office of Community Planning, 1981).

The Snohomish County growth management strategy has been linked on a local level with the identification and protection of environmentally sensitive areas. For instance, in the town of Sultan this has been accomplished through its comprehensive planning and zoning ordinance. Table 10.10 is an example of Newman's environmentally sensitive area classification system as it was applied to the town of the Sultan comprehensive plan and zoning ordinance.

The Snohomish, York, and Black Hawk counties examples illustrate how planning goals are carried

TABLE 10.10
ENVIRONMENTALLY SENSITIVE AREA CLASSIFICATION SYSTEM APPLIED TO SULTAN, WASHINGTON

Classification	Subclass	ESAs Delineated in the Planning Area
Ecologically critical areas	Natural wildlife habitat areas	Riparian forest
		Wetlands
		Oxbow pond
		Bald eagle winter concentration area
		Bald eagle communal night roost
	Scientific areas	Riparian forest
		Wetlands
		Oxbow pond
		Bald eagle winter concentration area
		Bald eagle communal night roost

(Continues)

TABLE 10.10 (Continued)
ENVIRONMENTALLY SENSITIVE AREA CLASSIFICATION SYSTEM APPLIED TO
SULTAN, WASHINGTON

Classification	Subclass	ESAs Delineated in the Planning Area
Perceptual and cultural critical areas	Scenic areas	Hillsides around the built-up area (slope greater than 25%)
		Shoreline areas (all areas covered by Shoreline Management Program)
		Alpine areas (beyond planning area boundary)
	Historic, archeological, cultural areas	The Knutson House
		Sultan River truss bridge
Resource production critical areas	Agricultural lands	Existing agricultural land use and prime agricultural soils meeting locally defined criteria
	Water quality areas	The watershed for the town's water supply system
Natural hazard critical areas	Flood-prone areas	Hydraulic floodway
		100-year floodplain
	Geologic hazard areas	Soils with severe erosion hazard
		Hillsides with landslide hazard (slopes greater than 25%)

SOURCE: Newman, 1982, pp. 51–52.

through to implementation. All three rely more on biophysical information than conventional planning processes. The York County sliding-scale system utilizes information about soils, geology, surface water, and vegetation. Suitability analysis played a central role in the implementation of the Black Hawk County zoning ordinance. Both the York and Black Hawk programs were undertaken to implement goals to protect farmland.

In Snohomish County, growth is managed to help protect environmentally sensitive areas as well as agricultural land. A wide range of ecologically, perceptual and cultural, resource production, and natural hazard critical areas have been identified. The philosophy is not antigrowth or no-growth, but rather managed growth, managed in such a way to protect the environment and valuable natural resources. Development and conservation need not be viewed as competing interests but rather as ultimately mutually dependent. Such a perspective requires the careful balancing of interests to administer implementation measures through time.

11

ADMINISTRATION OF PLANNING PROGRAMS

Once a plan and implementing measures have been adopted by the appropriate legislative body, it is usually necessary to establish some form of ongoing administration. This may be accomplished in several ways. One way to administer a plan and its implementing measures is through the use of commissions and review boards comprising elected or appointed citizens. Such groups often require technical assistance from a professional staff.

Administration presents many challenges for planners. As planning goals are institutionalized, a greater distance grows between the excitement of creation and the routine of everyday management. The typical office is isolated from the living landscape. Yet, for the landscape to be managed effectively there must be some set of rules of management and those who are responsible to ensure that the rules are indeed obeyed.

Local governments can effectively manage many land-use programs. However, local communities must be viewed in terms of larger and more complex interacting regions. The technological potentials for the exploitation of nature and the increase in knowledge about biophysical and sociocultural processes have resulted in the necessity for continued innovation in the administration of planning programs. Many efforts need to be addressed by multiple levels of government and by partnerships between government and nongovernment organizations. To be most effective and equitable, administration must be a two-way street—managers and planners must understand the people they serve and citizens must appreciate and monitor the bureaucrats.

This chapter will explore the current systems used to administer plans. The role of planning commissions, review boards, and planning staffs will be described. The impact of procedural requirements will be discussed briefly. One administrative tool is the budget. Three budgeting techniques will be described: the planning, programming, and budget system (PPBS); zero-base budgeting (ZBB); and capital improvement programming (CIP). Impact statements are an approach to evaluate government programs and projects. Two examples of planning administration are presented: the Boulder, Colorado, residential allocation system and court-mandated plan-review and administrative procedures in Oregon.

CURRENT PLANNING

The Role of Planning Commissions and Review Boards

Planning commissions originated in the early twentieth century. The idea was promulgated by municipal reformers dismayed by the corruption of big-city politics. Planning commissions were proposed as independent advisory boards of honest, civic-spirited citizens. The commissions were to make recommendations to elected officials. The concept was embodied in the model Planning Enabling Act of 1928 published by the U.S.

Department of Commerce and adopted by many state legislatures. Such commissions are created by ordinance by the appropriate city, special-use, county, regional, state, or federal jurisdiction. Usually planning commissions consist of five to nine members. The members are typically appointed by an elected official for a specific period of time.

Planning commissions usually have two functions. The first is advisory. They assist elected officials in establishing goals, objectives, and policy for the jurisdiction. In this capacity, they may conduct research and review options facing the planning area. The second function is administrative. In cities and counties, planning commissions review subdivision proposals to assure that they conform to regulations.

Planning commissions may also hold hearings to review proposed changes in zoning ordinances and comprehensive plans. Such hearings are quasi-judicial proceedings in some states and take on a courtlike format. Planning commission findings from hearings are passed on as recommendations to elected officials. If those people proposing changes are not pleased with the decision of the elected body, then they may appeal it to the court.

The relative ease of rezoning and amending comprehensive plans has been criticized as a weak link in the American planning process. Political pressure can be used to force appointed and elected bodies to approve such changes even if they are contrary to established goals and the conclusion of scientific and technical research. Anyone who has been involved in such hearings will testify that they are a very human procedure—the outcome often based more on the persuasive power of key individuals and emotion than on logic.

Another type of citizen body involved in planning administration is the review board. These are usually special-purpose groups. Examples include zoning review boards, boundary review boards, design review boards, and environmental quality councils. Zoning review boards, also called *boards of adjustments,* administer variances from zoning ordinances and conditional uses that may be permitted in the ordinances with special permission. Boundary review boards may be involved in such matters as annexations and capital improvements. Design boards may arbitrate aesthetic matters in a community and are often composed of architects, landscape architects, artists, and designers. Environmental boards review matters of environmental quality and are made up of individuals with an interest or training in the relevant sciences. Some review boards include some or all members who are elected officials or professionals rather than appointed citizens.

The Role of Planning Staffs

Many planning agencies are split into two divisions to handle separate long-range and current functions. The long-range division is responsible for research, projections, comprehensive planning, and special functions that may arise as a result of a specific issue. The current planning division is responsible for the administration of regulations. This function may be shifted to another department of government such as that responsible for public works.

The current planning staff is generally responsible for processing applications of those who want to change the use of their property or develop it for some purpose. The current planning staff often works with the property owner to ensure the application meets all the necessary requirements of the commission or review board. The staff may be responsible for presenting its findings to the commission or review board. They may also be responsible for the public notice of hearings to review such proposals. In many jurisdictions the current planning staff has the authority to process applications that meet specified requirements. In these municipalities and counties, commissions or boards review only those applications where a variance is needed.

In some jurisdictions, because of the weaknesses involved in rezoning through commissions or the sheer number of applications for zone changes, this has been made a staff responsibility. These *hearings examiners,* or *zoning adjustors,* have the administrative responsibility to approve zone changes on the merits of the case. Presumably, these decisions may be made in a more unbiased, professional manner than by a citizen board or commission. The rulings of hearings examiners, or zoning adjustors, are subject to appeal if the applicant or other party is not satisfied with the results.

In areas where performance standards have been adopted, it may be necessary for a team to visit sites to ensure the criteria have been met. For instance, for a proposed residential development in an agricultural area, such a team may comprise a staff planner, a soil scientist from the SCS, an engineer, and a health officer. These individuals are responsible for making a report of their findings concerning the conformance of the site to the standards.

The Impact of Procedural Requirements

The process that individuals must go through to meet the legal requirements of a jurisdiction obviously has an impact on their personal plans for the use of property. Procedural requirements should ensure that the laws of the jurisdiction are met, yet be fair and swift to minimize unnecessary costs to individuals proposing changes.

Generally, regulatory systems have three basic elements in common. First, there is a *pre-application stage* during which proponents of a land-use change discuss ideas with the planning staff. Second, there is a *technical staff review.* At this stage, proponents submit a formal application, often accompanied with plans and drawings. The planning staff reviews the application and makes recommendations to elected officials. Finally, there is the *official review* made by the appointed and/or elected officials or possibly by an administrator. Often proponents of a change are responsible for the costs involved in the technical and official reviews.

For those responsible for such reviews, it would be wise to remember that the word *administration* in its original Latin form meant to give help or service. There are numerous ways of helping people through the regulatory process. One way is to minimize the number of required permits. Another is to publish the procedural requirements in a straightforward format. Figure 11.1 is an example of the application procedure for a certificate of zoning compliance in Whitman County, Washington. The application forms should be easy for all to understand as well. Figure 11.2 is an example of an application for a certificate of zoning compliance in Whitman County, Washington. Finally, it is important for administrators to be courteous and friendly.

FIGURE 11.1 Procedure for application for a certificate of zoning compliance in Whitman County, Washington.

Date: _____

Case Number: _____

Purpose

Within the agricultural zoning district of Whitman County, residential land use must meet certain minimum-lot size requirements. The requirements are waived for homes proposed on lands not useful for commercial agricultural production. In their place are a number of "conditions" that must be met to qualify a site for development. Usually, a much smaller lot is possible by meeting these conditions than would normally be required.

To determine if a proposed site qualifies for the waiver, county and regional planning staff evaluate the site. If the criteria are met, a certificate is issued. The certificate entitles the recipient to secure building, sewer and water system permits.

Application

A complete application must be filed prior to the staff's review of the request. An application will not be accepted unless it is complete in the judgment of the administrative official and the application fee paid.

A complete application shall include:

_____ 1. Application for certificate of zoning compliance form.
_____ 2. Environmental checklist.*
_____ 3. Applicant's statements describing the site's compliance with the zoning ordinance requirements.
_____ 4. Application fees
      a. Certificate review fee $25.00
      b. Environmental impact statement (if necessary) cost
_____ 5. Site description
      A description of the site giving distance from the permanent landmarks adequate in detail for staff to visit the site and determine from the description its approximate boundaries. Permanent landmarks would include roads, section markers, power poles, etc. If a legal description is available, that should be given.

* The environmental checklist will be reviewed by the administrative official. Based upon that review, the designated "responsible official" will make a determination under the guidelines of the State Environmental Policy Act (SEPA) whether the proposed issuance of a certificate will have a significant or nonsignificant environmental impact. If it will be significant, the applicant will have to provide an environmental impact statement. At her or his option, the responsible official may convene the environmental review committee to aid in her or his determination of significance.

_____ 6. Site plan map

A site plan showing the approximate location of major site features.

_____ 7. Written permission

If the applicant is not the owner of the site, he must provide a statement from the owner giving their permission for the staff site survey and the issuance or denial of a certificate of zoning compliance.

NOTE: Special Help:

The administrative official will be happy to answer any questions. If in doubt about any portion of this application, please ask. Telephone Number: 397–4361.

Procedure

_____ 1. Submit completed application to the administrative official.

_____ 2. The administrative official provides the planning director with a completed application for her or his review.

_____ 3. The planning director has 14 days to render a decision if the site shall or shall not be granted a certificate of zoning compliance. If necessary, he or she may extend this period for an additional 14 days, and will notify the applicant of this additional review period.

During the review, the planning director will consult with health department, engineering, and Soil Conservation Service personnel to aid in her or his decision.

The decision will be provided to the administrative official, who shall notify the applicant in writing of the decision.

Failure of the planning director to render a decision within the period allotted, shall constitute a denial of the request.

_____ 4. If a certificate of compliance is issued, the administrative official shall notify property owners within 300 feet (91.5 m) of the proposed site that they have 20 days from the date of issuance to appeal the planning director's decision.

_____ 5. If a certificate of compliance is not granted, the administrative official shall notify the applicant that they have 20 days from the postal date to appeal the decision.

_____ 6. In the event of appeal, a hearing date will be set before the hearings examiner committee. The applicant and property owners within 300 feet (91.5 m) of the property will be notified of the hearing.

_____ 7. If the hearing results are challenged, that must occur by legal action by any affected party in a court of competent jurisdiction within 10 days of the committee's decision.

Consistency with the Zoning Ordinance

The following is excerpted from the county's zoning ordinance and is the basis for decisions called for by this application:

1. Two of the following three conditions must exist:
   a. Land whose near-surface geology consists of basalt or alluvium, or on slopes of greater than 20%, crystalline rock, all as defined by *Water Supply Bulletin No. 26* of the Washington Department of Ecology, *Reconnaissance of Geology and of Ground-Water Occurrence in Whitman County,* or any updated version of the document. Whenever difficulty exists in the verification of surface geological conditions from this map, reference shall also be made to the maps of detailed soil mapping units maintained by the Soil Conservation

(Continues)

FIGURE 11.1 *(continues)*

Service, which maps shall either indicate or not indicate a pattern of specific soil types which is known to be associated with basaltic, alluvial or crystalline surface geological conditions. All of these facts shall be verified by on-site inspection.

    b. The subject lot has not been cultivated, used for production of commercial forage for sale, commercial grazing of livestock for sale, or subjected to any agricultural practice designed to produce for sale in the preceding three years.

    c. The subject lot is within two distinct areas of land 15 acres (4.6 m) or less which is insufficient size, quality and/or accessibility to the efficiently used for agricultural production for income. "Distinct" shall mean that the subject area if substantially bounded by natural or man-made features which buffer this land from agricultural lands, such as: wooded areas, steep canyon walls, railroads, surface waters or public roads.

2. All of the following requirements must be met:

    a. The subject lot must have frontage on an improved county or state road of at least 200 feet (61 m). "Improved" shall mean a gravel surface or better.

    b. If a perennial surface water passes through, or along any boundary of the subject lot, there must be at least 200 feet (61 m) of frontage along such surface water.

    c. Less than one-half of the area of the subject lot shall be in an area of special flood hazard and/or floodway as designated on the flood hazard boundary map of the *Flood Insurance Study for Whitman County*.

    d. Construction plans for structures, parking areas and private roads on the subject lot shall leave a maximum amount of existing vegetation undisturbed.

    e. The area of the subject lot shall be no less than the minimum area required by the Whitman County Department of Environmental Health to safely accommodate water supply and on-site sewage disposal systems.

FIGURE 11.2 Application for certificate of zoning compliance in Whitman County, Washington.

Date Received: _____

Case Number: _____

1. **Applicant**

Name: _____

Address: _____

Telephone: _____

Status: (lessee of property, agent, owner, prospective purchase, etc.) _____

2. **Property Owner** (if different from the applicant)

Name: _____

Address: _____

Telephone: _____

For purposes of this application, "owner" shall mean

1. The mortgagee (person buying the land with a bank loan)
2. The contract seller (person holding a contract on the land and selling it to another person)
3. Person who holds clear title to the land
4. Corporation, partnership, estate that holds title to the land

3. **Property Owners within 300 Feet of the Property to be Included within the Certificate of Zoning Compliance**
   a. Name _____
      Address: _____
      Telephone: _____
   b. Name _____
      Address: _____
      Telephone: _____
   c. If additional parties, put information on a separate sheet of paper.

4. Description of Site
   This description will be used to locate the site and determine its boundaries:
   a. Township _____ Range _____ Section _____
   b. Major road intersection nearby is _____ and it is _____ miles to the site
      heading _____ (north, south, east, west).
   c. Provide the approximate boundaries of the site using permanent landmarks like roads, power poles, section lines, etc.

   _____
   _____
   _____

   If a legal description is available of the site, it should be attached. If it describes the property adequately, the above-requested description is not necessary.

5. **Site Plan**
   A site plan should be drawn. It need not be drawn professionally, but must be legible and drawn to an appropriate scale. It will be used by staff to evaluate the site to determine if it meets the zoning ordinance criteria. It should show:

   a. Boundaries with dimensions
   b. Proposed home location
   c. Drainfield location
   d. Well location
   e. Driveway location
   f. Stream or creek within site
   g. Areas of intended excavation
   h. Vegetation that will be removed
   i. Rock outcroppings
   j. Existing fencelines
   k. Existing buildings
   l. Names of property owners within 300 feet (91.5 m) on the property they own

6. **Statement of Zoning Ordinance Compliance**
   Review the requirements that must be met to achieve zoning ordinance compliance. They are found on the first page of the application instruction section. State if your proposal complies, does not comply or is not related to the stated criteria.

   _____
   _____
   _____
   _____
   _____

(Continues)

FIGURE 11.2 *(continues)*

_____
                        Applicant

_____
        Date

(To be completed if the applicant is not the owner of the property involved)

_____

Owner's Affidavit

State of Washington)

                    : ss.

County of Whitman)

   I, _____, being duly sworn, depose and say that I am the owner of property or his authorized agent, involved in this application, and that the foregoing statements and answers herein contained and the information herewith submitted are in all respects true and correct to the best of my knowledge and belief; and I grant my permission to the above-named applicant to apply for a certificate of zoning compliance for the above-described property; and for county staff to examine this subject property in the cause of their work related to this application.

Subscribed and sworn to before me   Signed: _____
this _____day of _____,
19 _____.   Address: _____
                                                      _____

                                             Telephone: _____

_____
Notary Public in and for the
State of Washington, residing
at _____.

THE BUDGET

Planning, Programming, and Budget System (PPBS)

The budget is perhaps the most effective way to administer planning programs. There are numerous techniques to manage budgets. In the early 1960s, the planning, programming, and budget system (PPBS) was initiated in the U.S. Department of Defense by Robert McNamara who brought the concept with him from his experience in the automobile industry (Graham, 1976; Hudson, 1979; & So, 1988). Otis Graham describes the system in the following way, "PPBS starts with the whole, not the parts; it forces explicit statements of assumptions; it begins with strategic goals, sets up alternative plans for their realization, qualifies costs and benefits" (1976, p. 172).

According to Frank So (1979, 1988) of the American Planning Association who is critical of PPBS, the system has four distinct characteristics. These include (1) focusing on the identification of the fundamental objectives of the program, (2) the explicit identification of future-year implications, (3) the consideration of all costs, and (4) the systematic analysis of the options involved (So, 1979).

According to So, PPBS has proven too complicated to be administered by local officials.

However, a number of more effective systems have evolved from PPBS. Frank So cites the example of the Dayton, Ohio, method, called *program strategies*. He contends that the purpose of this system "is to describe municipal services in a language elected officials and the community understand while at the same time allocating [financial] resources (local, state, and federal) in such a way as to classify expenditures on the basis of policies and programs" (1979, p. 126).

Table 11.1 lists the program strategies and 1981 resource allocations for community involvement for Dayton, Ohio. Table 11.2 is a more detailed analysis of specific activities for housing

TABLE 11.1

PROGRAM STRATEGIES AND 1981 RESOURCE ALLOCATIONS FOR COMMUNITY INVOLVEMENT IN DAYTON, OHIO

1981 program total resource allocation plan					$1,335,230
Activity	**Funding Source**	**1980 Budget**	**1981 Budget**	**1980/81 Staff**	**Notations**
1. Neighborhood affairs	CDBG	921,630	967,910	29/29	1980 CETA is a
	CETA	94,950	90,070	13/9	9-month budget
Housing and neighborhood affairs	TOTAL	1,016,580	1,057,980	42/38	
2. City Beautiful Council	General	77,090	64,190	3/2	1980 CETA is a
	CETA	54,520	64,470	5/5	9-month budget
Planning	TOTAL	131,610	128,660	8/7	
3. Neighborhood assistance officers	General	109,770	115,120	5/5	
Police	TOTAL	109,770	115,120		
4. Visiting artists	National Endowment Grant	21,500	21,720		
Planning	TOTAL	21,500	21,720		
5. Alternative spacing	State	9,500	11,750		
Planning	TOTAL	9,500	11,750		
Operating total	General	186,860	179,310	8/7	
	CDBG	921,630	967,910	29/29	
	CETA	149,470	154,540	18/14	
	Other	31,000	33,470		
	TOTAL	1,288,960	1,335,230	55/50	

SOURCE: City of Dayton.

TABLE 11.2

1981 DAYTON, OHIO, ORGANIZATIONAL OBJECTIVES BUDGET FOR HOUSING CONSERVATION

Group: Community Services	Responsible Agency: Housing and Neighborhood Affairs	Staff: 129	1981 Budget: $3,533,150

		Units	
Objectives	**Performance Criteria**	**1980 Estimate**	**1981 Estimate**
Management/Housing and Neighborhood Affairs			
*1. To ensure that an effective mechanism is established for 312 Loan Self-Approval Authority and that all 1981 312 loans are processed through that mechanism	1a. Date mechanism established		1/81
	b. Number of FY and UHDEM 312 loans not processed with self-approval		0
*2. To assist in the implementation of the Vacant Structure/Vacant Lot Task Force recommendations	2a. Date vacant structure inventory reports provided		1/81
	b. Number of vacant structures improved and reoccupied through 312 loans	7	
3. To implement a paint-up project using entirely donated resources	3a. Number of gallons of paint donated		500
	b. Number of houses painted		50
	c. Number of neighborhood workshops		4

Housing Conservation

		Units	
Geographic Housing Inspection			
*4. To close 2,500 structural housing cases including worst-first priorities and stimulate $2,000,000 in residential property improvements	4a. Number of cases closed in conformance with geographic concept	2,500	2,500
	b. Dollars invested in residential property improvements		$2,000,000
*5. To close 30% of those properties listed in the worst-first property inventory with at least 65% either closed or in legal stage by December 1981	5a. Number of properties in the worst-first inventory	2,500	2,500
	b. Number of worst-first cases closed		900
	c. Percent of worst-first cases closed	30%	30%
	d. Number of worst-first in legal stage		1,500
	e. Percent either closed or in legal stage	65%	65%
*6. To complete on-site investigation of 100% of all citizen structural complaints within 5 work days of receipt with 90% being investigated within 2 work days	6a. Number of complaints received		2,500
	b. Number of on-site investigations within 2 work days		2,500
	c. Percent within 2 work days	90%	90%
	d. Number of on-site investigations made within 3 to 5 work days		250
	e. Percent within 3 to 5 work days	10%	10%
7. To provide a housing condition statement to the city manager by March 1981	7. Date housing condition statement submitted		3/31/81
8. To initiate structural complaints on properties where violations exist and citizen complaints have not been received.	8. Number of inspector-initiated complaints		150
*9. To secure owner consent to demolish 150 garages under the garage demolition program	9a. Number of garages approved to be demolished in program	150	150
	b. Number of owner-consent forms referred by housing inspection	150	150

TABLE 11.2 *(continues)*

Objectives	Performance Criteria	Units	
		1980 Estimate	**1981 Estimate**
10. Through cooperation with other city agencies, solve 12 major neighborhood problems identified through housing inspection services	10a. Number of major neighborhood problems solved	6	12
	b. Date report submitted to city manager		12/81
11. To conduct an annual worst-first property survey for each inspection segment	11. Date survey submitted	12/29/81	1/1/81
Environmental Services			
12. To complete on-site investigation of 100% of all citizen environmental complaints within 5 work days of receipt	12a. Number of complaints received	5,000	5,700
	b. Number of on-site investigations	5,000	5,700
	c. Percent within 5 work days	100%	100%
	d. Number of citizen meetings attended		50

* High-priority objectives.
SOURCE: City of Dayton.

conservation. According to So, it "can be seen that specific objectives are presented in significant detail. This detail allows Dayton [officials] to determine, during the year, whether or not it is meeting its objectives by keeping track of the performance criteria" (1979, p. 127).

The administration of the program strategies method is the responsibility in Dayton of a strategy planning group comprising the city manager, the deputy city manager, the planning director, and three assistant city managers. Neighborhood citizens advisory boards review program strategies affecting their communities. In this way, budgets receive both agency and community-level review.

Zero-Base Budgeting (ZBB)

Another budget system is the *zero-base budgeting* (ZBB) concept, developed by the Texas Instruments Company and made popular as a result of its use by Jimmy Carter during his tenure as governor of Georgia. According to Frank So:

> The essence of ZBB strikes at the heart of traditional "nonrational" budget making: the practice of taking last year's budget as a given and adding a little for

inflation and expanding programs. Under ZBB, last year is a closed book; *everything* must be justified as though it were a new program. (1979, p. 129)

Zero-base budgeting is in some ways similar to the management by objectives (MBO) system used in the Nixon administration. In MBO all federal agencies annually listed their objectives and President Nixon selected those to be given top priority (Graham, 1976). The key difference is the "clean slate" aspect of ZBB. The major steps and elements of ZBB include:

- The isolation of "decision units"
- The analysis of the analysis into "decision packages"
- The ranking of the decision packages in order of priority by management
- The final compilation of the budget, based on the rankings (Leininger & Wong, 1976, p. 2)

Capital Improvement Programming

Capital improvement programming (CIP) was introduced in Chapter 10 as a technique to implement planning programs. Attention should be paid to the administration of CIP. Frank So (1979, 1988) outlines the following typical steps involved in CIP administration. The first step is an analysis of the fiscal resources of the community—the revenue and expenditure projections. The second step is a listing of all capital-improvement-projections-related projects in the jurisdiction. This listing is usually collected by the planning department or finance office.

The next step involves each department of the jurisdiction completing detailed project forms describing the capital improvements. Each department will rank its projects. Then a review group discusses all the department proposals. This group includes the planning director, finance officer, the local government manager, top elected officials, and department heads. Often public hearings are held concerning the proposed expenditures. From this stage a priority ranking of the projects is achieved.

The CIP is then presented to the appropriate legislative body. After this body determines its own expenditure priorities and choices, the CIP is adopted (So, 1979). Budgeting is a cyclical process, usually occurring annually. One of the strengths of CIP is that projects and programs can be linked to community goals and the ability of an area to sustain proposed capital improvements.

ENVIRONMENTAL IMPACT ASSESSMENTS

As a result of NEPA, a national policy for the environment and the Council on Environmental Quality (CEQ) were established. The central purposes of the act were

> to declare a national policy which will encourage productive and enjoyable harmony between man and his environment; to promote efforts which will prevent or eliminate damage to the environment and biosphere and stimulate the health and welfare of man; to enrich the understanding of the ecological systems and natural resources important to the Nation and to es-

tablish a Council on Environmental Quality. (U.S. Congress, 1969)

The requirements for *environmental impact statements* (EISs) were established by Section 102(2) of the National Environmental Policy Act as follows:

All agencies of the federal government shall—

A. Utilize a systematic, interdisciplinary approach which will insure the integrated use of the natural and social sciences and environmental design arts in planning and in decision making which may have an impact on man's environment;

B. Identify and develop methods and procedures in consultation with the Council on Environmental Quality . . . , which will insure that presently unquantified environmental amenities and values may be given appropriate consideration in decision making along with economic and technical considerations;

C. Include in every recommendation or report on proposals for legislation and other major federal actions significantly affecting the quality of the human environment, a detailed statement by the responsible official on—

   i. The environmental impact of the proposed action,

   ii. Any adverse environmental effects which cannot be avoided should the proposal be implemented,

   iii. Alternatives to the proposed action,

   iv. The relationship between local short-term uses of man's environment and the maintenance and enhancement of long-term productivity, and

   v. Any irreversible and irretrievable commitments of resources which would be involved in the proposed action should it be implemented. (U.S. Congress, 1969)

The purpose of an EIS is to serve as "an action-forcing device to insure that the policies and goals" defined in NEPA "are infused into the ongoing programs and actions" of the federal government. The EIS is to provide "full and fair discussion of significant environmental impacts" and is to "inform decision-makers and the public of reasonable alternatives which would avoid or minimize adverse impacts or enhance the quality of the human environment." According to the CEQ, "An environmental impact statement is more than a disclosure document. It shall be used by Federal officials in conjunction with other relevant material to plan actions and make decisions" (1986, p. 791).

Often the EIS (or less often a comprehensive review known as an *environmental assessment*) is prepared jointly between a federal agency and state or local governments. Since NEPA states that "major Federal actions significantly affecting the quality of the human environment" require an EIS, both federally funded projects and federal permits and licenses are subject to the law. The approval process for projects, permits, or licenses may affect how a local plan is implemented or administered. If, for instance, a county has a policy to protect farmland and environmentally sensitive lands, and a federal project is proposed, such as a dam or highway, then county officials may object during the EIS process. On the other hand, it may be county policy to provide new sources of water or transportation. In this case, the county may work with a federal agency to advocate water-supply and transportation options which would be studied through the EIS process. A developer may propose a project that requires a permit, for instance, Section 404 dredge and fill permits required through clean water legislation for wetlands. In such a case, county officials can comment during the EIS process concerning the consistency of such a proposal with local plans.

The CEQ has developed a recommended format for EISs that is similar to the ecological planning process being described in this text. The following standard format is to be used by federal agencies to prepare EISs:

- Cover sheet
- Summary
- Table of contents
- Purpose of and need for action
- Alternatives including the proposed action
- Affected environment
- Environmental consequences
- List of preparers
- List of agencies
- Index
- Appendixes

The cover sheet includes relevant information about the proposal, such as the responsible agencies, the title of the proposed action, contact people, the designation of the EIS as draft or final, an abstract, and the date by which comments must be received. The summary provides a synopsis of major conclusions, areas of controversy, and the issues to be resolved. The EIS is then to briefly specify the underlying purpose and need to which the agency is responding (Council on Environmental Quality, 1986).

The heart of the EIS is the description of the alternatives including the proposed action. Planners are to rigorously "explore and objectively evaluate all reasonable alternatives." Each alternative is to be considered in detail. An "alternative of no action" is to be included in the analysis. The agency is to identify its preferred alternative or alternatives and to include appropriate mitigation measures to address environmental impacts (Council on Environmental Quality, 1986).

The EIS is to describe "the environment of the area(s) to be affected or created by the alternatives under consideration." The affected environment section of an EIS is an inventory and analysis of the planning area, such as what was described in Chapters 3 and 4. The affected environment section is to be followed by detailed studies of the environmental consequences. The environmental consequences section "forms the scientific and analytic basis" for comparisons of alternatives.

The consequences are to include discussions of direct effects of the alternatives and their significance; indirect effects and their significance; energy requirements and conservation potential of various alternatives; natural or depletable resource requirements and conservation potentials; urban quality, historic and cultural resources, and the design of the built environment, including reuse and conservation potentials; and means to mitigate adverse environmental impacts. This section is also to address possible conflicts between the proposed actions and the objectives of federal, regional, state, local, and Indian land-use plans, policies, and controls for the area concerned (Council on Environmental Quality,1986).

In addition to the federal environmental protection law, 27 states, the Commonwealth of Puerto Rico, and many local governments have adopted impact statement or assessment requirements. According to Ortolano (1984), fourteen states use comprehensive statutory requirements, four have comprehensive executive or administrative orders, and nine states have special-purpose EIS requirements. In addition to the United States, many other nations have environmental impact assessment requirements. Westman (1985) identifies twenty-nine other nations with operational impact assessment programs.

A major criticism of environmental impact review in the United States at the federal level is that essentially the process is procedural rather than substantive. For instance, the Natural Resources Defense Council has observed:

> Environmentalists today are turning more attention toward the substantive quality of the NEPA statements which are prepared. Unfortunately, far too frequently the quality of these impact statements leaves much to be desired. For example, NEPA statements are sometimes silent on the most severe environmental effects caused by a proposed project. (1977, p. 28)

In some states with comprehensive statutory requirements, the EIS process has become some-what more substantive. In Washington State, its comprehensive State Environmental Policy Act (SEPA) contains substantive policies and goals that apply to all levels of government. A proposal may be denied under SEPA, if an agency finds that:

- The proposal would likely result in significant adverse environmental impacts identified in an EIS
- Reasonable mitigation measures are insufficient to ameliorate the identified impact (see Washington Administrative Code 197–11–660)

Thus, SEPA in Washington can be used by the state and local governments to permit or deny projects. Washington State courts have held that SEPA applies to comprehensive plans, preliminary plats, and all kinds of permits. Generally, however, the EIS process in many states, like at the federal level, tends to be more procedural than substantive.

In spite of these problems, environmental impact statements and environmental assessments can be an important administrative tool. Astute planning administrators can make use of EISs to justify and explain their projects to decision makers and the public. Such projects may be to implement the goals of their constituents. Conversely, during the process as state and local officials review EISs, they can comment about impact of a proposal on the programs and policies of their jurisdictions. Administrators may better gauge the impact of projects through a systematic use of environmental, economic, fiscal, and social analyses.

Environmental Impact Analysis

The CEQ has put in place a uniform EIS review with a standard terminology. These terms include the categorical exclusion, the environmental assessment and/or environmental impact statement, a finding of no significant impact, a scoping of issues, and process monitoring (Buskirk, 1986). In addition to the federal agencies that adopted the procedure and terminology recommended by the

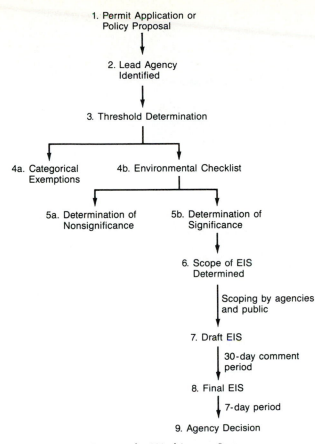

1. Permit Application or
   Policy Proposal

2. Lead Agency
   Identified

3. Threshold Determination

4a. Categorical
    Exemptions

4b. Environmental Checklist

5a. Determination of
    Nonsignificance

5b. Determination of
    Significance

6. Scope of EIS
   Determined

Scoping by agencies
and public

7. Draft EIS

30-day comment
period

8. Final EIS

7-day period

9. Agency Decision

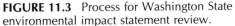

FIGURE 11.3 Process for Washington State environmental impact statement review.

CEQ, a number of states adapted the process. Washington is one such state.

The Washington Department of Ecology (DOE) explains its SEPA process, in part and paraphrased, as follows (Figure 11.3). The environmental review process generally begins when someone submits a permit application to an agency or when an agency proposes some activity, policy, plan, ordinance, or regulation. Once this occurs, a *lead agency* is selected that has the principal responsibility for implementing SEPA procedures for the specific proposal. The lead agency, which is normally the city or county where the proposal has been made, then makes a *threshold determination* to decide whether or not a proposal is likely to have a probable significant adverse environmental impact (Washington Department of Ecology, 1984).

Some categories of actions, which may indeed have significant environmental impacts, however, have been excluded by the Washington legislature for political reasons and thus are exempted from the process. If a proposal is not categorically exempt, then the proponent completes an *environmental checklist*. This checklist helps the lead agency identify environmental impacts that may result from the proposal and decide if the impacts are significant. If both the proponent and lead agency agree the impacts are indeed significant, then a checklist need not be completed and an EIS is instead completed (Washington Department of Ecology, 1984).

If, based on the checklist, the lead agency decides that the proposal would not have a probable significant adverse environmental impact, then it issues a *determination of nonsignificance* and no EIS is prepared. If the opposite is found, then the lead agency issues a *determination of significance* that would require an EIS to be prepared. There is some middle ground allowed. When some environmental impacts are foreseen that can be addressed with specific mitigation measures, then a *mitigated determination of nonsignificance* can be issued. Such a document would describe mitigation measures that will be implemented (Washington Department of Ecology, 1984).

If an EIS is to be prepared, then the lead agency must decide its scope, which means the range of actions, options, and impacts to be analyzed. This process is called *scoping*. The scoping process leads to a draft EIS, which is circulated to various government agencies and interested parties for a 30-day comment period. After considering the comments and revising the draft EIS accordingly, the lead agency issues a final EIS. All agencies must then wait for 7 days before acting on the

(Barry Kough, The Lewiston Morning Tribune)

permit or approval. After considering the appropriate environmental concerns and documents, along with other relevant factors, agencies may then act upon the permit or other approval required for a proposal to proceed (Washington Department of Ecology, 1984).

In Washington State the elements of the physical and human environment that must be considered in an environmental checklist and an EIS are contained in the State Environmental Policy Act and DOE guidelines. These elements are listed in Table 11.3. As can be seen, the elements are similar to those previously discussed in Chapters 3 and 4. As a result, the legal framework exists in Washington State to connect landscape inventory and analysis information to the administrative review of proposed projects and actions.

Economic Impact Analysis

Critics of impact analyses have argued that nonenvironmental elements are not adequately considered. As a result, techniques for economic,

fiscal, and social impact analyses have been developed and proposed. Economic impacts are those that affect the private sector, while fiscal impacts refer to those that affect the public sector. Ronald Faas, an economist, has noted that:

> Mining, industrial expansion, and energy facility construction affect the private sector of a community's economy. Such projects require new investment in plant facilities and lead to increased local employment, income, and sales. In addition, the new economic activity often stimulates local business. Commercial activities and residential housing expand to serve the new population. (1980, p. 1)

Faas stresses that economic impacts should be considered by both private-sector managers and public administrators. He points out that promoters of a particular project often emphasize the new jobs, increased payrolls, expanded sales, and new investments. These points can form a persuasive argument when public officials are asked to make a zoning change, grant a variance, or allow a tax concession. But, these claims should not be accepted at face value, but rather an objective evaluation of the economic impacts

TABLE 11.3

ELEMENTS OF THE PHYSICAL AND HUMAN ENVIRONMENT REQUIRED IN CHECKLISTS AND IMPACT STATEMENTS BY THE WASHINGTON STATE ENVIRONMENTAL POLICY ACT

WAC 197–11–444: Elements of the environment

1. Natural environment
   a. Earth
      (1) Geology
      (2) Soils
      (3) Topography
      (4) Unique physical features
      (5) Erosion/enlargement of land area (accretion)
   b. Air
      (1) Air quality
      (2) Odor
      (3) Climate
   c. Water
      (1) Surface water movement/quantity/quality
      (2) Runoff/absorption
      (3) Floods
      (4) Groundwater movement/quantity/quality
      (5) Public water supplies
   d. Plants and animals
      (1) Habitat for and numbers or diversity of species of plants, fish, or other wildlife
      (2) Unique species
      (3) Fish or wildlife migration routes
   e. Energy and natural resources
      (1) Amount required/rate of use/efficiency
      (2) Source/availability
      (3) Nonrenewable resources
      (4) Conservation and renewable resources
      (5) Scenic resources
2. Built environment
   a. Environmental health
      (1) Noise
      (2) Risk of explosion
         (3) Releases or potential releases to the environment affecting public health, such as toxic or hazardous materials
   b. Land and shoreline use
      (1) Relationship to existing land-use plans and to estimated population
      (2) Housing
      (3) Light and glare
      (4) Aesthetics
      (5) Recreation
      (6) Historic and cultural preservation
      (7) Agricultural crops
   c. Transportation
      (1) Transportation systems
      (2) Vehicular traffic
      (3) Waterborne, rail, and air traffic
      (4) Parking
      (5) Movement/circulation of people or goods
      (6) Traffic hazards
   d. Public services and utilities
      (1) Fire
      (2) Police
      (3) Schools
      (4) Parks or other recreational facilities
      (5) Maintenance
      (6) Communications
      (7) Water/storm water
      (8) Sewer/solid waste
      (9) Other governmental services or utilities
3. To simplify the EIS format, reduce paperwork and duplication, improve readability, and focus on the significant issues, some or all of the elements of the environment in 197–11–444 may be combined.

should be made.

Economists have developed techniques that can be helpful to measure such impacts. One tool is the economic multiplier. Multipliers are based on the interdependency between two types of businesses in the local economy—the export (or basic) and service (or nonbasic) sectors. Export activities produce goods and services for outside the local economy, while service activities sell goods and services within the local economy. An expansion of sales in the basic sector generally has a multiplier effect on the local service sector.

Economic multipliers may then be defined as the numerical relationship between an original change in economic activity and the ultimate change in activity that results as the money is spent and respent through various sectors of the economy (Faas, 1980). This concept is illustrated in Figure 11.4. Of $1 in wages, half may be spent locally, of which half again goes to wages. As a result, the original dollar generates another $.25 of income the first time it is respent.

Several types of multipliers have been identified, including employment multipliers, income

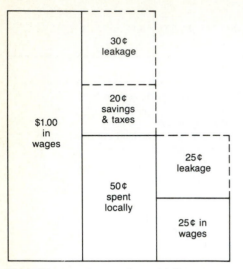

FIGURE 11.4 Economic multipliers. *(Source: Faas, 1980)*

multipliers, and output multipliers. An *employment multiplier* is the total change in full-time equivalent employment (FTE) generated in the local economy for each change of one FTE in an export sector of the local economy. A *household income* (or *earnings*) *multiplier* is the total change in household income throughout the local economy from a $1 change in household income payments by an export sector. An *output* (or *business*) *multiplier* is the total change in sales generated throughout the local economy by a $1 change in export sales (Faas, 1980).

There are many techniques for estimating economic multipliers. Two such techniques include the export-base approach and the input-output model (see Chapter 4). The amount of income generated in the local economy for the actual dollars spent will vary. The sophistication and type of technique used will differ with the local structure and the nature of the proposed project or program.

Fiscal Impact Analysis

Fiscal impact analysis refers to the study of the effect of proposed projects or actions on

government expenditures and revenues and on taxes. Theodore R. Siegler and Neil L. Meyer (1980) have presented a framework for fiscal impact analysis. They suggest starting with three key questions:

- How many people are expected to move into the community, how long will they stay, and where will they live?
- What costs will be generated providing public services and expanded capacities of public facilities to accommodate the growing population, and when will the costs be incurred?
- What revenues will be generated by the growth, and when will the revenues be available?
(Siegler & Meyer, 1980, p. 2)

The answers to some of these questions may exist if the community has developed an inventory and analysis of human factors. That information can then be used for the administrative review of proposed project actions. Siegler and Meyer have developed a worksheet (Table 11.4) for estimating additional operating and maintenance costs and capital costs associated with incoming population for services commonly provided by communities. Operating and maintenance costs may be estimated for the incoming population by examining the community budget. The total operating and maintenance costs for each service divided by the existing population represents the present per capita cost of providing each service. This per capita cost can be multiplied by the estimated size of the incoming primary (persons directly associated with the source of growth) and secondary or tertiary (workers and their families required in other sectors of the local economy to provide expanded or new services) population to provide what Siegler and Meyer term a "minimum estimate" of the total additional operating and maintenance costs associated with the new population.

Capital costs may be estimated for the incoming population in various ways. Local officials must estimate the capacity of existing facilities and then judge which facilities will require additional capital investment. By dividing the total expansion

TABLE 11.4
ESTIMATING ADDITIONAL OPERATING AND MAINTENANCE COSTS AND CAPITAL COSTS ASSOCIATED WITH INCOMING POPULATION FOR SERVICES COMMONLY PROVIDED BY COMMUNITIES

| | Operating and Maintenance Costs | | | | | Capital Costs | | |
| | | | | | | | Anticipated Expenditure | |
Public Service	Current Costs (a)	Costs per Capita (b)	Size of Incoming Population (c)	Change in Costs (b × c)	Capacity Needed	Year	Amount
General government							
Education							
Judicial							
Law enforcement							
Fire							
Libraries							
Public works							
Roads							
Sewer							
Water							
Solid waste							
Health							
Welfare							
Other							

SOURCE: Siegler & Meyer, 1980.

investment cost by the expected number of new residents, an investment cost for each new resident can be estimated (Siegler & Meyer, 1980). Siegler and Meyer have developed a checklist of revenue sources potentially affected by community population growth (Table 11.5). An analysis of potential revenues can help a community determine if the fiscal costs of growth will be borne by the proposed project or action.

The American Farmland Trust and Loudoun County, Virginia, designed a procedure for fiscal impact analysis, using county data, to estimate (1) the net public costs of new residential development and (2) whether these costs could be expected to vary significantly with the density of development. American Farmland Trust researchers pursued these objectives by (1) identifying the major categories of public costs and revenues for Loudoun County in metropolitan Washington, D.C., (2) developing a representative demographic profile of a new 1,000-household residential community, (3) projecting four different density distributions for the prototype community, and (4) analyzing costs and revenues for each of the four densities (American Farmland Trust, 1986).

The public costs and revenues were determined for major categories on a current annual basis, using the county budget and other published fiscal records. The researchers found that public education consumes most of the county budget (68 percent), followed by health and welfare (9 percent) and public safety (8 percent). General property taxes account for 48 percent of the county revenue, followed by state funds (31 percent) and other local taxes (9 percent) (American Farmland Trust, 1986).

For the American Farmland Trust study of Loudoun County, age-specific census data for tracts in

TABLE 11.5

REVENUE SOURCES POTENTIALLY AFFECTED BY COMMUNITY POPULATION GROWTH

	Current Revenue (a)	Current per Capita Revenue (b)	Size of Incoming Population (c)	Change in Revenue (b × c)	Date Revenue Will Be Available to Spend
Local					
Real property					
Personal property tax					
Permits					
Fines					
Service fees					
User charges					
Development fees					
Hookup charges					
Prepayment of taxes					
Negotiated impact payments from development					
Other					
State					
Motor vehicle tax					
Liquor tax					
Cigarette tax					
Sales tax					
Grants-in-aid					
Severance tax					
Other					
Federal					
Revenue sharing					
Grants					
Federal *en lieu* payments					
Special programs					
Other					

SOURCE: Siegler & Meyer, 1980.

different parts of the county were examined. These data enabled the researchers to construct a prototype community, which they divided into four possible density groups

Rural low density: 1 dwelling unit per 5 acres

Rural cluster: 1 dwelling unit per acre

Medium density: 2.66 dwelling units per acre

High density: 4.5 dwelling units per acre (American Farmland Trust, 1986)

While researchers held the total population, age structure, and number of dwellings constant, the dwelling unit density varied. The researchers were able to show that the cost for public services such as education, road maintenance and construction, and water and sewer facilities was significantly greater for rural low-density settlement than higher-density development. In addition, "slightly higher revenues were projected from the higher-density communities" (American Farmland Trust, 1986, p. 4).

The American Farmland Trust study found "that

higher net public costs are associated with lower-density residential development" (1986, p. 4). The Loudoun County study illustrates that fiscal impact analyses can be constructed "at the county level for a given residential development at different densities, using existing data for major categories of public costs and revenues." Furthermore, the research shows that for many densities "the ongoing public costs of new residential development will exceed the revenues from such development" (American Farmland Trust, 1986, p. 5). As a result, once a plan has been adopted and its implementing measures put in place, planning administrators should carefully analyze the fiscal impacts of proposed new development, especially those that require amending the adopted plan and implementing ordinances.

Social Impact Analysis

A straightforward way of assessing social impacts of a project is to ask who suffers and who benefits as a result of the proposal? One tool to analyze who suffers and who benefits is a matrix. The matrices introduced in Chapter 4 may provide a starting point. For example, a city in the west proposes the construction of a dam and reservoir in a mountain environment to supply water. Several groups will suffer and benefit from the proposal (Table 11.6).

City and suburban water users will both benefit and suffer from the proposal. They may benefit from more water but will suffer from added costs to pay for the facility. Developers stand to benefit because new areas will be open for development once new water is available. The on-site landowners whose land will be flooded by the dam will suffer. Some downstream, off-site landowners may be protected from floods and, as a result, benefit. Off-site farmers downstream will suffer from the decline of available water for irrigation. Water conservation advocates stand to suffer because there will be less of an incentive to conserve with new water supplies.

TABLE 11.6
WHO SUFFERS AND WHO BENEFITS

Affected Groups	Suffers	Benefits
City users	X	X
Suburban users	X	X
Developers		X
On-site landowners	X	
Off-site landowners		X
Farmers	X	
Water conservation advocates	X	
Sportspeople	X	X
Environmentalists	X	
Consultants		X
Scientists	X	

The stream which will be dammed is a natural trout habitat. The stream bank contains vegetation that provides wildlife habitat. As a result of the destruction of the stream and the riparian vegetation, sportspeople will suffer. New fish habitat may be created by the reservoir too, so some fishers may benefit. Environmentalists who appreciate the scenic beauty and natural qualities of the stream corridor will suffer. Consultants involved in the planning and design of the new dam will benefit. Scientists who conduct biological and geological research in the watershed will suffer.

Such a matrix helps clarify those who stand to gain from the proposal and those who will lose. Planning administrators can use such a matrix, with a written analysis, to assess social impacts. As a result, decisions can be made more fairly so that costs and benefits can be evenly distributed.

TWO EXAMPLES OF PLANNING ADMINISTRATION

Boulder, Colorado, Residential Allocation System

In 1977, the city of Boulder, Colorado, enacted a strong growth management policy in response to a ballot issue to limit new development. The economy of Colorado generally was vibrant and, with many people moving to the state, growth pressures on cities like Boulder were strong. With the goal to limit residential growth to 2 percent a year, the Boulder Growth Limitation Ordinance authorized the city to allocate an average of 450 dwelling units within each construction year. The program was referred to as the "Danish system" after Paul Danish, a councilman who advocated the system. The distribution of building permits was limited by geographic area. An average of 175 dwelling units was authorized annually for the central area of the city to encourage infill development. An average of 275 dwelling units was allocated for the periphery of the city (City of Boulder Planning Department, 1980).

A residential allocation system, administered by the city planning department, was used to implement this policy until 1981. The Danish system expired in 1981, and it was replaced with a new growth management program, which continues to evolve (Pollock, 1987). However, a review of the Danish system is worthwhile. The first step in the Danish system was to complete an application form (Figure 11.5). The written statement and site plan portions of the application were used as the basis for the city staff review. Each potential project was assigned points in accordance with a "merit system" (Figure 11.6). Applicants were encouraged to describe in detail how their proposed project meets the merit system criteria.

FIGURE 11.5 City of Boulder, Colorado, residential allocation system application form.

The Applicant is required to complete all parts of this application properly and to submit two copies of all required site plans and written material to the city planning office by the appropriate deadline (See Fig. 11.6). Late or incomplete filings will not be accepted. After the required site plans and written material have been submitted, they may not be changed or modified except for minor zoning corrections as directed by the planning staff prior to the submission of an application.

If the number of requested allocations exceeds the number of allocations available, the planning department will contact the applicant requesting thirteen (13) additional copies of all required site plans and written material.

I. **General Data**
   A. Number of units requested _____
   B. Name of development _____
      Location of development _____
   C. Name of owner: _____
      Address: _____ Telephone: _____
   D. Representative for development (if different from owner, e.g., architect, planner, engineer): _____
      Address: _____ Telephone: _____
   E. The project:

	Yes	No
1. Has received approval for annexation	_____	_____
2. Complies with the Boulder Valley Comprehensive Plan	_____	_____
3. Meets all land-use regulation requirements	_____	_____
4. Has preliminary plat or PUD approval	_____	_____
5. Is a PUD approved by city of Boulder prior to November 10, 1976	_____	_____
6. Is a subdivision or PUD approved by Boulder County prior to November 10, 1976	_____	_____

   F. *Development Schedule:* A project has eleven (11) months from the date of approval of the allocation request to secure a building permit for the entire allocation. If a project needs a longer development schedule, indicate the requested schedule below. Only planning board may approve an exception to the normal development schedule.

_____

_____

_____

G. If a phased development schedule is not approved by the planning board, indicate the number of units requested to be built within the normal development schedule: _____

	Yes	No

Will you accept a pro-rate allotment? _____ _____

H. If you are requesting credit for low and/or moderate income housing, the number of units: _____

II. Land-use Data for Present Allocation Request

A. Residential Types—Building Coverage

	Acres	Units	Density	% of Total Development
1. Single-family detached (Owner occupied)	_____	_____	_____	_____
2. Single-family attached (Owner occupied)	_____	_____	_____	_____
3. Multifamily	_____	_____	_____	_____
4. Other	_____	_____	_____	_____

B. Usable Open Space*

	Acres			% of Total Development
Common land (publicly owned)	_____			_____
Common land (privately owned)	_____			_____
Private land	_____			_____

	Acres	Units	Density	% of Total Development
C. Circulation				
Public streets	_____			_____
Garages, parking, and private drives	_____			_____
D. Miscellaneous				
_____	_____			_____
_____	_____			_____
E. Total (Should include total acreage in site)	_____	_____	_____	_____

III. Multiphased Projects

If the project requesting an allocation is part of a large multiphased project, fill in the following information;

A. Size of total project _____ acres.

B. Number of units for total projects _____ units.

C.

Housing Types	Number of Units
1. _____	_____
2. _____	_____
3. _____	_____
4. _____	_____

D. Overall Density _____

E. Expected development schedule of other phases: _____

_____

(*continues*)

FIGURE 11.5 *(continues)*

IV. **FEES** ($50 plus $5 per unit)   Amount: _____
V. **Persons in Interest**
   (Names of all persons and companies who hold an interest in the as described property, whether as owner,
   mortgagee, lessee, optionee, etc.)

Name	Address	Interest
_____	_____	_____
_____	_____	_____
_____	_____	_____
_____	_____	_____
_____	_____	_____

VI. **Certification**
   I certify that the information and exhibits herewith submitted are true and correct to the best of my knowledge and
   that in filing this application I am acting with the knowledge and consent of those persons listed above without
   whose consent the requested action cannot lawfully be accomplished.

   Name (*please print*) _____ Capacity: _____
   Signed: _____
   Address: _____ Telephone: _____

VII. **Staff Use Only**
   Application received by _____ Date/Time _____ Number _____
   Scheduled: P.S. _____ P.B. _____ C.C. _____
   Date of findings to: P.B. _____ C.C. _____
   Finding mailed to applicant: _____ Date approved/denied _____

* As defined in the land-use regulations.

   Potential projects had to be prepared to the point where they theoretically would be ready to apply for a building permit. This meant that the project should receive all necessary annexation, rezoning, and planned unit development approvals prior to submitting an application. The proposal also had to be consistent with the city comprehensive plan, and only minor modifications were allowed after applications were formally submitted (City of Boulder Planning Department, 1980).

   The city's planning commission scheduled a public hearing during the last month of each application period. Public notice of the hearing was required in the local newspaper at least 10 days prior to the hearing. The purpose of the hearing was designed to review the planning staff's evaluations of the various projects. The agenda of the hearings were restricted to the evaluation of the scores given the proposed projects.

   Attendance by the applicant, or a duly authorized representative, was encouraged at the hearing. Applicants had the opportunity to make a presentation about the merits of their proposal. The public was permitted to speak in favor of or opposition to each request, too (City of Boulder Planning Department, 1980).

   After reviewing each proposed development and a final determination of all point assessments, the planning commission approved the awarding of dwelling unit allocations. The permission to seek

FIGURE 11.6 City of Boulder, Colorado, residential allocation system checklist.

Name of Project: _____

The following checklist is intended to serve as a guideline for submitting an application for the merit system. Depending upon the particular project, not all of the information listed may be necessary. The project requesting an allocation of units will be reviewed by the planning staff against the criteria indicated in the merit system and this general checklist is intended to help that review.

Check if Submitted:

_____ A. Complete application

_____ B. Two (2) copies of a site plan (folded to 9″ × 12″) of the proposed development. If the number of allocations requested exceeds the number available, thirteen (13) additional copies (folded 9″ × 12″) will be requested. The site plan should contain the following information:

    _____ 1. The site plan shall be drawn on a sheet size of 24″ × 36″ at a scale of not less than 1″ = 100′; a variation of the sheet size may be approved by the planning staff.

    _____ 2. The date, north arrow, scale and name of proposed development shall be shown on the site plan. A vicinity map shall also be shown at a scale of 500 feet to the inch.

    _____ 3. The legal description of the property within the development.

    _____ 4. The existing topographic character of the land, including existing and proposed contours.

    _____ 5. The location and size of all existing and proposed buildings, structures and improvements with appropriate dimensions.

    _____ 6. The density and type of dwellings.

    _____ 7. The internal traffic and circulation system, off-street parking areas, service areas, trash receptacles, loading areas, major points of access to public rights-of-way with appropriate dimensions, bus facilities and access to existing bus service, pedestrian access to activity areas, i.e., schools, shopping.

    _____ 8. The location, height and size of proposed signs, lighting and advertising devices.

    _____ 9. Areas which are to be conveyed, dedicated or reserved as common park areas, including public parks and recreational areas, and as site for schools or other public buildings.

    _____ 10. Major drainageways and areas subject to 100-year flooding cycle.

    _____ 11. All existing and proposed utility lines.

    _____ 12. External lighting plan.

    _____ 13. Site relation map, showing the relationship of the development to the existing land uses and public rights-of-way in the surrounding area.

_____ C. Two copies of a preliminary utility plan, including:

    _____ 1. Drainage plan

    _____ 2. Water and sewer service

    _____ 3. Flood protection and improvements

_____ D. Two copies of a written statement—a written statement must be submitted with the application, containing the following information:

    _____ 1. A statement of present ownership and options;

    _____ 2. The development schedule indicating:

        a. The approximate date on which construction of project can be expected to begin.

        b. The stages in which the project will be built and the approximate date when the construction of each stage can be expected to begin.

        c. The anticipated rate of development (i.e., number of units per year, etc.).

(continues)

FIGURE 11.6 (*continues*)

         d. The approximate dates when the development of each of the stages in the development will be completed.

         e. The area and location of common open space that will be provided at each stage.

_____ 3. *Public facilities*—A written statement indicating how the project relates to the public facilities section of the merit system by including a description of the following aspects of the development: streets, parks, fire protection, flood control, water distribution, sanitary sewage collection, school capacity, police protection, public transportation, and special facilities and services.

_____ 4. *Low and/or moderate income housing*—If developer seeks to obtain points for low and/or moderate income housing, a written statement of how the criteria will be met.

_____ 5. *Environment element*—A written statement describing how the merit development meets the following critiera as outlined in the merit system: natural resources and natural areas, and conservation.

_____ 6. *Site design and relationship with surrounding area*—A written description of how the development meets the criteria as outlined in the merit system: open space and landscaping; circulation and parking, livability; relationship to surrounding area.

_____ E. Preliminary landscaping plan—A preliminary landscaping plan may be submitted at this time to be followed by a detailed landscaping plan prior to a building permit being approved, showing the spacing, sizes, costs, and specific types of landscaping material. The preliminary landscaping plan shall include the following:

    1. The location, type and size of major existing plant materials;

    2. Location, general type, minimum size and quantity of proposed plant and other materials;

    3. Scale shown on map for plant materials must reflect ¾ mature size;

    4. Location of irrigation system.

_____ F. Architectural intent drawings and statement—elevations and perspective drawings of all proposed structures and improvements, except single-family detached residences and their accessory buildings. The drawings need not be the result of final architectural designs and need not be in detail. They shall include colors, materials, view orientations, privacy provisions and other details necessary to review the project against the merit system.

_____ G. Copies of any special agreements, conveyances, restrictions, or covenants, which will govern the use, maintenance and continued protection of the development and any of its common park areas.

_____ H. The applicant may submit any other information or exhibits deemed pertinent in evaluating the proposed development.

building permits for approved allocations was valid for a period of 11 months (unless it was specifically modified by the planning commission at the public hearing). If, at the end of 15 months, no construction of actual structures for which the permits were given was initiated, then the allocation of those permits was deemed void and the applicant notified of such in writing. The applicant then had 14 days to file a written appeal to the planning board.

Once the units had been allocated to a particular project and developer, the intent was to have the developer construct the project. However, allocations could be sold within the same development or transferred within the time limit, subject to the terms and conditions under which the allocation was originally approved. The city of Boulder emphasized that applicants should understand the requirements of the merit system (City of Boulder Planning Department, 1980).

In 1981 and again in 1985, the residential allocation, or Danish, system was amended. The goal of the 1981 program was still to limit residential growth to 2 percent a year. The merit system was retained, but allocations were not split between the center and the periphery of the city. This program included a "trigger mechanism": the allocation system was not applicable until the growth rate reached the 2 percent level. Because of the demand for new development in the Boulder area, this level was reached rather quickly, leading to further refinements in the system. The most recent form of residential growth management dispenses with the merit system approach and uses a simple prorated method of allocating residential building permits. The number of allocations requested is divided into the number available; every development then receives an equal share of the allocations available. Through the 1985 prorated system, if builders apply for 400 permits total during a period when 200 permits are available, then each builder receives half its requested number (Raabe, 1989). Provisions are made for "banking" allocations over time for multiunit buildings. Aspects of the merit system, such as energy conservation and moderate-income housing, are required features of all developments.

By the late 1980s, the Colorado economy had changed dramatically. Demand for new houses in Boulder in 1988 had dropped by nearly two-thirds from its 1977 peak. Although the allocation system authorized the issuance of 989 residential permits in 1987, the city received requests for only 266 permits, because there was limited new housing demand (Raabe, 1988). But with the slower economic growth came a general acceptance of the allocation system by the real estate industry and the public. According to one home builder, "The development community has accepted the argument that limited growth enhances real estate values and maintains economic strength by preserving the city's attractive environment" (Raabe, 1988, p. 1-C). The chronology of Boulder's growth-control efforts can be summarized as follows:

1976: Ballot initiative for limited growth passes by razor-thin 500 vote margin out of 37,000 votes cast.

1977: Boulder enacts growth-control ordinance, the Danish system, that limits issuance of residential building permits to a 2 percent annual population increase. Allocation based on a system that awards points to builders based on location, density, and cost of housing.

1981: At urging of development community, ordinance revised. New system gives some permits on first-come basis; remainder of permits issued on point system.

1985: Ordinance revised again. New system awards permits to all applicants on prorated basis.

1985–1988: Sluggish economy results in surplus of available permits over number requested. (Adapted from Raabe, 1988, p. 1-C)

Court-Mandated Plan Review and Administrative Procedures in Oregon

The process of selecting among planning options in Portland, Oregon, was discussed in Chapter 6. This process resulted because of the Oregon statewide goals reviewed in Chapter 2. Those measures selected to implement the Oregon plan are subject to a review and administration procedure.

In Oregon, plan review and administration has been strongly affected by three landmark court decisions. It is necessary to review those decisions to understand how plans are administered in the state, such as the plan of the city of Portland. The first decision of the Oregon Supreme Court,

Fasano v. Board of County Commissioners of Washington County (1973), established procedures and criteria for consideration of applications for a zone change. The *Fasano* decision considered traditional zoning activity in relationship to a more recent comprehensive Washington County plan as it applied to a requested zone change in the county. In essence, the Oregon Supreme Court determined that planning and zoning, although containing many similar elements, were not of the same level of effect and should not be acted on in a like manner (Portland Bureau of Planning, 1980).

Planning was determined to be the establishment of general rules affecting a large body of citizens and land. Zoning was determined to be much more limited in nature, affecting specific parcels of land and specific people. In this light, the court declared zoning to be an implementing force for planning and determined that the procedures involved must be different. Planning, because of its general nature and wide scope, is a legislative function and requires only the usual legislative procedures to enact. Zoning, as a result of its more specific nature, requires a quasi-judicial procedure to protect the rights of individuals. According to Attorney General Lee Johnson:

> The court in classifying certain zoning actions as quasi-judicial rather than legislative indicated that the efficient implementation of that classification required that the action should not only be labeled as quasi-judicial but should be conducted in a manner similar to usually accepted procedures before the courts in trials and administrative agencies in contested case proceeding. (1974, p. 979)

Change of land use, particularly where a comprehensive plan had been enacted, was felt to require guidelines for the quasi-judicial procedure. Johnson laid out the standard points for proving the need for change as:

- The change must conform to the comprehensive plan.

- There must be a public need for the change in question.
- It must be shown that the public need will be served best by changing the zone classification of the property in question as opposed to other available property.
- The change must be shown to comply with the general welfare standard contained in the enabling legislation. (1974, p. 978)

The court went on to establish credence for comprehensive planning and establish once and for all its status in the realm of land-use regulation in Oregon. Again, according to Johnson, "*Fasano* establishes that the comprehensive plan is a basic general standard against which specific fact situations should be measured" (1974, p. 975).

Since *Fasano* the Oregon Supreme Court refined its approach to land-use planning and zone changes. In *Neuberger v. City of Portland* (1979), the court recognized the significant body of land-use planning statutes and administrative regulations adopted by the Oregon legislature and the LCDC. In *Neuberger v. City of Portland,* the Oregon Supreme Court reinforced the preeminence of LCDC goals and locally adopted comprehensive plans as the primary resource for determining zone-change decisions. While not invalidating all elements of the *Fasano* decision, the court did reject the requirement to show "public need" and consideration of other available property (Portland Bureau of Planning, 1980). However, the court did leave those two factors open to consideration if they are required by the local comprehensive plan. The court noted in its decision:

> We find, then, no statutory or LCDC requirement that a showing of either public need or a comparison with other available property is a specific and independent prerequisite to a zoning amendment. In light of the continuous legislative and agency attention to the planning and zoning process since the *Fasano* decision, we conclude that the legislature and LCDC have not found it necessary to impose such requirements.

That is not to say, however, that the considerations which they embodied are irrelevant. Under the present legislative scheme, each local government must adopt a comprehensive plan which is in compliance with the LCDC goals, and adopt zoning and other ordinances to implement it. Once the plan and its implementing ordinances have been adopted and have been acknowledged by LCDC to be in compliance with the goals, zoning amendments and other land use decisions will be governed by criteria in the plan and related ordinances or, in cases in which those criteria do not apply, by the goals themselves. (Oregon Supreme Court, 1979)

A third landmark decision of the Oregon Supreme Court was *Baker v. City of Milwaukie.* This decision established that zoning must comply with the limits set by a comprehensive plan. Thus, the land-use designations of a comprehensive plan are "superior" to a zoning map. In other words, the zoning map cannot allow land uses which are more intensive than those allowed by the comprehensive plan map (Oregon Supreme Court, 1975; Portland Department of Planning, 1980).

To summarize, the Oregon legislature and supreme court have determined that LCDC goals and locally adopted comprehensive plans are "superior" to other land-use controls. The other land-use controls, such as zoning, *must* comply with the limits and designations of the comprehensive plan but not at the expense of existing activities.

Decisions affecting a comprehensive plan are determined to be legislative in nature because of the scope and general application of such a plan. Zoning or other plan implementation measures, because of their specific nature—applying the general rules of a comprehensive plan—are determined to be a quasi-judicial procedure. A quasi-judicial procedure entitles the participants in a change request to the protection afforded by the judicial process and, obviously, also requires the participants to comply with judicial proceeding regulations and directives; i.e., the person or agency seeking a change must bear the burden of

proof, showing that such a change is consistent with the adopted comprehensive plan (Portland Department of Planning, 1980).

Because of these cases and the Oregon land-use legislation, cities, including Portland, and counties must administer comprehensive plans within a well-defined framework. This framework is illustrated in Table 11.7. At the legislative or rule-making level, LCDC is the highest level of the land-use hierarchy. Under authority of legislative mandate, LCDC has formulated the rules for statewide land-use planning. These general rules guide the action of re-

TABLE 11.7
ORGANIZATION OF COMPREHENSIVE PLANNING IN OREGON USING THE CITY OF PORTLAND AS AN EXAMPLE

Department of Land Conservation and Development

Governing body:	Land Conservation and Development Commission (appointed)
Responsibilities:	Statewide land-use goals and guidelines; and review and acceptance (or rejection) of constituent jurisdictions' comprehensive plans

Metropolitan Service District

Governing body:	Portland Metropolitan Service District Council (elected)
Responsibilities:	Coordination of regional planning within Metropolitan Service District boundary; and preparation and administration of regional plan

City of Portland

Governing body:	Portland City Council (elected)
Responsibilities:	Preparation and administration of local plan

Portland City Planning Commission

Governing body:	Portland City Planning Commission (appointed)
Responsibilities:	Advise preparation and administration of local plan

City of Portland Planning Staff

Responsibilities:	Assemble and disseminate information for preparation and administration of local plan

SOURCE: Adapted from Portland Bureau of Planning, 1980.

gional and local jurisdictions. In the Portland metropolitan area, a regional agency directs the coordination of area land-use planning and assures coordination and cooperation between local governments whose proximity is such that their internal activities will have an effect on surrounding or adjacent governments (Portland Bureau of Planning, 1980).

One such government in the metropolitan region is the city of Portland, which operates in both the legislative and quasi-judicial spheres of land-use control. Portland establishes general rules of land use through a legislative process and also must implement those regulations. The implementation of land-use rules is the activity addressed by the *Fasano* decision; making changes or variances to those rules is a quasi-judicial matter (Portland Bureau of Planning, 1980).

The expected sequence of events, for a person seeking to modify the structures or activity allowed on a piece of land, would begin at the Code Administration Section of the Portland Bureau of Planning. The staff would determine if the proposed change was allowable in the current zone in question. If not, an application for change could be submitted and a quasi-judicial hearing would be held before the hearings officer or the planning commission. Failing a satisfactory resolution of the issue at that level, an appeal could be made to the city council, again a quasi-judicial hearing. Although a land-use control decision made by the city council may be appealed, two levels of hearings are provided initially within the city's jurisdiction (Portland Bureau of Planning, 1980).

The Portland and Boulder examples illustrate that administration must be based on a solid legal foundation. Furthermore, planning administration relies on a competent staff, and administrative activities should be linked to other steps in the planning process. Planning administration in Oregon is guided by specific statewide goals.

Court cases have further articulated plan review and administrative procedures in Oregon. The development of such statewide goals for land-use planning has occurred relatively recently in the United States. When compared to more conventional planning processes, planning in Oregon goes much further in connecting state goals to local administrative decisions. Oregon has required greater consistency in the planning process—actions must be connected to detailed environmental information, which is mandated in the state goals.

Both the Oregon and Boulder examples help illustrate the importance of the staff in planning administration. The Boulder system has been subject to continued refinement. The staff has been flexible and creative. In Portland, the planning staff determines whether proposed zone changes are allowed, and a hearings officer oversees rezone requests.

The Boulder example illustrates a more comprehensive use of biophysical information in planning administration as compared with more conventional programs. As part of the residential allocation application process, open-space and land-use information had to be supplied. The topographic character of the land, natural drainageways, floodplains, and natural areas were considered in the review process. Boulder requires specific site design plans, such as those described in Chapter 9, for proposed projects.

Part of the success of planning in Portland and the rest of Oregon is due to the broad public understanding of its statewide goal. This is partially the result of the attention generated by the various referenda and court cases. Another reason for the visibility of planning in Oregon is the dedication of key political leaders, such as the charismatic former governor, the late Tom McCall. A third reason is that responsible officials have continually attempted to explain the law to the citizens of Oregon.

12
CONCLUSION

From within the planning community, there have been many critics of a normative, rationalist approach to planning. The normative perspective suggests a standard, model, or pattern of conduct for planners. Normative planning is where "planners subject both the ends and means of public policy to rational consideration" (Klosterman, 1978, p. 38). Critics of this rational approach contend it focuses on problem solving: "Take the problem, break it down into its component parts, and let's see what we can do about it" (Forester, 1982, p. 61). They argue, "this may serve well for relatively routine, conventional, stable problems—but perhaps not for most planning and policy problems" (Forester, 1982, p. 61).

Rationalists believe that "reason, independent of the senses, constitutes a superior source of knowledge" (Lai, 1988, p. 19). This belief leads to a model that should be applied a priori to any situation or setting. A rationalist tradition underlies the planning profession because of its foundation in the fields of architecture, landscape architecture, engineering, and law. In addition, the very definition of the word *planning* suggests rationality.

Herbert Gans was especially critical of the physical bias of planning prior to the 1960s. Yet, Gans espoused a rationalist perspective: "Planning must be and can be *rational*—rationality being achieved when planners develop plans or programs which can be proved to implement the goals that are being sought" (1968, p. ix). Gans was largely successful in his effort to wean planners from their architectural and site planning roots and lay the foundation for a social rationalist approach.

Lewis Mumford, who was certainly critical of the architectural rationalists, was nevertheless an advocate of the spatial, physical concepts of planning. He proposed an organic approach to planning:

Organic planning does not begin with a preconceived goal: it moves from need to need, from opportunity to opportunity, in a series of adaptations that themselves become increasingly coherent and purposeful, so that they generate a complex, final design. (1961, p. 302)

Mumford's organic approach foreshadows a contingency view. Contingency is the condition of being subject to chance. The concept of contingency has been explored by theorists in management, organization behavior, and planning. According to Kast and Rosenzweig:

The contingency view seeks to understand the interrelationships within and among subsystems as well as between the organization and its environment and define patterns of relationships or configurations of variables. It emphasizes the multivariate nature of organizations and attempts to understand how organizations operate under varying conditions and in specific circumstances. (1974, p. ix)

Human organizations and their interactions with each other and their settings are complex. The postmodern condition would lead some to conclude that humans are doomed to exist in chaos. Students of chaos, however, have detected that order exists in apparently chaotic situations (Prigogine & Stengers, 1984). Planners are faced with the task of making order out of chaos; they must be able to adapt to changing conditions and to act in a contingent manner.

In spite of the criticisms made by Gans two decades ago, many planners, or at least individuals who hold that title in local and even higher levels of government, are faced with situations concerning the physical ordering of the built and natural environments. Planners must address issues concerning the use of land and other natural resources. To be effective, they require a repertoire of approaches that can be applied to a variety of situations.

The model for planning presented here is a linear yet iterative process—identification of issues; establishment of goals; inventory and analysis of the biophysical and sociocultural environments at the regional and local levels; detailed studies such as suitability analysis; determination of options; development of a plan for the landscape; continued public participation and community education; detailed design; implementation; and administration. Such a linear approach is inadequate for most situations—after starting to implement a plan, the original goals may change or there may be new information discovered about the environment. A feedback process is necessary to reformulate and restudy issues. In many cases, this process of review may occur repeatedly. As a result, instead of having a linear planning process, in many cases one experiences a cyclic form of planning, reviewing previous stages again and again.

Such a cyclical process has occurred in Whitman County, Washington, which has been used as an example in several sections of this book. The Whitman County example helps illustrate how an ecological approach can be integrated into conventional planning processes. Whitman County is located in the region known as the Palouse in eastern Washington and northern Idaho. The county adopted its first comprehensive plan in 1960. This plan consisted of a few simple sentences designating the entire county for agricultural use. Rapid growth at Washington State University and its associated impact on the city of Pullman, industrial and

Snake River, Wyoming. *(Philip Maechling)*

was broad information gathering. A series of nine background reports were prepared by the planning staff from August through November of 1977. The background reports included information about population characteristics and forecasts, land and water resources, transportation, public facilities and services, conservation and natural hazards, economic structure, constraints to housing development, and citizen comments. During this time, a citizens advisory committee was organized, which included all the members of the planning commission in addition to other citizens. This advisory committee reviewed these background documents, which were then presented to the community in a series of five workshops. At each workshop a prepared set of questions concerning the citizens' views on the county's future was reviewed by the planning staff and advisory committee (Whitman County Regional Planning Council, 1978).

The second phase involved setting goals. This phase lasted from December 1977 through mid-February 1978 and involved the advisory committee and the planning staff. This group decided what elements to include in the plan. The Washington Planning Enabling Act requires land-use and transportation elements and permits several optional elements. In addition to the two required elements, four more are included in the Whitman County plan: economic development, environmental quality and natural conservation, parks and recreation, and implementation. Draft goals were written by the planning staff after the intent was established by the advisory committee. The advisory committee then reviewed the draft goals that were revised as needed (Whitman County Regional Planning Council, 1978). Once the goals were established, the final phase began. This third phase involved the establishment of specific policies to achieve the goals. These policies took two forms: planning guidelines and implementation guidelines. Planning guidelines addressed specific standards and concerns. Implementation guidelines outlined specific actions necessary to achieve the goals (Whitman County Regional Planning Council, 1978).

commercial port development on the Snake River, and the development of a county park system resulted in a new comprehensive plan in 1970.

After 1970, there were several events in the county that caused local officials to revise and update the comprehensive plan once again. Most of the concern was focused on the growth of Washington State University and the impact of that growth on the adjacent rich wheat fields of the Palouse. Several strategies were attempted by local officials to curb housing and commercial development, but these were recognized as only partially effective. There were also concerns about the impact of federal programs on the county in general and on its farmland specifically.

The revision of the comprehensive plan was organized by the local planning agency and accomplished in three phases: information gathering, goal making, and policy-making. The first phase

The Whitman County comprehensive plan included several important goals. Perhaps the most important goal in the plan is the protection of agricultural land. Since 1978, it has been the goal of Whitman County to "preserve productive agricultural land and the family farm as the prime economic and social resources of Whitman County by preventing land from being taken out of production by indiscriminate or excessive changes in land use" (Whitman County Regional Planning Council, 1978, p. 25).

This goal has been implemented through an ongoing farmland protection effort (Steiner, 1981). In addition to farmland protection, the plan articulated several other goals for the county. Limited, low-density living opportunities in unincorporated areas on nonagricultural lands were to be provided. Urban and suburban development outside of incorporated areas in the county was to be discouraged. A basis for decisions concerning *light* industrial land use was to be designed to help support the long-term economic health of the county. The corridor between Pullman and Moscow along Paradise Creek was identified as an opportunity area for *light* industrial land use. Areas on the Snake River were to be used for heavy industry. Retail and highway-oriented strip commercial land use was prohibited outside incorporated areas. Construction of major facilities by the state or federal government was to minimize impacts on farm and ranch operations. The extensive county road system was to be maintained and improved. Hazards for bicycle, equestrian, and pedestrian uses on roads were to be decreased. Air and water quality were to be maintained and improved. Critical environmentally sensitive areas were to be preserved, consistent with Washington's SEPA. Flood hazards were to be reduced. Park, recreation, and open space opportunities were to be provided to meet the needs of the entire Whitman County community.

Certainly, this is an ambitious set of goals, and, remarkably, much of the agenda established in 1978 has been achieved. Each goal in the comprehensive plan was backed up by a detailed goal rationale, specific planning guidelines, and a realistic implementation strategy.

The legacy created by the county commissioners, the planning commission, and the local planning agency in 1978 has largely been beneficial for the citizens of the Palouse. Land values of farmland did not inflate as rapidly as in other regions where speculation for nonagricultural uses drove the prices up, then sent them crashing down. Such unstable prices have caused widespread farm bankruptcies in other parts of the nation.

Land-use conflicts between farmers and nonagricultural users have been minimized. Whitman County farmers have not faced lawsuits for their use of chemicals, as farmers have elsewhere. (Although certainly farmers and others in the Palouse should question the excessive use of farm chemicals in the region.) Whitman County farmers have been free to farm without complaints from suburbanites about dust, farm odors, noise, late evening work, pesticides, or herbicides. Farm animals have not been harassed by suburban children. Except for an occasional prank by college students, Whitman County farms have been relatively free of vandalism. Through the plan, county officials have been able to influence the location of highways and public facilities to minimize the negative impacts on productive farmlands.

By the early 1980s, there was some concern about two land-use provisions in the Whitman County comprehensive plan, those regulating light industrial and heavy commercial land use. This concern coincided with the development of a LESA pilot study (see Chapter 5), and thus there was an opportunity to use the new system. The original planning guidelines restricted light industrial and heavy commercial uses to areas of thin soils, near floodplains, in the urban periphery, and in the same vicinity as other nonagricultural uses. All these guidelines were designed to help protect farmland. There was, however, concern from the county commissioners and planning commissioners that the first two of these criteria—thin soils and floodplains—were inappropriate. As a result, the

LESA system was explored as a means to evaluate light industry and heavy commercial uses while maintaining the county goal to protect agriculture. Since residential and light commercial uses have been regulated successfully, these uses were not evaluated.

The LESA project resulted in the amendment of planning guidelines to better regulate light industrial and heavy commercial uses and to protect farmland at the same time. The LESA system that emerged was different than the one described in Chapter 5. Much fine-tuning and public discussion and debate was necessary before a suitable LESA system was agreed upon by county officials. The resultant system has since been used by planners to provide options for these uses to the county commissioners.

The city of Pullman has benefited from the 1978 county plan because residential and commercial land uses have been encouraged within the city limits, rather than sprawling into the countryside. Meanwhile, the county has been able to maintain a fiscally conservative budget because there has not been a rapid demand for new services or the sudden expenditures for emergency services. For instance, in neighboring Spokane County, which permits scattered subdivisions in wooded rural areas, one forest fire cost the county approximately $7 million.

As successful as the plan has been, however, it should not be viewed as a panacea. The planning for the Pullman-Moscow corridor has not proceeded smoothly. The county plan identified the corridor as a *light* industrial opportunity area. The comprehensive plan also sought to minimize hazards for bicyclists on county roads. Another official county document, its parks plan, designates the corridor as an area of recreational potential. Nearly everyone in the region recognizes the corridor as a logical place to focus development activities. Disagreement has arisen over the type of development.

The county commissioners sought to have the corridor developed for heavy industrial use, mainly rock-crushing and strip-mining operations. A large group of citizens felt that such uses were inappropriate for the academic and agricultural character of the region. This group was not opposed to development but rather felt a greenway between the two cities could both provide recreational use and be a stimulus to light industrial development. The Palouse path conceptual design, described in Chapter 9, was an attempt to resolve this disagreement (Carlson et al., 1989).

The Palouse path concept was only partially successful. The state highway department, the cities of Pullman and Moscow, the University of Idaho, and Washington State University planners have used many of the ideas in their own plans and programs. The Whitman County planning commission adopted the recommendations as well, but their suggestions were ignored by the county commissioners. The county commissioners continued to rezone much of the corridor into heavy industrial use until they were replaced through the 1988 election by new commissioners more sympathetic to the path concept.

Whitman County has one of the worst soil erosion problems in the nation, which has a serious negative impact on regional water quality. The problem was recognized in the environmental quality and conservation element of the 1978 plan, but little has been done by the county to ameliorate it. Michael Jennings and John Reganold (1988) have provided a critical review of the county efforts to protect environmentally sensitive areas.

The Washington SEPA encourages environmental protection through a procedure review of many actions (see Chapter 11). Some actions, however, are specifically exempt from the EIS review required by SEPA. The state does allow, however, local governments to designate environmentally sensitive areas where exempt activities are subject to SEPA review (see Chapter 10). In its 1978 plan in the environmental quality and natural conservation element, the county acknowledged the importance of designating environmentally sensitive areas to promote environmental quality

(Washington State University College of Agriculture and Home Economics)

and to conserve natural resources.

Jennings and Reganold (1988) illustrate significant environmental problems in the county relating to geologic, soil, water, and biotic resources. According to Jennings and Reganold,

"Long-term local human health, safety, and well-being are directly related to these resources in terms of (a) sustainability of agricultural productivity and related economic structure, (b) ground and surface water quality, (c) flooding and related stream morphology, and (d) natural habitat and biological diversity" (1988, p. 378). The county could use an environmentally sensitive area designation to protect these resources, but it has not.

Independent of county government, however, planning efforts have been undertaken by the Palouse Conservation District to control erosion and improve water quality in the Missouri Flat Creek watershed. The Whitman County efforts that have been described did not follow the linear process used as the organizational basis for this book. In fact, only two of the examples used consciously followed this format: the Teller County, Colorado, growth management effort and the Missouri Flat Creek watershed conservation plan.

The Missouri Flat Creek watershed planning process was initiated by the local conservation district in 1985 (Steiner & Osterman, 1988). Through this process, the issues of soil erosion and sedimentation and the problems that result in terms of long-term agricultural productivity and water pollution were identified. The goal was established to eliminate pollution of the Missouri Flat Creek. This goal was compatible with state water quality and federal soil conservation policies and programs. Inventories and analyses were conducted of the Palouse River drainage basin and the Missouri Flat Creek watershed. Detailed studies were undertaken of highly erodible lands and of farmer attitudes about conservation. Concepts were developed about how to control erosion. These concepts were incorporated into a watershed-level plan that set specific strategies and actions for achieving the planning goals. Throughout the process, land users were involved

and were provided information. Detailed designs, in the form of farm-level conservation plans, were prepared for individual land users. These individual designs as well as the watershed plan were implemented through provisions of state and federal law. As of early 1990, the plan is being administered, monitored, and evaluated. The early indications are that the process has been a success and the vexing issue of soil erosion in the Palouse is being addressed. The Missouri Flat Creek project is now being used as an example for other watersheds with critical erosion problems.

The method described in this book reflects a middle-ground approach to landscape planning somewhere between a purely organic and a truly rational one. The method presented here is not suggested as a rigid, lockstep approach that is appropriate for every situation but rather a flexible, iterative method that can be used when a group of people identify an issue or set of issues. The method is a framework for problem solving. As the feedback arrows in Figure 1.1 indicate, there are many steps in the process where it may be adjusted or modified. Certainly, the steps may be reordered or skipped entirely depending on the situation. For instance, in some cases it may be appropriate to conduct inventories and analyses (steps 3 and 4) before establishing goals (step 2). The method represents "a series of adaptations," in Mumford's words.

The issue or set of issues may be viewed as symptoms of the problems and opportunities facing the planning area. The landscape planner then may make a diagnosis about the situation based on an understanding of the nature of the place in order to prescribe an appropriate intervention.

GLOSSARY OF ECOLOGICAL PLANNING TERMS

Abiotic   Those aspects dealing with nonliving matter.

Adaptation   A genetically determined characteristic that enhances the ability of an organism to better adjust to its surroundings.

Adiabatic lapse rate   A variation in temperature of a parcel of air up or down a change in elevation. This does not take into account exchanges of heat between the air parcel and the environment.

Administration   Execution of an organizational policy to reach predetermined objectives.

Advection   The transfer of an atmospheric property due to mass air motion along a gradient of the property in question; the horizontal spreading of local effects by wind.

Agricultural lands   Places used for crop or animal production or for silviculture.

Air mass   A widespread body of air that gains certain characteristics while set in one location. The characteristics change as it moves away.

Air parcel   A space of air over a certain area of land.

Air pollution areas   Places that require restraints on air pollution emissions due to periods of poor vertical air mixing and the subsequent entrapment of polluting substances.

Albedo   Reflected solar radiation factor.

Alluvium   The soil material deposited by running water.

Analysis   The examination of individual parts to find out their nature, function, and interrelationship with other parts.

Annexation   The addition of new territory to the jurisdiction of a municipality.

Aquifer   A water-bearing layer of permeable rock, sand, or gravel.

Aspect   Orientation toward some direction.

Basalt   A hard, fine-grained igneous rock caused by volcanism.

Base map   A reproducible map used to display various types of information.

Biogeochemical cycles   Mineral and nutrient cycles that are important to the biological community.

Biological   Those aspects dealing with living matter.

Biomass   The amount of living matter in a given unit of the environment.

Biophysical   Biological and physical factors.

Biosphere   The portion of earth and its atmosphere that can support life.

Biota   All living organisms that exist in an area.

Biotic community   An assemblage of plants and animals living in the same community, forming a system that is mutually sustaining and interdependent and influenced by the abiotic factors of the ecosystem. A biotic community is generally characterized by the dominant vegetation.

Board of adjustment   An independent board created to handle conditional uses, variances, and special applications of regulations established by a zoning ordinance and to hear and act on appeals.

Building code   The legal requirements pertaining to the building of structures.

Canopy layer   The uppermost layer of forest vegetation.

Capability   An evaluation based on a resource's inherent, natural, or intrinsic ability to provide for use and includes that existing ability which is the result of past alterations or current management practices. Often *capability* is used interchangeably with *suitability*.

Capability class   An evaluation made by the U.S. Soil Conservation Service concerning the agricultural management of a soil type.

Capital improvement programming (CIP)   The multiyear scheduling of public physical improvements. The scheduling is based on studies of fiscal resources available and the choice of specific improvements to be constructed for a period of 5 or 6 years in the future.

Carnivores   Animals that feed on other animals.

Carrying capacity   (1) In ecology, the number of individuals that the resources of a habitat can support. (2) In wildlife, the maximum number of animals an area can support during a given period of the year. (3) In recreation, the amount of use a recreation area can sustain without deterioration of its quality.

Citizen participation   The involvement of the public in the planning process.

Citizens advisory committee (CAC)   A group of citizens called together by an agency to represent the ideas and attitudes of their community in advising and giving consultation to the agency.

Clay   Soil particles smaller than 0.002 millimeters in diameter.

Climate   The set of meteorological conditions characteristic of an area over a given length of time.

Cognitive mapping   A process by which people acquire, code, store, recall, and decode information about the relative locations and attributes of phenomena in the everyday spatial environment.

Cohort-survival method   Popular method for making population projections based on fertility, mortality, and net migration.

Community   (1) In sociology, a variety of physical and social areas and institutions within which and with which people live. (2) In ecology, an association of interacting populations, usually determined by their interactions or by spatial occurrence.

Compensating wind   Wind originating above plains and flowing toward nearby mountains along a pressure gradient.

Competition   The use or defense of a resource by one individual which reduces the availability of that resource to other individuals.

Comprehensive plan   A document setting forth official governmental policy for the long-term future development of an area that considers all major determinants of growth and change—economic, political, social, and biophysical.

Comprehensive planning   A process for coordinating and establishing the policies set forth in a comprehensive plan.

Conditional use   A permitted use allowed in zoning ordinances that requires review by a board of adjustment or similar review agency.

Conifer   A cone-bearing plant whose needles remain on the tree all year.

Conservation   The management of human use of the biosphere to yield the greatest sustainable benefit to present generations while maintaining its potential to meet the needs and aspirations of future generations.

Critical areas   Places significantly affected by, or having an effect on, an existing or proposed major facility or other areas of major public investment; or containing or having a significant impact on historical, natural, or environmental resources of regional or statewide importance.

Cropland   Land regularly used for production of crops, except forestland and rangeland, including permanent pasture.

Cross section   A graphic tool that illustrates a vertical section of land.

Cumulative impact assessment   A comprehensive planning process whereby the rate or total amount of development is managed to stay below prestated threshold levels and is halted when such thresholds are reached.

Deadwater   Unflowing stream or river water.

Decomposers   The breakdown of matter by bacteria. It changes the chemical makeup and physical appearance of materials.

Delphi   A method for systematically developing and expressing the views of a panel of experts.

Detritus   Freshly dead or partially decomposed organic matter.

Detritus-feeding animals   Animals that ingest and break down fragments of organic matter.

Detrivores   Animals that obtain energy from decaying plant and animal matter.

Development   The modification of the biosphere and the application of human, financial, living, and nonliving resources to satisfy human needs and improve the quality of human life.

Dike   Hardened lava extending in a direction other than that of the flow.

Dominant species   A species that has a controlling influence on the local environment.

Drainage basin   A part of the earth's surface that is occupied by a drainage system, which consists of a surface stream or a body of impounded surface water together with all tributary surface streams and bodies of impounded surface water.

Drainage class   The relative terms used to describe natural drainage as follows:

Excessive: Commonly very porous and rapidly permeable soils that have low water-holding capacity.

Somewhat excessive: Very permeable soils that are free from mottling throughout their profile.

Good: Well-drained soils that are nearly free of mottling and are commonly of intermediate texture.

Moderately good: Moderately well-drained soils that commonly have a slow permeable layer in or immediately beneath the solum. They have uniform color in the surface layers and upper subsoil and mottling in the lower subsoils and substrata.

Somewhat poor: Soils wet for significant periods but not all the time. They commonly have a slowly permeable layer in the profile, a high water table, additions through seepage, or a combination of these conditions.

Poor: Soils wet for long periods of time. They are light gray and generally are mottled from the surface downward, although mottling may be absent or nearly so in some soils.

Drainage wind   A wind flowing from a higher elevation to a lower elevation.

Duplex   A detached structure containing two dwelling units.

Dwelling unit   An independent living space within a structure designed and intended for occupancy by not more than one family and having its own housekeeping and kitchen facilities.

Easement   The purchase of partial rights in a piece of land.

Ecological critical areas   Places containing one or more significant natural resources that could be degraded or lost as a result of uncontrolled or incompatible development.

Ecological planning   The application of ecological knowledge to community, regional, and resource planning.

Ecology   The reciprocal relationship of living things to one another and to their physical and biological environment.

Economic   Of or having to do with the management of the income and expenditures of a household, business, community, or government.

Economic multiplier   The numerical relationship between an original change in economic activity and the ultimate change in activity that results as the money spent and respent through various sectors of the economy.

Ecosystem   The interacting system of a biological community and its nonliving surroundings.

Ecotone   Transitional areas between two ecological communities, generally of greater richness than either of the communities it separates.

Elevation   The height of land (in feet or meters) above sea level.

Energy   That which does or is capable of doing work.

Environment   The sum of all external influences that affect the life, development, and survival of an organism.

Environmental impact statement (EIS)   A document required of federal agencies by the National Environmental Policy Act for major projects or legislative proposals. It is used in making decisions about the positive and negative effects of the undertaking and lists alternatives. Some states and several other nations also require impact statements.

Environmentally sensitive areas   Places vulnerable to negative environmental impacts, such as unstable soils, steep slopes, floodplains, wetlands, and certain plant and animal habitats.

Environmental thresholds   The level beyond which additional stress to an ecosystem results in a marked decrease in the system's performance or an adaptive change in the system's structure or both.

Eolian soils   Soils deposited by the wind.

Erosion   The process of diminishing the land by degrees by running water, wind, ice, or other geological agents.

Erosion, bank   The destruction of land areas from active cutting of stream banks.

Erosion, beach   The retrogression of the shoreline of large lakes and coastal waters caused by wave action, shore currents, or natural causes other than subsidence.

Erosion, gully   The widening, deepening, and headcutting of small channels and waterways due to erosion.

Erosion, rill   The removal of soil by running water with formation of shallow channels that can be smoothed out completely by normal cultivation.

Erosion, sheet   The removal of a fairly uniform layer of soil or materials from the land surface by the action of rainfall and runoff water.

Estuary   A semienclosed coastal body of water that has a free connection with the open sea; it is thus strongly affected by tidal action, and within it seawater is mixed (and usually measurably diluted) with fresh water from land drainage.

Evaporation   The loss of water to the atmosphere from the surface of a soil or a body of water.

Evapotranspiration   The sum of evaporation and transpiration during a specific time period.

Exotics   Plants or animals introduced into a community that are not normally constituents of that community.

Fault   A fracture line along which movements have occurred, causing the geologic units on either side to be mismatched.

Fauna   Animal life.

Fire hazard areas   Places identified by the U.S. Forest Service and state wildfire management agencies as being particularly susceptible to forest fires.

First-order stream   See *Stream orders.*

Flooding   The general and temporary condition of partial or complete inundation of normal dryland areas from the overflow of streams, rivers, and other inland water or from abnormally high tidal water resulting from severe storms, hurricanes, or tsunamis. Also, any relatively high stream flow overtopping the natural or artificial banks in any reach of a stream, or a relatively high flow as measured by either gauge height or discharge quantity.

Floodplain   The area of land adjoining a body of water that has been or may be covered by floodwater.

Flood-prone areas   Places identified on the basis of the frequency of flooding.

Floodway   The channel of a river or other watercourse and the adjacent land areas required to carry and discharge a flood of a given magnitude.

Flora   Plant life.

Fog   Suspended liquid particles formed by condensation of vapor.

Food chain   The interconnected feeding relationships of various species that transfer energy from an initial source through a series of organisms.

Forb   Herbs other than true grasses, sedges, and rushes and nongrasslike plants having little or no woody material.

Forestland   Land that is at least 10 percent stocked by trees of any size and land from which the trees have been removed to less than 10 percent stocking but that has not been developed for other use.

Frost pocket   A hollow in the topography into which cold air will flow, thereby lowering temperatures in the bottom of the hollow.

Geological hazard areas   Places characterized by a high frequency of earthquake shaking, landslides, fault displacements, volcanic activity, subsidence, or severe erosion.

Geology   The science dealing with the study of rocks, often in an attempt to learn more about the history of the earth.

Geomorphology   The science dealing with the interpretation of the relief features of the surface of the earth.

Goal   A concise statement of a community or organization's central aspirations in addressing a problem or an opportunity expressed in terms of a desired state or process that operating programs are designed to achieve.

Grass   Plant species with narrow leaves and jointed stems.

Greenbelts   Buffer zones created by restricting development from certain land areas.

Ground cover   Plants grown to keep soil from eroding.

Groundwater   Water that fills all the unblocked pores of material lying beneath the water table.

Groundwater recharge areas   Areas where additions are made to an aquifer by infiltration of water through the land surface.

Group dynamics   A generic term classifying a variety of interpersonal techniques used to foster group interaction and achievement of group goals and problem-solving techniques designed to clarify substantive issues.

Habitat   The sum of environmental conditions in a specific place that is occupied by an organism, population, or community.

Hedgerow   A group or row of trees and shrubs separating two grassy areas.

Herb   Any flowering plant that does not develop a persistent woody stem above ground, including forbs, grasses, and grasslike plants.

Herbicide   A chemical that controls or destroys undesirable plants.

Herbivores   Primary consumers or animals that obtain energy from plants.

Historic, archaelogical, and cultural areas   Sites important to the heritage of the community, region, state, or nation.

Human ecology   The interdisciplinary study of human-ecosystem relationships.

Humus   The semistable fraction of the soil organic matter remaining after the major portion of added plant and animal residues has decomposed, usually dark-colored.

Hydrograph   A graph showing the volume of water that passes a point of a stream over a certain period of time.

Hydrologic cycle   A recurring series of events involving the circulation of water through the environment. The cycle includes precipitation, storage, and evaporation.

Hydrology   The science dealing with the study of groundwater and surface water and the changes that occur during the hydrologic cycle.

Impact fees   A growth management technique that requires a developer to pay for public services necessary for new urban development.

Indicator species   A species (either plant or animal) generally limited to a particular environment so that its presence will usually indicate that environment or life zone.

Infiltration rate   The rate of speed at which water flows into soil through small pores.

Insolation   Incoming solar radiation that is absorbed by the land, largely dependent on landforms and wind direction.

Intrinsic suitability   The inherent capability of an area to support a particular land use with the least detriment to the economy and the environment.

Introduced species   A species brought into an area by people; one that is not a native.

Inventory   The gathering of data for future use.

Inversion   An atmospheric condition caused by a layer of warm air preventing the rise of cool air trapped beneath it.

Landscape   All the natural features such as fields, hills, forests, and water that distinguish one part of the surface of the earth from another part.   Usually a landscape is that portion of land or territory which the eye can comprehend in a single view, including all its natural characteristics.

Landscape architecture   The art and science of arranging land so as to adapt it most conveniently, economically, functionally, and gracefully to any of the varied wants of people.

Landscape ecology   A study of the structure, function, and change in a heterogeneous land area composed of interacting ecosystems.

Landscape plan   A written and graphic documentation of a community's goals, the strategies to achieve those goals, and the spatial consequences of the implementation strategies.

Land use   The occupation of an area for a particular purpose, such as rangeland or industrial areas.

Land-use need   A factor that is essential or beneficial for a particular land use.

Land user   Person using a land resource who may or may not own title to that land.

Langley   A measurement of solar radiation equivalent to one calorie per square centimeter over some increment of time.

Leaching   The process by which nutrient chemicals or contaminants are dissolved and carried away by water or are moved into a lower layer of soil.

Life cycle   The stages an organism passes through during its existence.

Life zone   A biotic region with a distinctive flora and fauna.   The region is based on climatic conditions, elevation, and other natural factors.

Limestone   A metamorphic rock formed from organic remains.

Limnology   The study of the physical, chemical, meteorological, and biological aspects of fresh water.

Loam   A soil mixture of sand, clay, and silt.

Loess   Predominately silt-sized particles that have been transported and deposited by the wind.

Lot   A parcel of land under one ownership, used or capable of being used under the subdivision regulations of a zoning ordinance, including both the building site and all required yards and open spaces.

Matrix   A graphic tool that plots two groups of interdependent factors against each other (one in rows and one in columns) to help illustrate their relationships.

Meandering stream   A stream that follows many S-shaped curves.

Metamorphic rock   A previously igneous or sedimentary rock that was exposed to conditions which entirely altered its original condition.

Metropolitan statistical area (MSA)   Following the 1980 U.S. Census, the term *standard metropolitan statistical area* (SMSA) was shortened to *metropolitan statistical area* (MSA). If any area has more than 1 million population and meets certain other specified requirements, then it is termed a *consolidated metropolitan statistical area* (CMSA), consisting of major components recognized as *primary statistical areas* (PMSAs).   In addition there are special New England county metropolitan areas (NECMAs) in that region of the United States.   MSAs, PMSAs, and NECMAs are categorized by their population size, as follows:

Level A: Areas of 1 million or more
Level B: Areas of 250,000 to 1 million
Level C: Areas of 100,000 to 250,000
Level D: Areas of less than 100,000

Metropolitan statistical areas are defined in two ways: a city of at least 50,000 population or an urbanized area of at least 50,000 population with a total metropolitan area population of at least 100,000.   MSAs are defined in terms of whole counties, except in the six New England states where they are defined in terms of cities and towns.   In addition to the county containing the main city, an MSA also includes additional counties having strong economic and social ties to the central county.

Microclimate   The climate from the surface of the earth to a height at which the local effects of the earth can no longer be distinguished from the general climate.

Migratory animals   Animals that periodically pass from one region or climate to another for feeding or breeding purposes.

Mineral extraction areas   Places that contain minerals or materials of commercial quality and quantity and include, but are not limited to, sand, gravel, clay, peat, rock, and ores.

Moratoriums   The prevention of the issuance of building permits until urban service capacity levels are attained or until plans and ordinances are completed.

Morphology   The study of land surfaces.

Multifamily dwelling A building containing three or more dwelling units.

Multiple use Harmonious use of land for more than one purpose, such as grazing of livestock, wildlife production, recreation, and timber production. It is not necessarily the combination that will yield the highest economic return or greatest unit output.

Natural ecological areas Places with ecosystem units that are either superlative examples of their type or areas that perform a vital function in maintaining the ecological integrity and environmental quality of a larger region.

Natural hazard critical areas Places in which incompatible development may result in the loss of life or property or both.

Natural selection The process of survival of the fittest by which organisms that adapt to their environment survive and those that do not disappear.

Natural system The biophysical factors, such as geology, soils, and wildlife.

Natural wildlife habitat areas Places essential to the preservation of either game species or unique, rare, or endangered species.

Neighborhood planning council A locally based organization that permits citizen participation in making policy decisions and in planning issues affecting their immediate geographic area.

Niche An area that provides the necessary elements for the existence of a particular organism.

Nominal-group workshop A citizen-participation technique based on the concept that people think most creatively while working in a group.

Nonconforming use Any lawful use of activity involving a building or land occupied or in existence at the effective date of a zoning ordinance that does not conform to the principal, accessory, or conditional uses permitted in, or the density provisions of, the zoning district in which it is located.

Non-point-source pollution Caused by residuals carried into streams, lakes, and estuaries by surface water as well as to groundwater zones by infiltration and percolation. These pollutants do not result from a direct release from a pipe or channel.

Nutrients Elements or compounds essential to growth and development of living things: carbon, oxygen, nitrogen, potassium, and phosphorus.

Objective A clear and specific statement of planned results to be achieved within a stated time period.

Oceanography The study of the sea in all its physical, chemical, geological, and biological aspects.

Omnivores Animals that obtain energy from plants and other animals.

Open space A relatively undeveloped green or wooded area provided usually within an urban development to minimize the feeling of congested living.

Organic Referring to or derived from living organisms. In chemistry, it is any compound containing carbon.

Organic matter Matter derived from living matter.

Organism Any living things.

Organization development A discipline involved in intervening in social networks to foster higher levels of cohesion and effectiveness.

Osmosis The tendency of a fluid to pass through a permeable membrane, as the wall of a living cell, into a less concentrated solution so as to equalize concentrations on both sides of the membrane.

Parent material The unconsolidated and chemically weathered mineral or organic matter from which soils are developed.

Pedon A three-dimensional soil sampling unit from 1 to 10 square meters, large enough so the nature of its soil horizons can be studied and the range of its properties identified.

Perceptual and cultural critical areas Places containing one or more significant scenic, recreational, archeological, historical, or cultural resources that could be degraded or lost as a result of uncontrolled or incompatible development.

Perched water table condition A layer of soil separated above the saturated zone by an impermeable layer.

Percolation The downward movement of water in a soil.

Perennial plant A species of plant that lives longer than 2 years.

Performance standards Criteria that are established and must be met before a certain use will be permitted. These criteria, or standards, may be a set of economic, environmental, or social factors or any combination of these factors.

Permeability The rate of speed at which water can move through soil.

Pesticide Any substance used to control pests ranging from rats, weeds, and insects to algae and fungi.

pH A measure of the acidity or alkalinity of a material, solid, or liquid. pH is represented on a scale of 0 to 14, with 7 being a neutral state, 0 most acid, and 14 most alkaline.

Photogrammetry The art or science of obtaining reliable measurements through photography.

Phyllite A rock similar in composition to silt and schist.

Physical In ecological planning, the abiotic elements of the environment, including geology, physiography, soils, hydrology, and climate.

Physiography The science dealing with the study of physical features of the land, in particular slope and elevation.

Planning The use of scientific and technical knowledge to provide choices for decision making as well as a process for considering and reaching consensus on a range of options.

Planning commission An appointed citizen body that advises elected officials on such matters as the comprehensive plan, zoning ordinances, and subdivision regulations.

Planning, programming, and budget system (PPBS) A complex annual budget system that involves the linkage of programs to the budgeting process.

Planning staff The professional staff for the planning commission.

Plant community An association of plants characterized by certain species occupying similar habitats.

Plat A map or plan, especially of a piece of land divided into building lots.

Plateau A large, flat area of land that is higher in elevation than some adjacent land.

Policy A definite course or method of action selected by a governmental agency, institution, group, or individual from among options and in light of given conditions to guide and usually determine present and future decisions.

Preferential tax policies Favorable taxation of land in exchange for an agreement to use that land for a certain use, such as agriculture, or for open spaces.

Process The action of moving forward progressively from one point to another on the way to completion.

Primary consumers Herbivores or animals that obtain energy from plants.

Pristine Pure and untouched.

Producers Organisms that can use solar energy to convert inorganic substances into organic substances.

Profile A graphic tool that shows a portion of the surface of the earth and the features on this portion.

Project planning Designing a solution to a specific problem such as a dam, highway, harbor, or a single building or group of buildings.

Public hearing An open forum where statements become part of official records. Public hearings are often required by law.

Public opinion poll (preference survey) A means of gathering information, attitudes, and opinions from a large number of people.

Purchase of development rights (PDR) The property owner's development interests are relinquished to the purchaser of the rights, who will control the use of the land.

Putative species The species expected to occur in an area based on habitat requirements.

Rain shadow An area that has decreased precipitation because it is to the leeward side of mountains.

Rangeland Land in grass or other long-term forage growth of native species used primarily for grazing. It may contain shade trees or scattered timber trees with less than 10 percent canopy. It includes grassland, land in perennial forbs, sagebrush land, and brushland other than sage. The term *nonforest range* is used to differentiate the nonforest range from the forest range when both are being discussed.

Recharge Process by which water is added to the zone of saturation, as recharge of an aquifer.

Recharge areas See *Groundwater recharge areas.*

Recreation Any experience voluntarily engaged in largely during leisure (discretionary time) from which the individual derives satisfaction.

Region (1) An uninterrupted area possessing some kind of homogenity in its core but lacking clearly defined limits. (2) A governmental jurisdiction or designation. (3) A frame for multidisciplinary research: a demand for the integration of data from many realms of ecological reality and, therefore, an opportunity for specialists to work together on theoretical conceptions of human ecology as a synthesis.

Regolith The predominately loose surficial material overlaying bedrock. It is roughly equivalent to what engineers term *soil* and may contain or be capped by a true soil pedon, as used by soil scientists.

Remote sensing The detection, identification, and analysis of objects of features through the use of imaging devices located at positions remote from the objects of investigation.

Resident Animals that remain in one region or climate through the year.

Residium Unconsolidated and partly weathered mineral materials accumulated by disintegration of consolidated rock in place.

Resource A substance or object required by an organism for normal maintenance, growth, and reproduction. If a resource is scarce relative to demand, then it is referred to as a *limited* resource. *Nonrenewable* resources (such as space) occur in fixed amounts and can be fully utilized; *renewable* resources (such as food) are produced at a fixed rate with which the rate of exploitation attains an equilibrium.

Resource production critical areas Places that provide essential products supporting either the local economy or economies of a larger scale.

Riparian Relating to a habitat on the banks of streams, rivers, and lakes.

River basin The land area drained by a river and its tributaries.

Rubble A mass of broken stones and rocks, often at the base of a cliff.

Runoff Water from rain, snowmelt, or irrigation that flows over the ground surface and returns to streams.

Sand Soil particles between 0.05 and 2.0 millimeters in diameter.

Scenic areas Places that contain natural features of sufficient aesthetic quality to warrant their preservation.

Scientific areas Places of geological interest or places that present ecological processes warranting study.

Secondary consumer Carnivore or animals that obtain energy from other animals.

Second-order stream See *Stream orders*.

Septic tank An enclosure in which the organic solid matter of continuously flowing wastewater is deposited and retained until it has been disintegrated by anaerobic bacteria.

Service districts The division of a jurisdiction into areas based on the level of urban and rural services with different rates of taxation.

Shale A sedimentary rock formed from tightly packed clays and silts.

Silt Fine soil particles between 0.05 and 0.002 millimeter in diameter that can be picked up by air or water and deposited as sediment.

Single-family dwelling A detached building containing one dwelling unit.

Slope The incline of the land surface, usually expressed in percentage of slope. Often slopes are expressed as follows:

0–3 percent	nearly level
3–7 percent	gently sloping
7–12 percent	moderately sloping
12–25 percent	strongly sloping
25–40 percent	steeply sloping
40–70 percent	very steeply sloping
70–100 percent and above	extremely steeply sloping

Slope wind Winds flowing up or down slopes along a temperature gradient.

Social Relating to human society and the interactions of the community.

Sociocultural A combination of the social and the cultural characteristics of an area.

Soil A natural, three-dimensional body on the surface of the earth that supports plants and has properties resulting from the integrated effect of climate and living matter acting upon parent material as conditioned by relief over periods of time.

Soil association Soils of different series found in the same area.

Soil catena A group of related soils that have developed from the same parent material but differ in drainage class due to different locations on a slope.

Soil depth The depth of soil material that plant roots can penetrate readily to obtain water and nutrients. It is the depth to a layer that, in physical or chemical properties, differs from the overlying material to such an extent as to prevent or seriously retard the growth of roots or penetration of water. The depth classes are (1) very deep, more than 60 inches; (2) deep, 40 to 60 inches; (3) moderately deep, 20 to 40 inches; (4) shallow, 10 to 20 inches; and (5) very shallow, 1 to 10 inches.

Soil profile A vertical section of the soil through all its horizons and extending into the parent material.

Soil series Soils from the same parent material having similar horizon characteristics.

Soil texture The relative proportions of sand, silt, and clay particles in a mass of soil. The basic textural classes, in order of increasing proportion of fine particles, are shown in the chart at the top of page 327.

Soil types Soils within a series having the same texture.

Solar radiation The energy from the sun that reaches the earth.

Solum The upper and most weathered part of the soil profile; and A and B horizons.

Species A group of closely related organisms potentially able to reproduce viable offspring.

Species diversity The number of different species occurring in a location or under the same conditions.

Sprawl Unplanned development of open land.

Standard A statement that describes a condition when a

General Terms	Basic Soil Textural Class Names
Sandy soils	
Coarse-textured soils	Sand
Moderately coarse- textured soils	Sandy loam Fine sandy loam
Loamy soils	
Medium-textured soils	Very fine sandy loam Loam Silt loam Silt
Moderately fine- textured soils	Clay loam Sandy clay loam Silty clay loam
Clayey soil	
Fine-textured soils	Sandy clay Silty clay Clay

job is done properly. Standards show how well something should be done rather than what should be done.

Strategy   The approach and/or methods through which problems are solved or minimized and objectives are achieved.

Stream   A general term for a body of flowing water. In hydrology, the term is generally applied to the water flowing in a natural channel as distinct from a canal. More generally, as in the term *stream gauging,* it is applied to the water flowing in any natural or artificial channel.

Stream, ephemeral   A stream that flows only in response to precipitation.

Stream, intermittent   A stream that flows only part of the time or through only part of its reach.

Stream orders   First-order streams are primary drainage-ways. Second-order streams are the confluence of two first-order streams. Third-order streams are the confluence of two second-order streams, and so on.

Stream, perennial   A stream that flows continuously.

Street   The entire width between property boundary lines of every way that provides for public use for the purpose of vehicular and pedestrian traffic and the placement of utilities.

Strip-cropping   Growing crops in a systematic arrangement of strips or bands that serve as barriers to wind and water erosion.

Structures, heavy   A building of generally great weight and size such as a mill or factory.

Structures, light   A building of generally slight weight and size such as a residence.

Subdivision   The division of a lot, tract, or parcel of land into two or more lots, plats, sites, or other divisions of land for the purpose, whether immediate or future, of sale or building development.

Subdivision regulation   The legal requirements pertaining to the subdivision of land.

Subsoil   The B soil horizon; the layer of soil below the layer in which grass roots normally grow.

Succession   The orderly progressive replacement of one community by another until a relatively stable community occupies an area.

Suitability analysis   The process of determining the fitness of a given tract of land for a defined use.   *Suitability* is often used interchangeably with *capability.*

Surface water   Water that remains on the top of land, such as lakes, rivers, streams, and seas.

Swale   An elongated depression in the land.

Synthesis   The combining of all the parts to form an interrelating whole.

Task force   An agency-sponsored citizen committee with a specific task and charge usually related to a single problem or subject.

Technical advisory committee (TAC)   A group of individuals with specific expertise, usually from various disciplines, brought together by an agency for giving advice and consultation.

Temperature gradient   The difference in temperature along some horizontal distance or up a vertical parcel of air.

Terracing   Dikes built along the contour of agricultural land to hold runoff and sediment, thus reducing erosion.

Third-order streams   See *Stream orders.*

Topoclimate   The term used when the topographic variations of the land on microclimate are considered.

Topography   The physical features of a surface area, including relative elevations and the position of natural and artificial features.

Town meeting   The traditional New England meeting of the people of a town.

Transfer of development rights (TDR)   The development rights are purchased to be used in another location, thereby separating the development rights from the land itself.

Transpiration   The loss of water to the atmosphere from plants.

Tree   A woody, perennial plant with a single main stem.

Trophic levels   The different levels through which energy flows from producers to consumers.

Understory Herbs and shrubs that grow beneath a forest canopy.

Urban growth boundary Line to which urban areas may grow based on population projections and physical conditions of the area.

USGS map U.S. Department of Interior Geological Survey map.

Valley wind Winds flowing up or down valleys along temperature gradients.

Variance A special situation that creates a need to deviate from the established zoning ordinances and requires review by a board of adjustment or similar review agency.

Vegetation Plant life: trees, shrubs, herbs, and grasses.

Ventilation The circulation of fresh air across the land, largely dependent on landforms and wind direction.

Voluntary covenants Agreements that limit what can be done with property.

Water A transparent, odorless, tasteless liquid, a compound of hydrogen and oxygen (H_2O) freezing at 32°F (0°C) and boiling at 212°F (100°C), which is more or less an impure state, that constitutes rain, oceans, lakes, rivers, and other such bodies. It contains 11.188 percent hydrogen and 88.812 percent oxygen by weight.

Water balance The ratio of water lost from a system and brought into a system.

Water quality areas Aquifer recharge areas, headwaters, stream corridors, and wetlands that function as a natural filter for surface waters.

Watershed A drainage area separated from other drainage areas by a dividing ridge.

Water table The upper surface of groundwater or that level below which the soil is saturated with water.

Wilderness recreation areas Isolated tracts of land that are large enough to support recreational activities like camping, hiking, and canoeing.

Wildlife Animals that are neither human nor domesticated.

Windchill The relationship between body heat loss and the cooling power of different wind and temperature combinations.

Zero-base budgeting (ZBB) An annual budget system, developed by the Texas Instruments Company, that involves developing budgets for programs from scratch each year.

Zoning Land-use controls such as limiting the use to which land in each area may be put, minimum lot size, and building types.

Zoning ordinance The legal document establishing the division of a municipality or other governmental unit into districts and the regulation within those districts.

ACRONYMS

ASCS	Agricultural Stabilization and Conservation Service
BLM	Bureau of Land Management
BPA	Bonneville Power Administration
CEQ	Council on Environmental Quality
CMSA	Consolidated metropolitan statistical area
DLCD	Department of Land Conservation and Development (Oregon)
DOE	Department of Ecology (Washington)
EIS	Environmental impact statement
EPA	Environmental Protection Agency
FAA	Federal Aviation Administration
FPPA	Farmland Protection Policy Act
FTE	Full-time equivalent employment
HUD	Department of Housing and Urban Development
LCDC	Land Conservation and Development Commission (Oregon)
LESA	Agricultural Land Evaluation and Site Assessment System

LE	Land evaluation
MSA	Metropolitan statistical area
NECMA	New England County Metropolitan Area
NEPA	National Environmental Policy Act
NOAA	National Oceanic and Atmospheric Administration
NPS	National Park Service
PMSA	Primary metropolitan statistical area
PNB	Pacific Northwest Bell
SA	Site assessment
SCS	Soil Conservation Service
SEPA	State Environmental Policy Act
SMSA	Standard metropolitan statistical area
USDA	U.S. Department of Agriculture
USFS	U.S. Forest Service
USGS	U.S. Geological Survey

REFERENCES

1. INTRODUCTION

Alinsky, Saul D. 1946. *Reveille for Radicals*. The University of Chicago Press, Chicago. 235 pp.

Anderson, James R., Ernest E. Hardy, John T. Roach, and Richard E. Witmer. 1976. *A Land Use and Land Cover Classification System for Use with Remote Sensor Data* (U.S. Geological Survey Professional Paper 964). 28 pp.

Berger, Jonathan, and John W. Sinton. 1985. *Water, Earth, and Fire*. Johns Hopkins University Press, Baltimore. 228 pp.

Berry, Wendell. 1972. *A Continuous Harmony, Essays Cultural and Agricultural*. Harcourt Brace Jovanovich, New York. 182 pp.

Boyden, Stephen. 1979. *An Integrative Ecological Approach to the Study of Human Settlements* (MAB Technical Notes 12). UNESCO, Paris. 87 pp.

Dickert, Thomas, and Robert B. Olshansky. 1986. "Evaluating Erosion Susceptibility for Land-Use Planning in Coastal Watersheds." *Coastal Zone Management* **13**(3/4):309–333.

Doornkamp, John C. 1982. "The Physical Basis for Planning in the Third World, IV: Regional Planning." *Third World Planning Review* **4**(2):111–118.

Duchhart, Ingrid. 1989. *Manual on Environment and Urban Development*. Ministry of Local Government and Physical Planning, Nairobi, Kenya. 86 pp.

Easter, William K., John A. Dixon, and Maynard M. Hufschmidt (eds.). 1986. *Watershed Resource Management*. Westview Press, Boulder, CO. 236 pp.

Eber, Ronald. 1984. "Oregon's Agricultural Land Protection Program" in *Protecting Farmlands*, Frederick R. Steiner and John E. Theilacker (eds.). AVI Publishing Company, Westport, CT, pp. 161–171.

Fabos, Julius Gy. 1979. *Planning the Total Landscape*. Westview Press, Boulder, CO. 181 pp.

Fox, Jeff. 1987. "Two Roles for Natural Scientists in the Management of Tropical Watersheds: Examples from Nepal and Indonesia." *Environmental Professional* **9**:59–66.

Friedmann, John. 1973. *Retracking America*. Anchor Press/Doubleday, Garden City, NY. 289 pp.

Gans, Herbert J. 1968. *People and Plans*. Basic Books, New York. 395 pp.

Glikson, Artur. 1971. *The Ecological Basis of Planning*. Matinus Nijhoff, The Hague, Netherlands. 115 pp.

Hall, Peter. 1975. *Urban and Regional Planning*. Halsted Press/John Wiley & Sons, New York. 312 pp.

Hills, G. A. 1961. *The Ecological Basis for Land-Use Planning* (Research Report No. 46). Ontario Department of Lands and Forests, Toronto. 204 pp.

Johnson, A. H. 1981. "Guest Editorial: Human Ecological Planning—Methods and Studies." *Landscape Planning* **8**:107–108.

———, Jonathan Berger, and Ian L. McHarg. 1979. "A Case Study in Ecological Planning: The Woodlands, Texas" in *Planning the Uses and Management of Land*, Marvin T. Beatty, Gary W. Petersen, and Lester D. Swindale (eds.). American Society of Agronomy, Crop Science Society of America, and Soil Science Society of America, Madison, WI, pp. 935–955.

Laslett, Peter (ed.). 1988. *John Locke: Two Treatises of Government* (student edition). Cambridge University Press, Cambridge. 464 pp.

Leopold, Aldo. 1933. "The Conservation Ethic." *The Journal of Forestry* **31**(6):634–643.

———. 1949. *A Sand County Almanac and Sketches Here and There*. Oxford, New York. 295 pp.

331

Lewis, Philip H. 1969. "Ecology: The Inland Water Tree." *American Institute of Architects Journal* **51**(8):59–63.

Lovejoy, Derek (ed.). 1973. *Land Use and Landscape Planning*. Barnes & Noble, New York. 308 pp.

Lowrance, Richard, Paul F. Hendrix, and Eugene P. Odum. 1986. "A Hierarchial Approach to Sustainable Agriculture." *American Journal of Alternative Agriculture* **1**(4):169–173.

MacDougall, E. Bruce. 1975. "The Accuracy of Map Overlays." *Landscape Planning* **2**:23–30.

MacKaye, Benton. 1940. "Regional Planning and Ecology." *Ecological Monographs* **10**(3):349–353.

Marsh, William M. 1983. *Landscape Planning*. Addison-Wesley, Reading, MA. 356 pp.

McDowell, Bruce D. 1986. "Approaches to Planning" in *The Practice of State and Regional Planning,* Frank S. So, Irving Hand, and Bruce D. McDowell (eds.). American Planning Association, Chicago, pp. 3–22.

McHarg, Ian L. 1969. *Design with Nature*. Doubleday/The Natural History Press, Garden City, NY. 197 pp.

———. 1981. "Human Ecological Planning at Pennsylvania." *Landscape Planning* **8**:109–120.

Meinig, D. W. 1979. "Introduction" in *The Interpretation of Ordinary Landscapes,* D. W. Meinig (ed.). Oxford University Press, New York, pp. 1–7.

Moore, Terry. 1988. "Planning without Preliminaries." *Journal of the American Planning Association* **54**(4):525–528.

National Agricultural Lands Study. 1981. *Final Report*. U.S. Department of Agriculture and Council on Environmental Quality. 94 pp.

Neckar, Lance M. 1989. "Developing Landscape Architecture for the Twentieth Century: The Career of Warren H. Manning." *Landscape Journal* **8**(2):78–91.

Novikoff, A. B. 1945. "The Concept of Integrative Levels and Biology." *Science* **101**:209–215.

Pease, James R. 1984. "Oregon's Land Conservation and Development Program" in *Planning for the Conservation and Development of Land Resources,*

Frederick R. Steiner and Hubert N. van Lier (eds.). Elsevier Scientific Publishing, Amsterdam, pp. 253–271.

Prigogine, Ilya and Isabelle Stengers. 1984. *Order Out of Chaos*. Bantam Books, Toronto, ON. 349 pp.

Quinby, Peter A. 1988. "The Contribution of Ecological Sciences to the Development of Landscape Ecology: A Brief History." *Landscape Research* **13**(3):9–11.

Ricklefs, Robert E. 1973. *Ecology*. Chiron Press, Newton, MA. 861 pp.

Roberts, John C. 1979. "Principles of Land Use Planning" in *Planning the Uses and Management of Land,* Marvin T. Beatty, Gary W. Petersen, and Lester D. Swindale (eds.). American Society of Agronomy, Crop Science Society of America, and Soil Science Society of America, Madison, WI, pp. 47–63.

Spirn, Anne Whiston. 1984. *The Granite Garden*. Basic Books, New York. 334 pp.

Steiner, Frederick. 1983. "Resource Suitability: Methods for Analyses." *Environmental Management* **7**(5):401–420.

Steinitz, Carl, Paul Parker, and Lawrie Jordan. 1976. "Hand-Drawn Overlays, Their History and Prospective Uses." *Landscape Architecture* **66**:444–455.

Stokes, Samuel N., A. Elizabeth Watson, Genevieve P. Keller, and J. Timothy Keller. 1989. *Saving America's Countryside*. Johns Hopkins University Press, Baltimore. 306 pp.

Tarlet, Jean. 1985. *La Planification Écologique: Méthodes et Techniques*. Economica, Paris. 142 pp.

Wallace, McHarg, Roberts, and Todd. 1971–1974. *Woodlands New Community* (4 volumes). Philadelphia. Various pages.

Wilkinson, Charles F., and H. Michael Anderson. 1985. "Land and Resource Planning in National Forests." *Oregon Law Review* **64**(1 & 2):1–373.

Young, Gerald L. 1974. "Human Ecology as an Interdisciplinary Concept: A Critical Inquiry." *Advances in Ecological Research* **8**:1–105.

———. 1976. "Environmental Law: Perspectives from Human Ecology." *Environmental Law* **6**(2):289–307.

———. 1978. *Human Ecology as an Interdisciplinary Domain: An Epitesmological Bibliography.* Vance Bibliographies, Monticello, IL. 62 pp.

——— (ed.). 1983. *Origins of Human Ecology.* Hutchinson Ross Publishing, Stroudsburg, PA. 415 pp.

———. 1989. "A Conceptual Framework for an Interdisciplinary Human Ecology." *Acta Oecologiae Hominis* **1**:1–136.

———, Frederick Steiner, Kenneth Brooks, and Kenneth Struckmeyer. 1983. "Determining the Regional Context for Landscape Planning." *Landscape Planning* **10**(4):269–296.

Zube, Ervin H. 1980. *Environmental Evaluation.* Brooks/Cole, Monterey, CA. 148 pp.

2. ESTABLISHING PLANNING GOALS

Alinsky, Saul D. 1946. *Reveille for Radicals.* University of Chicago Press, Chicago. 235 pp.

Berger, Jonathan, and John W. Sinton. 1985. *Water, Earth, and Fire.* Johns Hopkins University Press, Baltimore. 228 pp.

Bolan, Richard S. 1979. "Social Planning and Policy Development" in *The Practice of Local Government Planning,* Frank S. So, Israel Stollman, Frank Beal, and David S. Arnold (eds.). International City Management Association, Washington, DC, pp. 521–551.

Bosselman, Fred, and David Callies. 1971. *The Quiet Revolution in Land Use Control.* U.S. Government Printing Office, Washington, DC. 327 pp.

———, David Callies, and John Banta. 1973. *The Taking Issue.* U.S. Government Printing Office, Washington, DC. 329 pp.

Callies, David L. 1980. "The Quiet Revolution Revisited." *Journal of the American Planning Association* **46**(2):135–144.

Daniels, Thomas L., and Arthur C. Nelson. 1986. "Is Oregon's Farmland Preservation Program Working?" *Journal of the American Planning Association* **52**(1):22–32.

DeGrove, John M. 1984. *Land, Growth and Politics.* Planners Press, Chicago. 454 pp.

Delbecq, André L., Andrew H. Van de Ven, and David H. Gustafson. 1975. *Group Techniques for Program Planning, A Guide to Nominal Group and Delphi Processes.* Scott, Foresman, Glenview, IL. 192 pp.

Dillman, Don A. 1977. "Preference Surveys and Policy Decision: Our New Tools Need Not Be Used in the Same Old Ways." *Journal of the Community Development Society* **8**(1):30–43.

———. 1978. *Mail and Telephone Surveys: The Total Design Method.* Wiley-Interscience, New York. 325 pp.

Gil, Efraim, and Enid Lucchesi. 1979. "Citizen Participation in Planning" in *The Practice of Local Government Planning,* Frank S. So, Israel Stollman, Frank Beal, and David S. Arnold (eds.). International City Management Association, Washington, DC, pp. 552–575.

Institute for Participatory Planning. 1978. *Citizen Participation Handbook.* Laramie, WY. Various pages. (Sixth edition, 1989, Institute for Participatory Management and Planning, Monterey, CA.)

Land Conservation and Development Commission (LCDC). 1980. *Statewide Planning Goals and Guidelines.* Salem, OR. 24 pp.

Littrell, David. 1976. *The Theory and Practice of Community Development.* University of Missouri, Extension Division, Columbia. 39 pp.

MacNair, Ray H. 1981. "Citizen Participation as a Balanced Exchange: An Analysis and Strategy." *Journal of the Community Development Society* **12**(1):1–19.

Pease, James R. 1984. "Oregon's Land Conservation and Development Program" in *Planning for the Conservation and Development of Land Resources,* Frederick R. Steiner and Hubert N. van Lier (eds.). Elsevier Scientific Publishing, Amsterdam, pp. 253–271.

Pinelands Commission. 1980. *New Jersey Pinelands Comprehensive Management Plan.* State of New Jersey, New Lisbon, NJ. 446 pp.

Reps, John W. 1970. *Town Planning in Frontier America.* (Paperback ed.; orig. copyright 1969.) Princeton University Press, Princeton, NJ. 473 pp.

U.S. Department of Transportation. 1976. *Effective Citizen Participation in Transportation Planning. Volume II, A Catalog of Techniques.* Federal Highway Administration, Socio-Economic Studies Division, Washington, DC. 298 pp.

3. INVENTORY AND ANALYSIS OF THE BIOPHYSICAL ENVIRONMENT

Anderson, James R., Ernest E. Hardy, John T. Roach, and Richard E. Witmer. 1976. *A Land Use and Land Cover Classification System for Use with Remote Sensor Data* (U.S. Geological Survey Professional Paper 964). 28 pp.

Beach, Richard, Don Benson, Dave Brunton, Karen L. Johnson, Julie Knowles, Joanne Michalovic, Harry George Newman, Betsy J. Tripp, and Cheryl Wunschel. 1978. *Asotin County Ecological Inventory and Land Use Suitability Analysis.* Washington State University, Cooperative Extension Service, Pullman. 356 pp.

Berger, Jon, Arthur Johnson, Dan Rose, and Peter Skaller. 1977. "Regional Planning Notebook" (course guidelines). University of Pennsylvania, Department of Landscape Architecture and Regional Planning, Philadelphia. 132 pp.

——— and John W. Sinton. 1985. *Water, Earth, and Fire.* Johns Hopkins University Press, Baltimore. 228 pp.

Brunton, Dave, Theda Scheibner, Jill Stanton, Tom Blanchard, and Julie Knowles. 1977. "Albion Ecological Inventory" (class project). Washington State University, Department of Horticulture and Landscape Architecture and Program in Environmental Science and Regional Planning, Pullman. No page numbers.

Churchill, Sherry, Terri Jacobson, Misa Kiyota, Beth Kringen, Richard Lane, Rob MacDougall, Laurel Macha, and Elaine Montague. 1986. "Rose Creek Watershed" (class project). Washington State University, Department of Horticulture and Landscape Architecture and Program in Environmental Science and Regional Planning, Pullman. 241 pp.

Cowardin, Lewis M., Virginia Carter, Francis C. Golet, and Edward T. LaRoe. 1979. *Classification of Wetlands and Deepwater Habitats in the United States.* U.S. Department of Interior, Fish and Wildlife Service. 103 pp.

Daubenmire, Rexford. 1970. *Steppe Vegetation of Washington.* Washington State University, Washington Agricultural Experiment Station, Technical Bulletin 62, Pullman. 131 pp.

Donaldson, Norman C. 1980. *Soil Survey of Whitman County, Washington.* U.S. Department of Agriculture. 185 pp.

Geiger, Rudolf. 1965. *The Climate Near the Ground.* Harvard University Press, Cambridge, MA. 611 pp.

Higashi, Irvin, Nancy Hopkins, Rick Nishi, Jani Raymond, and Susan Vogt. 1978. "Parvin Ecological Study" (class project). Washington State University, Department of Horticulture and Landscape Architecture and Program in Environmental Science and Regional Planning, Pullman. No page numbers.

Holdridge, L. R. 1967. *Life Zone Ecology.* Tropical Science Center, San Jose, Costa Rica. 206 pp.

Hunt, Charles. 1967. *Physiography of the United States.* W. H. Freeman, San Francisco. 725 pp.

Jacobs, Allan B. 1985. *Looking at Cities.* Harvard University Press, Cambridge, MA. 153 pp.

Johnson, L. C., B. L. Carlile, D. L. Johnstone, and H. H. Cheng. 1973. *Surface Water Quality in the Palouse Dryland Grain Region.* Washington State University, Washington Agriculture Experiment Station, Pullman. 38 pp.

Kaiser, Verle G. 1967. "Soil Erosion and Wheat Yields in Whitman County, Washington." *Northwest Science* **41**(2):86–91.

Ledwitz, Martin W. 1977. "Washington State Climatology for Grape Production." Washington State University, Department of Horticulture and Landscape Architecture, Pullman. No page numbers.

Lovelock, J. E. 1979. *Gaia.* Oxford University Press, Oxford. 157 pp.

Morisawa, Marie. 1968. *Streams.* McGraw-Hill, New York. 175 pp.

Nassar, E. G., and Kenneth L. Walters. 1975. *Water in the Palouse River Basin, Washington* (Water Supply

Bulletin No. 39). Washington State Department of Ecology, Olympia. 246 pp.

Odum, Eugene P. 1971. *Fundamentals of Ecology*. W. B. Saunders, Philadelphia. 574 pp.

Pacific Rim Planners. 1980. *Makah Coastal Zone Management Program*. Seattle. 137 pp.

Pielke, R. A., and R. Avissar. 1990. "Influence of Landscape Structure on Local and Regional Climate." *Landscape Ecology* (forthcoming).

Pinelands Commission. 1980. *New Jersey Pinelands Comprehensive Management Plan*. State of New Jersey, New Lisbon. 446 pp.

Quinby, Peter A. 1988. "The Contribution of Ecological Science to the Development of Landscape Ecology: A Brief History." *Landscape Research* **13**(3):9–11.

Ricklefs, Robert. 1973. *Ecology*. Chiron Press, Newton, MA. 861 pp.

Rogers, Golden, and Halpern, Inc. 1986. *Reforestation in the Pacific Islands*. U.S. Peace Corps, Washington, DC. Each chapter paged.

Satterlund, Donald R., and Joseph E. Means. 1979. *Solar Radiation in the Pacific Northwest* (Bulletin 874). Washington State University, College of Agriculture Research Center, Pullman. 10 pp.

Strahler, A. N. 1957. "Quantitative Analysis of Watershed Geomorphology." *Transactions, American Geophysical Union* **38**:913–920.

University of Pennsylvania. 1985. "Landscape Architecture and Regional Planning 501 Course Primer" (course guidelines). Department of Landscape Architecture and Regional Planning, Philadelphia. Unpaged.

U.S. Department of Agriculture. 1978. *Palouse Co-Operative River Basin Study*. Soil Conservation Service; Forest Service; and Economics, Statistics and Cooperatives Services, Spokane, WA. 182 pp.

Vroom, M. J., J. B. Struik, and M. W. M. van der Toorn. 1980. *Landscape Planning in Coastal Areas* (Annex-B). Agricultural University, Department of Landscape Architecture, Wageningen, Netherlands. 90 pp.

Waananen, A. O., J. T. Limerinos, W. J. Kockelman, W. E. Spangle, and M. L. Blair. 1977. *Flood-Prone Areas and Land-Use Planning—Selected from the San Francisco Bay Region* (U.S. Geological Survey Professional Paper 942). 75 pp.

Walters, Kenneth, and P. A. Glancy. 1969. *Reconnaissance of Geology and Ground-Water Occurance in Whitman County, Washington* (Water Supply Bulletin, No. 26). Washington State Department of Water Resources, now the Department of Ecology. Prepared in cooperation with the U.S. Geological Survey, Water Resources Division, Olympia. 169 pp.

4. HUMAN COMMUNITY INVENTORY AND ANALYSIS

Berger, Jon, Arthur Johnson, Dan Rose, and Peter Skaller. 1977. "Regional Planning Notebook" (unpublished course guidelines). University of Pennsylvania, Department of Landscape Architecture and Regional Planning, Philadelphia. 132 pp.

——— and John W. Sinton. 1985. *Water, Earth, and Fire*. Johns Hopkins University Press, Baltimore, MD. 228 pp.

Bonneville Power Administration (BPA). 1976. *Population, Employment and Housing Units Projected to 1995, Washington*. Portland, OR.

Chapin, F. Stuart, and Edward J. Kaiser. 1979. *Urban Land Use Planning*. University of Illinois Press, Urbana. 656 pp.

Dillman, Don A. 1978. *Mail and Telephone Surveys, The Total Design Method*. John Wiley & Sons, New York. 325 pp.

Forman, Richard T. T. and Michel Godron. 1986. *Landscape Ecology*. John Wiley & Sons, New York. 619 pp.

Gibson, Lay James. 1975. "Local Impact Analysis: An Arizona Case Study." *Arizona Research* **24**(1):1–10.

Hightower, Henry C. 1968. "Population Studies" in *Principles and Practice of Urban Planning,* William I. Goodman and Eric C. Freund (eds.). International City Manager's Association, Washington, DC, pp. 51–75.

Hirschman, Joan. 1988. ''Bird Habitat Design for People: A Landscape Ecological Approach'' (master's thesis). University of Colorado, Denver, Program in Landscape Architecture and Urban Design. 147 pp.

Jackson, Joanne Barnes and Frederick R. Steiner. 1985. ''Human Ecology for Land-Use Planning.'' *Urban Ecology* **9**:177–194.

Jacobs, Allan B. 1985. *Looking at Cities.* Harvard University Press, Cambridge, MA. 153 pp.

Kartez, Jack D. 1981. ''Community Economic Base Analysis'' (mimeograph). Washington State University, Program in Environmental Science and Regional Planning, Pullman. 7 pp.

Land Conservation and Development Commission (LCDC). 1980. *Statewide Planning Goals and Guidelines.* Salem, OR. 24 pp.

Litton, R. Burton, Jr. 1968. *Forest Landscape Description and Inventories—A Basis for Land Planning and Design.* U.S. Forest Service, Pacific Southwest Forest and Range Experiment Station, Berkeley, CA.

Long, John. 1981. *Population Deconcentration in the United States.* U.S. Government Printing Office, Washington, DC.

Lynch, Kevin. 1960. *The Image of the City.* MIT Press, Cambridge, MA. 194 pp.

McKenzie, Ricki. No date. *The Pinelands Scenic Study* (Summary Report). U.S. Department of Interior, Philadelphia, PA. 27 pp.

Morrell, Terri A. 1989. ''Small Social Spaces in the Netherlands'' (paper). School of Architecture and Planning, University of Colorado, Denver. 36 pp.

Pacific Northwest Bell (PNB). 1976. *Population and Household Trends in Washington, Oregon, and Northern Idaho 1975–1990.* Seattle, WA.

Pacific Rim Planners. 1980. *Makah Coastal Zone Management Program.* Seattle, WA. 137 pp.

Pinelands Commission. 1980. *New Jersey Pinelands Comprehensive Management Plan.* State of New Jersey, New Lisbon. 446 pp.

Ricklefs, Robert E. 1973. *Ecology.* Chiron Press, Newton, MA. 861 pp.

Rose, Dan, Frederick Steiner, and Joanne Jackson. 1978–1979. ''An Applied Human Ecological Approach to Regional Planning.'' *Landscape Planning* **5**(4):241–261.

Steinitz, Carl. 1988. ''When Visual Quality and Ecological Integrity Are Mutually Supportive or in Conflict (and What to Do about It): A Case Study Based on (Still-in-Progress) Research in Acadia National Park.'' Paper presented at the Third Annual Landscape Ecology Symposium, Albuquerque, NM.

Sudman, Seymour, and Norman M. Bradburn. 1983. *Asking Questions, A Practical Guide to Questionnaire Design.* Jossey-Bass, San Francisco. 397 pp.

Survey Research Center. 1976. *Interviewer's Manual* (rev. ed.). University of Michigan, Institute for Social Research, Ann Arbor. 143 pp.

U.S. Bureau of the Census. 1950, 1960, 1970, 1980a. *U.S. Census of Population.* U.S. Department of Commerce.

————. 1980b. *Data User News* (June).

U.S. Congress. 1969. *National Environmental Policy Act of 1968* (Public Law 91–190).

U.S. Forest Service. 1973. *National Forest Landscape Management* (Volume 1, Agricultural Handbook Number 434). U.S. Government Printing Office, Washington, DC. 77 pp.

————. 1974. *National Forest Landscape Management* (Volume 2, Agricultural Handbook Number 462). U.S. Government Printing Office, Washington, DC. 47 pp.

Wardwell, John M., and C. Jack Gilchrist. 1980. ''The Distribution of Population and Energy in Nonmetropolitan Areas: Confluence and Divergence.'' *Social Science Quarterly* **61**(3 and 4):567–580.

Washington Office of Program Planning and Fiscal Management (OPP & FM). 1976. *Pocket Data Book 1976.* Olympia.

————. 1977. *Preliminary Population Forecasts.* Olympia.

Washington State University. No date. *WSU Comprehensive Plan.* Pullman.

Whitman County Regional Planning Council. 1978. *Whitman County Comprehensive Plan.* Colfax, WA. 64 pp.

———. No date a. *Population Part I: Trends and Characteristics.* Colfax, WA. 18 pp.

———. No date b. *Population Part II: Projections.* Colfax, WA. 18 pp.

5. SUITABILITY ANALYSIS

Barnhart, Clarence L. (ed.). 1953. *The American College Dictionary.* Harper & Brothers, New York. 1,432 pp.

Bartelli, L. J., A. A. Klingebiel, J. V. Baird, and M. R. Heddleston, (eds.), 1966. *Soil Surveys and Land-Use Planning.* Soil Science Society of America, Madison, WI. 179 pp.

Beach, Richard, Don Benson, Dave Brunton, Karen L. Johnson, Julie Knowles, Joanne Michalovic, Harry George Newman, Betsy J. Tripp, and Cheryl Wunschel. 1978. *Asotin County Ecological Inventory and Land-Use Suitability Analysis.* Washington State University, Cooperative Extension Service, Pullman. 356 pp.

Beek, K. J. 1978. *Land Evaluation for Agricultural Development* (Publication 23). International Institute for Land Reclamation and Improvement, Wageningen, Netherlands. 333 pp.

Beeman, Larry E. 1978. "Computer-Assisted Resource Management" in *Integrated Inventories of Renewable Natural Resources: Proceedings of the Workshop,* H. G. Lund, V. J. LaBau, P. F. Ffolliot, and D. W. Robinson (eds.). U.S. Forest Service, Tucson, AZ, pp. 375–381.

Belknap, Raymond K. and John G. Furtado. 1967. *Three Approaches to Environmental Resource Analysis.* The Conservation Foundation, Washington, DC. 102 pp.

——— and ———. 1968. "Hills, Lewis, McHarg Methods Compared." *Landscape Architecture* 58(2):145–147.

Berger, Jon, Arthur Johnson, Dan Rose, and Peter Skaller. 1977. "Regional Planning Notebook" (course guidelines). University of Pennsylvania, Department of Landscape Architecture and Regional Planning, Philadelphia. 132 pp.

Brady, Nyle C. 1974. *The Nature and Properties of Soils.* MacMillan, New York. 639 pp.

Brinkman, R., and A. J. Smyth (eds.). 1973. *Land Evaluation for Rural Purposes* (Publication 17). International Institute for Land Reclamation and Improvement, Wageningen, Netherlands. 116 pp.

Cannon, T. M. and B. R. Hunt. 1981. "Image Processing by Computer." *Scientific American* 245(4):214–225.

Catton, William. 1983. "Social and Behavioral Aspects of the Carrying Capacity of Natural Environments" in *Behavior and Natural Environment* (Volume VI of Human Behavior and Environment), Irwin Altman and Joachim F. Wohwill (eds.). Plenum, New York, pp. 269–306.

Coombs, Donald B., and J. Thie. 1979. "The Canadian Land Inventory System" in *Planning the Uses and the Management of the Land,* Marvin T. Beatty, Gary W. Petersen, and Lester R. Swindale (eds.). American Society of Agronomy, Crop Science Society of America and Soil Science Society of America, Madison, WI, pp. 909–933.

Davis, Paul E., Norbert Lerch, Larry Tornes, Joseph Steiger, Neil Smeck, Howard Andrus, John Trimmer, and George Bottrell. 1976. *Soil Survey of Montgomery County, Ohio.* U.S. Department of Agriculture, Soil Conservation Service. 107 pp.

Dickert, Thomas G., and Andrea E. Tuttle. 1985. "Cumulative Impact Assessment in Environmental Planning, A Coastal Wetland Watershed Example." *Environmental Impact Assessment Review* 5:37–64.

Dideriksen, Raymond I. 1984. "SCS Important Farmlands Mapping Program" in *Protecting Farmlands,* Frederick Steiner and John Theilacker (eds.). AVI Publishing, Westport, CT, pp. 233–240.

Donahue, Roy, Raymond W. Miller, and John C. Schickluna. 1977. *Soils: An Introduction to Soils and Plant Growth.* Prentice-Hall, Englewood Cliffs, NJ. 626 pp.

Fabos, Julius Gy., and Stephanie J. Caswell. 1977.

Composite Landscape Assessment (Research Bulletin Number 637). University of Massachusetts, Massachusetts Agricultural Experiment Station, Amherst. 323 pp.

Food and Agriculture Organization of the United Nations. 1977. *A Framework for Land Evaluation* (Publication 22). International Institute for Land Reclamation and Improvement, Wageningen, Netherlands. 87 pp.

Gordon, Steven I., and Gaybrielle E. Gordon. 1981. "The Accuracy of Soil Survey Information for Urban Land-Use Planning." *Journal of the American Planning Association* **47**(3):301–312.

Hills, G. A. 1961. *The Ecological Basis for Land-Use Planning* (Research Report No. 46). Ontario Department of Lands and Forests, Toronto. 204 pp.

Hopkins, Lewis D. 1977. "Methods for Generating Land Suitability Maps: A Comparative Evaluation." *Journal of the American Institute of Planners* **43**(4):386–400.

International Union for the Conservation of Nature and Natural Resources. 1980. *World Conservation Strategy* (published in Cooperation with the United Nations Environment Programme and The World Wildlife Fund.) Gland, Switzerland. Various pages.

Juneja, Narenda. 1974. *Medford.* University of Pennsylvania, Department of Landscape Architecture and Regional Planning, Center for Ecological Research in Planning and Design, Philadelphia. 64 pp.

Killpack, Charles. 1981. "Computer Mapping, Spatial Analysis, and Landscape Architecture." *Landscape Journal* **1**(1):41–48.

Laird, Raymond T., Jeanne B. Perkins, David A. Bainbridge, James B. Baker, Robert T. Boyd, Daniel Huntsman, Paul E. Staub, and Melvin B. Zucker. 1979. *Quantitative Land-Capability Analysis* (U.S. Geological Survey Professional Paper 945). 115 pp.

Lime, D. W. 1979. "Carrying Capacity." *Trends in Rivers and Trails* **16**:37–40.

——— and G. H. Stankey. 1971. "Carrying Capacity: Maintaining Outdoor Recreation Quality" in *Forest Recreation Symposium Proceedings,* Northeast Forest Experiment Station, Upper Darby, PA, pp. 174–184.

Lynch, Kevin. 1971. *Site Planning.* MIT Press, Cambridge, MA. 384 pp.

——— and Gary Hack. 1984. *Site Planning* (3d ed.). MIT Press, Cambridge, MA. 499 pp.

MacDougall, E. Bruce. 1975. "The Accuracy of Map Overlays." *Landscape Planning* **2**:23–30.

McCormack, D. E. 1974. "Soil Potentials: A Positive Approach to Urban Planning." *Journal of Soil and Water Conservation* **29**:258–262.

McHarg, Ian L. 1969. *Design with Nature.* Doubleday/Natural History Press, Garden City, NY. 197 pp.

Meester, R., and J. L. M. van der Voet. 1980. *Carrying Capacity, Goal or Result of a Policy Concerning Water-Based Recreation Areas.* Agricultural University, Department of Land and Water Use, Wageningen, Netherlands. 6 pp.

Meyers, C. R., Jr. 1971. *Regional Modeling Abstracts* (3 volumes). Oak Ridge National Laboratory, Oak Ridge, TN. Various pages.

Meyers, Charles R., Michael Kennedy, and R. Neil Sampson. 1979. "Information Systems for Land-Use Planning" in *Planning the Uses and Management of Land,* Marvin T. Beatty, Gary W. Petersen, and Lester D. Swindale (eds.). American Society of Agronomy, Crop Science of America, and Soil Science Society of America, Madison, WI, pp. 889–907.

Miller, Fred P. 1978. "Soil Survey under Pressure: The Maryland Experience." *Journal of Soil and Water Conservation* **33**(3):104–111.

Ministry of Transport and Public Works. No date. *Room at Last.* IJsselmeerpolders Development Authority, Lelystad, Netherlands. 48 pp.

National Agricultural Lands Study. 1981. *Final Report.* U.S. Department of Agriculture and Council on Environmental Quality. 94 pp.

Palmer, Arthur E. 1981. *Toward Eden.* Creative Resource Systems, Winterville, NC. 417 pp.

Pfister, R. E. and R. E. Frenkel. 1975. *The Concept of Carrying Capacity: Its Application for Management of Oregon's Scenic Waterway System* (Publication No. WRRI–32). Water Resources Research Institute,

Oregon State University and Oregon State Marine Board, Salem, OR. 155 pp.

Reganold, John P., and Michael J. Singer. 1978. *Defining Prime Agricultural Land in California* (Environmental Quality Series No. 29). University of California, Institute of Government Affairs, Davis. 45 pp.

———— and ————. 1979. "Defining Prime Farmland by Three Land Classification Systems." *Journal of Soil and Water Conservation* **34**(4):172–176.

Schneider, Devon M., David R. Goldchalk, and Norman Axler. 1978. *The Carrying Capacity Concept as a Planning Tool* (PAS Report No. 338). American Planning Association, Chicago. 26 pp.

Singer, Michael J., Kenneth K. Tanji, and J. Herbert Snyder. 1979. "Planning Uses of Cultivated Cropland and Pastureland" in *Planning the Uses and Management of Land,* Marvin T. Beatty, Gary W. Petersen, and Lester D. Swindale (eds.). American Society of Agronomy, Crop Science Society of America, Soil Science of America, Madison, WI. pp. 225–271.

Soil Conservation Service. 1975. *National Soils Handbook.* U.S. Department of Agriculture. No page numbers.

Soil Survey Staff. 1951, 1975a. *Soil Survey Manual* (USDA Handbook 18). U.S. Department of Agriculture. 200 pp.

————. 1975b. *Soil Taxonomy—A Basic System of Soil Classification for Making and Interpreting Soil Surveys* (USDA Agricultural Handbook 436). U.S. Department of Agriculture. 754 pp.

Stankey, George H., and David W. Lime. 1973. *Recreational Carrying Capacity: An Annotated Bibliography* (General Technical Report INT-3). U.S. Forest Service, Intermountain Forest and Range Experiment Station, Ogden, UT. 45 pp.

Steiner, Frederick. 1981. "Farmland Protection in the Netherlands." *Journal of Soil and Water Conservation* **36**(2):71–76.

————. 1987. "Agricultural Land Evaluation and Site Assessment: An Introduction." *Environmental Management* **11**(3):375–377.

———— and John Theilacker. 1979. "Locating Feasible Areas for Rural Housing in Whitman County, Washington." *Journal of Soil and Water Conservation* **34**(6):283–285.

————, Richard Dunford, and Nancy Dosdall. 1987. "The Use of the Land Evaluation and Site Assessment System in the United States." *Landscape and Urban Planning* **14**(3):183–199.

Tahoe Regional Planning Agency. 1982. *Environmental Impact Statement for the Establishment of Environmental Threshold Carrying Capacities.* South Lake Tahoe, CA. 140 pp.

University of Pennsylvania. 1985. *Landscape Architecture and Regional Planning 501 Course Primer.* Department of Landscape Architecture and Regional Planning, Philadelphia. Various pages.

U.S. Congress. 1979. "National Forest System Land and Resource Management Planning." *Federal Register* **44**(181):53983–53999.

U.S. Department of Agriculture. 1983. *National Handbook Land Evaluation and Site Assessment Handbook.* Soil Conservation Service. 120 pp.

van Lier, H. N. 1973. *Determination of Planning Capacity and Layout Criteria of Outdoor Recreation Projects.* Centre for Agricultural Publishing and Documentation, Wageningen, Netherlands. 156 pp.

————. 1980. "Outdoor Recreation in the Netherlands. II. A System to Determine the Planning Capacity of Outdoor Recreation Projects Having Varying Daily Attendance." *Landscape Planning* **7**(4):329–343.

———— and Frederick Steiner. 1982. "A Review of the Zuiderzee Reclamation Works: An Example of Dutch Physical Planning." *Landscape Planning* **9**(1):35–59.

Ventura, Steve. 1988. *Dane County Soil Erosion Control Plan.* Dane County, WI. 109 pp.

Vink, A. P. A. 1975. *Land Use in Advancing Agriculture.* Springer-Verlag, New York. 394 pp.

Wagner, J. Alan. 1974. "Recreational Carrying Capacity Reconsidered." *Journal of Forestry* **72**(5):274–278.

Walters, Kenneth, and P. A. Glancy. 1969.

Reconnaissance of Geology and Ground-Water Occurrence in Whitman County, Washington (Water Supply Bulletin No. 26). Washington Department of Water Resources, Olympia. 169 pp.

Whitman County Regional Planning Council. 1978. *Whitman County Comprehensive Plan.* Colfax, WA. 64 pp.

Wright, Lloyd. 1981. "Agricultural Land Evaluation and Assessment Systems: Pilot Program" (unpublished briefing paper). U.S. Department of Agriculture, Soil Conservation Service.

———, Steve Aradas, Ron Darden, Sue Pfluger, and Warren Zitzmann. 1982. "Farmland: Want to Protect?" *Planning* **48**(7):20–21.

6. PLANNING OPTIONS AND CHOICES

Davidoff, Paul, and Thomas Reiner. 1962. "A Choice Theory of Planning." *Journal of the American Institute of Planners* **28**(May):103–115.

Dillman, Don A. 1977. "Preference Surveys and Policy Decisions: Our New Tools Need Not Be Used in the Same Old Ways." *Journal of the Community Development Society* **8**(1):30–43.

Hill, Morris. 1968. "A Goals-Achievement Matrix for Evaluating Alternative Plans." *Journal of the American Institute of Planners* **34**(1):19–29.

Hirschhorn, Larry. 1980. "Scenario Writing: A Developmental Approach." *Journal of the American Planning Association* **46**(2):172–183.

Johnson, James A. 1984. "Wisconsin's Farmland Preservation Program" in *Protecting Farmlands,* Frederick R. Steiner and John E. Theilacker (eds.). AVI Publishing, Westport, CT, pp. 147–159.

Manuwoto, Peter Rodd, Kathy Rumsey, and Vicki Vine. 1978. "Focus: Walworth County" in *Farmland Preservation Planning,* Peter W. Amato (ed.). University of Wisconsin-Extension, Madison, pp. 205–212.

Miller, Donald. 1980. "Project Location Analysis Using the Goals Achievement Method of Evaluation." *Journal of the American Planning Association* **46**(2):195–208.

Pease, James. 1984. "Oregon's Land Conservation and Development Program" in *Planning for the Conservation and Development of Land Resources,* Frederick R. Steiner and Hubert N. van Lier (eds.). Elsevier Scientific Publishing, Amsterdam, pp. 253–271.

Portland Bureau of Planning. 1977. *The City Planner Handbook.* Portland, OR. (November). 117 pp.

———. 1980. *Citizen Involvement* (Comprehensive Plan Support Document: No. 9 of 11 documents.) Portland, OR. (September). 23 pp.

Sistrom, Peter. 1979. "The Comp Plan Goes Political." *Willamette Week* **6**(3):1, 5. (November 26).

West, James. 1978. "Walworth County Case Study— An Addendum" in *Farmland Preservation Planning,* Peter W. Amato (ed.). University of Wisconsin-Extension, Madison, pp. 101–105.

7. LANDSCAPE PLANS

Ansbro, John, Joseph Bell, Meghan Gallione, Karen Karpowich, Johnny Patta, Michael Reis, Gretchen Schalge, Maria Valdez, and David Wood. 1988. *Ecological Inventory and Analysis, Teller County, Colorado.* School of Architecture and Planning, University of Colorado, Denver. 249 pp.

Bell, Joseph, Meghan Gallione, Gretchen Schalge, and David Wood. 1989. *Visions for the Teller County Landscape.* School of Architecture and Planning, University of Colorado, Denver. 79 pp.

Bowie, Robert, Cathy Chin, Jim Estus, Rita Gerou, Bruce Guerard, Jeff Hardcastle, George Hernandez, Judith Karinen, and Susan Maxberry. 1988. *Woodland Park, Colorado: Ecological Inventory and Analysis.* School of Architecture and Planning, University of Colorado, Denver. 91 pp.

deFranceaux, Cynthia. 1987. "National Park Service Planning." *Trends* **24**(2):13–19.

Land Conservation and Development Commission. 1980. *Statewide Planning Goals and Guidelines.* Salem, OR. 24 pp.

Osterman, Douglas A. 1988. *The Missouri Flat Creek Watershed: The Natural and Social Systems, Erosion and Water Quality Problems, Farmers' Perception of*

Highly Erodible Land, and Water Quality Management Plan. State of Washington Department of Ecology, Pullman. 99 pp.

————, Frederick Steiner, Theresa Hicks, Ray Ledgerwood, and Kelsey Gray. 1989. "Coordinated Resource Management and Planning of the Missouri Flat Creek Watershed." *Journal of Soil and Water Conservation* **44**(5):403–406.

Petersen, Kip, Terri Morrell, and Larry Larsen. 1989. *Growth Management Plan, Teller County, Colorado* (Draft). Teller County Planning Department and City of Woodland Park Planning Department, Cripple Creek and Woodland Park, CO. Various pages.

Pinelands Commission. 1980. *New Jersey Pinelands Comprehensive Plan*. New Lisbon, NJ. 446 pp.

Steiner, Frederick R., and Douglas A. Osterman. 1988. "Landscape Planning: A Working Method Applied to a Case Study of Soil Conservation." *Landscape Ecology* **1**(4):213–226.

————, David C. Wood, and Robert Bowie. 1989. "The Use of Ecological Planning Information for Growth Management Planning: The Teller County/ Woodland Park, Colorado Case Study" (paper). School of Architecture and Planning, University of Colorado, Denver. 30 pp.

U.S. Bureau of Census. 1983. *1980 Census of Population, Volume 1, Characteristics of the Population, Chapter C, General Social and Economic Characteristics, Part 7, Colorado*. U.S. Department of Commerce.

Verburg, Edwin A., and Richard A. Coon. 1987. "Planning in the U.S. Fish and Wildlife Service." *Trends* **24**(2):20–26.

Whitman County Regional Planning Council. 1978. *Whitman County Comprehensive Plan*. Colfax, WA. 64 pp.

8. CONTINUING CITIZEN INVOLVEMENT AND COMMUNITY EDUCATION

Domack, Dennis. 1981. *The Art of Community Development*. University of Wisconsin—Extension, Madison. 60 pp.

Land Conservation and Development Commission. 1980. *Statewide Planning Goals and Guidelines*. Salem, OR. 24 pp.

Lassey, William R. 1977. *Planning in Rural Environments*. McGraw-Hill, New York. 257 pp.

Living Systems. 1977. *Practical Use of the Sun*. Winters, CA.

McGregor, Gloria Shepard. 1984. "The Davis, California, Energy Program" in *Planning for the Conservation and Development of Land Resources: Case Studies*, Frederick R. Steiner and Hubert van Lier (eds.). Elsevier Scientific Publishing, Amsterdam. pp. 189–207.

Pinelands Commission. 1980. *New Jersey Pinelands Comprehensive Management Plan*. New Lisbon, NJ. 446 pp.

Thayer, Robert L., Jr. 1989. "The Experience of Sustainable Landscapes." *Landscape Journal* **8**(2): 101–110.

U.S Congress. 1979. "National Forest System Land and Resource Planning." *Federal Register* **44**(181):53,983–53,999.

U.S. Department of Transportation. 1976. *Effective Citizen Participation in Transportation Planning, Volume I, Community Involvement Processes*. Federal Highway Administration, Socio-Economic Studies Division, Washington, DC. 129 pp.

9. DETAILED DESIGNS

Alesch, Richard. 1987. "Evaluating and Managing Cultural Landscapes in the National Park System" in *Aesthetics of the Rural Renaissance* (Conference proceedings). California Polytechnic State University, San Luis Obispo, pp. 161–165.

Bell, Joseph, Meghan Gallione, Gretchen Schalge, and David Wood. 1989. *Visions for the Teller County Landscape*. School of Architecture and Planning. University of Colorado, Denver. 79 pp.

Carlson, Christine, and Dennis Canty. 1986. *A Path for the Palouse*. National Park Service, U.S. Department of Interior, Seattle. 29 pp.

————, ————, Frederick Steiner, and Nancy Mack.

1989. "A Path for the Palouse: An Example of Conservation and Recreation Planning." *Landscape and Urban Planning* **17**(1):1–19.

City of Lakewood. 1988a. *West Colfax Avenue Design Guidelines.* Planning Division, Lakewood, CO. 26 pp.

————. 1988b. *West Colfax Avenue Pedestrian Streetscape Demonstration Project.* Planning Division, Lakewood, CO. 9 pp.

Corbett, Marjorie J. (ed.). 1983. *Greenline Parks.* National Parks & Conservation Association, Washington, DC. 142 pp.

Lynch, Kevin. 1962. *Site Planning* (1st ed.). MIT Press, Cambridge, MA. 248 pp.

———— and Gary Hack. 1984. *Site Planning* (3d ed.). MIT Press, Cambridge, MA. 499 pp.

New Jersey State Planning Commission. 1988. *The Preliminary State Development and Redevelopment Plan for the State of New Jersey* (Volume 2), Trenton. 85 pp.

Olin, Laurie. 1988. "Form, Meaning, and Expression in Landscape Architecture." *Landscape Journal* **7**(2):149–168.

Ortolano, Leonard. 1984. *Environmental Planning and Decision Making.* John Wiley & Sons, New York. 431 pp.

Raintree, John. 1987. *D. & D. Users Manual.* International Council for Research in Agroforestry. Nairobi, Kenya. 55 pp.

Spirn, Anne Whiston. 1988. "The Poetics of City and Nature: Towards a New Aesthetic for Urban Design." *Landscape Journal* **7**(2):108–126.

————. 1989. " 'Deep Structure:' On Process, Pattern, Form, and Design in the Urban Landscape" in *Linking Landscape Structure to Ecosystem Process* (Conference abstracts). Colorado State University, Fort Collins. p. 40.

Sutro, Suzanne. 1984. *Farmland Protection Strategies for the Connecticut River Valley of Massachusetts.* Mid-Atlantic Regional Office, U.S. National Park Service, Philadelphia. 128 pp.

U.S. National Park Service. 1985. *Connecticut Valley Action Program, Landowner Survey Report.* Mid-Atlantic Regional Office, Philadelphia. 29 pp.

————. 1986. *Zoning Review for the Connecticut River Valley of Massachusetts.* Mid-Atlantic Regional Office, Philadelphia. 90 pp.

U.S. Soil Conservation Service. 1978. *National Conservation Planning Manual.* U.S. Department of Agriculture, Washington, DC. Various pages.

Yaro, Robert D., Randall G. Arendt, Harry L. Dodson, and Elizabeth A. Brabec. 1988. *Dealing With Change in the Connecticut River Valley: A Design Manual for Conservation and Development.* Center for Rural Massachusetts, University of Massachusetts, Amherst. 181 pp.

10. PLAN AND DESIGN IMPLEMENTATION

American Law Institute. 1974. *A Model Land Development Code.* Philadelphia. Various pages.

Barron, James C. 1975. *Transferable Development Rights* (E. M. 3939). Washington State University, Cooperative Extension Service, Pullman. 7 pp.

Butler, Stuart M. 1981. "Enterprise Zone Theorist Calls for Unplanning." *Planning* **47**(2):6.

Callies, Davis L. 1980. "The Quiet Revolution Revisited." *Journal of the American Planning Association* **46**(2):135–144.

Canham, Ronald R. 1979. *Interagency Coordination and Rapid Community Growth* (WREP 22). Oregon State University, Western Rural Development Center, Corvallis. 4 pp.

Center for Natural Areas, Smithsonian Institution. 1974. *Planning Conservation for Statewide Inventories of Critical Areas: A Reference Guide* (Report 3). U.S. Army Corps of Engineers, Washington, DC.

Clark, Janice M. 1977. "Agricultural Zoning in Black Hawk County, Iowa," in *Land Use: Tough Choices in Today's World.* Soil Conservation Society of America, Ankeny, IA., pp. 149–154.

Conn, William J. 1984. "Techniques for Protecting

Prime Agricultural Land, Zoning Applications in York County, Pennsylvania" in *Protecting Farmlands,* Frederick Steiner and John Theilacker (eds.). AVI Publishing, Westport, CT, pp. 97–108.

Coughlin, Robert E., and John C. Keene (Senior authors and eds.). 1981. *The Protection of Farmland: A Reference Guidebook for State and Local Governments* (National Agricultural Lands Study). U.S. Government Printing Office, Washington, DC. 284 pp.

Daniels, Thomas L., and David E. Reed. 1988. "Agricultural Zoning in a Metropolitan County: An Evaluation of the Black Hawk County, Iowa, Program." *Landscape and Urban Planning* **16**(4):303–310.

De Chiara, Joseph, and Lee Koppelman. 1975. *Urban Planning and Design Criteria.* Van Nostrand Reinhold, New York. 646 pp.

Dunford, Richard W. 1984. "Property Tax Relief Programs to Preserve Farmlands" in *Protecting Farmlands,* Frederick Steiner and John Theilacker (eds.). AVI Publishing, Westport, CT, pp. 183–194.

Emory, Benjamin R. 1985. "Report on 1985 National Survey of Government and Non-Profit Easement Programs: Executive Summary." *Land Trusts' Exchange* **4**(3):2.

Fletcher, W. Wendell. 1978. *Agricultural Land Retention: An Analysis of the Issue. A Study of Recent State and Local Farmland Retention Programs and Discussion of Proposed Federal Legislation.* Library of Congress, Congressional Research Service, Washington, DC. 52 pp.

Green, Philip P., Jr. 1968. "Land Subdivision" in *Principles and Practice of Urban Planning,* William I. Goodman and Eric C. Freund (eds.). International City Manager's Association, Washington, DC, pp. 443–484.

Harris, Dianne Chandler. 1988. "Growth Management Reconsidered." *Journal of Planning Literature* **3**(4):466–482.

Huddleston, Jack. 1981. "Tax Increment Financing in Wisconsin." *Planning* **47**(11):14–17.

Humphreys, John A. 1985. "Breckenridge, Point Systems: Keeping Score." *Planning* **51**(10):23–25.

Iowa Northland Regional Council of Governments. 1975. *County Living Study.* Black Hawk County, Waterloo, IA. 50 pp.

Jaffe, Martin, and Duncan Erley. No date. *Protecting Solar Access for Residential Development.* U.S. Government Printing Office, Washington, DC. 154 pp.

Jennings, Michael D., and John P. Reganold. 1988. "Policy and Reality of Environmentally Sensitive Areas in Whitman County, Washington, USA." *Environmental Management* **12**(3):369–380.

Johannsen, Sonia A., and Larry C. Larsen. 1984. "Corn Suitability Ratings: A Method of Rating Soils for Identifying and Preserving Prime Agricultural Land in Black Hawk County, Iowa" in *Protecting Farmland,* Frederick Steiner and John Theilacker (eds.). AVI Publishing, Westport, CT, pp. 109–127.

Kartez, Jack D. 1980. "A Zoning Administrator's View of Farmland Zoning." *Journal of Soil and Water Conservation* **35**(6):265–266.

Kendig, Lane. 1977. "Carrying Capacity: How It Can Work for You." *Environmental Comment* (December):4–6.

Kleymeyer, John E. No date. "Some Aspects of Land-Use Control" (class notes). University of Cincinnati, Department of Community Planning, Cincinnati. 8 pp.

Leary, Robert M. 1968. "Zoning" in *Principles and Practice of Urban Planning,* William I. Goodman and Eric C. Freund (eds.). International City Manager's Association, Washington, DC, pp. 403–442.

Lewis, James A. 1980. *Landownership in the United States, 1978.* U.S. Department of Agriculture, Washington, DC. 98 pp.

McHarg, Ian L. 1969. *Design With Nature.* Doubleday/Natural History Press, Garden City, NY. 197 pp.

Meyer, Neil L. 1980. *Programming Capital Improvements* (WREP 30). Oregon State University, Western Rural Development Center, Corvallis. 12 pp.

National Agricultural Lands Study. 1981. *Final Report.* Department of Agriculture and Council on

Environmental Quality. 94 pp. Washington, DC.

National Committee on Governmental Accounting. 1968. *Governmental Accounting, Auditing and Financial Reporting.* Municipal Finance Officers Association of the United States and Canada, Chicago. 234 pp.

Nellis, Lee. 1980. "Planning with Rural Values." *Journal of Soil and Water Conservation* 35(2):67–71.

———. 1981. "The Bottom Line: Implementation of Regional Landscape Planning Through Effective Citizen Participation and An Innovative Legal and Administrative Technique" in *Regional Landscape Planning,* Julius Gy. Fabos (ed.). American Society of Landscape Architects, Washington, DC, pp. 72–80.

Newman, Harry George, III. 1982. "An Environmentally Sensitive Area Planning Model for Local Government in the State of Washington" (unpublished master of regional planning thesis). Washington State University, Program in Environmental Science and Regional Planning, Pullman. 115 pp.

O'Harrow, Dennis. 1954. *Performance Standards for Industrial Zoning.* National Industrial Zoning Committee, Columbus, OH.

Pinelands Commission. 1980. *New Jersey Pinelands. Comprehensive Management Plan.* State of New Jersey, New Lisbon. 446 pp.

Reps, John W. 1964. "Pomeroy Memorial Lecture: Requiem for Zoning" in *Planning 1964.* The American Society of Planning Officials, Chicago, pp. 56–67.

———. 1970. *Town Planning in Frontier America.* (Paperback edition, original copyright 1969.) Princeton University Press, Princeton, NJ. 473 pp.

Snohomish County Office of Community Planning. 1981. *Snohomish County Growth Management Strategy.* Everett, WA. 399 pp.

State of Washington. 1984. *State Environmental Policy Act Rules.* Department of Ecology, Olympia. 56 pp.

Steiner, Frederick, and John Theilacker (eds.). 1984. *Protecting Farmland.* AVI Publishing, Westport, CT. 312 pp.

Toner, William. 1978. *Saving Farms and Farmlands: A Community Guide* (PAS Report No. 333). American Planning Association, Chicago. 45 pp.

———. 1981. *Zoning to Protect Farming: A Citizens' Guidebook* (National Agricultural Lands Study). U.S. Government Printing Office, Washington, DC. 32 pp.

U.S. Bureau of Land Management. 1988. *Public Land Statistics 1987.* U.S. Department of Interior, Washington, DC. 124 pp.

Weber, Bruce, and Richard Beck. 1979. *Minimizing Public Costs of Residential Growth* (WREP 17). Oregon State University, Western Rural Development Center, Corvallis. 5 pp.

Whitman County Regional Planning Council. 1979. *Whitman County Zoning Regulations, Revised.* Colfax, WA. 62 pp.

Wickersham, Kirk, Jr. 1978. "Reform of Discretionary Land-Use Decision-Making: Point Systems and Beyond." *Zoning and Planning Law Report* 1(9):65–71.

Wisconsin Supreme Court. 1972. *Just vs. Marinette County* (4 ERC 1842).

11. ADMINISTRATION OF PLANNING PROGRAMS

American Farmland Trust. 1986. *Density-Related Public Costs.* Washington, DC. 44 pp.

Buskirk, E. Drannon, Jr. 1986. "Environmental Impact Analysis" in *The Practice of State and Regional Planning,* Frank S. So, Irving Hand, and Bruce D. McDowell (eds.). American Planning Association, Chicago, pp. 238–254.

City of Boulder Planning Department. 1980. *Residential Allocation System.* Boulder, CO. 46 pp.

Council on Environmental Quality. 1986. "Environmental Impact Statement." *Code of Federal Regulations* 40, Ch. V (7-1-86 edition).

Faas, Ronald C. 1980. *What Does the Impact Statement Say About Economic Impacts?* (WREP 31). Oregon State University, Western Rural Development Center, Corvallis. 7 pp.

Graham, Otis L., Jr. 1976. *Toward a Planned Society.* Oxford University Press, London. 357 pp.

Hudson, Barclay M. 1979. "Comparison of Current Planning Theories: Counterparts and Contradictions." *Journal of the American Planning Association* **45**(4):387–398.

Johnson, Lee. 1974. *Attorney General's Opinion on Fasano v. Board of County Commissioners of Washington County.* State of Oregon, Department of Justice, Salem.

Leininger, David L. and Ronald C. Wong. 1976. "Zero-Base Budgeting in Garland, Texas." *Management Information Service Reports* **8**(4A):2.

Natural Resources Defense Council. 1977. *Land Use Controls in the United States.* Elaine Moss (ed.). The Dial Press/James Wade, New York. 362 pp.

Oregon Supreme Court. 1973. *Fasano v. Board of County Commissioners of Washington County.*

———. 1975. *Baker v. City of Milwaukie.*

———. 1979. *Neuberger v. City of Portland.*

Ortolano, Leonard. 1984. *Environmental Planning and Decision Making.* John Wiley & Sons, New York. 431 pp.

Pollock, Peter. 1987. Planner, City of Boulder, CO. (Telephone interview, January 14.)

Portland Bureau of Planning. 1980. *Plan Review and Administration.* Portland, OR. 48 pp.

Raabe, Steve. 1988. "Boulder Builders Mellow Toward Slow-Growth Policy" *The Denver Post* (November 21, 1988), pp. 1-C and 7-C.

Siegler, Theodore R., and Neil L. Meyer. 1980. *Assessing Fiscal Impact of Rural Growth* (WREP 29). Oregon State University, Western Rural Development Center. Corvallis. 5 pp.

So, Frank S. 1979. "Finance and Budgeting" in *The Practice of Local Government Planning,* Frank S. So, Israel Stollman, Frank Beal, and David S. Arnold (eds.). International City Management Association, Washington, DC, pp. 115–149.

———. 1988. "Finance and Budgeting" in *The Practice of Local Government Planning* (2d ed.), Frank

S. So and Judith Getzels (eds.). International City Management Association, Washington, DC, pp. 435–471.

U.S. Congress. 1969. *National Environmental Policy Act of 1969* (Public Law 91–190).

Washington Department of Ecology. 1984. *State Environmental Policy Act Rules* (chap. 197–11, Washington Administrative Code). Olympia, WA. 56 pp.

Westman, Walter E. 1985. *Ecology, Impact Assessment, and Environmental Planning.* John Wiley & Sons, New York. 532 pp.

12. CONCLUSIONS

Carlson, Christine, Dennis Canty, Frederick Steiner, and Nancy Mack. 1989. "A Path for the Palouse: An Example of Conservation and Recreation Planning." *Landscape and Urban Planning* **17**(1):1–19.

Forester, John. 1982. "Understanding Planning Practice: An Empirical, Practical, and Normative Account." *Journal of Planning Education and Research* **1**(2):59–71.

Gans, Herbert J. 1968. *People and Plans.* Basic Books, New York. 395 pp.

Jennings, Michael D., and John P. Reganold. 1988. "Policy and Reality of Environmentally Sensitive Areas in Whitman County, USA." *Environmental Management* **12**(3):369–380.

Kast, Fremont E., and James E. Rosenzweig. 1974. *Organization and Management: A Systems and Contingency Approach* (3d ed., 1979). McGraw-Hill, New York. 644 pp.

Klosterman, Richard E. 1978. "Foundations for Normative Planning." *Journal of the American Institute of Planners* **44**(1):37–46.

Lai, Richard Tseng-yu. 1988. *Law in Urban Design and Planning.* Van Nostrand Reinhold, New York. 470 pp.

Mumford, Lewis. 1961. *The City in History.* Harcourt, Brace, World, New York. 657 pp.

Prigogine, Ilya, and Isabelle Stengers. 1984. *Order Out of Chaos*. Bantam Books, New York. 349 pp.

Steiner, Frederick. 1981. *Ecological Planning for Farmlands Preservation*. Planners Press, Chicago. 122 pp.

———— and Douglas A. Osterman. 1988. "Landscape Planning: A Working Method Applied to a Case Study of Soil Conservation." *Landscape Ecology* **1**(4):213–226.

Whitman County Regional Planning Council. 1978. *Whitman County Comprehensive Plan*. Colfax, WA. 64 pp.

Abiotic, 60, 63, 92, (fig.) 93, 319
Adams, Ansel, 7
Administration, 3, 9, (fig.) 10, 19, 150, 279–308, 312, 319
Administrative planners, 6–8
Advocacy, 196
Advocacy planners. See also Adversary planners, 6–8, 194
Aerial photographs, 43, (fig.) 44, 68, 74, 97, 150, 164, (photo) 165, 169
Affected environment, 174, 181, 291
Africa, 208
Afro-Americans, 81, 99. See also Blacks
Agriculture, 12, (fig.) 16, 17, 27, 30, (table) 36–37, 53, 66, (fig.) 79, 96, 101, 102, (table) 110, 111, 122–123, 124, (table) 126, 132–140, (fig.) 142, (fig.) 143, 145, (fig.) 146, 150, (fig.) 153, 154, 155–159, 161, 162, (figs.) 163, 164, 168, 182, 184, 215, 245, 258, 260, 261, 263–264, 267, (table) 272, 282, (figs.) 283–286, (table) 295, 316
Agricultural lands, 11, 17, 33–34, (fig.) 74, 122, 132–140, 141, 169, 176–177, 181, 223, 243, (table) 250, 251, (table) 276, 281, 314, 319. See also Farmland
Agricultural Land Evaluation and Site Assessment (LESA) System, 135–140, 251, 314–315, 329
Agricultural production areas, 182–183
Agricultural Wastes Grant Program, 177–178
Agricultural zoning, 242, 261, 282, (figs.) 283–286
Agroforestry, 208–209
Air, 141, (table) 295
    pollution areas, (table) 250, 252, 319
    quality, 12, (table) 36, 83, 169, 184, 215, 248, (table) 295, 314
Airports, 262
Alabama, (table) 264
Alaska, 73, 89, 103, 248, (table) 264
Albany, (fig.) 260, (fig.) 270
Albion, Washington, 42–81, 100, (table) 101, 102, 157, 162, (figs.) 163, (fig.) 164, 178, (fig.) 180, 268–269
Alluvial deposits, 49, (fig.) 50
Alluvium, (fig.) 49, 156, (table) 245, (fig.) 283–284, 319
Alinsky, Saul, 7, 8, 24
American, 4, 5–8, 12, 27, 30, 41, 75, 81, 124, 164, 173, 205, 222, 241, 252, 280
American Farmland Trust, 268, 297–299
American Indians. See Indians
American Law Institute, 248, 249

American Planning Association, 287
American Revolution, 255
American Society of Planning Officials, 245
Amsterdam, (fig.) 147, (fig.) 148
Analysis, 3, 150, 319
Animals, (table) 36, 42, 51, 71–72, (fig.) 73, (table) 84–85, (table) 87, 92, 151, 249, 250, (table) 253, (table) 254, (table) 295. See also Wildlife
Annapolis, (fig.) 270
Annexation, 33, 177, 180, 266–267, 281, (fig.) 300, 302, 319
Appleyard, Donald, 120
Aquicludes, 76
Aquifer, 55, 58, 76, (fig.) 86, 154, 319
Aquifer recharge areas, 58, 252
Areawide water quality commission, 269
Architecture, 162, 173, 196, 197, 208, (fig.) 304, 311
Argyris, Chris, 25
Arizona, 17, (table) 264
Arkansas, (table) 264
Arterials, (figs.) 143, (fig.) 144
Artists, 281, (table) 287
Asian, 103
Asotin County, Washington, (table) 101, (table) 102, (table) 103, (tables) 105, (table) 106, 111, (fig.) 112, (fig.) 113, 141, (figs.) 143, (fig.) 144, (fig.) 146
Aspect, 53
Athletic fields, 133
Atlantic City, 125, (fig.) 183
Atlantic Coastal Plain, 83
Atlantic County, New Jersey, (table) 125, (table) 129, (table) 254
Atlantic Ocean, (fig.) 35, (fig.) 147, (fig.) 152, (fig.) 183, 222
Attorneys. See Lawyers
Audubon Society, 223, 268
Aurora, Colorado, 220
Automobiles, 151
Avalanche, 250

Babylonian, 255
Baker v. City of Milwaukie, 244, 307
Baltimore, 261, 270
Basalt, 48, (fig.) 50, 76, 156, 157, (fig.) 158, 162, (table) 245, (fig.) 282–284, 319
Base map, 42, 43, 319
Bassett, Edward M., 242
Beaches, 35
Beck, Richard, 266
Bedrock, 4, 51, 62, 134, 157
Bedroom community, 162, (fig.) 164, 181, 184
Belgium, (fig.) 147

Benefit-cost analysis. See Cost-benefit analysis.
Bennis, Warren, 25
Berger, Jonathan, 8, 93, 124, 128, 141
Berry, Wendell, 8
Best-management practices, 269
Bettman, Alfred, 242
Biblical, 255
Bicyclists, 213, 214, 216, (fig.) 224, 314, 315
Bill of Rights, 7
Biosphere, 290, 319
Biotic, 60, 63, 92, (fig.) 93, 319
Bitterroot Mountain Range, 44, (fig.) 46
Bivariate relationships, 76–80, 121–123
Black Hawk County, Iowa, 18, 242, 269–273
Blacks, 8, 103, (table) 116, (table) 117, 124. See also Afro-Americans
Block diagram, 51, (fig.) 52
Board of adjustment, 268, (fig.) 269, 281, 319
Boating, (fig.) 153, (fig.) 154
Boise, Idaho, (fig.) 274
Bonneville Power Administration, 106, 329
Boston, 255, (fig.) 260
Boston, (table) 98, 99
Boulder, Colorado, 248, 280, 299–305, 308
Boulder Growth Limitation Ordinance, 300–305
Boundary review boards, 280, 281
Brandywine Valley Association, 268
Breckenridge, Colorado, 248
Breckenridge Development Code, 248
British Conservative Party, 266
Bucks County, Pennsylvania, 245, (table) 246–247
Budget, 266, 280, 286–290, 297
Builders, 157, 197, 200
Building
    codes, 33, 158, 200, 241, 252, 255–256, (table) 257, 319
    permits, 33, 107–108, 256, 267, (fig.) 282, 300, 302, (fig.) 304, 305
Bureaucrats, 280
Burlington County, New Jersey, (table) 125, (table) 129, (fig.) 152, (table) 254
Bush, George, 8
Business. See Commercial land use
Butler, Stuart M., 266
Byrne, Brendan T., 35

Cable television, 165, 197
California, 17, (table) 98, 99, 200, 205, 242, 256, (table) 264
Camden County, New Jersey, (table) 125, (table) 129
Camden, New Jersey, 152
Campsites, 133
Canada, 44, (fig.) 45, (fig.) 87
Canadian, 8, 141
Canadian Land Inventory System, 141

Canham, Ronald, 266
Canty, Dennis, 211, 212
Capability, 131, 319. *See also* Land capability *and* Suitability analysis
Cape May County, New Jersey, (table) 125, (table) 129
Capital improvement program (*also* Capital improvement budget), 33, 184, 242, 262–263, 266, 274, 280, 281, 289–290, 319
Caribbean, 80
Carlson, Christine, 211, 212
Carrying capacity, 34, 132, 150–151, 174, 319–320
Carter, Jimmy, 7, 35, 269, 289
Cascade Mountains, 44, (fig.) 46, 48, 273
Case law, 242, 249, 268, 305–307
Casino gambling, 125
Catchment area, 12, 42
Catenas, 61, 63, 326
Catton, William, 150–151
Cedar Falls, Iowa, 271
Cemeteries, 133
Census data, 97, (table) 98, 99, 100, 297–298
Center for Ecological Research in Planning and Design, 152
Center for Population Research, 170
Center for Rural Massachusetts, 223–226, (fig.) 227, (fig.) 228, (fig.) 229, (figs.) 230, (fig.) 231, (figs.) 232, (fig.) 233, 235, 236
Central Park, 7
Central place, 200, (table) 201
Chambers of commerce, (table) 98, 200
Change agent, 7, 25
Charrette, 162, 164, 171, 194
Chester County, Pennsylvania, 268
Chicago, 7, 168, (fig.) 273
Chinese, 242
Chinook winds, 78
Choices, 17, 161–171, 174
Cincinnati, (table) 98, 99
Citizen
    honoraria, 194
    involvement (*also* Citizen participation), 9, (fig.) 10, 18, 24–25, (fig.) 28, 30–32, 161–171, 182, 184, 191–205, 248, 268, 312, 320
    referendum, 162, 165–166, 194
    review boards, 194
    training, 194
Citizens, 17, 19, 24, 25, 166, 167, 169, 170, 171, 184, 191–205, 207, 211, 221, 267, 279, 280, 306, 308, 315
    advisory committees, 23, 24, 27, 162, 165, 167, 171, 192, 194, 195, 196, 289, 320
City
    council, 17, 30, 31, 167, 170, 175, 192
    manager, (table) 288, 289
    officials, 134, 287
City Beautiful Movement, 7
The City Planner Handbook, 169
Civil engineering, 242
Civil engineers. *See* Engineers
Civil rights, 7, 8
Clark, Janice, 271
Clay, 62–63, 76, 145, (fig.) 148, 320
Climate, (fig.) 13, 43–48, 60, 63, 65–67, 68,

76, (fig.) 77, 78, 80–81, 83, 87, 88, 89, 92, 96, (fig.) 121, (fig.) 122, 133, (fig.) 143, 145, 256, (table) 295, 320. *See also* Micro-climate and Regional climate
Clubs, (table) 98, 99, 100, 118–119, 195–196
Coastal areas, 35, 87–93, 102, 124, 125–128, 169, 244, 252
Coastal Zone Management Act (CZMA), 7, 88
Costa Rica, 80
Cohort-survival, 100, 105–106, (fig.) 107, 320
Colfax Avenue, 220–221, (fig.) 225, (fig.) 226, (fig.) 227
Colfax, Washington, (table) 101, (table) 105
Colleges. *See* Universities
Colorado, 76, 184–188, 208, 248, (table) 264, 300, 305
Colorado Springs, 184, (fig.) 185, 186
Columbia River, 56
Columbia River Basin Commission, 42
Columnar section, 49, (fig.) 50
Commercial land use (*also* Business), 36, (table) 37, (fig.) 74, 106, 141, (fig.) 143, (fig.) 146, 162, (fig.) 163, (fig.) 164, 168, 169, 176, (fig.) 180, 181, 186, (table) 201, (table) 202, (table) 203, 208, 215, 221, 227, 243, 244, (table) 246, 263, 266, 267, (table) 275, 312–313, 314–315
Common law, 256
Community, 9, 97, 186, 194, 268, 287, 290, 296, 298, 314, 320
    colleges, 97, 99–100, 192, 195, 197
    -consensus study, 198–199, 200
    education, 3, 18, 178, 179, 191–205, 268, 312
    development, 134, 192, 197–205, 263
    involvement, 3, 25–27, 287
    needs assessments, 97, 122–123, 196
    organization, 192
    organizations, 97, (table) 98, 99, 100, 118–119, 169, 194–196
Comprehensive planning/plans, 4, 17, 23, 30, 32–38, 81, 83–87, 124–125, 137, (table) 139, 155, 159, 162, 169–171, 173–184, 197, 211, 242, 243, 244, 248, 254, 269, 274, 275, 280, 281, 292, (fig.) 300, 302, 306, 307, 312–317, 320
Computers, 15, 27, 51, 132, 145–146, 149–150, 210
Concepts, 3, 9, (fig.) 10, 17, 180, 186, 210–219, (fig.) 220–221, 315
Concord, New Hampshire, (fig.) 260
Condemnation, 242, 258, 261
Conditional use permits, 281, 320
Conferences, 193, 194, 195
Connecticut, 222, 260, (table) 264
Connecticut River, 222
Connecticut River valley, 208, 210, 221–226, (fig.) 227, (fig.) 228, (fig.) 229, (figs.) 230, (fig.) 231, (figs.) 232, (fig.) 233, 234–236
Conn, William, 270
Conservation, 63, 145, (figs.) 163, (fig.) 164, 168, 176–181, 211, 212, 214, 215, 218, 222, 223, 259, 276, 292, (table) 295, 320

districts, 132, 176, 209, 269, 317
easements. *See* Easements
plans, 137, 178, 179, 208–209, 267, 317
policy, 132
Conservationists, 60, (fig.) 72, 132, 133, 134, 135, 139, 162, 209
Constraints, (table) 141, 143, (fig.) 146, 154, 157, 181, 185, 186
Construction, (table) 110, 138, (figs.) 143, (fig.) 144, 208, (table) 245, 256, (table) 257, (fig.) 284, 298, 304, 314
Consulting firms (*also* Consultants), 6, 24, 27, 31, 81, 87, 97, (table) 98, 99, 104, 116, 124, 167, 170
Contingency planning, 312
Contract documents, 208
Cooperative Extension Service, 195, 196, 197–205
"Coping with Growth," 196–197
Corbett, Mike, 200
Corvallis, Oregon, 197
Cost-benefit analysis, 166
Cost estimate, 208
Cost sharing, 179
Council on Environmental Quality, 7, 290, 291, 292–293, 329
County
    commission, 17, 30, 31, 155, 175, 176, 192, 261
    commissioners, 155–156, 158, 176, 261, 268–269, 314, 315
    recorder, 175
Covenants, 241, 256, 258, 260, 268, (fig.) 304
Cowboys, 96, 186
Critical areas protection, 241, 248–252, 255, 320. *See also* Environmentally sensitive lands
Cripple Creek, Colorado, (fig.) 185, 186, (fig.) 187, 228, 234
Cropland. *See* Agriculture
Cross compliance, 267
Cross section, 51, (fig.) 52, 320
Crop Suitability Rating, 271
Crystalline rock, 48, (fig.) 50, 76, 156, (table) 245, (fig.) 283–284
Cultural resources (*also* Cultural areas), 137, 143, (fig.) 146, 184. (*See also* Historic, archaeological, and cultural areas)
Cumberland County, New Jersey, (table) 125, (table) 129
Cumulative environmental impacts, 151, 320
Current planning, 280–286

Dalles, 96
Danish, Paul, 300
Danish system, 300, 304–305
Dane County Land Records Project, 150
Dane County, Wisconsin, 150, 197–205
Daubenmire, Rexford, 68–69
Davis, California, 192, 200, 205, 256
Dayton, 8, 133, 287–289
Declaration of Independence, 6, 7
Deed restrictions, 256
Deep Structure, 207, 234
Deerfield, Wisconsin, (fig.) 198
Deferred taxation, 264, (table) 265
Deforestation, (fig.) 153
DeKalb County, Illinois, 134

Delaware, (table) 264, (fig.) 270
Delaware Bay, (fig.) 152, (fig.) 183
Delaware River Basin Commission, 42
Delphi, 23, 26–27, 194, 320
Democracy, 194
Demonstration projects, 208, 219–221, (fig.)
    225, (fig.) 226, (fig.) 227
Denver, (fig.) 185, 220
Dependency ratios, 103–104, (table) 105
Des Moines, Iowa, (fig.) 273
Design, 3, 9, (fig.) 10, 18, 186, 198, 200, (fig.)
    204, 207–238, 244, 263, 312,
    315, 317
    education, 164
    guidelines, 186, 235
    review, 210
        boards, 280, 281
    simulation, 208
    standards, 216, 220, (fig.) 225, (fig.) 226,
        244
Designers, 281
Design with Nature, 141, 260
Detailed studies, 9, (fig.) 10, 14–17, 131, 181,
    312, 317
Determination of nonsignificance, 282*n.*, 293
Determination of significance, 282*n.*, 293
Developers, 134, 152, 197, 225, 244, 248,
    252, 254, 264, 291, 299, (fig.)
    304
Development, 36, (table) 37, 96, 143, 145, (fig.)
    153, 181, 183, 222, 223, 224–
    225, (fig.) 227, (fig.) 228, (fig.)
    229, (figs.) 230, (fig.) 231, (fig.)
    232, (fig.) 233, 235, (table) 245–
    246, 248, 261, 271, 276, 297–
    299, (fig.) 300–302, (fig.) 303–
    304, 305, 315, 320
    credits, 184, 261
    projections, 106–108, 110, 180, 181, 185
Diagnosis and design, 208–209
Dickert, Thomas, 151
Dillman, Don, 27, 29, 116, 118, 166
Divide, Colorado, 227
Dover, Delaware, (fig.) 270
Downtown, 215
Drainage, 42, 51, 55, 61, 63, 78, 89 (figs.) 143,
    (fig.) 144, (fig.) 146, (fig.) 153,
    (table) 155, (table) 156. *See also*
    Watersheds
    basin, 7, 9, 12, 42, 55, 58, 86, 178, 317,
        320
    patterns, 56, (fig.) 57
Dredge and fill permits, 291
Due process, 6, 307
Dunford, Richard, 264
Dust bowl, 132
Dutch, 17, 145

Earthquake. *See also* Scenic easements
    hazards, 143, 250, 252
    zones, 51
Easements, 18, 222, 225, 242, (table) 246, 258–
    259, 260–261, 268, 270, 321
École des Beaux-Arts, 162, 164
Ecological critical areas, 182, 249, (table) 250,
    (table) 253, (table) 254, (table)
    275, 276, 321
Ecologists, 151
Ecology, 4, 20, 41, 80, 151, 188, 195, 196,
    321

Economically critical areas, 249
Economic
    analysis, 96, 110–111, (table) 114
    base, 96, 110, (table) 114
    characteristics, 175
    development, 100–101, 102, 104–105,
        111, 113, 176, 181–182, 199–
        200, 223
    impact analysis, 292, 294–296
    information, (table) 109, 110
    multipliers, (table) 114, 295–296, 321
    studies, 95, 96, 110–111, 123, 125
Economics, 96, 169, 197, 273
Economists, 265, 294, 295
Ecosystem, 12, 42, 72, 92, 128, 152, 249, 250,
    (table) 253, (table) 254, 321
Ecotones, 69, (fig.) 70, 71, 321
Education. *See* Community education
Eighteenth century, 225
Election boards, 97, (table) 98
Elevation, 43, 51, 53, (fig.) 54, 56, 76, 78, (fig.)
    88, (fig.) 146, 321
Eminent domain, 262
Employment multiplier, 295–296
Enabling legislation, 181, 268. *See also* State
        enabling legislation
Endangered species, 143
Energy, 79, 292, 294, (table) 295, 321
    conservation, 12, 35, 78, 169, 196, 200,
        205, 256, 263, 305
    crisis, 255
    planning, 192, 200, 205
Engineers, 7, 97, (table) 98, 133, 173, 254,
    281, (fig.) 300
England, 5, 7, 30
English, 5, 7, 8, 197, 255, 256
Entrepreneurship, 266
Enterprise zones, 263, 266
Environmental
    assessments, 17
    checklists, (fig.) 282, 293, 294, (table) 295
    consequences, 174, 291, 292
    design arts, 120, 290
    impact, 249, 266, 282*n.*, 291–292
        analysis, 292–294
        assessment, 269, 290–292
        statements, 7, 174, 193, (fig.) 282, 290–
            294, (table) 295, 315, 321, 329
    management, 20
    mitigation, 291–292, 293
    quality, 158, 176, 181–182, 250, 281, 315
        councils, 280
    review, 249, 281
    threshold, 151
Environmentally sensitive areas, 6, 102, 120,
        168, 180–181, 184, 185, 186,
        211, 241, 244, 248–252, 261,
        263, 269, 275, (table) 276, 291,
        314, 315–317, 321
Eolian disposition, 48, (fig.) 50, 321
Erosion, (fig.) 16, 56, 61, 62, 63, 76, 78, 89,
        133, 134, (fig.) 142, (figs.) 143,
        (fig.) 144, (fig.) 146, 150, 175–
        176, (photo.) 177, 178–181,
        209, 223, 252, 268–269, (table)
        276, (table) 295, 315, 317, 321
    control plans, 12, 150
    hazard, 62, 63, 134, (fig.) 144
Estuarine resources, 35, 56, 58, (fig.) 59
Estuary, 56, 58, 321

Ethnicity, (table) 14, 99, 100, 103, 115, (fig.)
    116, (fig.) 117, 118, 119, 124
Euclid v. Ambler Reality Co., 242
Europe, 5, (fig.) 147
European, 222, 252, 255
Europeans, 5, 81, 124, 127
Evapotranspiration, (fig.) 55, 80, (fig.) 81, 321
Everett, Washington, 166–167
Evergreen Station, Colorado, 227
Exclusive farm-use zones, 33, 268–269
Extension agents, 17, 63, 67, 197
Ezekiel, 252

Faas, Ronald, 294
Face-to-face interviews, 115, 118–119
Family farm, 155, 314
*Fasano v. Board of County Commissioners of
    Washington County,* 244, 306,
    308
Farm Bureau, 98, 169
Farm Council, 169
Farmers, 11, 17, 18, 48, 67, 72, 75, (fig.) 77,
    78, 121, 123, 128, 132, 152,
    157, 159, 169, 175–176, 178,
    179, 209, 224, 244, 258, 260,
    267, 299, 314, 317
Farmland, 73, 102, 132–140, 224–225, 244,
    263, 273, 314. *See also* Agricul-
    tural lands
    protection, 18, 138–140, 155–159, 162,
        (fig.) 163, 168–169, 171, 180–
        181, 196, 225–226, 235, 244,
        268–273, 276, 314–315
Farmland Protection Policy Act (FPPA), 138,
    329
Fault zones, 51
Federal Aviation Administration (FAA), 46, 60,
    67, 329
Fee-simple purchase, 241–242, 258, 261, 268
Fire
    and police services, 33, 274, (table) 275,
        (table) 295, (table) 297, (fig.)
        304
    hazard areas, (table) 250, 252, 321
    management, 184
    prevention, 256
First-order streams, 56, (fig.) 57
Fiscal impact analysis, 196–197, 292, 294,
    296–299
Fisheries, 34, 60, 89, (fig.) 91, (fig.) 92, 93,
    (table) 110, (table) 124, 249,
    (table) 295
Fishing, 96, 111, 125, 127, 128, (fig.) 153, (fig.)
    154, 179
Flood
    control, 249, 262, (fig.) 304
    hazard, 157, (table) 245, (fig.) 284, 314
    -prone areas, 41, 244, (table) 250, 252,
        (table) 276, 322
Flooding, 8, 41, 56, 137, (table) 246, 252,
    (table) 295, 299, (fig.) 303, 316–
    317, 322
Floodplains, 53, 55, 56, (fig.) 144, (fig.) 158,
    164, 168, 171, 181, 243, (table)
    246, 249, 252, 263, (table) 276,
    308, 314, 322
Florida, 32, (table) 264, 267
Florissant, Colorado, 227
Florissant Fossil Beds, (fig.) 185, (fig.) 187
Fog and frost, 65, 66, 76, 78, 322

Food Security Act, 138, 175, 178, 179–180, 267
Food webs, 72, (fig.) 73, 79, 114
Ford, John, 7
Forest and Rangeland Renewable Resources Planning Act, 132
Forestry (*also* Forests), 34, (table) 37, 76, (table) 110, 124, (fig.) 153, 154, 169, 171, 182–183, 184, 225, (table) 246, 251–252, 263, (table) 275, 322
Forman Richard T. T., 121
Foundations, (fig.) 153, (fig.) 154, (table) 156
4-H Clubs, 195, 196
Freeways. *See* Highways
French, 8, 162, 164
Friedmann, John, 4, 17
Front Range, 76
Frost-heave susceptibility, (table) 156
Full-time equivalent employment (FTE), 111

Gaia hypothesis, 67–68
Gans, Herbert, 11, 242, 312
Garden clubs, 196
Gas stations, 97, (table) 98
Geddes, Patrick, 8
Geiger, Rudolf, 65, (fig.) 66
General plans, 17
Geographic information systems (GIS), 150
Geological hazard area, 49, (table) 250, 252, (table) 276, 322
Geology, (fig.) 13, 42, 48–51, 55, 63, 68, 76–77, (fig.) 77, 83, 88, (fig.) 89, 93, (fig.) 122, (fig.) 123, 132, (fig.) 143, (fig.) 146, 154, 156–157, 171, (table) 245, 251, 276, (fig.) 283–284, (table) 295, 316, 322
Georgia, (table) 264, 289
Geraldine R. Dodge Foundation, 83
German, 65
Germans, 124
Germany, (fig.) 147
Gibson, Lay, 110
Gil, Efraim, 30
Glickson, Artur, 8
Glouchester County, New Jersey, (table) 125, (table) 129
Goal rationale, 176, 181, 314
Goals, 3, 9, (fig.) 10, 11–12, 14, 17, 18, 19, 23–38, 118, 122, 155–156, 161, 162, 165, 166–167, 168, 171, 173, 175–181, 182, 194, 205, 209, 211, 221, 242, 243, 263, 268–269, 273, 275–276, 280, 287, 290, 305, 307, 308, 311, 313, 314, 317, 322
Goals-achievement matrix, 162, 166–167, 170
Godron Michel, 121
Government agencies. *See* Public agencies
Grade schools, 192, 195. *See also* Schools
Graham, Otis, 286–287
Grange, (table) 98, 169
Gravel pits, 162, (fig.) 163
Great Lakes, 242
Great Plains, 76
Greek, 26
Greenbelts, 8, 322
Greenline planning, 221–222

Greenway, 315
Grid cells, 149–150
Groundwater, (fig.) 13, (table) 36, (fig.) 55, 58, 76–77, (fig.) 77, 78–79, (fig.) 86, (figs.) 143, (fig.) 144, 184, (table) 295, 316, 322
Group dynamics, 23, 25, 322
Growth management, 95, 100–101, 102, 105, 106, 182–188, 226–228, 234–235, 242, 266–267, 273–276, 299–305, 317
Guthrie, Woody, 7

Habitat, 72, 78–79, (table) 84–85, (table) 87, 141, (fig.) 146, 151, (fig.) 163, 215, 217, 218, 249, 250, (table) 295, 299, 317, 322. *See also* Wildlife
Hack, Gary, 208
Harrisburg, Pennsylvania, (fig.) 260
Hartford, Connecticut, (fig.) 260
Hawaii, 32, (table) 264
Hazardous areas, 34, (fig.) 144, (fig.) 146, (fig.) 153
Hazardous waste site, 29
Health. *See* Public health, safety, and welfare
Hearings examiners, 281, (fig.) 283, 308
Highly erodible land, 150, 162, 175, 181, 209, 267, 317
High schools, 192, 195. *See also* Schools
Highways, 97, 102, 134, 151, 162, (fig.) 163, (fig.) 164, 228, 262, 314
Hill, Morris, 166–167
Hills, G. Angus, 8, 141
Hirschhorn, Larry, 167
Historic
    areas (*also* Historic buildings), 111, 137, 141, 143, 154, 186, (fig.) 187, 195, 226, 228, 234, 244, 248, 260
    archaeological, and cultural areas, (table) 36, (fig.) 146, (fig.) 154, (table) 155, 183, 249, (table) 250, 251, (table) 276, 292, 322
    preservation, 196, (table) 295
Histories, 74, 76, 97, (table) 98, 100, 182, 197
Holdridge Life-Zone System, 80–81
Holdridge, L. R., 80–81
Holland. *See* The Netherlands
Home
    builders, 305
    sites, 133
Homeowners, 31, 152, 258
Hopkins, Lewis, 141
Horticulture. *See* Agriculture
Household income (or earnings) multiplier, 296
Housing, 5, 11, 12, (fig.) 16, 17, 34, (table) 37, 78, 96, 101, 106–108, 110, 115, 122–123, (fig.) 142, 161, 162, (figs.) 163, (fig.) 164, 169, (fig.) 180, 184, 186, (table) 199, 208, 224, 226, 227, 244, 245, 248, 267, 271, (table) 272, 275, 287, (table) 288–289, 294, (table) 295, (fig.) 301, (fig.) 304, 305
Howard, Ebenezer, 8
Human
    ecology, 14, 20, 73, 322

health, safety, and welfare. *See* Public health, safety, and welfare
    rights, 7
Hunt, Charles B., 51
Hurricanes, 56, 252
Huxtable, Ada Louise, 242
Hydroelectric power, 56, 262
Hydrologic cycle, 53, (fig.) 55, 322
Hydrology, (fig.) 13, 51, 53, 55–60, 68, 77, (fig.) 82, 83, (fig.) 86, 93, (fig.) 122, (fig.) 123, 132, (fig.) 143, 154, 256, 322

Idaho, 3, 44, (fig.) 45, (fig.) 46, (fig.) 87, 111, 157, (fig.) 176, 178, (fig.) 213, (table) 264, (fig.) 274, 312
Igneous rock, 49
IJsselmeer polders, 145, (fig.) 147, (fig.) 148
Illinois, (table) 264, (fig.) 273
Image processing, 149–150
Impace fees, 266–267, 274, 322
Implementation, 3, 9, (fig.) 10, 17, 18–19, 32–35, 168, 171, 176, 179, 181–182, 193, 194, 241–276, 306, 307, 308, 312, 313, 314
    matrix, 242, 268–269
Income multipliers, 295–296
Indiana, (table) 264
Indians, 30, 74, 87–93, 103, 124, 125–128, (table) 129, 193
Industrial:
    development, 162, 265, 294, 312–313
    land use, 36, (table) 37, (fig.) 74, 115, 141, (fig.) 143, (fig.) 144, (fig.) 146, (fig.) 153, 169, 176, 179, 181, 186, 211, 215, 243, 244, 245, (table) 246, 258, 267, (table) 275, 314–315
    revolution, 256
Industry, 99, (table) 114, (fig.) 163, 164, 168, 263, 266
    primary, 96, 111
    secondary, 111
    tertiary, 96, 111
Infill development, 300
Information
    collection, 192–194
    dissemination, 192–194
Initiative planning, 192–194
Inner city, 266
Institute for Participatory Management and Planning (formerly Institute for Participatory Planning), 25–26, 27
Interagency coordination (*also* Intergovernment coordination), 182, 266–267
Interstate 70, 220
Interstate highway. *See* Highways
Interviews, 27, 74, 76, 96, 97, (table) 98, 120, 121, 170, 171. *See also* Face-to-face interviews
Inventories, 3, 9, (fig.) 10, 17, 19, 41–129, 131, 141, 150, 152, 157, 158, 167, 168, 171, 182, 186, 196, 209, 291, 294, 317, 323
    biophysical, 41–93, 150, 185, 312
    human community, 95–129, 185, 296, 312
Iowa, 209, (table) 264, 269–273
Iowa Northland Regional Council of Governments, 271
Irrigation, (fig.) 153

Israeli, 8
Italians, (table) 116, (table) 117, 124

Jacobs, Allan, 74, 119
Jazz, 20
Jefferson, Thomas, 5–6
Jennings, Michael, 315–316
Jerusalem, 252
Jews (also Jewish), (table) 116, (table) 117, 124
Jobs, 169
Joggers, 214, 216
Johannsen, Sonia, 271–272
John Deere and Company, 271
Johnson, Arthur, 9
Johnson, Lee, 306
Journalists (also Reporters), 195, 196, 197
Journal of the American Planning Association, 167
Juneja, Narendra, 152, 154
Just compensation, 261
Just v. Marinette County, 249

Kansas, (fig.) 185, (table) 264
Kartez, Jack, 111
Kennett region, Pennsylvania, 115, (table) 116, (table) 117
Kentucky, 248, (table) 264
Key informants, 118–119
Kiev, 255
King County, Washington, 18, 260
King Hammurabi, 255
Köppen climatic classification, 44, 46

Labor, 7
    force, 110–111
        participation, 102, 104–105, (table) 106
        unions, (table) 98
Lacustrine, 58, (fig.) 59
Lake Geneva, 168
Lakewood, Colorado, 220, 221
Land, 108, 137, 141, 161
    acquisition, 184
    capability, 131, 132–140, 182
    classification, 13, 113, 131–159
    cover, (table) 15, 68, 113, 152
    evaluation, 135–140, 329
    -grant university, 100, 196–197
    purchase, 18
    use, 4, 20, 72–76, (fig.) 77, 78, (fig.) 79, 97, 121, 124, (table) 125, 136, 137, (table) 139, (table) 141, 143, (fig.) 144, (fig.) 146, 150, 154, 155, 159, 168, 174, 176–177, 180, 186, 243, 244, (table) 246, 252, 268, 281, (fig.) 300–301, (fig.) 303, 306, 307, 308, 314, 323
        conflicts, (table) 124, 177, 215, 314
        map, (fig.) 74, 97, (table) 98
        plan, 18, 164, 169–171, 174–175, 188, 258, 292, (table) 295
        planning, 19, 23, 32, 33, 134, 169–171, 306
        users, 17, 72–76, 96, 97, 111, 113–115, 121, (table) 141 150, 177, 180, 207–209, 215, 317, 323
    plan, 208–209
Land Conservation and Development Commission (LCDC), 19, 32–35, 36, 165n., 171, 306–307, 329

Landowner (also Property owner), 72, 150, 184, 209, 223, 249, 258, 261, 263–264, 265, 267, 271, 281, (fig.) 283, (fig.) 284–286, 299, (fig.) 300–302
Landscape, 4, (photo) 5, 20, 42, 51, 55, 61, 76, 92, (fig.) 93, 96, 113, 119, 120–121, 125, (fig.) 127, 145, 161, 178, 185, 195, 207, 212, 213, 214, 217, 218, 224, 234–235, 249, 251, 279, 323
    analysis, 12–14, 41–93, 185, 188
    architects, 8, 17, 97, (table) 98, 120, 133, 141, 173, 197, 211, 225, 254, 281
    ecology, 44, 120–121, 188, 235, 236, 323
    patterns, 97, 120–121
    plans, 9, (fig.) 10, 17–18, 32, 173–188, 192, 208, 228, (fig.) 304, 312, 323
Land Trust Exchange, 259
Larsen, Larry, 271–272
Lassey, William, 191–192
Latah County, Idaho, (fig.) 45, 111, (fig.) 113, (fig.) 213, (fig.) 221
Latin, 282
Law, 6, 242, 256, 311
Lawns, 133, (figs.) 143, (fig.) 144, (fig.) 153, (table) 155
Laws of the Indies of 1573, 252
Lawyers, 111, 241, 242
Layer-cake relationships, (fig.) 13, (fig.) 79, 80, (fig.) 82
Lead agency, 293
League of Women Voters, (table) 98, 99, 200
Leary, Robert, 243
Lely, Cornelis, 145
Lenape, 124
Leopold, Aldo, 8
Lewin, Kurt, 25
Lewis, Philip, 8, 141
Libraries, 48, 51, 53, 60, 63, 67, 71, 76, 97, 195, (table) 297
Library of Congress, 97, (table) 98
Life zones, 80–81, (fig.) 82, (fig.) 146, 323
Limestone, 134, 323
Limnology, 56, 154, 323
Linkage, 267
Litton, R. Burton, 120
Living Systems Company, 200
Loam, 62–63, 323
Locke, John, 5
Loess, 48, 323
Logging, 96, 111
London, 255
Long Beach Island, New Jersey, (fig.) 183
Long Island, 260
Loudoun County, Virginia, 297–299
Louisiana, (table) 264
Lovelock, J.E., 67–68
Low- and moderate- income housing. *See* Housing
Lucchesi, Enid, 30
Lynch, Kevin, 120, 208–209

McCall, Tom, 32, 308
MacDougall, E. Bruce, 15, 146, 149
McGregor, Gloria Shepard, 200, 205
McHarg, Ian, 8, 9, 10, 13, 14–15, 132, 141–146, 152, 157, 261

MacKaye, Benton, 8
McKenzie, Ricki L., 124–125
MacNair, Ray, 31
McNamara, Robert, 286
Madison, (fig.) 168, (fig.) 273
Madison Area Surveyors Council (Wisconsin), 150
Mailings, 192, 193, 199
Mail surveys, 115, 116, 118, 169, 193
Maine, (table) 264
Makah Indian Reservation, 42, 87–93, 97, 125–128, (table) 129
Makah Indians, 87–93, 125–128, (table) 129
Management, 4
    by objectives (MBO) system, 289
    plans, 173–174
Man and the Biosphere Programme, 13
Manning, Warren, 15
Manufacturing, (table) 110
Maps, 97, 100, 119, 121, 134, 141, 143, 146, 149, 152, 154, 164, (photo) 165, 169, 170, 180–182, 185, 243, 244, (table) 245, 252, (fig.) 284, 307. *See also* Base maps
Marine, 58, (fig.) 59
Marinette County, Wisconsin, 249
Maryland, 260, (table) 264, (fig.) 270
Massachusetts, 208, 222–226, 234, 260, (table) 264
Massachusetts Department of Environmental Management, 223
Master plans, 173
Medford Township, New Jersey, 132, 152–155, (table) 156, 158
Meetings. *See* Public meetings
Meinig, Donald W., 20
Metamorphic rock, 49, 323
Metzenbaum, James, 242
Meyer, Neil L., 296–297
Miami Conservancy District, 7–8
Michigan, (fig.) 168, (table) 264
Microclimate, 51, 63, 65–67, 76, (figs.) 143, (fig.) 144, (fig.) 153, 154, 255, 323
Middletown, Wisconsin, (fig.) 198
Military installations, 182–183
Miller, Donald, 166–167
Milwaukee, 168
Mineral extraction areas (also Mineral resources), 51, (table) 250, 252, 323
Mining, 27, 96, (table) 110, 111, 184, 186, (fig.) 187, 228, 234, 248, 294, 315
Minnesota, (fig.) 168, (table) 264, (fig.) 273
Miocene, 48
Mississippi, (table) 264
Missoula Flood, 157
Missouori, (table) 264
Missouri Flat Creek watershed, 175–180, 209, 317
Missouri Ozarks, 248
Mitigated determination of nonsignificance, 293
Model Land Development Code, 248
Moratoriums, 266–267, 323
Montana, (table) 265
Monterey, California, 27
Montgomery County, Ohio, 133–134
Montpelier, Vermont, (fig.) 260
Morgan, Arthur, 7

Moscow, Idaho, (fig.) 46, 157, 178, 211–219, (fig.) 221, 315
Motorists, 213
Mumford, Lewis, 8, 312, 317
Munich, 255

Nassau County, New York, 260
National Agricultural Lands Study, 14, 134, 269
National Conservation Planning Manual, 209
National Council on Goverment Accounting, 262
National electrical code, 256
National Environmental Policy Act (NEPA) 4, 120, 174, 193, 263, 290–292, 329
National Forest System, 193
National Parks and Recreation Act of 1978, 35
National Oceanic and Atmospheric Administration (NOAA), 46, 67, 329
National Register of Historic Places, 186
National Trust for Historic Preservation, 268
National Weather Service, 46, 67
Natural
    areas, 151, 260
    ecological areas, (table) 250, 324
    hazard critical areas, 249, (table) 250, 324
    wildlife habitat areas, (table) 250, (table) 275, 324
Natural Resources Defense Council, 292
Nature Conservancy, 268
Nebraska, (fig.) 185, (table) 265
Neighborhood
    associations, 169–170
    planning councils, 23, 24, 27, 195, 323
    quality, 169
Nellis, Lee, 245
The Netherlands, 103, 132, 145, (fig.) 147
Neuberger v. City of Portland, 306
Nevada, (table) 265
New Deal, 8
New England, 6, 30
New Hampshire, 222, 260, (table) 265
New Jersey, 23, (fig.) 35, 36–38, 42, 81, 83–87, 96, 97, 124–125, (table) 126, 152–155, (table) 156, 175, 182–184, 194, 210, (figs.) 211, 260, (table) 265, (fig.) 270
New Jersey Coastal Plain, 76, 77
New Jersey Legislature, 182–183
New Jersey State Planning Commission, 210
Newman, George, 249, 250, 275
New Mexico, (fig.) 185, (table) 265
Newsletters, 99, 165, 193, 194
Newspapers, 27, 76, 97, (table) 98, 99, 100, 115, 165, 167, 192, 196, 199, 200, 205, 302
New towns, 8
New West, (table) 98, 99
New York, (fig.) 35, (fig.) 152, 260, (table) 265, (fig.) 270
New York City, 7, (fig.) 35, (table) 98, 99, (fig.) 152, 242, 260
New York Supreme Court, 244
Nielsen ratings, 30
Nineteenth century, 7, 145, 173, 184, 242
Nixon, Richard, 4, 7, 289
Nominal-group workshops, 23, 25–26, 324
Nonconforming uses, 243
Nongovernment strategies, 242, 267–268
Non-point-source pollution, 178–181, 324

North America, 42, 255
North Carolina, (table) 265
North Dakota, (table) 265
North Sea, 145, (fig.) 147, (fig.) 148
Nuclear power plant, 7, 29, 125, (fig.) 127, (fig.) 128

Objectives, 176, 178–179, 324
Ocean County, New Jersey, (table) 125, (table) 129, (table) 254
Oceanography, 56, 324
Ocean resources, 35
Odum, Eugene, 42, 56
Office of Coastal Zone Management, 60, 88
Office of Federal Statistical Policy and Standards, 14
O'Harrow, Dennis, 245
Ohio, (table) 265
Oklahoma, (fig.) 185, (table) 265
Old Testament, 252
Olin, Laurie, 236
Olmsted, Frederick Law, 7
Olympia, Washington, (fig.) 274
Olympic Mountains, (fig.) 87
Olympic Peninsula, 88, 89
1000 Friends of Oregon, 19, 268
Open space, 5, 33, 34, (fig.) 74, (fig.) 79, 137, (table) 139, 162, (figs.) 163, (fig.) 164, 180, 181, 186, 235, 243, 244, (table) 246–247, 263–264, 267, (fig.) 301, (fig.) 304, 308, 314, 324
Opportunities, (table) 141, 143, 154, 181, 185, 186
Options, 3, 9, 17, 161–171, 180, 186, 194, 209, 305, 312, 315
Oral histories, 97
Orchard. *See* Agriculture
Oregon, 11–12, 17–18, 19,23,32–35, 36–38, (fig.) 45, (fig.) 46, (fig.) 87, 96, 122–123, 162, 165n., 169–171, 174–175, 182, 192–193, (table) 265, 267, 268, (fig.) 274, 280, 305–308
Oregon legislature, 32, 33, 175, 306, 307
Oregon State University, 197
Oregon Supreme Court, 244, 305–307
Oregon, Wisconsin, (fig.) 198
Ordinances, 33, 179, 182. *See also* Zoning ordinance
Organic planning, 312, 317
Organization development, 24–25, 324
Outcome measures, 179
Outdoor recreation, 151, 186. *See also* Recreation
Output (or business) multiplier, 296
Overlay technique, 15, 17, (table) 141, 146, 149

Pacific Northwest Bell, 106, 329
Pacific Ocean, (fig.) 87, 89, (fig.) 90, (table) 91, 127
Pacific Rim Planners, 87, 93, 127
Palissy, Bernard, 53
Palouse, 3, 44–81, 175–181, 211–219, 268–269, 312, 313, 314, 317
Palouse Conservation District, 177, 178, 209, 317
Palouse formation, 49

Palouse path, 211–219, (fig.) 220–221, (fig.) 222, (fig.) 223, (fig.) 224, 315
Palouse Range, 178
Palouse River, (fig.) 52, 55, 56, 78, (fig.) 176, 178, (fig.) 212–213, 215, 317
Palustrine, 58, (fig.) 59
Paradise Creek, (fig.) 212–213, 215, 218, 314
Paris, 162
Parking, (table) 199, 225, 228, 243, (table) 245, 265, (fig.) 284, (table) 295, (fig.) 301, (fig.) 303, (fig.) 304
    lots, 133
Parks, 101, 102, 105, 133, 151, 168, 174, 176, 181–182, 199, 215, 217, 219, 222, 228, 262, 263, 274, (table) 295, (fig.) 304, 313, 314, 315
Participation observation, 96, 97, (table) 98, 115, 119–120, 121, 194
Pasture, 133, (fig.) 143, (fig.) 144, (fig.) 146, (fig.) 153, 154, (figs.) 163, (fig.) 164, (fig.) 180
Peach Bottom Township, Pennsylvania, 271, (table) 272
Pedestrians, 214, (fig.) 225, (fig.) 226, (fig.) 227, 228, 314
Pennsylvania, 5–6, (fig.) 35, 115, (table) 116, (table) 117, (fig.) 152, (fig.) 260, (table) 265, 268, 269–273
People, 6, 9, (fig.) 13, 72–76, 79, 95–129, 145, 159, 161, 169, 171, 175, 192, 194, 196, 198, 205, 280, 296
Perceptually and culturally critical areas, 249–250, (table) 276, 324
Performance standards, 18–19, 152–155, 186, 235, 241, 244–245, (table) 246–247, 248, 252, 266, 281, 324
Periodicals, (table) 98, 99, 100
Permeability, 55, 63, 78, 324
Permits, 256, 282, 291, 292, 293, 294, (table) 298, 305
Permit systems, 245, 248
Petaluma, California, 248
pH, 78, 86, (fig.) 143, 324
Philadelphia, 6, (fig.) 35, 73, (table) 98, 99, 152, (fig.) 183, 222, 270
Philip II, 252
Phone books, 97, (table) 98, 99
Photomotage, 210
Photoretouching, 210
Physiognomic profiles, 69, (fig.) 70, 71
Physiography, (fig.) 13, 44, 48, 51–53, (figs.) 54, 63, 76–77, (fig.) 77, 78, (fig.) 122, (fig.) 123, (fig.) 143, 154, 325
Physiography of the United States, 51, 53
Pike National Forest, (fig.) 185
Pinchot, Gifford, 19
Pine Barrens, 35, (photo.) 83, 93, 128, (fig.) 153, 182, 188, 195
Pinelands, 23, (photo.) 34, 35–38, 42, 51, 81, 83–87, 91–93, 97, 124–125, (table) 126, (fig.) 127, (fig.) 128, (tables) 129, 152, 175, 182–184, 188, 194–196, 252, (table) 253, (table) 254, 261
    towns and villages, 182–183
Pinelands Planning Commission, 35–38, 81, 83, 86–87, 182, 194–196, 249, (table) 250
Plan elements, 176–177, 178, 313

Planned unit development (PUD), 241, 244, (fig.) 300, 302
Planners, 6–8, 17, 19, 20, 30, 58, 72, 86, 95–96, 104, 116, 119, 133, 134, 135, 136, 151, 166, 167, 171, 184, 185, 191, 193, 195, 196, 197, 205, 207, 208, 211, 221, 226, 228, 241, 244, 248, 279, 280, 281, (fig.) 300, 315
Planning, 4, 23, 38, 41–42, 91–93, 95–96, 128, 131–132, 133–134, 145, 151, 159, 161–162, 165n., 171, 173–174, 188, 191–192, 196, 205, 207–208, 209, 236, 241–242, 263, 265, 275–276, 279–280, (table) 287, 306, 308, 311–317, 325
   agency (*also* department), 6, 24, 27, 97, (table) 98, 151, 167, 194, 196, 197, 254, 268–269, 290, (fig.) 300, 314
   commission, 24, 27, 31, 167, 170, 176, 197, 244, 252, 254, 268–269, 280–281, 302, 304, 308, 314, 315, 325
   education, 164
   director, (fig.) 283, 289, 290
   guidelines, 176, 179, 313, 314–315
   project, 4, 95–96, 149
   staff, 167, 168, 169, 170, 254, 280, 281, (fig.) 282, (fig.) 300, 302, (fig.) 303, 308, 325
Planning Enabling Act, 280
   planning, programming, and budget system, 280, 286–289, 325
Planning Standards in Industrial Zoning, 245
Plants, (table) 36, 51, 92, 133, 214, 215, 249, (table) 253, (table) 254, (table) 295, 325. *See also* Vegetation
Plat, 254, 292, 325
Pleistocene, 157
Pliocene, 48
Point systems, 186, 248, 299–305
Polders, 145, (fig.) 147
Police, 33, 262, (table) 287, (table) 295, (table) 297, (fig.) 304
   powers, 6, 242, 249
Policies, 18, 27, 175, 176–181, 182, 194, 207, 210, 243, 263, 280, 290, 292, 293, 311, 313, 325
Policy plans, 173–174
Political parties, (table) 98
Politicians, 241
Polygons, 149–150
Pope, Alexander, 131
Population, 151, 161, 256, 296–297
   characteristics, 96, 99, 102–104, (tables) 105, (table) 106, 175
   growth, 184, 186, 273–274, (table) 298
   projections, 96, 104–106, (fig.) 107, (table) 108, (tables) 129, 180, 181, 185
   pyramid, 100, 103, (fig.) 104
   studies, 95, 96, 123, 125, 196
   trends, 96, 100–102
Portland Bureau of Planning, 308
Portland, Oregon, 162, 169–171, 305–308
Portland State University, 170
Powell, John Wesley, 42
Practical Use of the Sun, 200

Precipitation, 45–46, (fig.) 47, (fig.) 55, 78, 80–81, (fig.) 82, 89
Preference surveys, 27–30, 171, 197
Preferential assessment, 264, (table) 265, 267, 325
Preservation areas, 182–184, 261
Press releases, 196
Prigogine, Ilya, 20
Prime farmland (*also* Prime agricultural land), 17, 86, 111, 134–140, 162, (figs.) 163, (fig.) 164, 167, (fig.) 180, 251, 271, (table) 276
Private land, 256, (fig.) 259, 261
Problems and opportunities, 3, 9, (fig.) 10, 11, 14, 19, 23, 32, 175, 181, 317. *See also* Opportunities
Procedural requirements, 281–282
Program strategies, 287–289
Property, 5–6, 74, 157, 256, 258, 259, 261–262, 263–266, 281
   acquisition, 261–262
   deed, 254, 256, 261
   owner. *See* Landowner
   values, 261
Protection areas, 182–184
Public
   administration, (table) 110, 242
   administrators, 241, 294
   agencies, 24, 30–31, 169, 170
   facilities (*also* services), 33, 35, (table) 139, 176, 177, 181–182, 197, 248, 265, 266, 274–275, (table) 295, 296, (table) 297, (fig.) 303–304
   funds, 262
   health, safety, and welfare, 19, 134, 143 (fig.) 146, 151, 152, 180, 192, 245, 249, 256, 266, 297, 316
   hearings, 23, 30–31, 157, 159, 162, 167–168, 170, 171, 194, 196, 197, 280, 281, (fig.) 283, 290, 302, 304, 308, 325
   lands, (fig.) 144, 174–175, 186, (fig.) 187, 242, 258
   meetings, 169, 171, 192, 193, 194, 196, 198, 199, 205
   opinion polls, 23, 27–30, 194, 197, 325
   property management, 263
   transportation, (table) 199
Publications, 196–197, (fig.) 198
Puerto Ricans, 124
Puerto Rico, 292
Puget Sound, 273
Pullman-Moscow corridor, 211–219, (fig.) 220–221, 314, 315
Pullman, Washington, (fig.) 46, (table) 101, 102, (table) 105, 157, 158, 162, 211–219, (fig.) 220, 312, 315
Purchase of development rights (PDR), 242, 258, 259–261, 270, 325
Pure Milk Association, 169
Puritans, 30

Quakers, (table) 116, (table) 117, 124
Quasi-judicial proceedings, 280, 306, 307, 308
Quinby, Peter, 42

Radio, 192, 194, 197, 199
Radon-prone deposits, 49
Railroads, 102, 157, 162, (fig.) 163, (table) 245, (table) 246, (fig.) 284

Rainfall, 41
Raintree, John, 208–209
Ramapo, New York, 248
Ranchers, 209
Ranching, 96
RAND Corporation, 26
Rangeland, 133, (fig.) 143, (fig.) 144, (fig.) 146, 186, (fig.) 187, 227, 325
Rational planning, 311–312, 317
Reactive planning, 192–194
Reagan, Ronald, 7, 8
Real estate agents, 97, (table) 98, 157, 197
Reclamation, 133, 145
Recreation, 5, 11, 17, 34, (table) 37, 56, 118, 133, 137, 141, (fig.) 143, (fig.) 146, 151, 154, (table) 155, 161, 168, 176, 181–182, 184, 195, 211, 212, 213, 214, 215, 216, 217, 219, 223, 244, (table) 246–247, 250, 267, (table) 295, 314, 315, 325. *See also* Outdoor recreation
Reganold, John, 315–316
Region, 12, 42, 97, 325
Regional
   climate, 42, 43–48, (figs.) 46–47, 76, 255
   design system, 210, (figs.) 211
   context map, 43, (fig.) 45
   growth areas, 183
Regolith, 49, 51, 325
Regulation, 6, 19, 33, 137, 151, 168, 184, 192, 222, 224, 236, 241, 242–258, 261, 266, 280, 281, 293, 307
Renaissance, 255
Reporters. *See* Journalists
Reps, John, 30, 242, 252
Residential land use, 36, (table) 37, (fig.) 74, 138, 141, (fig.) 143, (fig.) 144, (fig.) 146, 155–159, 168, 169, 181, 184, 186, (fig.) 187, 215, 226, 227, 243, 244, 245, (table) 246–247, 261, 266, 267, 280, 281, 282, (figs.) 283–286, 299–305
Resource production critical areas, 249, (table) 250, (table) 276, 326
Restrictive covenants, 256
Retail, 96, (table) 110, (table) 201, (table) 202, (table) 203
Retirees, 8, 125, 168
Reveille for Radicals, 7
Review boards, 268, 279, 280–281. *See also* Zoning review boards
Rezoning, 243, 261, 272–273, 280, 281, 302, 308, 315
Rhodehamel, E.C., 83
Rhode Island, 260, (table) 265
Ricklefs, Robert E., 67
Riparian corridors. *See* Stream corridors
Riverine, 58, (fig.) 59
Roads, 134, 157, 158, 162, (fig.) 180, 186, (table) 199, 214–218, (fig.) 220, (fig.) 222, 226, 228, 235, (table) 245, (table) 246, 259, 262, 263, 265, 274, (fig.) 282, (fig.) 284, (fig.) 285, (table) 297, 314, 315
Rock crushing, 162, (fig.) 163, 315
Rocky Mountain, (table) 98, 99
Rocky Mountains, 44, (fig.) 46, 48, 76, 77, 184, 248

Rogers, Carl, 25
Rogers, Golden, and Halpern, 252
Romans, 145, 252, 255
Rome, 255
Roosevelt, Franklin, 132
Roosevelt, Theodore, 7
Rotary Club, 200
Rules of combination, 141–142, (table) 155, (table) 156
Rural, 4, 101 (table) 102, 124, (fig.) 143, (fig.) 146, (fig.) 154, 186, 199, 223, 224, 243, 244, 267, 274
　character, 226
　development areas, 182–184
　housing, 155–159, 162 (figs.) 163, 176–177, (fig.) 180, (table) 245, 268–269, 298
Russians, 124

Safety. *See* Public health, safety, and welfare
St. Paul, (fig.) 168, (fig.) 173
Salem, Oregon, 274
Sand, 62–63, (fig.) 153, 326
San Francisco Bay, 78
Sanitary landfills, 133
Satellite photographs, 150
Scenarios, 17, 125, 161, 167, 170, 208
Scenario writing, 167, 171
Scenic, 151, (fig.) 153, (table) 156, 186, 258
　areas, 34, (table) 36, 141, (figs.) 143, (fig.) 144, 154, 184, 249–250, 251, (table) 276, (table) 295, 326
　easements, 222. *See also* Easements
　roadways, 186, (fig.) 187
Schein, Edgar, 25
School districts, 97, (table) 98, 265
Schools, 101, 102, 105, 137, 199, 200, 205, 215, (table) 275, (table) 295, (fig.) 303
Scientific areas, 250, (table) 275, 326
Scoping, 292–293
Scottish, 8
Scouts, (table) 98, 195, 196
Sea-grant university, 60, 100
Seattle, 87, 273
Second-order streams, 56, (fig.) 57
Second World War, 151
Sedimentary rock, 49
Sedimentation, 56, 175–176, 179, 209, 317
Seminars, 193
Septic tanks, 33, 78, 86, 133, 134, 245
Service districts, 266
Services, 96, (table) 110. *See also* Public facilities and Water and sewer systems
Settlement pattern diagrams, (fig.) 75, (table) 98
Settlement patterns, 74–75, 76, (fig.) 77, 97, 124
Seventeenth century, 30, 145
Sewage (facilities, lagoons, systems, and treatment), 78, 124, 133, 137, (figs.) 143, (fig.) 144, (fig.) 153, (fig.) 154, 157, 162, (table) 245, 262, 266, (table) 297, (fig.) 304. *See also* Water and Sewage systems
Shopping centers, 134, 137
Shorelines, 87–93, 127, (fig.) 146, 168, 171, 249, (table) 276, (table) 295

Shrink-swell potential, (table) 156
Sidewalks, 220, 221, (fig.) 225, (fig.) 226, 228, 262, 265
Siegler, Theodore R., 296–297
Sign ordinances, 33, 242
Silt, 62–63, (fig.) 64, 326
Simulation, 167, 208, 210, (figs.) 211
Sinton, John, 93, 124, 128
Site
　assessment, 135–140, 329
　design, 208–209, 210, 215, 266, (fig.) 304, 308
　plan/planning, 208–209, 224, 235, (fig.) 283, (fig.) 285, 300, (fig.) 303, 311
Sixteenth century, 30, 53
Skaller Peter, 69
Slope, (fig.) 16, 51, 53, (fig.) 54, 61, 63, 76, 78, (fig.) 79, 89, 132, 134, (fig.) 142, (figs.) 143, (fig.) 144, (fig.) 146, (table) 156, 157, 158, 181, 244, (table) 245, (table) 246, 249, 255, (table) 276, 326
Smith, Joan, 170
Smithsonian Institution, 249, (table) 250
Snake River, 56, 179, (photo) 313, 314
Snohomish County, Washington, 242, 273–276
Snohomish, Washington, (fig.) 274
Social impact analysis, 196–197, 292, 294, 299
Socioeconomic analysis, 95–129
So, Frank, 287, 289, 290
Solar, 256
　energy, 53, 200
　orientation, (fig.) 255
　radiation, 65, 66, 67, 78
Soil, (fig.) 13, (table) 36, 51, 60–63, (fig.) 66, 68, 69, 71, 76–78, (fig.) 79, 83, 86, 88, 89, 93, 96, 121, (fig.) 122, (fig.) 123, 132–140, (fig.) 143, (fig.) 144, 145, 154, (table) 155, (table) 156, 157, 158, 171, 178–181, 211, 245, 249, 250, 251, 271, (table) 272, (table) 276, (table) 295, 314, 315, 316, 326
　association, 61, 63, 326
　capability class, 33, 61, 63, 131–140, 145, 164, 168, 251, (table) 272
　conservation. *See* Conservation
　conservationists. *See* Conservationists
　conservation practices, 162, (figs.) 163, (fig.) 164, 178, (fig.) 180, 181
　erosion. *See* Erosion
　horizon, 62
　mapping units, (fig.) 61, 132–140, (table) 245, (fig.) 283–284
　phase, 61
　potential, 135–140
　productivity, 133, 135–140, (figs.) 143, (fig.) 144, 251
　profile, 61–62, 63, (fig.) 64, 326
　scientists, 131, 281
　series, 61–63, 157, 326
　surveys, 13, 60–63, 89, 132–140, 145
　texture, 61, 62–63, 78, 89, 326
Soil and Water Conservation Society, 63
Soil Erosion Service, 132
South Carolina, (table) 265
South Dakota, (table) 265
Southern Living, (table) 98, 99, 196

Southwestern Wisconsin Regional Planning Commission, 168
Spanish, 252
Speakers Bureau, 196
Special-use permits, 243
Spirn, Anne, 8, 207–208, 234–235
Springfield, Illinois, (fig.) 273
Spokane County, Washington, 315
Spokane Flood, 157
Staatsbosbeheer, 17
Standard Zoning Enabling Act, 242
State enabling legislation, 242–243, 254, 256
State Environmental Policy Act (SEPA), 249, 282*n*.
Steinitz, Carl, 15
Stengers, Isabelle, 20
Strahler stream-ordering system, 55–56
Strait of Juan de Fuca, (fig.) 87, 89, (figs.) 90, (table) 91
Strategies, 18, 178–182, 210, 317, 327
Stream
　banks, 179, 218, 223, 299
　corridors, 6, 215, 217, 252
　orders, 55–56, (fig.) 57, 327
Street, 133, (table) 199, 262, (fig.) 301, (fig.) 304, 327
　furniture, 221, 228, 234
　trees, 220–221, (fig.) 225, (fig.) 226, 265
Strip-mine reclamation, 27
Students, 185, 186, 195, 199, 226
Subdivision regulations, 33, 168, 197, 252, 254–255, 256, 327
Suburban development, 4, 11, 124, (fig.) 143, (fig.) 146, (fig.) 154, (table) 156, 171, 176–177, 274, 314, 315
Suburbanization, 102, 134
Suffolk County, New York, 18, 260
Suitability analysis, 3, 9, 14–17, (fig.) 16, 131–159, 161, 162, 164, 165, 167, 174, 180, 181, 185, 263, 276, 312, 327
Sulton, Washington, 275, (table) 276
Sunset, (table) 98, 99
Surface water, (fig.) 13, (table) 36, 55, 58, 76, (fig.) 77, 78–79, 86, (figs.) 143, (fig.) 144, 157, 171, 184, (table) 245, 252, 268–269, 276, (fig.) 284, (fig.) 285, (table) 295, 316, 327
Surficial deposits, 49, 51
Surveyor, 254
Survey Research Center, Institute for Social Research, 118
Surveys, 96, 116, 120, 121, 165, 167, 170, 178, 185, 194, 198–200. *See also* Mail surveys *and* Telephone surveys
Sustainability, 145
Swimming, (fig.) 153, (fig.) 154
Synchronized surveys, (fig.) 29, 118, 162, 165–166, 170

Tahoe Regional Planning Agency, 151
Taking clause, 6, 261
Tarlet, Jean, 8
Task forces, 23, 24, 31, 162, 165, 167, 194, 195, 327
Tax assessor, 74, 76, 97, (table) 98
Tax increment financing, 265
Taxpayers, 184

Taxes, 18, (table) 124, 137, (table) 139, 241, 242, 249, 258, 263–266, 267, 268, 270, 294, 297, (table) 298
Teachers, 195
Technical advisory committees, 23, 24, 27, 162, 165, 167, 327
Telephone surveys, 115, 116, 118
Television, 30, 116, 150, 165, 192, 194, 195, 197, 199
Teller County, Colorado, 175, 184–188, 208, 210, 226–228, 234–238, 317
Temperature, 41, 44–46, (fig.) 47, 80, (fig.) 81
Tennessee, (table) 265
Tennessee, Valley Authority, 8, 42
Texas, 96, (table) 265
Texas Instruments Company, 289, 328
Third-order streams, 56, (fig.) 57
Thoreau, Henry David, 7
Threshold determination, 293
Threshold-level analysis, 198, 200 (table) 201
Tolerable soil loss (T values), 62, 178, 209
Toner, William, 270–271
Topoclimate, 65, 327
Topographic profiles, 51, (fig.) 52
Topography, (table) 36, 48, 65–66, 86, (figs.) 143, (fig.) 144, (fig.) 153, 225, 227, 251, 252, 271, (table) 295, (fig.) 303, 308, 327
Tourism, 76, 118, 186, 228
Town meeting, 23, 30–31, 170, 327
Townships, 132, 152–156, 159, 168–169
Trade area, 199
    survey, 198–199
Traffic, (table) 199
Transfer of development rights (TDR), 18, 184, 258, 259–261, (fig.) 262, 270, 327
Transportation, 5, 12, 35, (table) 110, 137, 157, 169, 174, 176, 181–182, 210, 211, 213, 214, 266, 291, (table) 295, (fig.) 304
Trenton, New Jersey, (fig.) 35, 152, (fig.) 260, (fig.) 270
Tropical Science Center, 80
Trust for Public Land, 268
Tsunamis, 56
Tugwell, Rexford, 8
Tuttle, Andrea, 151
Twain, Mark, 7
Twentieth century, 7, 30, 173, 256, 280
Two Treaties of Government, 5

Udell v. Haas, 244
UNESCO, 13, (table) 14
Uniform building code, 256, (table) 257
United Nations, (table) 98
United States, 4, 5–8, 12, 13, 17, 30, 42, 43, 63, 68, 78, 97, 102, 108, 125, 132, 133, 134, 135, 151, 152, 209, 241, 242, 258, 261–262, 263, 270, 292, 308
U.S. Agricultural Stabilization and Conservation Service (ASCS), 60, 63, 329
U.S. Army Corps of Engineers, 42, 60, 252
U.S. Bureau of Economic Analysis, (table) 109
U.S. Bureau of Indian Affairs, 88
U.S. Bureau of Land Mangement (BLM), 18, 174, 263, 329
U.S. Bureau of the Census, 76, 97, (table) 98, 103, (table) 109

U.S. Census, 10
U.S. Coast Guard, 60
U.S. Congress, 4, 7, 35, 138, 209
U.S. Constitution, 6, 7, 261
U.S. Department of Agriculture (USDA), 60, (table) 98, (table) 109, (fig.) 140, 329
U.S. Deparment of Commerce, 60, 88, 97, (table) 98, 242, 280
U.S. Department of Defense, 286
U.S. Department of Housing and Urban Development (HUD), (table) 98, 200, 329
U.S. Department of Interior, 88, 125
U.S. Department of Transportation, (table) 98, 193–194
U.S. Environmental Protection Agency (EPA), 55, 60, 329
U.S. Fish and Wildlife Service, 13, 56, 58, (fig.) 59, 60
U.S. Forest Service (USFS), 12, 13, 18, 19, 34, 42, 60, 68*n.*, 71, 72, 120, 132, 174, 193, 251–252, 263, 329
U.S. 40, 220
U.S. Geological Survey, 13, 51, 53, 55, 60, 71, 76, 97, (table) 98, 132, 329
    Land Use and Land Cover Classification System, 14, (table) 15, 68, 74, 113
    quadrangel maps, 43, 328
U.S. Internal Revenue Service, (table) 109
U.S. National Park Service (NPS), 18, 42, 120, 174, 195, 211, 223, 235, 263, 329
    Mid-Atlantic Regional Office, 222
U.S. Secretary of Interior, 35
U.S. Soil Conservation Service (SCS), 12, 13, 33, 42, 55, 60, 63, 71, 72, 74, 76, 86, 89, 97, (table) 98, 132–140, 145, 157, 158, 168, 169, 177, 178, 208–209, 223, (table) 245, 251, 267, 269, 281, (fig.) 283–284, 329
    Important farmland classification system, 86, 134–140
U.S. Supreme Court, 6, 242
Universal soil-loss equation, 62
Universities (*also* Colleges), 48, 51, 53, 60, 63, 67, 71, 72, 76, 97, (table) 98, 99–100, 157, 192, 195, 197, 224, 242
University of Amsterdam, 145
University of California, Berkeley, 74, 120, 151
University of Colorado at Denver, 185, (fig.) 187, 226, 236
University of Idaho, 157, 211, (fig.) 213, 215, 315
University of Massachusetts, 223–226
University of Michigan, 118
University of Pennsylvania, 10, 141–145, 152
University of Washington, 166
University of Wisconsin-Extension, 168, 192, 197–205
University of Wisconsin-Madison, 8, 141, 150
Urban, 4, (table) 102, 134, 137, (fig.) 143, (fig.) 144, (fig.) 146, (fig.) 153, 168, 176–177, 186, (fig.) 187, (fig.) 225, 258, 267, 274, 314
    visitors, 168
Urban Land Institute, (table) 109
Urbanization, 6, 17, 35, 124, 154, 169, 273

Utah, (fig.) 185, (table) 265
Utilities, 221, 223, (table) 246, 258, (fig.) 303
Utility extension policies, 18

Vancouver Island, (fig.) 87
Variances, 243, 268, 281, 294, 308, 319, 328
Vegetation, (fig.) 13, 41, 42, 58, 65, (fig.) 67, 68–71, 72, 74, (fig.) 77, 78–79, 80–81, 83, 86–87, (fig.) 122, (fig.) 123, 137, (figs.) 143, (fig.) 144, 152, (fig.) 153, 154, (table) 155, 184, 217, 218, 227, 244, (table) 245, 251, (table) 253, (table) 254, 255, 256, 276, (fig.) 284, (fig.) 285, 299, 328. *See also* Plants
Ventilation, 65–66, 328
Vermont, 32, 222, (table) 265, 267
Victor, Colorado, (fig.) 185, 186, (fig.) 187, 228, 234
Victorian, 227, 228, 234
Views. *See* Scenic
Village centers, 226
Vink, A.P.A., 145
Virginia, 6, (table) 265
Visual
    analysis, 120–121, 125, (fig.) 127, (fig.) 129, (fig.) 198, 199, 200
    character, 216, 221, 248
    impact, 95
    patterns, 120–121
    quality, 219, 226
    types, 125, (fig.) 127, (fig.) 128
Volcanoes, 252
Voluntary covenants, 18, 256, 328
Voluntary restrictive agreements, 264, (table) 265
Voting, 23, 26, 165

Wallace, David, 261
Wallace-McHarg Plan, 261
Walla Walla County, Washington, (table) 101, (table) 102, (table) 103, (table) 105, (table) 106, 111, (fig.) 112, (fig.) 113
Walworth County, Wisconsin, 162, 168–169, 171
Washington, 3, 42–81, 87–93, (table) 98, 99, 100–108, (table) 110, 111, 138, (table) 139, 155–159, (fig.) 176, 177, (fig.) 213, (table) 265, 268–269, 273, (fig.) 274, (fig.) 286, 292–294, (table) 295, 312
Washington Conservation Commission, 177
Washington County, Oregon, 306
Washington, D.C., 135, 255, 297
Washington Office of Program Planning and Fiscal Management, 106
Washington legislature, 293
Washington Planning Enabling Act
Washington State Department of Ecology, 88, 177, (table) 245, 269, 293–294, 329
Washington State Environmental Policy Act (SEPA), 249, 292–294, (table) 295, 314, 315, 329
Washington State University, 27, 74, (table) 101, 102, 104, 111, (fig.) 112, 157, 177, 211, (fig.) 212, 215, 312, 313, 315

Waste management, 184
Water, (table) 37, 43, 78, 96, 108, 110, 121,
        133, 141, (fig.) 146, (fig.) 153,
        154, (table) 156, 184, 211, 249,
        250, 259, 266, 291, (table) 295,
        299, 316, 328
    and sewer systems, 60, 137, (figs.) 143,
        (fig.) 144, (fig.) 153, 158, 162,
        169, 263, 265, (fig.) 282, (fig.)
        284, (table) 297, 298, (fig.) 303,
        (fig.) 304
    availability, 60
    budget, 53, (fig.) 55, 86
    pollution, 175, 249, 317
    quality, 12, (table) 36, 55, 56, 58, 60, 86,
        169, 175, 178, 215, 223, 248,
        268–269, (table) 295, 314, 315,
        317
    areas, (table) 250, 252, (table) 276, 328
    recreation, 186, (fig.) 187
    table, 55, 58, 86, 154, 245, 328
Waterloo, Iowa, 271, (fig.) 273
Watersheds, 7, 8, 9, 12, 42, 55, 58, 175–181,
        209, 223, 248, 258, 268, (table)
        276, 317, 328. *See also* Drain-
        age basins
    protection, 183
Weber, Bruce, 266
Welfare (*see* Public health, safety, and welfare)
West Colfax Pedestrian Improvement Demon-
        stration Project, 220–221, (fig.)
        225, (fig.) 226, (fig.) 227
Western Hemisphere, 252
Western Rural Development Center, 196–197

West Virginia, (table) 265
Wetlands, 6, 11, 124, 137, 184, 244, (table)
        246, 249, 252, (table) 275, 291
Whites, 103
Whitman County, Washington, 18, 42–81, 100–
        108, 110–111, (figs.) 112, (fig.)
        113, 132, 134, 155–159, 175–
        181, 211, 245, 268–269, 282,
        (figs.) 283–286, 312–317
Whitman, Walt, 7
Wholesale, 96, (table) 110
Wickersham, Kirk, 245
Wild and Scenic Rivers Act, 223
Wilderness: 174, 251, 263
    recreation areas, (table) 250, 251, 328
Wildfires, 227
Wildlife, (fig.) 13, 34, (table) 37, 60, 71–72,
        (fig.) 73, (fig.) 77, 78–79, 83,
        (table) 84–85, 87, 133, 141,
        (figs.) 143, (fig.) 144, (fig.) 153,
        154, (table) 155, 157, 158, (fig.)
        163, 164, 184, 214, 215–216,
        249, 250, 259, 263, 328. *See
        also* Animals
    ecology, 151
Willamette River, 32, 35
Williams, F.B., 242
Wind, 46, 48, 65, 67, 78
Wind-erosion equation, 62
Windfalls and wipeouts, 261
Windshield survey, 120–121
Wisconsin, 150, 163, 168–169, 171, 197–205,
        209, (table) 265, (fig.) 273
Wisconsin Power and Light, 150

Wisconsin Supreme Court, 249
Woodland. *See* Forestry
Woodland Park, Colorado, 184–188
Working plans, 19–20
Workshops, 178, 193, 194
World Conservation Strategy, 143, 145
World's Columbian Exposition, 7
Wright, Lloyd E., 135
Wyoming, (fig.) 185, (table) 265

Yakima County, Washington, 167
Yankee, 224
York County, Pennsylvania, 242, 269–273
York County Planning Commission, 270
York, Pennsylvania, (fig.) 270
Young, Gerald, 14

Zero-base budgeting, 280, 289, 328
Zoning, 18, 136, 137, (table) 139, 152, 154,
        158, 169, 174, 176, 222, 223,
        224, 241, 242–244, (table) 245,
        248, 258, 260, 261, (table) 264–
        265, 266, 267, 268–273, 294,
        (fig.) 300, 306, 307, 328
    adjustors, 281
    compliance, 282, (figs.) 283–286
    districts, 243, 245, (table) 246–247, 248,
        249
    ordinance, 165*n.*, 168–169, 197, 242,
        243, 248, 254, 255, 256, 266,
        271, 275, 280, 281, (figs.) 282–
        286, 307, 319, 328
    review boards, 280–281
Zuider Zee, 145, (fig.) 147, (fig.) 148